LAW AS AN ARTIFACT

Law as an Artifact

Edited by
LUKA BURAZIN
KENNETH EINAR HIMMA
CORRADO ROVERSI

OXFORD
UNIVERSITY PRESS

OXFORD
UNIVERSITY PRESS

Great Clarendon Street, Oxford, OX2 6DP,
United Kingdom

Oxford University Press is a department of the University of Oxford.
It furthers the University's objective of excellence in research, scholarship,
and education by publishing worldwide. Oxford is a registered trade mark of
Oxford University Press in the UK and in certain other countries

First Edition published in 2018

Published in the United States of America by Oxford University Press
198 Madison Avenue, New York, NY 10016, United States of America

British Library Cataloguing in Publication Data
Data available

Library of Congress Control Number: 2018936198

ISBN 978–0–19–882197–7

Contents

Editors' Introduction

The idea that law is an artifact is commonly accepted among legal theorists. For example, Brian Leiter and Frederick Schauer reject an "essentialist" approach to analyzing the concept of law on the ground that law is an artifact and hence subject to change.[1] John Gardner analyses the relationship between law as a genre of artifacts, on the one hand, and legal systems (basic units) and laws (sub-units) as artifacts belonging to this genre, on the other.[2] Neil MacCormick and Kenneth Ehrenberg advocate the functional analysis of law since, in the case of artifacts, functions seem to play an important role.[3] Leslie Green rejects the possibility of applying an intention-based analysis to the "law" as such but endorses this kind of analysis in the case of particular norms, branches of law or legal institutions.[4] Surprisingly, for all these statements, a complete analysis of what the claim that law is an artifact ontologically entails and what consequences, if any, this claim has for philosophical accounts of law has yet to be made.

This state of affairs is more surprising given the fact that the general philosophical discussion about the nature of artifacts is very rich and tends to alternate between four different notions relevant to law—namely, intention, function, history, and action. Most conceptual theories of artifacts highlight, in some way, the concept of intention as playing a role in the existence conditions for artifacts. Indeed, Risto Hilpinen explicates the nature of artifacts in terms of an author's intentions, thus considering the concepts of "author" and "authorship" as central when accounting for the artifactual domain.[5] Lynne Rudder Baker situates the author's intention within a necessary functional framework, connecting the existence of an artifact with the author's intention to produce an object able to perform a specific

[1] See Brian Leiter, 'The Demarcation Problem in Jurisprudence: A New Case for Scepticism' (2011) 31 *Oxford Journal of Legal Studies* 663; Brian Leiter, 'Why Legal Positivism (Again)?' (University of Chicago, Public Law Working Paper No. 442) <http://ssrn.com/abstract=2323013> accessed 20 March 2017; Frederick Schauer, ' On the Nature of the Nature of Law' (2012) 98 *Archiv für Rechts- und Sozialphilosophie* 457.

[2] See John Gardner, 'The Legality of Law' (2004) 17 *Ratio Juris* 168.

[3] See Neil MacCormick, *Institutions of Law* (Oxford University Press 2007); Kenneth M. Ehrenberg, 'Defending the Possibility of a Neutral Functional Theory of Law' (2009) 29 *Oxford Journal of Legal Studies* 91; Kenneth M. Ehrenberg, *The Functions of Law* (Oxford University Press 2016).

[4] See Leslie Green, 'The Functions of Law' (1998) 12 *Cogito* 117.

[5] See Risto Hilpinen, 'Authors and Artifacts' (1993) 93 *Proceedings of the Aristotelian Society* 155.

"essential" function.[6] Randall Dipert instead frames the role of intentions in the ontology of artifacts in historical terms—namely, by highlighting the connection that objects of this sort have with a "deliberative" history eventually rooted in human intentions and activities—and another kind of historical approach has been framed on evolutionary grounds, for example, by Beth Preston.[7] Further, action-oriented theories of artifacts, like that advocated by Wybo Houkes and Pieter E. Vermaas, underline the connection between the author's intention and use, showing that an account of the ontology of artifacts depends on the "use plan" for which an artifact is built.[8] Finally, artifacts have been investigated in their abstract dimension, particularly in connection with fictions, for example by Amie Thomasson.[9]

Even if significant recent work in legal theory has been inspired by the theory of artifacts, there is still no comprehensive treatment of the various implications of the claim that philosophical investigations concerning artifacts can improve our understanding of the law.[10] This volume attempts to remedy this gap in the literature on legal theory. In doing so, the volume seeks to enrich the ongoing legal-theoretical debates with essays by some of the most important participants in these debates that explore how the idea of law's artifactuality informs and otherwise bears on their respective positions. The rationale of this volume is, thus, to present the first comprehensive collection of papers attempting to fully explore and evaluate the idea that law is an artifact and its important implications for legal theory.

The volume begins with the foundational question of identifying the methodological consequences of law's artifactuality for the theory of law. In "Legal Positivism about the Artifact Law: A Retrospective Assessment," Brian Leiter argues that the artifactuality of law entails that law cannot have essential attributes (not even functional ones) and thus defends a

[6] See Lynne R. Baker, 'The Ontology of Artifacts' (2004) 7 *Philosophical Explorations* 99.

[7] See Randall Dipert, *Artifacts, Art Works, and Agency* (Temple University Press 1993); Beth Preston, 'Why is a Wing Like a Spoon? A Pluralist Theory of Function' (1998) 95 *The Journal of Philosophy* 215; Beth Preston, 'Philosophical Theories of Artefact Function' in Anthonie Meijers (ed.), *Philosophy of Technology and Engineering Sciences* (Elsevier 2009).

[8] See Wybo Houkes and Pieter E. Vermaas, *Technical Functions: On the Use and Design of Artifacts* (Springer 2010).

[9] See Amie L. Thomasson, *Fiction and Metaphysics* (Cambridge University Press 1999).

[10] Some works about the relevance of the theory of artifacts for law are: Luka Burazin, 'Can There Be an Artifact Theory of Law?' (2016) 29 *Ratio Juris* 385-401, Jonathan Crowe, 'Law as an Artifact Kind' (2014) 40 *Monash University Law Review* 737-757, Kenneth M. Ehrenberg, *Functions of Law* (Oxford University Press 2016), Corrado Roversi, 'Legal Metaphoric Artifacts' in Bartosz Brożek, Jerzy Stelmach and Łukas Kurek (eds.), *The Emergence of Normative Orders* (Copernicus Center Press 2015) 215-280. See also Mark C. Murphy, 'Two Unhappy Dilemmas for Natural Law Jurisprudence' (2015) 60 *The American Journal of Jurisprudence* 121-141 at 124-127.

metaphysically-deflated version of legal positivism as the theory that best captures Hart's benchmark for theoretical adequacy. In "Law as a Malleable Artifact," Frederick Schauer argues that the artifactuality of law entails that the content of the concept of law is determined by contingent contextual considerations that call for a continuous process of creation and re-creation of this concept. On his view, both descriptive and prescriptive approaches to the concept of law are legitimate and complementary: the first attempts to understand what the concept of law is in a given context, the second to prescribe how that concept should be understood and possibly changed.

The artifactuality of law has a methodological bearing not only on legal theory but also on legal science in general. In "Law, Fiction, and Reality," Andrei Marmor argues that law is (like fictions and games) an intangible compound artifact that creates closed prefixed contexts by elaborating on David Lewis's distinction between prefixed and non-prefixed statements. It follows from this characterization of law that genuine disagreements about what law is are not possible because collective acceptance is constitutive of what artifacts are. This, of course, entails that people cannot be mistaken about the essential features of law, but it does not entail that disagreements about the internal structure of law are impossible. Kevin Toh takes up a similar question in his "Law, Morality, Art, the Works," where he argues that, even if we assume that laws are artificial creations, we do not necessarily have to trace the truth conditions of judgments of legal validity to behavioral or psychological facts. By applying Kendall Walton's theory of implied fictional truths, he shows that there is a third way between psychologism and Dworkinian principlism.

After this methodological discussion, the second part of the book focuses on the ontology of law as an artifact. In "On the Artifactual—and Natural—Character of Legal Institutions," Corrado Roversi analyses several possible models of the ontology of artifacts as applied to the law, and puts forward a conception of artifacts in terms of their "deliberative histories," along the lines introduced by Randall Dipert for works of art. By drawing on this theory, Roversi shows that a theory of law as an artifact can act as a bridge between legal positivism and legal realism and, when combined with some contemporary findings about conceptual metaphors, can also account for some intuitions of natural law theory. In "Legal Systems as Abstract Institutional Artifacts," Luka Burazin shows that the emergence of law is grounded on a social practice based on a we-mode collective recognition of a social norm defining the status of officials; however, he argues, recognition is necessary but not sufficient for the existence of a legal system because, without a significant degree of success and effectiveness in the actual behavior of people, recognition could create nothing more than an abstract set of concepts. With

Kenneth Einar Himma's "The Conceptual Function of Law: Law, Coercion, and Keeping the Peace," the focus of discussion shifts from the need for recognition to the problem of function. Himma considers the issue of whether, like other artifact-types, law has a conceptual function that is performed by all conceptually possible legal systems, arguing that the conceptual function of law is to keep the peace so as to make societal living possible. Moreover, Himma argues that law performs this function by backing some norms with authorized coercive enforcement mechanisms, thus drawing a necessary connection between law and coercion on the grounds of law's artifactual nature.

The third part of the book deals with the bearing that an artifact theory of law can have on the problem of law's normativity. In his "Obligations from Artifacts," Brian Bix raises the crucial question of how legal systems conceived as artifacts can provide moral reasons for actions—a question that he conceives as a variant of how we can derive normative conclusions from descriptive premises. Bix considers the views advanced by several authoritative contemporary legal theorists in connection with this question, and in the end concludes that the reason-giving nature of law, when coupled with its artifactual nature, is still one of the most persistent problems for legal philosophy. In "Law Is an Institution, an Artifact, and a Practice," Kenneth Ehrenberg attempts to solve this problem by showing that, if we conceive law in terms of abstract artifacts, then we are able to understand how the practice of officials can be normative without any violation of Hume's law, because artifacts come with an inbuilt normativity regulating their recognition. Moreover, Ehrenberg argues, law is an institutionalized abstract artifact, namely an artifact built to create and manipulate reasons for action. The connection between artifacts and reasons is also at the core of Veronica Rodriguez Blanco's "Processes and Artifacts: The Principles are in the Author Herself." By elaborating on Elizabeth Anscombe's concept of intention and on Aristotle's distinction between actuality and potentiality, Rodriguez Blanco argues that the nature of any artifact can accurately be understood only in the light of practical reason. This entails explicating why authors design and use it, as well as identifying the way in which authors order their actions to achieve their ends. As a consequence, legal systems as artifacts must be understandable by their citizens in light of the "good-making" characteristics that law-makers intended to produce.

The final part of the book focuses on some caution or skepticism about the idea that law, legal systems, and legal institutions can fruitfully be conceived as artifacts. In his "A Strange Kind of Artifact," Giovanni Tuzet argues that law is, if artifactual, a strange kind of abstract and normative artifact that is not created by any individual and hence is not reducible to anyone's intentions. Moreover, he argues, if we conceive of law and legal institutions as artifacts, we cannot avoid the circularity that emerges between claims about the function and the nature of law. In Tuzet's view, however, this circularity is not necessarily vicious, as it points instead to a necessary integration of answers in addressing law's ontology. Finally, Dan Priel's "Not All Law Is an Artifact: Jurisprudence Meets the Common Law," argues that the idea of law's artifactuality is based on a set of ideological assumptions shared by contemporary legal positivism and natural law theory, namely, that law is an instrument designed by humans to achieve moral improvement. In Priel's view, this ideology is fit to explain law as an outcome of legislation, but it cannot account for common law or customary law, as it conveys a rather one-dimensional view of the practice legal philosophers aim to describe.

The essays collected in the four parts of this volume—methodology, ontology, normativity, and skepticism—are not, of course, meant to be an exhaustive treatment of all the possible issues and conceptions that can be connected with the idea of law's artifactuality. They do, however, show the far-ranging and deep implications this idea can have. Despite its seeming obviousness, the artifactuality of law can have a significant impact on the way we conceive of legal institutions, legal systems, legal science, and legal theory. We hope this collective work will give the reader the analytical tools to determine whether this impact is coherent with what the law is, in fact, and what it ought to be.

Luka Burazin
Kenneth Einar Himma
Corrado Roversi

List of Contributors

Brian H. Bix is the Frederick W. Thomas Professor of Law and Philosophy at the University of Minnesota. He holds a DPhil (doctorate) from Balliol College, Oxford University and a JD from Harvard University. He teaches in the areas of jurisprudence, contract law, family law, and constitutional law. His publications include *Jurisprudence: Theory and Practice* (7th edn., Sweet & Maxwell 2015), *Oxford Introductions to U.S. Law: Family Law* (Oxford University Press 2013), *Contract Law: Rules, Theory, and Context* (Cambridge University Press 2012), *A Dictionary of Legal Theory* (Oxford University Press 2004), and *Law, Language, and Legal Determinacy* (Oxford University Press 1993). He is a Member of the Bars of the States of Minnesota, Connecticut, and Massachusetts, and a Member of the American Law Institute.

Luka Burazin is assistant professor at the University of Zagreb, Faculty of Law and lecturer at the masters program of the Tarello Institute for Legal Philosophy (University of Genoa). He has published a number of papers in legal theory and philosophy of law and co-edited the book *Law and State: Classical Paradigms and Novel Proposals* (Peter Lang Publishing, Frankfurt am Main 2015). He is co-editor of *Revus—Journal for Constitutional Theory and Philosophy of Law.*

Kenneth M. Ehrenberg is currently Reader in Public Law and Legal Theory at the University of Surrey, School of Law, having moved there in 2017 from the University of Alabama, Department of Philosophy. His 2016 book, *The Functions of Law* (also published by Oxford University Press), advances an artifactual (and institutional) theory of the ontology of law, as well as a methodological argument that its nature is best further understood in terms of the social functions it performs.

Kenneth Einar Himma lectures at the School of Law and the Information School at the University of Washington. He has published more than 100 articles in philosophy of law, information ethics, philosophy of religion, applied ethics, bioethics, and philosophy of mind. He is author of *Morality and the Nature of Law* (Oxford University Press forthcoming). He is an editor (with Matt Adler) of *The Rule of Recognition and the US Constitution* (Oxford University Press 2009), an associate editor (Jules Coleman and Scott Shapiro eds.) of *The Oxford Handbook of Jurisprudence and Philosophy of Law* (Oxford University Press 2004), editor of *The Nature of Law: Philosophical Issues in Conceptual Jurisprudence and Legal Theory* (Foundation Press 2011), and editor (with Herman Tavani) of *The Handbook of Information and Computer Ethics* (Wiley 2008).

Brian Leiter is Karl N. Llewellyn Professor of Jurisprudence and Director of the Center for Law, Philosophy, and Human Values at the University of Chicago. He is the author of *Naturalizing Jurisprudence* (Oxford University Press 2007), *Why*

Tolerate Religion? (Princeton University Press 2013), and *Nietzsche on Morality* (2nd edn., Routledge 2015). He is also the founding co-editor of *Oxford Studies in the Philosophy of Law.*

Andrei Marmor is the Jacob Gould Schurman Professor of Philosophy and Law at Cornell University. Prior to joining Cornell in 2015, he was Professor of Philosophy and Maurice Jones Jr. Professor of Law at the University of Southern California. His research interests span philosophy of law; moral, social, and political philosophy; and philosophy of language. Marmor has published dozens of articles, six book monographs, and a number of edited volumes. His most recent books include *Social Conventions: From Language to Law* (Princeton University Press 2009), *Philosophy of Law* (Princeton University Press 2011), and *The Language of Law* (Oxford University Press 2014). His books and articles also appeared in numerous translations, including in Chinese, Spanish, Portuguese, Hebrew, and Italian. Marmor is the founding editor of the *Journal of Ethics and Social Philosophy*, and the editor of several important volumes in legal philosophy, including, most recently, *The Philosophical Foundations of Language in the Law* (with Scott Soames, Oxford University Press 2011), and *The Routlege Companion to Philosophy of Law.*

Dan Priel is associate professor at Osgoode Hall Law School. He has published articles in legal theory, tort law, and restitution, among other subjects. His current research interests are focused on ways of connecting currently popular jurisprudential theories to political theory as well as to other interdisciplinary perspectives, especially those coming from the natural sciences and engineering.

Veronica Rodriguez-Blanco is Professor of Moral and Political Philosophy (Jurisprudence) at the University of Surrey Centre for Law and Philosophy, UK. She studied law and legal philosophy at Oxford University (MJur) and the University of Cambridge (PhD). She is the author of numerous articles, the edited books *Dignity in the Legal and Political Philosophy of Ronald Dworkin* (Oxford University Press forthcoming), *Reasons and Intentions in Law and Practical Agency* (Cambridge University Press 2015), and the monograph *Law and Authority Under the Guise of the Good* (Hart Publishing 2014, paperback 2017). She has been awarded fellowships and grants from the British Academy, the Alexander Von Humboldt Foundation, the European University Institute (Fernand Braudel Fellow), FAPERJ, Cambridge Overseas Trust, and the British Council. She is co-editor of the journal *Jurisprudence: An International Journal of Legal and Political Thought.*

Corrado Roversi is Assistant Professor in Legal Philosophy at the University of Bologna. He holds a PhD in analytic philosophy and the general theory of law (awarded by the *Università Statale* in Milan) and has spoken at several international conferences and seminars. He is assistant editor of *Ratio Juris* (Oxford, Wiley-Blackwell) and has worked on the project *A Treatise of Legal Philosophy and General Jurisprudence* (Berlin, Springer), of which he has edited the last volume (along with Enrico Pattaro), titled *Legal Philosophy in the Twentieth Century: The Civil Law World* (2016). His publications include: "Constitutive Rules in Context," *Archiv für*

Rechts- und Sozialphilosophie (2010); "On Constitutive Normativity," in *New Essays on the Normativity of Law* (Hart Publishing 2011); "Acceptance Is Not Enough, but Texts Alone Achieve Nothing: A Critique of Two Conceptions of Institutional Ontology," *Rechtstheorie* (2012); "How Social Institutions Can Imitate Nature," *Topoi* (2015).

Frederick Schauer is David and Mary Harrison Distinguished Professor of Law at the University of Virginia. Formerly for nineteen years the Frank Stanton Professor of the First Amendment at Harvard University and a Fellow of the American Academy of Arts and Sciences, he is the author of six books, including *Playing By the Rules: A Philosophical Examination of Rule-Based Decision-Making in Law and in Life* (Clarendon/Oxford, 1991), *Profiles, Probabilities, and Stereotypes* (Harvard University Press 2003), *Thinking Like a Lawyer: A New Introduction to Legal Reasoning* (Harvard University Press 2009), and, most recently, *The Force of Law* (Harvard University Press 2015).

Kevin Toh teaches in the Faculty of Laws at University College London. He previously taught in the philosophy departments of San Francisco State University and Indiana University in Bloomington, and has held visiting fellowships at the Institute for Advanced Studies in the Humanities at the University of Edinburgh, the University of Texas at Austin School of Law, and University College, University of Oxford. He is the author of a number of articles in philosophy of law.

Giovanni Tuzet studied law and philosophy in Turin and Paris and wrote his PhD thesis on Peirce's theory of inference. Formerly post-doc researcher at the universities of Lausanne and Ferrara, he is presently Associate Professor of Philosophy of Law at Bocconi University in Milan, where he teaches Evidence and Economic Analysis of Law. His areas of interest include epistemology, pragmatism, argumentation theory, philosophy of law, and economic analysis of law.

PART I

METHODOLOGY

1

Legal Positivism about the Artifact Law

A Retrospective Assessment

*Brian Leiter**

1. Introduction

Hans Kelsen and H.L.A. Hart, the two giants of twentieth-century jurisprudence, are long dead. Ronald Dworkin, Hart's most persistent critic, passed away several years ago. John Finnis, our leading natural law theorist, has recently issued his collected papers and a second edition of his 1980 book *Natural Law and Natural Rights*. Joseph Raz, Hart's torch-bearer, long ago stopped writing primarily about issues in general jurisprudence, in large part because he thought (correctly in my view) that most of the main issues had been settled (as best as such issues can be settled, about which more below). Although academic life, in the modern research university, continues to follow Max Weber's century-old diagnosis of increasing specialization, now seems a particularly apt moment to reflect more synoptically upon what we learned from the legal philosophy of the past century given that the major contributors have, as it were, finished their contributions, and almost all recent work on these topics reads as footnotes, sometimes long and tedious footnotes, to their contributions, especially Hart's.[1]

* Earlier versions of portions of this material were presented to the work-in-progress luncheon at the University of Chicago Law School in December 2013; as a keynote address at the annual meeting of the Australasian Society of Legal Philosophy at the University of Sydney in August 2013; as the Mary Oliver Woods Lecture in the Department of Philosophy & Religious Studies at Western Illinois University in September 2010; and at a session on "Legal Positivism: For and Against" at the annual meeting of the Association of American Law Schools in New Orleans in January 2010. I am grateful for questions and challenges on all these occasions, and should thank, especially, Tom Campbell, Jonathan Crowe, Dale Smith, and Michael Stokes. I also benefited from discussion of some of these issues with Max Etchemendy, and from his comments, and those of Luka Burazin and Ken Himma, on the penultimate draft. Finally, I thank Taylor Coles, University of Chicago Law School class of 2018, for research assistance.

[1] I am hopeful that the new English translation of Alf Ross's *On Law and Justice*, forthcoming from Oxford University Press, will effect a shift in philosophical interests about law in Anglophone

Law as an Artifact. First Edition. Edited by Luka Burazin, Kenneth Einar Himma, and Corrado Roversi. Chapter 1 © Brian Leiter 2018. Published 2018 by Oxford University Press.

I propose to add my own long footnote, though hopefully not too tedious. Mine shall be less a systematic defense of legal positivism of the Hartian/Razian kind, than a synoptic explanation of what makes that view of the nature of law so plausible, one that all its critics—from Ronald Dworkin and John Finnis in the past, to Stephen Perry and Jeremy Waldron in the present—find they must contest again and again. A frequent target is not necessarily the correct view, to be sure, but in this case, I think it is: the critics return to it again and again because, even more than fifty years after Hart's seminal book, it is clearly the most sensible view to hold. I conclude with some partly sociological reflections about why resistance to legal positivism remains a live issue in certain quarters.

What distinguishes my long footnote is that I will also emphasize an important metaphysical point: namely, that law is a human artifact, not a natural kind. I have touched on that idea previously,[2] but here I want to explore in more detail the philosophical significance of that fact, given the growing interest in that topic as reflected by this very volume.

2. Legal Positivism, Some Preliminaries

Positivist theories of law, if we may put their core idea quite simply, treat law as a human *posit*: some norm—"Don't rob banks" or "Don't go faster than 55 miles per hour on the highway"[3]—is a law (or *legally valid*, as I will henceforth say) because of actions undertaken by human beings (not necessarily actions *intended* to produce legally valid norms, a point to which we return). Laws are not God's commands, they are not handed down from "on high": their existence and character is due to nothing more than certain kinds of human activity.[4] Human beings, of course, do and say lots of things; not all

legal theory. The new edition will correct some of the mistranslations that facilitated the uncharitable reception of the work in Anglophone philosophy after H.L.A. Hart's influential review. Ross has continued to have a huge influence in Continental jurisprudence, where, interestingly, naturalism and ethical non-cognitivism continue to loom large, and where I have always found a very warm reception for my own work aimed at (as a collection of my papers is called) *Naturalizing Jurisprudence* (Oxford University Press 2007).

[2] See Brian Leiter, "The Demarcation Problem in Jurisprudence: A New Case for Skepticism" (2011) 31 *Oxford Journal of Legal Studies* 663, 666–7.

[3] These are obviously proscriptions, but many legal norms are permissions, prescriptions about how to acquire powers, and so on.

[4] Writers who deny this, like Ronald Dworkin, are not theists, but they do think that the content of the law follows from objective moral considerations that no one may have recognized. Moral realism has more in common with theism than its believers acknowledge, a point Nietzsche first diagnosed more than a century ago. Cf. Brian Leiter, "The Death of God and the Death of Morality" *The Monist* (forthcoming).

of them create "laws." But, by the same token, there is no reason to think that because human beings have said or done things that do create laws that what they have done is good, or sensible, or fair, or just, or ought to command our obedience, or even our allegiance. What the law is in our society is one thing; what it morally ought to be, whether we ought to obey it or endorse it, is wholly another. We would do well not to confuse the two, says the positivist; we would do well, for example, not to think that because the U.S. Supreme Court says the law is X, that we have any moral obligation to comply with X or to celebrate it or defer to it. Or, as Jeremy Bentham was concerned to argue, we should never confuse the fact that certain rules were duly enacted by Parliament and so constitute "law" with the question whether these laws are any good, whether they make most people better off, whether they should be respected or, instead, ridiculed and repealed.

That is the simple way of putting the core thought underlying Legal Positivism. But let us now state it a bit more formally. Law is, in H.L.A. Hart's famous formulation, "the union of primary and secondary rules." Primary rules are the rules that tell citizens what they can and cannot do, what powers they can exercise, and how, but a legal system requires more: it also requires rules by which we can change the rules, adjudicate disputes about the rules, and, most importantly, figure out what the rules of *our* legal system actually are. The rule discharging this latter function Hart dubs "the Rule of Recognition": it is the rule that specifies the criteria of legal validity, the criteria all other rules must satisfy to count as rules of the legal system. Those criteria might include "enactment by the legislature" or "decided by a court" or "found in the Constitution." What these criteria are will vary from legal system to legal system. Of course, if the "rule of recognition" is just another rule, like all the others, then the question can naturally arise: how do we know *this rule of recognition* is the rule of our legal system? The answer had better not be: in virtue of satisfying the criteria of validity in a meta-rule of recognition, for then an infinite regress would loom.

But the Rule of Recognition, according to Hart, is a special kind of rule, what he calls a "social rule." A "social rule" is Hart's label for a social practice that has two distinguishing characteristics. A "social rule" exists when: first, there is a convergent practice of behavior among a group of people; and second, those engaged in the behavior *believe* themselves to be *obligated* to engage in that behavior (in Hart's terminology, those engaged in the behavior take an "internal point of view" toward what they are doing). The first criterion—convergent practice of behavior—is characteristic of lots of mindless group behavior: all the children choose chocolate at the ice cream parlor; all the worker ants serve the queen ant. No one thinks the children have an *obligation* to choose chocolate, it just happens that they are in the habit of doing so. And the worker ants certainly do not think they *must* protect the queen ant; they just do what they do!

The Rule of Recognition is different. To be sure, it involves a convergent practice of behavior: judges in the U.S., for example, treat the fact that Congress enacted a piece of legislation (and the President signed it) as *obligating* them to decide issues that come before them in accord with the rules in that legislation. So judges *converge* on "enacted by Congress and signed by the President" as a criterion of legal validity. But judges are not like the kids who habitually choose chocolate or the worker ants serving their queen. Judges do not just "mindlessly" happen to treat Congressional enactments as legally binding; rather they believe that they have an *obligation* to treat such enactments as binding. That is the second crucial component for the existence of a social rule in Hart's sense. The Rule of Recognition is a social rule, which means that for a Rule of Recognition to exist there must be *both* a convergent practice among officials of applying certain criteria of legal validity in deciding which norms are law, but also that the officials adopt an "internal point of view" toward this practice, that is, they believe they have an *obligation* to do this.

So now we have a much richer account of the sense in which law is a product of human actions: a norm is legally valid in some society when it satisfies the criteria of legal validity in that society's Rule of Recognition, and a Rule of Recognition exists in virtue of a complex sociological and psychological fact, namely, that certain officials of the system apply those criteria and *believe* they *ought* to apply them. Notice that the positivist theory of law does *not* claim that they are *correct* to believe that they ought to apply those criteria; the theory claims only that *when law exists* in some society, we find a social rule that is the Rule of Recognition. (Confusion about this point, I am afraid, accounts for almost all the major criticisms of positivism, from John Finnis to Ronald Dworkin.[5]) This leaves open the possibility—*importantly so*—that the officials of the system are *mistaken* in thinking they *ought* to apply the criteria of legal validity they actually apply. That, of course, is what any positivist would have said about judges in Nazi Germany or in the "Jim Crow" American South: to the extent those judges took themselves to have a moral obligation to apply rules enforcing the second-class status (or worse) of Jews or African-Americans or socialists, they had made a moral mistake. The valid laws of their system were morally reprehensible, and warranted disobedience, not enforcement. But whether Alabama had a legal system in 1950 is a separate question from whether it was a *good* legal system: no

[5] On Finnis, see Leiter, *Naturalizing Jurisprudence* (n. 1) 162–4; on Dworkin, see ibid. at 158–9.

significant legal positivist I can think of would have answered the second question in the affirmative.

Let us summarize the preceding even more succinctly. Legal positivism is a theory that answers the question: of all the norms in human societies, what distinguishes the norms that are part of the law, i.e., that are legally valid? According to the positivist, (1) norms are *legally valid* only in virtue of having certain sources (e.g., judicial pronouncement or legislative enactment) and without regard for their *merits*, that is, without regard for whether the norms are fair or just or efficient or sensible (call this, borrowing Raz's terminology, the "Sources Thesis"); and (2) the relevant sources of law in each society are fixed by a contingent practice of officials of the legal system (call this the "Conventionality Thesis").[6] One consequence of the Sources and Conventionality Theses is that, as the famous slogan has it, "there is no necessary connection between law and morality," which means, more precisely, that either (1) it is not necessary for a norm to be legally valid that it satisfy a moral criterion (as Hart would have it), or (2) it is necessary that morality *not* be a criterion of legal validity (as Raz would have it). (My statement of the Sources Thesis favors Raz's formulation, but I think both versions have all the virtues I attribute to the positivist theory in what follows.) As Leslie Green and John Gardner have emphasized in recent years[7]—and as Hart himself acknowledged with his minimum content of natural law thesis some fifty years ago—there are lots of senses in which law and morality *are* necessarily connected, but the familiar slogan about "no necessary connection" has always been meant to pick out either Hart's or Raz's theses about the criteria of legal validity, one of which is shared by everyone, I take it, who thinks that legal positivism gives us the best account of the nature of law.

3. Methodological Interlude: Why Law's Artifactual Nature Matters

So why accept legal positivism as the correct account of law? Sometimes legal philosophers make extravagant claims on behalf of the theory, and I want to

[6] More precisely, the sources are those that officials accept and which they take themselves to have an obligation to consult in deciding questions of legal validity. What Hart calls the "rule of recognition" just is this official practice.

[7] See, e.g., Leslie Green, "Positivism and the Inseparability of Law and Morals" (2008) 83 *NYU Law Review* 1035, and John Gardner, "Legal Positivism: 5 ½ Myths" (2001) 46 *American Journal of Jurisprudence* 199, 222–5.

start by scaling back the ambitions of the claim I am making. Julie Dickson, following Raz, says that

A successful theory of law ... is a theory which consists of propositions about the law which (1) are necessarily true, and (2) adequately explain the nature of law.... I am using "the nature of law" to refer to those essential properties which a given set of phenomena must exhibit in order to be law.[8]

Scott Shapiro, an ambivalent or quasi-positivist,[9] puts the claim even more strongly, declaring that legal philosophers want to "supply the set of properties that make (possible or actual) instances of [law] the things that they are"[10] and offers the example of water being H2O: "Being H2O is what makes water *water*. With respect to law, accordingly, to answer the question 'What is law?' on this interpretation is to discover what makes all and only instances of law instances of *law* and not something else."[11] In addition, says Shapiro (here again echoing Dickson who is following Raz), "to discover the law's nature" is also "to discover its necessary properties, i.e., those properties that law could not fail to have."[12]

Comparing "law" to "water" ought to strike philosophers as mad: water is a *natural kind*, and law is not. Indeed, on most accounts (Dworkin's is the exception), law is a *human artifact*, somewhat like cars, chairs, and computers (though with some important differences to which we will

[8] Julie Dickson, *Evaluation and Legal Theory* (Hart Publishing 2001) 17. Dickson faithfully follows Raz's lead here, though he has not always been so immodest. Thus, in the earlier essay "Legal Positivism and the Sources of Law," reprinted in Joseph Raz, *The Authority of Law* (2nd edn., Oxford University Press 2009), Raz notes that it is no part of the argument for the Sources Thesis "that a similar conception of legal systems is to be found in all cultures and in all periods." Ibid. 50. That is only one kind of theoretical modesty, for one might still think that it is possible to state necessary truths that explain the essential nature of a culturally and temporally bounded human practice; as noted in the text, our experience in the philosophy of science in the twentieth century invites skepticism.

[9] Shapiro self-identifies as a positivist, of course, and in his earlier work—see, e.g., "On Hart's Way Out" (1998) 4 *Legal Theory* 469, 494–5—offered a new argument for "hard" or "exclusive" legal positivism, a variation on Raz's authority argument, but with thinner (and more plausible) assumptions. But his more recent work makes so many confused criticisms of Hart's positivism and concedes so much to the anti-positivist views as to make it unclear whether the resulting theory really honors the Sources and Conventionality Theses. A useful short discussion of the problems is John Gardner and Timothy Macklem's review of Shapiro's *Legality*. John Gardner and Timothy Macklem, "Scott J Shapiro: *Legality*" (*Notre Dame Philosophical Review*, December 8, 2011) <http://ndpr.nd.edu/news/27609-legality/> accessed November 10, 2016.

[10] Scott Shapiro, *Legality* (Harvard University Press 2013) 8–9.

[11] Ibid. 9.

[12] Ibid. The preceding quotations should be read in light of Leslie Green's surprising claim that "no sensible legal philosopher, today or thirty years ago, is looking for properties of law that will 'distinguish it from morality in all cases'." Leslie Green, "The Morality in Law" in Luis Duarte d'Ameida, James Edwards, and Andrea Dolcetti (eds.), *Reading HLA Hart's* The Concept of Law (Hart Publishing 2013) 199.

return).[13] Artifacts can be made of almost anything; natural kinds, by contrast, typically have distinctive micro-constitutions, whether characterized in chemical, molecular, or genetic terms. To be clear, I am a Quinean about natural kinds: "natural kinds" just pick out those ways of grouping things over which the sciences can produce lawful generalizations, groupings we would be especially loathe to abandon given the disruption to the rest of our theoretical picture of how the world works. That is the only sense of "natural kind" that can make sense for empiricists and fallibilists, and it's the sense I endorse here. That means, of course, that at bottom, "natural kinds" also answer to human interests—the various pragmatic interests that inform theory-choice given the underdetermination of theory by evidence and logic[14]—and so the difference between them and artifacts will be ones of degree. But differences of degree can still be vast and theoretically and practically significant, and that is true about the way we demarcate stuff with a distinctive micro-constitution from stuff that is notable mainly for how human beings use it.

Things on the artifact side of the divide, needless to say, do not have distinctive micro-constitutions, but perhaps they can have essential or necessary properties of some other kind? Perhaps, for example, the essential property of an artifact is its function? Let us consider a recent paper by the legal philosopher Luka Burazin, who has given the most systematic account of law's artifactual nature in the jurisprudential literature and its relationship to claims about function.[15] Burazin begins with a well-known philosophical account of artifacts due to Risto Hilpinen, according to which an artifact is "an object that has been intentionally made for a certain purpose."[16] This way of thinking about artifacts poses an immediate difficulty in the case of law, due

[13] On traditional natural law views, *positive* law is a human artifact, but the moral law, of course, is not.

[14] On this see generally, W.V.O. Quine and Joseph Ullian, *The Web of Belief* (Random House 1978).

[15] Luka Burazin, "Can There Be an Artifact Theory of Law?" (2016) 29 *Ratio Juris* 385–401. For a somewhat similar account, see Jonathan Crowe, "Law as an Artifact Kind" (2014) 40 *Monash University Law Review* 737–57. Crowe's account has the virtue of acknowledging the problem that law does not necessarily involve an author, but his positive account is similar to Burazin's, and faces similar difficulties. (Crowe also aims to vindicate a natural law theory, which is no part of Burazin's ambition.)

[16] Risto Hilpinen, "Artifact," *The Stanford Encyclopedia of Philosophy* (2011) <http://plato.stanford.edu/entries/artifact/> accessed November 11, 2016, quoted in Burazin (n. 15) 388. A different account of artifacts as functional kinds holds only that the function is the one the artifact has "historically reproduced to serve." Beth Preston, "Philosophical Theories of Artifact Function" in Anthonie W.M. Meijers (ed.), *Philosophy of Technology and Engineering Sciences* (Reidel 2009) 226. Such a proposal runs into the difficulties discussed below in the text regarding the idea that law's function is to "guide conduct."

to the ambiguity of what "law" refers to. *Particular laws*—say, a particular statute or a particular court decision—may be created intentionally "for a certain purpose," though in the case of legislation, *what* purpose that is a particularly vexed question.[17] (It can also be vexed in the case of a judicial decision, since what law is created by the decision may be different from what the judges intended, and it may be unclear whether the purpose was, e.g., a fair resolution of the dispute before the court or to create a rule that will influence subsequent behavior.) But the positivist theory of law is not a theory about *particular laws*, it is rather a theory about why "particular laws" are tokens of a type "law." And the type law is a social phenomenon that is only implicit and inchoate in the actual practice of judges, lawyers, and ordinary citizens familiar with "modern municipal legal systems," as Hart put it.[18] This is a crucial problem for the traditional way of thinking of artifacts due to Hilpinen, and which Burazin follows. For it is not the case that the *type law*—the phenomenon of law captured by our concept of it—was "intentionally made for a certain purpose."[19] The difficulty becomes apparent when Burazin says that "the intention of legal officials to create an instantiation of the legal system is based on their substantive concept of the legal system."[20] But there is no evidence that legal officials have any such intentions let alone a substantive concept "of the legal system"—even if some philosophers do!

Law is not even alone in being an artifact without an intentional creator. Think of etiquette: even the particular norms of etiquette are rarely intentionally created, and the institution of regulating the boundaries of informal social interaction by, for example, norms of politeness, respect, and courtesy[21]—"etiquette"—is a kind of human social practice that was not created by anyone or any group for any particular purpose, though it serves several in most societies (e.g., reducing social friction, preserving hierarchy, marking degrees

[17] See generally Frank H. Easterbrook, "Judicial Discretion in Statutory Interpretation" (2004) 57 *Oklahoma Law Review* 1. Cf. Richard Ekins, *The Nature of Legislative Intent* (Oxford University Press 2016).

[18] H.L.A. Hart, *The Concept of Law* (3rd edn., Oxford University Press 2012) 7.

[19] Burazin, following other authors, allows that "an artifact can have properties ... acquired through its use in practice," but this is secondary to the primary properties, which are due to the author's intentions. Burazin (n. 15) 391. Burazin also denies that "patterns of behavior or behavioural regularities alone can constitute institutional artifacts" (law being an institutional artifact), again insisting that "a substantive concept" of that artifact must be intentionally applied and recognized by the community. Ibid. 395. But an inchoate concept, like the concept of law (or etiquette), cannot satisfy that demand, since agents have the concept only partially and inchoately.

[20] Ibid. 398.

[21] Note that the instantiation of such norms varies wildly by culture: crossing legs, showing one's feet, sitting down at a particular moment can all violate etiquette norms or be compatible with them.

of intimacy in relationships, among others). Yet etiquette, like law, does not exist without humans producing it, and what comes into existence is not reducible to or even supervenient upon any cluster of natural properties about which the sciences can identify nomic regularities. Yet the practice "etiquette" is still a human artifact, not only because humans produce it, but because *humans care about it*. So I suggest we think of the category of "artifacts" more broadly, as the category of phenomena that *result from human action*, which are *responsive to human interests*, and which are not otherwise natural kinds.[22] That captures both law and etiquette. Hilpinen's and Burazin's error is to define artifactuality in terms of intentionality, and then to suppose that the distinctive function is supposed to be traceable to intention.

Notice that law and etiquette are no different than "science" in this regard. No one set out to create the domain of human inquiry we now call "science" to serve a particular function; what happened, of course, in the scientific revolution is that individuals set out to try to discover different kinds of regularities in nature, and found out that they could do so through certain methods, with the resulting amalgamation of theories being deemed "science." Science is a human artifact too, but like law and etiquette, it has no intentional maker of the type of social phenomenon it is, though people and whole political cultures care about science immensely. Is there a distinctive *function* of science nonetheless? Certainly initially, it seemed to be *prediction and control* of nature, but that will hardly help explain the sense in which much of geology, evolutionary biology, and cosmology are part of science. Indeed, as Larry Laudan has shown,[23] there is no criterion at all, let alone a functional one, that adequately demarcates science from non-science. As I have argued elsewhere,[24] those of us working in general jurisprudence should all be given special pause by the failure of twentieth-century philosophy of science to identify the essential features of science, one of the most important human artifacts of modernity.[25] The two major attempts in the twentieth century are both recognized as abject failures. "Verificationist" theories (propounded by various logical positivists) held that scientific propositions were genuinely meaningful, that is, empirically verifiable. These theories, however, ran into trouble because, on the one hand, as Larry Laudan observes, "many statements in the sciences

[22] Some words pick out phenomena that lead dual existences. A "wolverine" can be a biological kind of animal, but it is also an artifact: the mascot for the University of Michigan sports teams.

[23] Larry Laudan, "The Demise of the Demarcation Problem" in R.S. Cohen and Larry Laudan (eds.), *Physics, Philosophy and Psychoanalysis: Essays in Honor of Adolf Grünbaum* (Springer 1983). Cf. the discussion in Leiter, "The Demarcation Problem in Jurisprudence" (n. 2) 667–70.

[24] Leiter, "The Demarcation Problem in Jurisprudence" (n. 2).

[25] See Laudan (n. 23).

[are] not open to exhaustive verification (e.g., all universal laws),"[26] while many false statements—like "the Earth is flat"—are verifiable (though false!) since "we can specify a class of possible observations which would verify" the statement.[27] Karl Popper's alternative, eschewing verification in favor of falsifiability, ran into different problems: it could not explain the scientific status of most "singular existential statement[s]" (e.g., "there exists a Black Hole") and it deems "scientific" "every crank claim which makes ascertainably false assertions."[28] Since the human practice of science is disciplined by far more demanding criteria than the human practice of law—criteria like successful "prediction and control" (the rockets need to go up and come down where expected!)—should we really expect an attempt to demarcate the essential characteristics that distinguish "law" from non-legal norms to fare better?

Leslie Green has recently expressed skepticism about what lesson we should draw from the preceding about the prospects for individuating artifact types by their functions. He gives the amusing purported counter-example of a "printer-driver":[29] "no string of code is a printer-driver," he observes, "unless it is written in order to, or has or could have some capacity to, drive a printer."[30] As a matter of the metaphysics, we can agree with Green that artifacts, like other entities, are self-identical, which is all his purported analysis of the function shows. The real question is whether there is any account of the *functional kind* an artifact is that does not trade on self-identity and which does not avert to the intentions of the creator—which for the reasons already noted, is not available in the case of law. In short, could phenomena that are produced by humans and are responsive to human interests still have distinctive functions, where distinctive means "type-individuating" functions?

One possibility, it might seem, is that facts about the etiology of the artifact *apart from the intentions of a creator* could individuate a function characteristic of the type. We are of course familiar with this idea from selectionist accounts not of artifactual but biological kinds. Yet even in the latter context,

[26] Ibid. 120. [27] Ibid. 121.

[28] Ibid. It is possible Popper's view could deal with singular existential statements by noting their dependence on theoretical claims that were, themselves, vulnerable to falsification. Still other objections, however, were raised to Popper's falsificationism. Paul Feyerabend called attention to the commitment of natural scientists to theories some of whose predictions had actually been falsified. The so-called Duhem-Quine thesis about the underdetermination of theory by evidence suggests that no theoretical claim can ever be falsified, since there is always a choice, when confronted with recalcitrant evidence, to reject *either* the claim being tested *or* the background assumptions underlying the test. (Laudan, however, is a critic of the Duhem-Quine thesis: see, e.g., Larry Laudan, *Science and Relativism* (The University of Chicago Press 1990)).

[29] Leslie Green, "The Morality in Law" in d'Ameida, Edwards, and Dolcetti, *Reading HLA Hart's* The Concept of Law (n. 12) 200.

[30] Ibid.

the claim is controversial. As the philosopher of biology David Hull asked, in an influential paper a quarter-century ago:

> [W]hat is the normal function of the [human] hand? We can do many things with our hands. We can drive cars, play the violin, type on electronic computers, scratch itches, masturbate, and strangle one another. Some of these actions may seem normal; others not, but there is no correlation between commonsense notions of normal functions and the functions which hands were able to fulfill throughout our existence. About all a biologist can say about the function of the human hand is that anything that we can do with it is "normal."[31]

Hull's view is by no means uncontroversial,[32] but I mention it only to underline that even in the biological domain, function talk is complicated. What then of artifacts, which have no biological etiology (and no intentional creator), how are their functions to be determined?

Law, like etiquette, serves many functions, and no evolutionary story—certainly none with the explanatory power of natural selection—picks out any distinctive one. When we untether artifacts from creators, I fear, functions are always hostage to rather variable interests, since that is all that is left to us to individuate the artifacts. The essential function of a chair, one might say, is to provide support to those who want to sit. But does that mean that the boxes in my new apartment are chairs because I rest on them while getting settled? And does it mean that decorative chairs are not chairs, because no one should or will sit on them? The worry can be generalized: I am not aware of a single, widely accepted analysis of the essential properties of any artifact that does not rely on appeal to intentions of the creator in a context where it seems we should defer to those. If there is one, I would like to hear it.

Sometimes it is said that the "essential" function of law is to guide conduct,[33] but perhaps we should pause for a moment to make clear why this will not work. Many valid laws do not, of course, guide conduct (think of laws against jay-walking, at least in many places). But even if we say the essential function of law is to *try* to guide conduct, there is the obvious problem that

[31] David Hull, "On Human Nature" in Stephen M. Downes and Edouard Machery (eds.), *Arguing about Human Nature* (Routledge 2013) 31.

[32] Cf. Edouard Machery, "A Plea for Human Nature" in ibid. especially at 65–8 explaining the relevance of etiology to function talk.

[33] Those influenced by speculative evolutionary psychology and anthropology sometimes think that law's function is a certain kind of "social coordination," which is an even more demanding standard than the fairly thin idea of "guiding conduct." I do not consider such proposals here, given how thin the scientific evidence is that this picks out a distinctive function of law. Consider: if law's function were really "social coordination," then why does the actual content of the law in societies at similar levels of economic development differ so dramatically? Evolutionary functionalists need to answer that question.

morality and advertising, for example, also try to guide conduct, but neither is (necessarily) law. Advertising, one might object, tries to guide conduct indirectly (i.e., not by telling subjects explicitly what to do), while law and morality try to do so directly. But law and morality also share that aim with the differing sets of rules that govern the Catholic Mass, dining in a fancy restaurant, and playing cricket. So if law were "essentially" about guiding conduct, that by itself would not pick it out from other normative systems. More problematically, however, law serves other functions besides attempted guidance of conduct: for example, some laws are meant to signal the values or aspirations of a community, and some are simply ceremonial (think of commemorations of national heroes). Law sometimes guides conduct, often attempts to guide conduct, but it cannot claim that as its distinguishing essential function, since it shares guidance and attempted guidance with too many other normative systems, and, itself, discharges other functions as well.

Green also accuses me of a *tu quoque* fallacy: "Leiter even holds," he says, "that it is a necessary feature of something being an artefact that it has no (other) necessary features"[34] and then claims that this shows, *contra* my skepticism, that there is, in fact, a necessary difference between law and morality since, as Green asserts, "morality does *not* owe its existence to human activities intended to create morality."[35] Green takes as his target here an earlier paper in which I mistakenly claimed that artifacts had to be *intentional* human creations,[36] a view I now repudiate for the reasons given earlier. My worry then was about human babies, which are not, it seems, artifacts, but are human creations, although not always intentional. But human babies are biological kinds, just like calves and lion cubs, and so are not artifacts in the sense proposed earlier: they result from human actions, human beings care about them, but they are biological kinds, so not artifacts.

But Green's objection does not depend on the specific claim about intentionality: it depends on my thinking there is a way to mark the artifact/natural kind distinction, which seems to commit me to artifacts having some necessary features after all. Everything turns here on the sense of "necessity": if the artifact/natural kind distinction is theoretically fruitful, as I think it is, then we need to say what that distinction is. As with natural kinds themselves, on the Quinean view, the boundaries could shift: in that sense, they are not necessary. But as theorizing stands today, if artifacts have essential features

[34] Green (n. 29) 200. [35] Ibid.

[36] Leiter, "The Demarcation Problem in Jurisprudence" (n. 2) 666.

or functions, then someone should name them![37] Green does not, and no one has.[38]

4. What Positivism Explains

Enough by way of methodological preamble to my defense of legal positivism. Let us deflate our ambitions in a way suitable to the subject matter and the history of attempts to develop essentialist accounts of artifacts. Human artifacts answer to human interests, thus their nature and character is hostage to changing needs and wants. Even so, we can try to take a conceptual snapshot of these artifacts that answers to our current concerns. We can try to say what an artifact is *here and now*, with the boundaries of the characterization to be specified. Hart himself proposed the "modern municipal legal system," meaning his theory would be agnostic about "primitive" law, ancient law, and so on. Any such temporally and/or culturally circumscribed snapshot will no doubt have fuzzy borders, and will likely be vulnerable to creative counterfactual intuition pumps, but nothing more can be expected: human interests can be well-served by imprecise concepts, and law is likely one. But with our theoretical ambitions so deflated, it is easy to say why legal positivism seems our best theory of law, without meaningful competition. Three theoretical desiderata appear decisive and critics of positivism really should make clear which ones they mean to reject.

First, if we take seriously Hart's *explicit* theoretical aim of doing justice to what the ordinary man understands about the modern municipal legal system,[39] then we have no better theory than positivism: it captures remarkably well the familiar distinctions between law and morality, law and policy, and legal knowledge and moral wisdom, the kinds of distinctions jurists, lawyers, and educated laymen draw all the time. Any controversial court decision in

[37] Alternatively, theorists could do something else! Cf. for one example, Frederick Schauer, *The Force of Law* (Harvard University Press 2015).

[38] This is more minor, but it is not my view that morality "does not owe its existence to human activities"—like law and etiquette it does not owe its existence to *intentional* human activities, but it is a wholly conventional normative system. I do not think this is a point of disagreement between myself and Green.

[39] See Hart, *The Concept of Law* (n. 18) 79. Despite my earlier doubts about Hart's methodological posture (e.g., Leiter, *Naturalizing Jurisprudence* (n. 1), especially chs. 4 and 6), I now think there is a sound rationale for his method, once we recognize that law is a social fact in Searle's sense, and thus constituted by linguistic practices. For sympathetic discussion of that way of rationalizing Hart's approach, see Alex Langlinais and Brian Leiter, "The Methodology of Legal Philosophy" in Herman Cappelen, Tamar S. Gendler, and John Hawthorne (eds.), *The Oxford Handbook of Philosophical Methodology* (Oxford University Press 2016), especially 674–7.

the United States can be met with the charge by its critics that the judges did not apply the law, but were influenced by extra-legal considerations. That charge is not unintelligible, and any serious theory of law should be able to explain it. We all think judges can have legal competence, but bad moral judgment: once again, any serious theory of law should explain the distinction. We all recognize the cogency of the complaint, "there ought to be a law" governing some wrongdoing that involves no legal sanction, but it again supposes that there is a difference between conduct which is normatively objectionable and that which is legally proscribed. I am not aware of any competitor theories to legal positivism that have satisfactory accounts of these "ordinary" distinctions.

Raz's "authority argument" for positivism[40] has attracted important criticism over the last generation—from Stephen Perry, Thomas Christiano and Stefan Sciaraffa, and Michael Sevel,[41] among others—but it is less often remembered that Raz's earliest, and more persuasive, arguments for positivism turned only on its ability to explain precisely these kinds of distinctions.[42] Positivism, as he observed, "reflects and explicates our conception of the law," for example the fact that we distinguish between "the legal skills of the judge" and his or her "moral character,"[43] and between "deciding cases regarding which the law is unsettled" and those "where the law is settled" such that judges need only "us[e] their legal skills in applying the law."[44] Positivism does so through its Social and Conventionality theses: to have "legal skill," for example, is to know what the laws are according to the extant conventions, or to know how to find out what they are. Anyone who has ever seen a confirmation hearing for a Justice of the United States Supreme Court can readily

[40] In condensed form: all law claims to be authoritative, yet given the nature of authority, law could not even *claim* to be authoritative if the criteria of legal validity were anything other than positive sources of law. The argument turns on Raz's "service" conception of authority, according to which a practical authority purports to adjudicate among all the relevant practical reasons and then issue its own directive about what ought to be done, one which will enable the subject of the authority to better do what he really ought to do. It is implausible, however, that law claims authority in the service conception sense, and such a thesis is inconsistent with the naturalistic outlook that otherwise commends legal positivism as I argue in Brian Leiter, "Legal Positivism as a Realistic Theory of Law" in Patricia Mindus and Torben Spaak (eds.), *The Cambridge Companion to Legal Positivism* (Cambridge University Press forthcoming).

[41] Stephen R. Perry, "Political Authority and Political Obligation" in Leslie Green and Brian Leiter (eds.), *Oxford Studies in Philosophy of Law, Vol. 2* (Oxford University Press 2013); Thomas Christiano and Stefan Sciaraffa, "Legal Positivism and the Nature of Legal Obligation" (2003) 22 *Law & Philosophy* 487; Michael Sevel, "Essays on Authority" (PhD Thesis, University of Texas at Austin 2010).

[42] Joseph Raz, "Legal Positivism and the Source of Law" in Joseph Raz, *The Authority of Law* (Oxford University Press 1979).

[43] Ibid. 48. [44] Ibid. 49.

confirm that these distinctions are, indeed, central to the popular conception of law in the United States. But in legal systems where the judiciary is more disciplined by virtue of its civil-service character—this is true in Britain and Australia—such distinctions are also quite familiar. Positivism explains the distinctions: as Raz puts it, "the law on a question is settled when legally binding sources provides its solution" and "since it is source-based, [the law's] application involves technical, legal skills in reasoning from those sources and does not call for moral acumen."[45]

Positivism, for similar reasons, also has an easy time explaining the most important fact about modern legal systems: namely, that despite their complexity, there exists massive agreement about what the law is in the vast, vast majority of legal questions that arise in ordinary life.[46] One may think of the universe of legal questions as a pyramid, with the very pinnacle of the structure captured by the judgments of the highest court of appeal, and the base represented by all those possible legal disputes that enter a lawyer's office. This is, admittedly, a very strange-looking pyramid, as the ratio of the base to the pinnacle is something like a million to one. It is, of course, familiar[47] that the main reason the legal system of a modern society does not collapse under the weight of disputes is precisely that *most* cases that are presented to lawyers never go any further than the lawyer's office; that *most* cases that lawyers take do not result in formal litigation; that *most* cases that result in litigation settle by the end of discovery; that most cases that go to trial and verdict, do not get appealed; and that most cases that get appealed do not get appealed to the highest court.

Massive and *pervasive* agreement about the law throughout the system explains these phenomena.[48] It is precisely because almost everyone agrees

[45] Ibid. 49–50.

[46] Cf. Brian Leiter, "Explaining Theoretical Disagreement" (2009) 76 *University of Chicago Law Review* 1215, 1227.

[47] Consider Administrative Office of the U.S. Courts, Statistical Tables for the Federal Judiciary, Table C-4 (December 2007) <http://www.uscourts.gov/statistics-reports/statistical-tables-federal-judiciary-december-2007> accessed November 13, 2016 (reporting that out of 236,256 cases in 2007, 53,581 were resolved without court action, and only 9,858 were resolved by the court at trial); Administrative Office of the U.S. Courts, *Judicial Case Load Indicators: 12-month Periods Ending March 31, 1998, 2003, 2006, and 2007* (March 2007) <www.uscourts.gov/file/13497/download> accessed November 13, 2016 (reporting that in 2007, 254,850 cases were terminated in the U.S. district court system and that only 60,668 appeals were filed in the U.S. court of appeals system).

[48] The point was made in the jurisprudential literature against reckless claims about legal indeterminacy by the Critical Legal Studies writers a generation ago. See, e.g., Frederick Schauer, "Easy Cases" (1985) 58 *Southern California Law Review* 399–440; Ken Kress, "Legal Indeterminacy" (1989) 77 *California Law Review* 283–337; Brian Leiter, "Legal Indeterminacy" (1995) 1 *Legal Theory* 481–92. There is a certain irony in now needing to re-emphasize a similar point against Dworkin, the true believer in global legal determinacy! The difficulty, of course, is that Dworkin's

about the law that lawyers can tell most prospective clients who wander through the doors that they have no claim, and should go home; it is precisely because just about everyone agrees about the law that most cases settle after discovery, since by then the facts are clear and both sides know what the legally required result will be (and so the only question is putting a price tag on the resolution); it is precisely because just about everyone agrees about the law that most cases are not appealed; and so on. To be sure, there are a variety of strategic and other considerations that may explain why some parties litigate and appeal verdicts quite independent of agreement about the law, but if there were not massive convergence about *what the law is*, we should expect the universe of legal cases to look less like a pyramid and more like a lopsided square, whose base was perhaps somewhat bigger than its top.[49]

One of the great theoretical virtues of legal positivism as a theory of law is that it explains why the universe of legal cases looks like a pyramid precisely because its Conventionality and Sources Theses explain how *massive legal agreement* is possible. Legal professionals agree about what the law requires so often because, in a functioning legal system, *what the law is* is fixed by a discernible practice of officials who decide questions of legal validity by reference to criteria of legal validity on which they recognizably converge. Only as we approach the pinnacle of the pyramid do we approach those cases where the practice of officials breaks down, and the "law" is up for grabs. Indeed, there is an obvious "selection effect" in favor of appealing the cases where the law is not clear and so judges have room for discretion and thus room for siding with the appellant's version of the case.

A second, more abstract theoretical consideration in favor of legal positivism deserves notice. It should count in favor of an account of the nature of law that it complements, and perhaps even wins support from, work in the empirical sciences. In the history of philosophy, one thing we have learned is that armchair confidence about reality often has to retreat in the face of scientific success. Kant took it to be a priori that space necessarily had the structure described by Euclidean geometry; a posteriori discoveries have insured that no one believes Kant any longer. A theory of law that makes explicit the tacit or inchoate concepts at play in scientific research is probably to be preferred to its competitors. Positivism is that theory. If one surveys, for example, the now vast empirical literature on adjudication,[50] which aims to explore the

belief in the determinacy of legal reasoning is only a *metaphysical* thesis, not an *epistemological* one—were it epistemological, then there would be no room, of course, for theoretical disagreement.

[49] I simplify, unavoidably, the complexity of considerations that influence parties in a modern legal system.

[50] See Jeffrey Segal and Harold Spaeth, *The Supreme Court and the Attitudinal Model Revisited* (Cambridge University Press 2002); Cass Sunstein et al., *Are Judges Political? An Empirical*

relative contributions of legal versus non-legal norms to decision-making by courts, that literature *always* demarcates the distinction in positivist terms.[51] The current predictive power of that literature is mixed, though better than the alternatives, but the striking fact is that the research program presupposes a positivist theory of law.

A third, and final, consideration in support of the positivist theory of law pertains to its ontological austerity. In all other domains of inquiry, it is taken to be a theoretical virtue to understand a phenomenon in ways that do not involve unnecessary, controversial, or incredible metaphysical commitments. So, for example, it would be a serious problem for a theory of law that it made the nature of law dependent on the will of God, since we have neither good reason to think God exists, nor reliable epistemic access to his will (even if he did exist). It is a virtue of legal positivism that its picture of the world is ontologically austere (though not as austere as some pictures!): it requires only persons and their psychological states to explain the social phenomenon of law.[52] Moral truths and transcendental norms play no role in the Hartian picture, though the former are required by the views of Finnis and Dworkin, and the latter by Kelsen's theory.[53] Since the existence of either is controversial at best and incredible at worst, it constitutes a theoretical virtue of Hartian legal positivism that it has no need for such an ontology.

Now admittedly the last two theoretical considerations I have adduced in favor of positivism take for granted what is often called "naturalism" in philosophy. But naturalism, and this bears emphasizing, is *our* world view, where "our" means we post-Enlightenment folk. It is easy to lose sight of the "background" of intelligibility of our theoretical endeavors, since we have no position outside that background from which to leverage or "ground" its credibility. Yet even the most religiously devout respect the epistemic demands of naturalism in their ordinary lives (e.g., sense perception is a generally reliable way to predict the future course of experience), and since the scientific revolution, the rest of culture and thought has gradually been disciplined by naturalistic considerations in one guise or another. In favoring a theory that

Investigation of the Federal Judiciary (Brookings 2006); Thomas Miles and Cass Sunstein, "The New Legal Realism" (2008) 73 *University of Chicago Law Review* 823; etc. Cf. Richard Posner, *How Judges Think* (Harvard University Press 2010) for an overview.

[51] Cf. Leiter, *Naturalizing Jurisprudence* (n. 1) 54–7.

[52] This was the great innovation of Hart's positivism as against Kelsen's NeoKantian variety, and together with his normative non-cognitivism and anti-behaviorism in psychology, allowed Hart to also displace the Scandinavian Realist theory of law as well.

[53] Kelsen's theory admits of a different, *epistemic* interpretation, which would vitiate this particular objection.

explains an artifact naturalistically, we favor a theory that is most likely to find a place within our most general theoretical accounts of how the world works.

5. Alternatives to Positivism?

What theories, then, stand opposed to the positivism that fares so well by the measures just noted? "Natural law" theories are not really competitors to positivism any longer, I believe. Their most prominent proponent, John Finnis, has already conceded that the legal positivist satisfies the first desideratum (roughly, explaining what the common man means),[54] and he has never been able to make good on the more ambitious claim that no general, descriptive theory of law is possible.[55] Finnis claimed that to do general jurisprudence, one not only needed to focus on the central cases of law—namely, law as understood from an internal point of view—but on the central case of the "internal point of view" itself. And that central case, according to Finnis, was the case in which officials did not simply believe the law to be obligation-imposing, but in which they believed so correctly. Thus, to describe *that* kind of law, one would first have to do normative philosophy to answer the question what kind of legal system would yield genuine moral obligations to comply with its directives. Unfortunately, Finnis never explained why the central case of the internal point of view had to be interpreted his way. Hart agrees that to understand a social practice one has to understand the point of view of participants in the practice. And Hart agrees that this internal point of view is central to understanding law, but for descriptive not normative reasons: recall that Hart's objection to Holmes (and, mistakenly, to the Scandinavian Realists) was not that the point of view of the "Bad Man" was morally wrong, but that it was descriptively false as an account of the internal point of view on law, given that citizens and especially officials talk in terms of an "obligation" to do what the law requires. For Hart, the central case of the internal point of view is the one that is actually present in all modern municipal legal systems, namely, that officials of the system treat the rules of the system as obligation-imposing. That descriptive thesis may be wrong, but Finnis has no argument that it is. Finnitian Natural Law, charitably understood, is just doing something different, trying to explain the features of

[54] John Finnis, "On the Incoherence of Legal Positivism" (2000) 75 *Notre Dame Law Review* 1611.

[55] See Leiter, *Naturalizing Jurisprudence* (n. 1) 162–3. Contemporary natural law theorists have, correctly, focused on attacking the possibility of descriptive jurisprudence as the key issue confronting positivism. See, e.g., Stephen Perry, "Hart's Methodological Positivism" (1998) 4 *Legal Theory* 427.

morally ideal legal systems. That is a good project, even if Finnis's meta- and normative ethics are, as it seems to me, implausible. But it states no dispute with positivism as a theory of law. Finnis's challenge is now plainly moribund outside certain Catholic sects.

If not natural law theory, then what? American Legal Realism, as I have argued for many years, is not only compatible with positivism as a theory of the nature of law, but *presupposes it* in its explanation of the indeterminacy of legal reasoning.[56] American Realists claimed that judicial decision-making had to be explained by the influence of non-legal norms on the judges, since the legal norms underdetermined the decision required. In so arguing, they assumed that only source-based norms could be legally binding ones, and that the only legally binding ones were those explicitly acknowledged by the courts in their opinions or embodied in statutes. They then argued that since there existed equally legitimate but incompatible ways of interpreting the sources, legal reasoning was indeterminate, at least in some range of cases. Their arguments for legal indeterminacy, in short, presupposed a positivist view of which norms were legally binding on judges.

Scandinavian Legal Realism is also, I believe, orthogonal to the claims the Hartian positivist is defending. Unlike the Americans, the Scandinavians' motivation was explicitly metaphysical and epistemological: they wanted to understand what legal norms could be, and how anyone could know them, in a world that was assumed not to include norms in its ontology.[57] The Scandinavians were in many ways severe naturalists, though unlike Quine, who thought that only physically observable stuff, like behavior, really exists, the Scandinavians were willing to countenance psychological states in their ontology. Rather than try to capture the common-sensical notion of law, Alf Ross, for example, was explicit that his basic account of law as a prediction of what legal actors will do was stipulative, intended to show how we could make sense of legal systems in a world thought to be norm-free—though not free of psycho-physical facts about human behavior. Ross's aim, in short, was not to make sense of what the "ordinary" person knows about the modern municipal legal system, and so, at that level, his theory was in no competition with Hart's positivism.[58]

[56] Leiter, *Naturalizing Jurisprudence* (n. 1) ch. 2.

[57] See Brian Leiter, "Legal Realisms, Old and New" (2013) 47 *Valparaiso Law Review* 949.

[58] Here I have been influenced by the work of Jakob Holtermann, who is editing the new English edition of Ross's *magnus opus.*

6. The Case of Dworkin-Lite

So that leaves us, as far as I can see, with just one familiar contender against positivism: Dworkin's theory of "law as integrity,"[59] as he came to call it, according to which the law is whatever follows from the best "constructive interpretation" of the institutional history of the legal system, that is, whatever follows from the principles that provide the best explanation and justification for what the courts and legislature have done so far. But Dworkin's theory fails along each dimension of theoretical adequacy noted earlier. For example, not only can it not explain why any judicial reference to morality is not in fact legally binding,[60] it even entails the bizarre and counter-intuitive possibility that no one in any legal system actually knows what the law is on any point, since it may be that no one has figured out the best constructive interpretation yet. Dworkin's theory figures as the background to no empirical research program into adjudication, and it demands that there be objectively right answers to *all* moral questions. It fails, in short, to explain what the ordinary man understands about the modern municipal legal system, and it does so with a theoretical edifice that plays no role in scientific research and which requires highly contentious metaphysical claims.[61]

This is not to deny that Dworkin's views have enjoyed a kind of popular resonance in many constitutional democracies, though this appears to be mainly due to a superficial understanding of Dworkin's actual views. Many constitutional lawyers find Dworkin's theory appealing, for example, because they like that it makes moral considerations obviously relevant to the resolution of momentous constitutional questions, and in what appears a principled way. The memorial notice for Dworkin by Cass Sunstein,[62] a leading American public law scholar, is illustrative. Here is Sunstein:

> Consider a question about which people fiercely disagree: Does the U.S. Constitution require states to recognize same-sex marriages? In answering that question, judges

[59] Ronald Dworkin, *Law's Empire* (Harvard University Press 1996).

[60] At best, the Dworkinian can say that any particular reference to morality is not *really* part of the best constructive interpretation of the law. But we often think we *know* that some moral references are extra-legal, and on the epistemic point, Dworkin's theory can not offer any explanation at all.

[61] The same applies to even more baroque, and less plausible, recent interventions, such as Mark Greenberg, "The Moral Impact Theory of Law" (2014) 123 *Yale Law Journal* 1118, which abandons even the pretense of being a theory of what anyone, academic or lawyer, understands by law.

[62] Cass Sunstein, "The Most Important Legal Philosopher of Our Time" (Bloomberg News, February 15, 2013) <https://www.bloomberg.com/view/articles/2013-02-15/the-most-important-legal-philosopher-of-our-time> accessed November 13, 2016.

have to deal with many precedents. For example, the Supreme Court has ruled that states can't criminalize sexual acts between people of the same sex. The court has also forbidden states from banning racial intermarriages. At the same time, the court allows states to forbid polygamous marriages.

In resolving the same-sex marriage dispute, how can judges deal with such precedents? Here Dworkin introduced an arresting metaphor. Suppose that you are a participant in writing a chain novel. Others have written earlier chapters. Now it's your turn. How shall you proceed?

Dworkin's answer is that you have to engage in an act of interpretation. You can't disregard what has come before. If your predecessors have started to write a romance, you can't suddenly turn it into a work of science fiction without doing violence to what they have done. You owe a duty of fidelity to their work.

But your task is not mechanical. You have to fit the existing materials, and you have to justify them, by writing a new chapter that makes the emerging novel, taken as a whole, the best it can be.

Dworkin thinks that judging is a lot like that. Precedents are like the existing chapters, and a new case is an opportunity to produce a fresh one. Judges can't just make the law up. But at least in hard cases, they can't merely "follow the law," because there isn't anything to "follow." What they have to do is produce a principle that both fits and justifies the existing legal materials. This is Dworkin's conception of law as integrity.

This does, indeed, seem like one sensible recommendation about how judges should proceed when the law leaves a question unsettled (such that there is no law to "follow," as Sunstein puts it), and nothing in the theory of law known as legal positivism actually takes issue with such a recommendation. Where the law is unsettled—as it often is in momentous constitutional cases—positivists certainly think moral considerations are pertinent to the best resolution of the question; and even where the law is settled, positivists also think that moral considerations can override the settled law: no serious positivist theory holds that settled law imposes non-defeasible obligations on officials or citizens.[63]

Dworkin's theory of law, *contra* Sunstein, is not simply the view that in an area which is "fiercely contested," one should apply the fit-justification method of interpretation. This completely elides the quite radical and implausible character of Dworkin's views about the nature of law. According to Dworkin, what the law is (not simply what a court should do in a hard case, but *what the law in any given jurisdiction really is*) is whatever follows from the

[63] What the law is, that is one thing; what the law *ought* to be is another. Every legal positivist from Bentham onwards takes that idea very seriously. One might even say that it is essential to the positivist view to defeat the assumption that legal validity entails moral obligation, by citizen or judge.

best constructive interpretation (in roughly the fit-justification sense glossed by Sunstein) of the institutional history of the legal system, i.e., the prior legislative enactments, court decisions, and so on. That means, among other things, that some prior legislative enactments and prior court decisions *might not really be law*, since they might not follow from the best constructive interpretation of the system. Indeed, it means that no one may actually *know* what the real law is in the United States, or in any other jurisdiction, since no one may have yet figured out the best justification for the institutional history of the legal system. A theory of law that entails that no one might actually know what the law is faces a serious, shall we say, *reductio ad absurdum* problem.

The trademark Dworkinian move in his decades-long battle with legal positivism was always to run together questions about what the law is (on which he and positivists had opposing views) with the question how courts should decide particular cases (where positivists could often agree with Dworkin). Here is how I put it in reviewing Dworkin's collection of essays, *Justice in Robes*, a decade ago:[64]

Dworkin organizes his reply [to Hart's criticisms of Dworkin in the "Postscript" to *The Concept of Law*] around a hypothetical case involving "Mrs. Sorenson," who has been injured by a defective drug whose precise manufacturer she cannot identify because many companies produced the same product. Common-law courts responded to this kind of problem by inventing a new doctrine, "market-share liability," requiring manufacturers to pay damages for harm based on their 'market share' of

[64] Brian Leiter, "The Theory of Esoteric Law" (2006) 56 *Journal of Legal Education* 675. It is perhaps worth noting that in the 2004 version of his essay on Hart's *Postscript*, Dworkin wrote:

Hart's sources thesis [the thesis that "the existence and content of law can be identified by reference to the social sources of law"] is very far from neutral between the parties in Mrs. Sorenson's case.... No "source" of the kind Hart had in mind had provided that people in Mrs. Sorenson's position are entitled to recover damages on a market-share basis, or stipulated a moral standard that might have that upshot or consequence. So if Hart is right Mrs. Sorenson cannot claim that law is on her side.... Mrs. Sorenson's lawyers argued to the contrary. They denied the sources thesis: they said that general principles inherent in the law entitled their client to win. So Hart's view is not neutral in the argument: it takes sides. It takes sides, in fact, in every difficult legal dispute, in favour of those who insist that the legal rights of the parties are to be settled entirely by consulting the traditional sources of law.

After I criticized this misreading in a notoriously polemical critique of Dworkin—Brian Leiter, "The End of Empire: Dworkin and Jurisprudence in the 21st Century" (2004) 36 *Rutgers Law Journal* 165—Dworkin rewrote the passage to make the mistake less obvious, omitting the last few lines, and now claiming only that for Hart, "So far as the law is concerned, he would have said, she must lose." Ronald Dworkin, *Justice in Robes* (Harvard University Press 2008) 144. That is closer to being accurate, but still gives the misleading impression, as does Dworkin's whole discussion, that Hart would have counselled that Mrs. Sorensen lose her case. Unsurprisingly, there was no citation indicating the reason for Dworkin's revision, which was, alas, typical of Dworkin's unscholarly *modus operandi*.

the dangerous product without requiring individualized proof by the plaintiff that defendant's version of the product caused the injuries in question. Dworkin thinks Mrs. Sorenson was legally entitled to this remedy even before clever judges crafted the new rule, and—more to the point here—he thinks Hart was committed to denying Mrs. Sorenson was entitled to such a remedy, since the existing legal authorities did not explicitly establish it. "Hart and I hold opposite opinions about the same issue," says Dworkin.

But this is false, if the issue is, as it appears to be, the remedy that ought to be awarded Mrs. Sorenson. For Dworkin runs together the question "What is the law in this jurisdiction?" with the question "How ought a particular case be decided?" Positivists have always been clear that a judge's legal duty to apply valid law can be overridden by moral or equitable considerations in any particular case, and Hart's general theory ("the sources thesis") that "laws" are distinguished by their source—by their being enacted, for example, by a legislative body or figuring in the holding of a court—is simply silent on how the wronged Mrs. Sorenson should be treated. On Dworkin's [theory], however, it seems every moral wrong must have a preordained *legal* remedy—even though no one knew the law required it!—so that forward-looking jurists who craft new legal rules in response to real-world problems are really only "discovering" a legal remedy that already existed in Dworkinian Heaven.

Sunstein's Dworkin—who is, I think, the Dworkin that has been influential in most Anglophone constitutional theory—is Dworkin-lite, though I intend nothing pejorative by that label: think "coca cola lite," which is still quite good (it's what I drink) but not the "real thing" as the advertising says. Dworkin-lite is not the real Dworkin, since it obscures from view the counter-intuitive commitments of his conception of the nature of law. But it is the bit of Dworkin that seems most appealing, and helps make sense of one way in which constitutional lawyers and theorists argue. Only atrocious public relations for legal positivism—aided and abetted by decades of misrepresentation by Dworkin—has led so many casual consumers of the jurisprudential literature to think otherwise. This poses an interesting sociological question about jurisprudence, but perhaps not an interesting philosophical one.

7. Philosophy or Sociology?

Let me take that back, slightly. Philosophers, due to their Socratic delusions,[65] often think there is a hard line between sociological and philosophical

[65] Cf. Brian Leiter, "The History of Philosophy Reveals that "Great" Philosophy is Disguised Moral Advocacy: A Nietzschean Case Against the Socratic Canon in Philosophy" in M. van Ackern (ed.), *Proceedings of the British Academy: Philosophy and the Historical Perspective* (Oxford University Press 2018).

considerations. I do not. The sociology of philosophy often illuminates philosophy, because what "intuitions" seem plausible, what "argumentative moves" seem decisive, are often sociological artifacts, not deliverances of reason.[66] That sociological and philosophical considerations are on a continuum does not mean that some considerations are not irrational and that some claims are not just artifacts of professional stratification that we ought to dismiss. It is the middle ground on that continuum about which we need to be careful, and so, in that spirit, I would like to conclude with some speculative reflections on the sociology of jurisprudence.

First, we should be mindful of the effects the sociology of academic life has on scholarly inquiry quite generally. PhD students are tasked with making a "contribution to knowledge," and that means that even if a particular theory is hugely successful and plausible, doctoral students will have reasons of professional self-preservation to find fault with the consensus. In a Millian spirit, this is surely not a bad thing, but it can also cause mischief. Sometimes it is reasonable to treat a philosophical problem as solved, lest philosophy just turn into an endless merry-go-round of sophistical mischief. It is hard for me not to read most of the Dworkinian and natural law critiques of positivism without thinking that sophistical mischief now rules the roost.

Second, there are some odd facts about Anglophone jurisprudence that deserve comment in this regard. There is no other area of Anglophone philosophy apart from general jurisprudence where Oxford reigns supreme: not metaphysics, epistemology, ethics, political philosophy, or philosophy of language, mind, or logic. Michael Dummett, for example, dominated Oxford-style philosophy of language for a generation, yet on my side of the Atlantic the work was often thought to involve confusions of metaphysical and epistemological issues, and so never exerted anything like the influence it did in England. Rawlsian political liberalism has never had any traction in Oxford, despite its huge influence on my side of the Atlantic. Oxford philosophy of mind has had a longstanding hostility to the naturalist approaches that are dominant in America and Australia. And so on.

Oxford, however, has truly dominated Anglophone general jurisprudence from the 1960s to, perhaps, the present. Those of us in the provinces, whether New Haven or Sydney, responded to the pronouncements from those close to High Street. Perhaps this is ending, but even so it is important to think about

[66] Being a naturalist and thus empiricist, I think there are almost no "deliverances of reason," except, perhaps, for some logical truths (e.g., the law of non-contradiction): everything is up for grabs, and only psychological and sociological considerations delimit the terrain. (Quine thought even logic was open to revision, but so far toward the center of our "web of belief" as to be largely untouchable.)

the import of the history. If Dworkin had not ascended to the Professorship of Jurisprudence after Hart, where he was able to enjoy the bully pulpit Hart had legitimized, would we still be talking about his criticisms of legal positivism?[67] The history could have been otherwise, and perhaps Hart wished it were. As Nicola Lacey revealed in her illuminating biography *The Nightmare and the Noble Dream*, Hart was frustrated by "Dworkin's fluid and sometimes elusive analytic style" and came to feel "that there was something wilful or even lacking in honesty about Dworkin's reading of his work."[68] Hart's posthumously published "Postscript" to *The Concept of Law*, with its painstaking accounting of the multiple instances where Dworkin misstated Hart's views, betrays an exasperation that must have been embarrassing to its target.

Dworkin, himself, was not adverse to such sociological speculations, we should remember. Late in his career, he levelled a remarkable *ad hominem* charge at legal positivists, namely, that their real motive was to preserve "legal philosophy as an independent, self-contained subject and profession." In other words, Dworkin suggested that legal positivists accepted their view of the nature of law not because they thought it true, but because it made it possible for them to have a career![69] Dworkin continued in this vein: "Positivists since Hart ... have defended with great fervor a guild-claim: that their work is conceptual and descriptive in a way that distinguishes it from a variety of other crafts and professions."[70] Hart, to be sure, did believe that his work was conceptual and descriptive in a distinctive way, but Dworkin might have

[67] Michael Sevel points out to me, not wrongly, that we might not still be talking as much about Hart's positivism were it not for Dworkin's criticisms! In any case, the Jurisprudence Chair is now in decline.

[68] Nicola Lacy, *A Life of HLA Hart: The Nightmare and the Noble Dream* (Oxford University Press 2006) 330, 350. Lacey's revelation of Hart's humiliating but fair response to Dworkin has been politely sidestepped by Dworkin's handful of remaining defenders. Nicos Stavropoulos, in an essay purporting to review the Hart-Dworkin debate, passes over in silence Hart's reaction to Dworkin's dishonesty. See Nicos Stavropoulos, "The Debate That Never Was" (2017) 130 *Harvard Law Review* 2082. Even more surprisingly, Stavropoulos says that the Hart-Dworkin debate began with Dworkin's attack on positivist "theories that purport to explain obligation in law" (ibid. at 2083), even though Hart's theory aimed to explain the concept of law, not that of obligation. To dispute my obviously correct claim that most jurisprudential scholars viewed Dworkin as having decisively lost the Hart-Dworkin debate, Stavropoulos (ibid. at 2085, n. 15) cites one Dworkin student and one critic of Dworkin who ultimately ends up rejecting Dworkin. These defensive maneuvers are more sad than intellectually interesting. Dworkin was a very gifted sophist, in the pejorative sense of that term Plato bequeathed us. His handful of remaining devotees should be content with that.

[69] There are layers of irony here, especially in the American context. Conceptual and descriptive work about the nature of law has never been warmly received in U.S. law schools; by contrast, moralizing "readings" or emendations of the U.S. Constitution has been a vibrant field, one for which Dworkin can claim some credit.

[70] Dworkin, *Justice in Robes* (n. 64) 213.

noted that Hart did not think this distinguished his method from the craft and profession of *philosophy*, at least as then conceived.

The difficulty with Dworkin's sociological speculations, in short, was that they were manifestly absurd, not that they interjected sociology into philosophical disputes. Alas, their absurdity has not stopped some who should know better, like Dworkin's student, Jeremy Waldron, from repeating them.[71] That Dworkin did not lose all credibility for putting forth such silly ad hominems is, itself, telling about the lax intellectual standards in Anglophone jurisprudence[72] and the role that the warped sociology of the field has played in scholarly discussion. For example, it is inconceivable—or at least nomically impossible!—that anyone would have attacked Frank Jackson's defense of conceptual analysis in ethics and metaphysics some twenty years ago on the grounds that it makes philosophy independent of other disciplines, and thus Jackson's real motivation must be to preserve a professional niche for philosophers! And someone who followed that up with the claim that Jackson had made the subject "boring"—Dworkin's final salvo at Hart—would have been laughed off as an anti-intellectual Richard Rorty wannabe. But that has not happened in response to Dworkin's nonsense, or Waldron's repetition of parts of it, a fact that cries out for sociological explanation.

None of the preceding, obviously, shows that Dworkin's arguments on the merits are not successful. But the defects of those arguments are the subject of a voluminous literature by now.[73] Let me then step back from sociology, and return to the main ambition of this chapter. Legal positivism, as defined by the Social and Conventionality Theses, gives an illuminating and plausible account of the "ordinary" concept of law, it does so in a way that can be deployed fruitfully in the empirical sciences, and it does so without controversial or incredible metaphysical assumptions. With respect to any analysis of a human artifact, it is hard to imagine how one could do better. The positivist theory is not immune to clever counterfactual intuition pumps, and it is, like any theory about an artifact, hostage to social, economic, and historical changes that will influence our interests in the subject. But if there is a reason not to be a legal positivist today, it is incumbent upon the critics to identify the theoretical point on which positivism fails. Remarkably, the critics have failed to do so.

[71] See, e.g., the astonishing first part of Jeremy Waldron, "Can There be a Democratic Jurisprudence?" (2009) 58 *Emory Law Journal* 675.

[72] Lax by comparison to other areas of philosophy, not other areas of academic legal scholarship.

[73] I rehearse most of them in Leiter, "The End of Empire" (n. 64) and in Leiter, *Naturalizing Jurisprudence* (n. 1) ch. 6.

2

Law as a Malleable Artifact

Frederick Schauer

1.

Except perhaps from a very strong version of a classical natural law position,[1] law is not a natural kind. Whatever law is, it is importantly different from water, gold, or elephants, all of which are delivered to us by nature in whatever form nature chooses to give them to us.

What makes law different from water, gold, and elephants is that law is a creation of human beings, and is thus an *artifact*. Like chairs, art, and music, law is created by people, and without people such creations would simply not exist. Moreover, it is not just that human beings create individual chairs, or particular works of art, or specific pieces of music. Rather, the very ideas (or concepts, if you will) of chairs, of art, and of music are human creations, and are consequently unlike gold, water, and elephants—all of which could and would exist without human beings.[2] And although none of the foregoing observations is specifically about law, what is legally and jurisprudentially important about the distinction

[1] I refer here to the possibility—and it is no more than a possibility—that human law or positive law (or a legal system), under some version of a natural law theory, could be understood as emanating from God, or in some other way being part of the furniture of the world. Aquinas plainly did not believe this, see John Finnis, *Natural Law and Natural Rights* (Clarendon Press 1980) 363–4, but it is possible that Cicero and some others did. See A.P. d'Entreves, *Natural Law* (2nd edn., Hutchinson University Library 1970) 22–36; Brian Bix, "Natural Law: The Modern Tradition" in Jules Coleman, Kenneth Einar Himma, and Scott Shapiro (eds.), *The Oxford Handbook of Jurisprudence and Philosophy of Law* (Oxford University Press 2002) 61–103, at 63–8. It is also possible, however, that no one has ever actually believed that human positive law and the human institutions that make, interpret, and enforce it are truly natural in any important ontological sense.

[2] See Lynne Rudder Baker, "The Ontology of Artifacts" (2004) 7 *Philosophical Explorations* 99; Paul Bloom, "Intention, History, and Artifact Concepts" (1996) 60 *Cognition* 1; Risto Hilpinen, "Authors and Artifacts" (1993) 93 *Proceedings of the Aristotelian Society* 155; Amie L. Thomasson, "Artifacts and Human Concepts" in Eric Margolis and Stephen Laurence (eds.), *Creations of the Mind: Theories of Artifacts and Their Representation* (Oxford University Press 2007).

Law as an Artifact. First Edition. Edited by Luka Burazin, Kenneth Einar Himma, and Corrado Roversi. Published 2018 by Oxford University Press.

between the natural and the artifactual is that not only specific laws, specific legal sources, and specific legal institutions but also the very idea of law itself lies on the artifactual side of the line between the artifactual and the natural.

All of this may seem obvious and banal, but the implications are both interesting and important. Specifically, recognizing that the idea of law itself is an artifact entails the conclusion that what humans have created humans could have created differently, and what humans could have created differently is what humans, subject to all of the constraints of path dependence, can still, to some extent, change. And thus an important implication of recognizing the artifactual nature of law is recognition of the capacity that humans possess to remake or at least modify that which they themselves have made. It is not simply that humans can remake or modify particular laws, or reconstruct or alter all or part of some legal system, but that humans can remake or modify the very concept of law that exists within some community. And that is the basic premise on which the analysis that follows will rest.

2.

A prominent form of jurisprudential inquiry—legal philosophy[3]—in the analytical tradition is what commonly goes by the name of conceptual analysis. For practitioners of this enterprise, one task of jurisprudence[4] is to describe the concept of law that exists within a culture. How does some society, or some culture, understand law? The inquiry is not into how some society understands *its* law, but rather how some society or culture understands law wherever, whenever, and however it exists. And so although conceptual

[3] For reasons I have articulated elsewhere (see Frederick Schauer, "Law's Boundaries" (forthcoming 2017) 130 *Harvard Law Review*; Frederick Schauer, "(Re)Taking Hart" (2006) 119 *Harvard Law Review* 852), I resist the now common conflation of the terms "jurisprudence" and "philosophy of law." Insofar as jurisprudence is the theoretical examination of law itself, and not just particular laws or law in particular communities, such an examination might be pursued from historical, sociological, economic, evolutionary, or other perspectives and not solely by the use of philosophical methods. As a result, it seems preferable to understand the enterprise of legal philosophy as being a branch or subset of jurisprudence rather than being understood as congruent with it.

[4] For some it is the only task. "The sociology of law provides a wealth of detailed information and analysis of the functions of law in some particular societies. Legal philosophy has to be content with those few features which all legal systems necessarily possess." Joseph Raz, *The Authority of Law: Essays on Law and Morality* (Clarendon Press 1979) 104–5. More or less to the same effect, although not stated quite as starkly, is Julie Dickson, *Evaluation and Legal Theory* (Hart Publishing 2001) 17–25; Scott J. Shapiro, *Legality* (Harvard University Press 2011) 2–22; Julie Dickson, "Methodology in Jurisprudence: A Critical Survey" (2004) 10 *Legal Theory* 117.

analysis is provincial or local in the sense that the analyst is seeking to locate and explain *our* concept of law,[5] and not some other culture's concept of law, and not everyone's concept of law, conceptual analysis is universal in the sense that the local concept of law that the analyst seeks to identify and analyze is a concept that, for the community that uses the concept, extends to all possible legal systems in all possible worlds.[6]

The enterprise of conceptual analysis, whether with reference to the concept of law or with reference to concepts generally, has been the subject of considerable controversy.[7] Some of the skeptics, especially those with naturalistic or Quinean sympathies, argue that concepts themselves are mysterious, elusive, or simply fictitious entities, or that they are simply definitions.[8] As a result, say the concept-skeptics, the very task of conceptual analysis is a non-starter at the outset. Others might (grudgingly) accept the existence of concepts, but find the enterprise of conceptual analysis to be misguided, especially insofar as it uses non-empirical philosophical tools or armchair empirical inquiry to engage in what is essentially a descriptive empirical enterprise best pursued by the use of serious empirical methodology.[9] If we are trying to determine how some collection of individuals understands some idea, or talks about some idea, then perhaps, so it is said, the inquiry is best left to the empirical linguists, the sociologists, the anthropologists, and the psychologists, rather than having philosophers take on a task ill-suited to their skills and training.[10]

These skeptical responses have in turn generated counter-responses, and the defenders of conceptual analysis have sought to explain that locating and then analyzing our concepts is only in the shallowest sense empirical,

[5] See Joseph Raz, *Ethics in the Public Domain* (Oxford University Press 1994) 217.

[6] See Joseph Raz, "Can There Be a Theory of Law?" in Martin P. Golding and William A. Edmundson (eds.), *The Blackwell Guide to the Philosophy of Law and Legal Theory* (Blackwell 2005).

[7] For good overviews of the issues and controversies, see David Braddon-Mitchell and Robert Nola (eds.), *Conceptual Analysis and Philosophical Naturalism* (MIT 2009); Ernest Sosa, "Experimental Philosophy and Philosophical Intuition" (2007) 132 *Philosophical Studies* 99.

[8] Willard van Orman Quine, *Word and Object* (MIT 1960). See also Edouard Machery, *Doing without Concepts* (Oxford University Press 2009).

[9] See Stephen Stich, *The Fragmentation of Reason* (MIT 1990); William Ramsey, "Prototypes and Conceptual Analysis" in Michael R. DePaul and William Ramsey (eds.), *Rethinking Intuition: The Psychology of Intuition and Its Role in Philosophical Inquiry* (Rowman & Littlefield 1998) 161–78; Gilbert Harman, "Doubts About Conceptual Analysis" in Michaelis Michael and John O'Leary-Hawthorne (eds.), *Philosophy in Mind* (Kluwer 1994).

[10] While not doubting the enterprise of conceptual analysis of the concept of law, Kenneth Himma argues that existing conceptual analyses pay insufficient attention to how actual people use the concept, and thus argues that coercion may figure more in our concept of law than many (most? almost all?) contemporary legal theorists are willing to acknowledge. Kenneth Einar Himma, "Could There Really be Laws in a Society of Angels?," available at <https://papers.ssrn.com/sol3/papers.cfm?abstract_id=2839942> (2016), accessed April 10, 2018.

and necessarily draws on philosophy to draw distinctions, identify deep similarities among seeming dissimilar items, and engage in all of the tasks that have occupied philosophers from the time of Plato to the present.[11]

Some of the debates about the possibility, value, and methods of conceptual analysis take on a different cast when the concepts under discussion are no longer the concepts of natural kinds or mathematical functions. While there are skeptics about the value of philosophical conceptual analysis even for natural kinds and mathematical functions,[12] the frequency and degree of skepticism increase exponentially when we turn from natural kinds to artifacts. There may well be essential (or necessary) properties of water and gold, say some of the skeptics, but the search for the essential properties of human creations is a fool's errand.[13]

Not so, rejoin the defenders. As long as we actually use the concepts that demarcate the artifacts, they say, it remains necessary to understand what we are talking about, and doing so requires just the kind of conceptual analysis that would apply to natural kinds.[14] The only difference, they say, is that the concepts of artifacts are culturally and temporally contingent, such that the concept of chair may be different today than it was a century ago, and may be different in Paris than it is in Somalia. But that does not detract from the fact that in a particular place at a particular time there are concepts connected with our artifacts, and that it is the job of the philosopher to locate and analyze them.

3.

The debates about conceptual analysis generally are important, as are the debates about conceptual analysis of artifacts. And because law is almost without question an artifact, the debates about conceptual analysis of artifacts apply to the conceptual analysis of the concept of law, with some theorists arguing that such an enterprise is hopeless[15] while others insist that conceptual

[11] See Frank Jackson, *From Metaphysics to Ethics: A Defense of Conceptual Analysis* (Oxford University Press 1998); Colin McGinn, *Truth by Analysis: Games, Names, and Philosophy* (Oxford University Press 2011); David J. Chalmers and Frank Jackson, "Conceptual Analysis and Reductive Explanation" (2001) 110 *Philosophical Studies* 315.

[12] See Joseph Almog, "Nature without Essence" (2010) 107 *Journal of Philosophy* 360.

[13] From the perspective of experimental cognitive psychology, see Steven A. Sloman and Barbara C. Malt, "Artifacts Are Not Ascribed Essences, Nor Are They Treated as Belonging to Kinds" (2003) 18 *Language and Cognitive Processes* 563. From philosophy, see Penelope Mackie, *How Things Might Have Been* (Oxford University Press 2006). For a contrary view, see Brandon Warmke, "Artifact and Essence" (2010) 38 *Philosophia* 595.

[14] See Warmke, "Artifact and Essence" (n. 13).

[15] See especially Brian Leiter, "Beyond the Hart/Dworkin Debate: The Methodology Problem in Jurisprudence" in *Naturalizing Jurisprudence: Essays on American Legal Realism and Naturalism*

analysis of the concept of law is not only possible but is also a necessary precursor to any other variety of inquiry about law.[16] Such inquiries can get off the ground, it is said, only if we know at the outset what we are investigating, and thus engaging in conceptual analysis to identify the concept of law is an essential prerequisite to any other form of jurisprudential or empirical inquiry about law.

Although I, along with others, have expressed doubts about the enterprise of searching for the necessary or the essential properties of the concept of law,[17] it is useful to distinguish the task of conceptual analysis from the activity of searching for necessary or essential properties. Even if we assume that law is, for example, a cluster concept with no essential properties,[18] it might nevertheless be useful to inquire into the nature of the cluster, even if the product of that inquiry is simply an identification of multiple properties, none of which is strictly necessary to the concept of law. Or if it turns out that law is a concept that comes in degrees, such that certain collections of properties produce more "law-ness" than others, it still may be valuable—or even necessary—to identify those properties, even if, again, none is strictly necessary, and even if law cannot be defined in terms of some set of necessary and sufficient properties. Relatedly, insofar as law is a concept involving degrees of distance from some prototype or paradigm,[19] it may still be useful or necessary to identify the prototype or paradigm case, even as we recognize that other proper applications of the concept may exist around and not within the prototype or paradigm.

in Legal Philosophy (Oxford University Press 2007); Brian Leiter, "The Demarcation Problem in Jurisprudence: A New Case for Scepticism" (2011) 31 *Oxford Journal of Legal Studies* 663.

[16] See Leslie Green, "Duty, Coercion, and Power" (2016) 29 *Ratio Juris* 164; Torben Spaak, "Schauer's Anti-Essentialism" (2016) 29 *Ratio Juris* 182. See also, albeit less explicitly, Jules L. Coleman, *The Practice of Principle: In Defence of a Pragmatist Approach to Legal Theory* (Oxford University Press 2001) 118–19, 173–4; Jules L. Coleman, "Incorporationism, Conventionality, and the Practical Difference Thesis" in Jules L. Coleman (ed.), *Hart's Postscript: Essays on the Postscript to the* Concept of Law (Oxford University Press 2001) 99, 107–8.

[17] Frederick Schauer, *The Force of Law* (Harvard University Press 2016) 37–41; Frederick Schauer, "On the Nature of the Nature of Law" (2012) 98 *Archiv für Rechts- und Sozialphilosophie* 457.

[18] The idea of a cluster concept appears to have originated in Max T. Black, *Problems of Analysis: Philosophical Essays* (Cornell University Press 1954) 28, and was further developed and made more prominent by John Searle, *Speech Acts: An Essay in the Philosophy of Language* (Cambridge University Press 1969) 162–74. Cluster concepts are closely related to Wittgenstein's idea of "family resemblance" (Ludwig Wittgenstein, *Philosophical Investigations* (G.E.M. Anscombe, P.M.S. Hacker, and Joachim Schulte (trans.), 4th edn., Blackwell 2009) 66–7), as to which the most prominent objection is Bernard Suits, *The Grasshopper: Games, Life and Utopia* (Broadview 2005) (1978).

[19] On paradigm or prototype cases and concept construction, see William Ramsey, "Prototypes and Conceptual Analysis" (1992) 11 *Topoi* 59; Eric Margolis and Stephen Laurence, "Concepts" in E.N. Zalta (ed.), *The Stanford Encyclopedia of Philosophy* (Spring 2014 edn.).

4.

Although the debates about conceptual analysis of law remain interesting and instructive, I want to assume here that descriptive conceptual analysis of the concept of law is both possible and valuable. I want to assume, therefore, that (most) cultures have a concept of law, and that attempting to discover what that concept is, as well as analyzing the concept's component parts, is an enterprise that will illuminate our understanding of the concept and also of the social phenomenon that the concept captures.

Even with this assumption in place, there are debates about the extent to which the enterprise of conceptual analysis of the concept of law is or can be entirely descriptive.[20] Although proponents of the view that conceptual analysis is a descriptive enterprise acknowledge that the analyst must identify the features of the concept that are important as well as necessary,[21] the proponents deny that the identification of importance or the process of conceptual analysis of the concept of law more broadly need involve a normative, and especially morally normative, dimension.[22] Against this view, however, is the view, embodied most prominently in the works of Ronald Dworkin[23] and Stephen Perry,[24] that normative moral considerations are necessarily part of the enterprise of conceptual analysis of the concept of law, and that what appears to some as a solely descriptive dimension in fact has an important morally normative aspect.

[20] A good summary of the positions is in Danny Priel, "Evaluating Descriptive Jurisprudence" (2007) 52 *American Journal of Jurisprudence* 139. See also Veronica Rodriguez-Blanco, "The Methodological Problem in Legal Theory: Normative and Descriptive Jurisprudence Revisited" (2006) 19 *Ratio Juris* 26.

[21] See especially Dickson, *Evaluation and Legal Theory* (n. 4). See also Leslie Green, "Positivism and the Inseparability of Law and Morals" (2008) 83 *New York University Law Review* 1035, 1043; Kevin Walton, "Jurisprudential Methodology: Is Pure Interpretation Possible?" in Jordi Ferrer Beltrán, José Juan Moreso, and Diego M. Papayannis (eds.), *Neutrality and Theory of Law* (Springer 2012).

[22] See Coleman, "Incorporationism, Conventionality, and the Practical Difference Thesis" (n. 16), at 107–8; Green, "Positivism and the Inseparability of Law and Morals" (n. 21), at 1036–7.

[23] Ronald Dworkin, *Justice in Robes* (Harvard University Press 2006); Ronald Dworkin, *Law's Empire* (Harvard University Press 1986); Ronald Dworkin, "Thirty Years On" (2002) 115 *Harvard Law Review* 1655.

[24] Stephen R. Perry, "Hart's Methodological Positivism" in Coleman, *Hart's Postscript* (n. 16); Stephen R. Perry, "Interpretation and Methodology in Legal Theory" in Andrei Marmor (ed.), *Law and Interpretation: Essays in Legal Philosophy* (Oxford University Press 1995). See also Stephen Guest, "Two Strands in Hart's Theory of Law: A Comment on the 'Postscript' to Hart's *The Concept of Law*" in Stephen Guest (ed.), *Positivism Today* (Dartmouth Publishing 1996); John Tasioulas, "Hart on Justice and Morality" in Luís Duarte d'Almeida, James Edwards, and Andrea Dolcetti (eds.), *Reading HLA Hart's* The Concept of Law (Hart Publishing 2013).

Again, this debate is important, but noting it is merely prologue. For although the debate just mentioned is a prominent and instructive part of contemporary jurisprudence, the debate is about the idea of the normative in only one sense. That is, the debate is about the morally normative in the sense of the claim on one side of the debate that offering what appears to be a descriptive claim is in fact one that presupposes certain normative commitments. But even if we reject this side of the debate, and thus assume that offering a morally inert description of the concept of law is possible,[25] and perhaps even desirable,[26] there is still another form of normative project that remains open. That is the project of conceptual revision,[27] or, more accurately, the project of prescribing conceptual revision, or simply of prescribing conceptual change.

5.

Once we grasp that law is an artifact, it follows that how a culture understands the idea or phenomenon of law is in a sense artifactual as well. Suppose, for example, that one society understands the idea, the phenomenon, or the concept of law as including the rule-like norms of etiquette, while another society, which also has rule-like norms of etiquette, does not consider those norms, or questions about compliance with them or enforcement of them, as in any way part of or even connected with law. In the former society, law consists of a wide array of social norms, including the norms of etiquette, the socially accepted norms of morality, and the official norms of behavior issued by the state and enforced by the state's mechanisms of application, interpretation, and coercive enforcement. In the latter society, the norms of morality and etiquette are understood as simply part of a different system. And because each of these societies' own concept of law is a concept about law wherever and whenever it appears, those societies' understanding of law frames not only their understanding of what did or did not count as law within their own society, but also what did or did not count as law whenever and wherever it appears.

[25] See Brian Leiter, "Beyond the Hart/Dworkin Debate: The Methodology Problem in Jurisprudence" (2003) 48 *American Journal of Jurisprudence* 17; Andrei Marmor, "Legal Positivism: Still Descriptive and Morally Neutral" (2006) 26 *Oxford Journal of Legal Studies* 683. An interesting variant is Kenneth Ehrenberg, "Defending the Possibility of a Neutral Functional Theory of Law" (2009) 29 *Oxford Journal of Legal Studies* 91.

[26] As suggested by the title (and less by the content) of Neil MacCormick, "A Moralistic Case for A-Moralistic Law" (1985) 20 *Valparaiso University Law Review* 1. See also Liam Murphy, "The Political Question of the Concept of Law" in Coleman, *Hart's Postscript* (n. 16).

[27] See Green, "Positivism and the Inseparability of Law and Morals" (n. 21) 1039.

One of the implications of acknowledging the artifactual nature of law is recognition of the fact that both of these concepts are possible. Just as there is no a priori reason why some society could not understand the concept of chair as including everything upon which people sat, including the backs of horses and the seats of bicycles, there is no reason why some society could not adopt more or less inclusive concepts of law.

Once we recognize the cultural contingency of a concept of law, we see that there are ways in which that concept might vary from culture to culture in addition to being more or less expansive. Even assuming that legal positivism is correct, and thus that moral acceptability is not a necessary property of law[28] as understood by *our* concept of law, there is no reason, for example, why a different concept of law could not treat moral acceptability, as in the classical version of natural law, as a necessary property of law in all possible legal systems in all possible worlds, and thus as a necessary property of law wherever and whenever it appears. Similarly, there is no reason why a different concept of law could not consider aesthetic beauty, or defeasibility, or non-defeasibility, or pretty much anything else as necessary properties (or, for that matter, necessary exclusions) of the concept of law.

6.

If there can be different concepts of law, or if different cultures can thus have different concepts of law, then there is no reason why one culture might not decide that it preferred the concept of law of some other culture. Indeed, if we

[28] I put aside here the debates between inclusive and exclusive positivists about whether under *our* concept of law morality could be a contingent property of law. For the inclusive positivists, morality (and more or less anything else) can be part of law as long as there is a social fact (and not a necessary natural fact) that makes it so. See, e.g., Wilfrid J. Waluchow, *Inclusive Legal Positivism* (Oxford University Press 1994); Kenneth Einar Himma, "Inclusive Legal Positivism" in Jules L. Coleman, Kenneth Einar Himma, and Scott J. Shapiro (eds.), *The Oxford Handbook of Jurisprudence and Philosophy of Law* (Oxford University Press 2004); Jules L. Coleman, "Beyond Inclusive Positivism" (2009) 22 *Ratio Juris* 359. By contrast exclusive legal positivism maintains that law, properly understood, includes only those norms or sources that are in some way distinctively legal, and that although these legal norms or sources might refer to morality, the moral norms to which legal norms might refer are not themselves law. See, e.g., Raz, *The Authority of Law* (n. 4); Andrei Marmor, *Positive Law and Objective Values* (Oxford University Press 2001); Joseph Raz, "The Problem of Authority: Revisiting the Service Conception" (2006) 90 *Minnesota Law Review* 1003; Scott J. Shapiro, "On Hart's Way Out" (2008) 4 *Legal Theory* 469. Good overviews of the debates include Brian Bix, "Patrolling the Boundaries: Inclusive Legal Positivism and the Nature of Jurisprudential Debate" (1999) 12 *Canadian Journal of Law and Jurisprudence* 17; Jules L. Coleman and Brian Leiter, "Legal Positivism" in Dennis Patterson (ed.), *A Companion to Philosophy of Law and Legal Theory* (2nd. edn., Blackwell 2010).

jettison the baggage associated with the word "concept," and with concepts themselves, we might just think instead about how a culture understands an idea, or understands a social phenomenon. And if we look at the question in this somewhat more down-to-earth way, we can then posit that there is no reason why a culture might not choose to understand some phenomenon differently from the way it now understands that phenomenon. Suppose, for example, that a society came to see that so many people were sitting on the backs of horses for so many different purposes that the distinction between "chair" and "back of horse" became unimportant. Were that the case, that society might then, over time, choose[29] to revise its concept of chair such that it included the backs of horses. And if "horse's back" has too many natural kind connotations, think about, to use a few Dworkinian examples, the phenomenon of honor, or of etiquette. Here again it might be that ideas of honor and etiquette changed so dramatically over time that what counted as honor or etiquette at one time did not count at some other time. Again, this is not about actual examples of etiquette in particular societies—it is how a particular society at a particular time viewed the concept of etiquette, and thus how that society at that time views etiquette at all times and all places. Although the understanding of the phenomenon would very likely be influenced by local examples, the understanding of the extension of the phenomenon would not be local, and a change in understanding in the particular culture would change how that culture viewed the instances (or non-instances) of the phenomenon in other cultures.

If concepts can change in this way, and no one appears to have argued that the concepts attached to artifacts are in some mysterious way non-revisable or immutable, then there is no reason to believe that the concept of law cannot change in much the same way. It is true that legal conceptual change does not follow inexorably from change in the law or in legal institutions. Even in the face of doctrinal or institutional change, a culture might nevertheless retain the same understanding of the phenomenon of law. It would just be that the instantiations of the concept changed, but not that the concept itself changed.

But it is also possible that the concept itself changed, perhaps as a result of dramatic change in the phenomenon that the concept is a concept of, and perhaps as a result of some instrumental reason for conceiving of the concept in a new way. And as long as this possibility exists, we can now

[29] Here and throughout, I use "choose" and its equivalents in a somewhat metaphorical sense. Contingent social norms, e.g., are in some diffuse and collective way chosen by the society in which they exist, although there is never a single act of a choice by an identifiable chooser. And so too with a society's concepts, including its concept of law.

glimpse a different kind of normative legal theoretic enterprise, one that has at times been referred to as "concept revision."[30] Because our concepts might be at some future time different from what they now are, then there is, in theory, an enterprise of concept revision, and, therefore, another enterprise that would consist of *prescribing* what some revised concept ought to be. Such prescriptions might be morally based, but need not be. Perhaps concepts different from the ones we now have would recommend themselves because they would be easier to grasp, or would explain more of the world, or in some other way serve non-moral purposes better than the concepts we now have. But whatever the basis for the prescription, it is in theory open to someone—theorist, or anyone else—to urge that it would be preferable to understand some phenomenon differently from the way it is now understood—to have a different concept from the one we now have.

Insofar as all of this applies as much to law as to any other artifact, we can now see that one form of normative legal theory would be that of prescribing what our concept of law ought to be. How should a culture understand law, and should it understand law in a way that is different from the way it now understands it? Insofar as a theorist might wish to answer or at least address this question, she can be said to engage in a particular form of prescriptive or normative legal theory, prescriptive or normative not at the level of specific laws or legal institutions, but at the level of a more global understanding of the concept of law itself.

7.

An exegetically controversial example of the just-described phenomena of conceptual change and conceptual revision is one understanding of the 1958 debate between H.L.A. Hart and Lon Fuller,[31] in particular that part of the debate that was concerned with the relative merits of a natural law and a legal positivist concept of law. Under one understanding of the debate, Hart and Fuller agreed that it is unfortunate when citizens, lawyers, and judges obey iniquitous official directives, as was often the case in Nazi Germany. And thus both Hart and Fuller can be seen to have agreed that it would be preferable were citizens, lawyers, and judges not to conform their behavior to such iniquitous official directives. Where Hart and Fuller differed, under

[30] See Jules L. Coleman, *The Practice of Principle* (n. 16), 4 at note 3.

[31] Lon L. Fuller, "Positivism and Fidelity to Law—A Reply to Professor Hart" (1958) 71 *Harvard Law Review* 630; H.L.A. Hart, "Positivism and the Separation of Law and Morals" (1958) 71 *Harvard Law Review* 593.

this understanding, is in how this preferable state of affairs might be brought about. For Fuller the route to this outcome was for people—a culture—to have a natural law understanding of the concept of law, such that members of that culture would be unwilling to label such directives as "law," and thus unlikely to attach their predispositions to obey the law[32] to that which was, for reasons of its moral deficiency, not law at all.[33]

Hart, of course, disagreed. For Hart the best route to the shared end was for people to understand that the concept of law was morally inert, and thus that some directive being law, or being labeled "law," said nothing about whether it should be followed.[34] Hart believed that a legal positivist understanding of the concept of law would sharpen citizen focus on the question of moral obligation, and thus make it more likely that iniquitous official directives would be disobeyed.

It is not my purpose here to offer views about whether it was Hart or Fuller who was right on this particular point. Rather, I want to use their debate as a way of illustrating a broader debate about concept revision, or about concept formation. Both Hart and Fuller appeared under the interpretation offered here to be arguing about what the concept of law *ought* to be, and consequently disagreed only about which concept of law would better facilitate what appears to have been their shared goal. And thus both of them can be understood as engaging in the project of normative conceptual prescription, a project that might include prescription about what some concept ought to

[32] An important link in the chain of Fuller's argument is his assumption that people have, as an empirical matter, a predisposition to obey that which is labeled or understood as law, and that this predisposition cannot realistically be altered. See Frederick Schauer, "Positivism as Pariah" in Robert P. George (ed.), *The Autonomy of Law: Essays on Legal Positivism* (Clarendon Press 1996), 31, at 38–44. For a similar assumption, see Anthony D'Amato, "The Moral Dilemma of Positivism" (1985) 20 *Valparaiso University Law Review* 43.

[33] See also Lon L. Fuller, *The Morality of Law* (rev. edn., Yale University Press 1969); Gustav Radbruch, "Statutory Lawlessness and Supra-Statutory Law" (2006) 26 *Oxford Journal of Legal Studies* 1. Although Fuller most often offered his arguments in the context of his own procedural version of natural law theory, much that he argued about natural law and obedience applies to more traditional substantive versions of natural law theory as well.

[34] It is important to note that Hart's position is agnostic rather than negative on the question whether there is a moral obligation to obey the law just because it is the law. One could believe that the fact of law did not by definition entail an obligation of obedience but also that the fact of law, for reasons other than the definition of "law," created a moral obligation of obedience. Or one could believe, with the so-called philosophical anarchists (see A. John Simmons, *Moral Principles and Political Obligations* (Princeton University Press 1979); Robert Paul Wolff, *In Defense of Anarchism* (Harper & Row 1970); M.B.E. Smith, "Is There a Prima Facie Obligation to Obey the Law?" (1973) 82 *Yale Law Journal* 950), that the fact of law did not in any way bear on the subject's decision about what to do. And thus Hart's insistence on separation of the questions does not exclude an obligation to obey the law, but nor does it demand it.

be from the outset, or, more realistically, how some existing concept ought to be revised.

This understanding of the Hart-Fuller debate as being a normative one about what our concept of law ought to be is, as I noted above, not without controversy. For some theorists, Hart and Fuller were simply arguing about what our concept *is*, and merely observing incidentally from their own perspectives the advantages—the favorable incidental—consequences of his own non-prescriptive description.[35] But although such a view might gain some support from some of the language in the "Postscript" to *The Concept of Law*,[36] it is a strained understanding of the 1958 debate, and an even more strained understanding of the principal (1961) text of *The Concept of Law*, where Hart discusses the "attractive[ness]" and respective "practical merits" of the alternative concepts, and makes it clear that the question is about which alternative a society should "adopt."[37]

To repeat, I am not on this occasion primarily (or even secondarily) interested in Hartian exegesis. As Julie Dickson observes, the potential disparity between Hart's 1958 and 1961 views, on the one hand, and his later views in the *Postscript*, on the other, is best understood as being, in Dickson's term, "awkward."[38] But even if we discount the early texts and thus do not credit Hart with taking a normative position on what concept of law a society ought to have, it is no less the case that some theorists could have taken the position that I attribute to Hart.[39] That is, it is possible (and more than merely possible for Fuller) that a theorist could believe that certain beneficial moral, pragmatic, or other consequences could flow to a society from having one concept of law rather than another, or from having a concept of law different from the one that it now has. A particular view about obedience to morally iniquitous (or, for that matter, morally beneficial) directives might be an example of such a consequence, but it is only an example. We might think, for example, that a society having a particular concept of law would lead talented people to gravitate to working within the institution marked

[35] This interpretation is advanced in, e.g., Green, "Positivism and the Inseparability of Law and Morals" (n. 21).

[36] H.L.A. Hart, *The Concept of Law*, Penelope A. Bulloch, Joseph Raz, and Leslie Green (eds.), (3rd edn., Oxford University Press 2012) (1961), 240. See also Jules L. Coleman, "Methodology" in Coleman, Himma, and Shapiro, *The Oxford Handbook of Jurisprudence and Philosophy of Law* (n. 1); John Gardner, "Legal Positivism: 5 ½ Myths" (2001) 46 *American Journal of Jurisprudence* 199, 205.

[37] Hart, *The Concept of Law* (n. 36), at 208–12.

[38] Julie Dickson, "Is Bad Law Still Law? Is Bad Law Really Law?" in Maksymilian Del Mar and Zenon Bankowski (eds.), *Law as Institutional Normative Order* (Ashgate 2009) 161, at 164.

[39] See Liam Murphy, "The Political Question of the Concept of Law" in Coleman, *Hart's Postscript* (n. 16), at 371. A softer version of the claim is in Liam Murphy, "Better to See Law This Way" (2008) 83 *New York University Law Review* 1088.

by the concept, or, in contrast, to avoiding that institution. But the point is only that concepts can have consequences, or that choices among possible concepts can have consequences, and those consequences might be for the better or for the worse. And if concepts have consequences—if how a society understands or conceptualizes a social institution can make a difference to something—then those consequences might be germane to how some society forms its concepts, and to how some society might choose to revise the concepts that at some particular point of time it has inherited.

None of this is to suggest that our concepts can change abruptly or dramatically. Although such dramatic change is in theory possible, the likelihood of such an occurrence, for pretty much any concept, is vanishingly small. Far more likely is conceptual change that is slow and incremental, with conceptual shifts being virtually invisible in the short term and only noticeable over longer spans of time. As a result, the process of conceptual revision is almost always gradual and diffuse, and there is no more reason to believe that such changes can be attributable to particular events or particular moments in time than that they can be traced to particular actions by particular individuals.

What makes this last point of some interest is the charge against Fuller, and perhaps against others, that they mistakenly—or absurdly—believed that the writings of legal theorists can have substantial causal effect on conceptual change within the larger society.[40] More specifically, Fuller is charged with believing that either particular legal positivists—Hans Kelsen, most prominently—or positivist legal theorists generally brought about the acceptance of a positivist understanding of law that in turn had, according to Fuller, detrimental and, indeed, catastrophic, social consequences.

Although Fuller did follow Gustav Radbruch in believing that a legal positivist understanding of the nature of law was a significant cause of the willingness of citizens, lawyers, and judges to comply with iniquitous Nazi directives,[41] there is no evidence whatsoever that Fuller was so naïve as to think that the writings of Kelsen or anyone else had very much, if anything, to do with the creation of this unfortunate understanding.[42] What Fuller's

[40] See Green, "Positivism and the Inseparability of Law and Morals" (n. 21), at 1043.

[41] On the relationship between the accounts of Radbruch and Fuller, and on whether either was accurate in depicting German legal theory at the relevant time, see Stanley L. Paulson, "Lon L. Fuller, Gustav Radbruch, and the 'Positivist' Theses" (1994) 13 *Law and Philosophy* 313. On the (theoretical) relationships among Fuller, Hart, and Radbruch regarding Nazi law, see also Kristen Rundle, *Forms Liberate: Reclaiming the Jurisprudence of Lon L Fuller* (Hart Publishing 2013) 66–78.

[42] Much of Lon L. Fuller, *The Law in Quest of Itself* (The Foundation Press 1940) is a polemic against legal positivism, and Kelsen is often mentioned, but even a slightly charitable reading makes clear that Fuller's target is a long positivist tradition—and not necessarily a strictly academic one—rather than particular contemporary theorists.

critics misunderstand is the distinction between a social understanding and the contribution of theorists to creation of that understanding. Fuller and Radbruch did charge a positivist concept of law with playing a role in the unfortunate tendency to obedience, but neither ever claimed that Kelsen's writings, or anyone else's, did very much to create the concept that they so vehemently criticized. As a prominent theorist, perhaps Kelsen and his writings contributed some small amount to how the concept of law was understood in Germany and Austria in the 1920s, 1930s, and 1940s, and perhaps Kelsen's writings were evidence of the existing concept of law he attempted to explain, and perhaps his writings emerged out of—were caused by—a particular understanding of law, but there is no evidence for the proposition that Fuller believed that legal positivist academic writings were the cause of an unfortunate (to Fuller) concept of law, or that academic legal positivists could be blamed for more than a miniscule contribution to Nazi atrocities.

If I am right that Fuller, at the very least, and probably also Hart in 1958 and 1961, were engaged in normative prescription of conceptual revision, then a comparison with normative moral or political philosophy is apt. *A Theory of Justice* is a work of academic moral and political philosophy,[43] but John Rawls was not naïve enough to think that his book would bring about substantial short or intermediate change in the moral and political behavior of the people in the societies within his purview, and even less did Kant imagine that his proscription of lying would have a noticeable effect on the truth-telling activities of the inhabitants of Königsberg. Rather, like all but the most self-delusional or hubristic academics, they believed that their academic writings might, over time, and in combination with the work of others, eventually bring about some small change in actual behavior, but nothing more immediate or dramatic than that.

This is not the place to delve deeply into the nature or value of academic influence on non-academic public behavior, but it remains important to make clear that the process of academic prescription of conceptual change should not be understood any differently from any other prescriptive academic enterprise.[44] Academic prescriptions might make some small difference in the long run, but that is all we can and should expect, and that is likely all that Kelsen, Fuller, Hart and many others arguably engaged in prescriptions for conceptual revision had in mind.

[43] John Rawls, *A Theory of Justice* (Harvard University Press 1971).

[44] Moreover, we should not ignore the way in which academic writings that might have somewhat of a prescriptive voice remain essentially scholarly works designed to increase our understanding far more than influence our behavior. See Kenneth Einar Himma, "Substance and Method in Conceptual Jurisprudence and Legal Theory" (2002) 88 *Virginia Law Review* 1119.

8.

The most important feature of artifacts is their contingency. The artifacts we have did not have to exist, and at some point they may no longer exist. And because artifacts are contingent, so too is our understanding of them, including the concepts we use to grasp them, define them, frame them, and understand them. Because artifacts are contingent, therefore, our concepts of them are contingent as well.

Recognizing that concepts are contingent entails recognizing that it is within our power, certainly theoretically and occasionally practically, to create concepts, to eliminate concepts, and, more realistically, to revise concepts.[45] The enterprise of conceptual revision is not, critics notwithstanding,[46] the enterprise of imagining that our concepts are what we would like them to be. Rather, it is the enterprise of urging that our concepts be revised to become what we would like them to be. Like much of prescriptive scholarship, the academic pursuit of conceptual revision may well be forced to set its sights on, at best, small gains over a vast expanse of time. And so it is with the pursuit of conceptual revision of the concept of law. But those who pursue it are not seeking to imagine the existing world as it ought to be. They are seeking to imagine a future word as it might be, or criticize an existing world for falling short of what it might be. Such an endeavor might make a difference only at the tiniest of margins and only with the smallest of probabilities, but there is nothing confused about it.

[45] See, in a slightly different context, Sally Haslanger, "What Are We Talking About? The Semantics and Politics of Social Kinds" (2005) 20 *Hypatia* 10; Sally Haslanger, "Gender and Race (What) Are They?; (What) Do We Want Them to Be?" (2000) 34 *Nous* 31. Natalie Stoljar draws on Haslanger, among others, in her "What Do We Want Law to Be? Philosophical Analysis and the Concept of Law" in Wil Waluchow and Stefan Sciaraffa, *Philosophical Foundations of the Nature of Law* (Oxford University Press 2013), and reaches conclusions substantially congenial to what I offer here.

[46] Dickson, *Evaluation and Legal Theory* (n. 4), at 83–102, charges me, among others, with confusing the description and analysis of the existing concept of law with the identification of the "beneficial moral consequences" of one or another concept of law. My response, which is the precursor to the more extensive analysis offered here, is Frederick Schauer, "The Social Construction of the Concept of Law: A Reply to Julie Dickson" (2005) 25 *Oxford Journal of Legal Studies* 493.

3

Law, Fiction, and Reality

Andrei Marmor

1. Introduction

There is some sense in which laws clearly exist. We talk about the law being this or that; we can say that there *is* a law that such and such, or there isn't, etc., etc. Furthermore, laws' existence is spatiotemporal. There might be a law that requires X in New York state but not in California right now; there are new laws that had not existed before, and old laws that get repealed or nullified. Laws vary by location and time. There is, however, also a sense in which laws do not exist. Laws do not form part of the fabric of the natural universe, as it were. Without human society and culture, there are no laws; there cannot be any. In some fundamental sense, the law is in our minds. Kelsen made this point a long time ago, when he suggested that law *is* essentially a scheme of interpretation, it consists in meanings we attribute to certain actions and events in the world.[1] So the question that motivates my discussion in this chapter is how to reconcile these two truisms: the fact that laws' existence is, at some foundational level, entirely in our minds, and the fact that laws' existence is essentially spatiotemporal, very closely tied to particular jurisdictions. My argument is going to be that law is an intangible artifact, like fiction, but of a kind that has some special features. And I would

[1] See, e.g., Hans Kelsen, *Pure Theory of Law* (1st edn., 1934), in English: (Paulson & Paulson trans.) *Introduction to the Problems of Legal Theory* (Oxford University Press 2002) 10. Kelsen was well aware of the spatiotemporal aspect of legal norms (ibid. 12), though he thought that all norms regulating human conduct are spatiotemporal, which is much more doubtful, of course. For a more detailed view of Kelsen's theory of law, see Andrei Marmor, *Philosophy of Law* (Princeton University Press 2011) ch. 1; Andrei Marmor, "The Pure Theory of Law" in E.N. Zalta (ed.), *The Stanford Encyclopedia of Philosophy* (Spring 2016 edn.).

Law as an Artifact. First Edition. Edited by Luka Burazin, Kenneth Einar Himma, and Corrado Roversi. Published 2018 by Oxford University Press.

like to show that there are some interesting conclusions that follow from the artifact nature of law.[2]

2. Intangible Artifacts

An artifact is an object created by humans for some purpose.[3] There are many kinds of artifact in the world we inhabit. There are chairs, cars, computers, houses, novels, poems, and countless other objects, tangible and intangible, deliberately created to serve some function or purpose in our lives. We often use them for their intended purposes and sometimes for other purposes, perhaps not intended; we can modify their uses in various ways. It is generally thought that artifacts are objects deliberately created for some purpose, with that purpose in somebody's mind, as it were. And that is surely correct about most ordinary artifacts we use in our daily lives. But deliberate creation for a purpose is not necessary for an artifact to have come into existence. Some artifacts may have been created by chance, or later significantly modified by repeated use, without any deliberate design. Or they may have been created for one purpose and later used for another.[4] What is essential for an object to be an artifact, I will assume here, is that it has been created by humans and that it is used by humans for some typical or designated purpose or other.

Now the ontology of artifacts is a tricky matter, and I will have nothing to say about some contentious metaphysical problems here. Consider this familiar example: you take a lump of clay and knead it into a shape of a horse, thereby, we assume, creating a statue. You brought a statue into existence. There is an ongoing debate about ontology here: is the statue a different object from the clay? Are there two objects now, the clay you started with, that is still there, unmodified, in some sense, and the statue that you just created? (E.g., you can easily destroy the statue without altering in any way the properties of the clay,

[2] Some of the themes in this chapter I have also developed, though in somewhat different directions, in Andrei Marmor, "Law as Authoritative Fiction" [draft] (July 13, 2017) *Cornell Legal Studies Research Paper No. 17-10*. Available at SSRN: <https://papers.ssrn.com/sol3/papers.cfm?abstract_id=2921943>. (Andrei Marmor, *Law and Philosophy* (2018), <https://doi.org/10.1007/s10982-018-9331-y>.)

[3] I am aware of the fact that some animals also make tools. I think it would be a stretch to say that animals have artifacts, but nothing in this chapter hangs on this. I will gracefully ignore nonhumans in this chapter.

[4] Artifacts change functions and uses over time, sometimes almost unnoticeably, sometimes quite radically, e.g., Chinese fireworks became rudimentary explosive devices around the thirteenth century, though gradually and in different places. At some point, this obviously became a radical change, creating a new kind of artifact. Saying when new uses of roughly the same object-type becomes a new artifact is often impossible. Changes are often very gradual and there's a great deal of inevitable vagueness about types and categories here.

apart from its shape, of course.) Some say yes and some say no.[5] But this, and similar metaphysical controversies, will be set aside here. My metaphysics in this chapter is going to remain shallow, and thus hopefully uncontroversial. I will assume, however, that artifacts have a sufficient degree of conceptual (viz. linguistic and cultural) independence from their natural building blocks, at least to the extent that the things we can intelligibly say about artifacts are constrained by their properties, qua artifacts of a certain kind. About a chair, for example, we can say that it is comfortable or pretty, but not that it is fast, or smart or canny. Chairs are neither fast nor slow; they are certainly not stupid or smart, and so on and so forth. Computers can be fast (or slow) and perhaps in some sense, computers can be smart (though not canny). And this applies to all artifacts; there are things we can say about them, ways in which we can relate to them, and uses to which we can put them. And these sayings and doings are constrained by the kind of artifact it is.[6]

Many of the artifacts we have are intangible: novels, poems, legends, gods and, generally, narratives, would be prime examples. Stories, myths, and legends are created by human beings. They have authors, even if, sometimes, the authors are not known or difficult to individualize. What makes stories artifacts is the fact that they are created by humans, with their particular properties or content, if you will.[7] Now there's another philosophical controversy here that I don't want to expand on, but cannot bracket entirely either: some would argue that the creator's intention in making an artifact of a certain kind or with certain properties has a constitutive role to play with respect to the artifact created. Michelangelo's David is David, some think, because the statue was intended by Michelangelo to be the biblical character we refer to as David. But suppose we discover a letter that Michelangelo wrote by which it transpires that the statue was meant to be his secret lover. Does it make any difference to what the statue is? Perhaps we don't have very clear intuitions about this, and this may have something to do with the nature of art. But the question is not confined to works or art; is the carpenter's intention to make a chair part of what makes his creation a chair or is the intention irrelevant? I hope we can proceed by assuming that the intentions with which an object is created are not necessarily constitutive of what that object is. We can certainly grant that artifacts, tangible and intangible, come into existence intentionally. They are intentionally created as objects of a certain kind. But the word "created" should not be taken too narrowly; it is not always

[5] See, e.g., Peter van Inwagen, *Material Beings* (Cornell University Press 1990) ch. 13.

[6] An old Eastern European joke has a guy asking: "Can you have sex with an open window?" "In principle yes," the interlocutor says, "but it's better to do it with a woman."

[7] See Amie L. Thomasson, *Fiction and Metaphysics* (Cambridge University Press 1999).

the original creation of an object that makes it an artifact of a certain kind. Something that was created or otherwise came about as an X, may become a Y-artifact by repeated and widespread Y-uses of it. Creation is sometimes no more than recurrent and widespread intentional use.[8] (I am not saying that this is always enough, far from it. It takes a lot of deliberate planning and design to make an iPhone, for example, it doesn't come about without it.)

Intangible artifacts supervene on tangible things. A novel has to be written, there is a tangible text that gets it going, so to speak. Even a myth or a legend has had to be told by someone at some point: sentences in some natural language have to be expressed, whether written down or voiced. And then we can descend further, from the words on paper to the paper and ink, and further down till we get to atoms and quarks and whatnot. No need for any of that here. All we need to bear in mind is that "intangibility" is a relative notion. Artifacts, of all kinds, are created or brought into existence by some human acts attended by beliefs, intentions, plans, etc., anchored in the fabric of the natural universe. Somebody does or says something that is taken up by others, used in certain ways, and under complex conditions, an artifact becomes existent, used and talked about.

Generally speaking, though exceptions are possible, artifacts exist and persist when there is a population or a community that treats them as such.[9] Chairs are the kind of artifacts they are because we use them as such, to sit on, mostly. Imagine a world in which there are chair-shaped objects, but nobody uses them for sitting on or, let us assume, for anything at all. They are just there, scattered around. In that world there are no chairs, only chair-shaped objects. And the same goes for intangible artifacts. Imagine a world in which people are not psychologically capable of suspending belief in the alleged truth of what they hear; they just take every statement as a straightforward proposition, intending to describe how things really are. In such a world, there may be stories but no fiction. The artifact of fiction requires suspension of belief. We have to be able to use a story or a narrative in certain ways (in our minds, mostly) for fiction to be possible. The ways in which we actually use artifacts is constitutive of what they are, as artifacts.

[8] A nice example, I think, is the incorporation of African warrior masks into the European art world in the early decades of the twentieth century. The masks, as far as we can tell, were not created as works of art—at least not as the idea of art was understood in the Western world—but the artistic interest in them by influential European artists and their display in art galleries changed this, making them, as it were, works of art, at least in the West.

[9] Can there not be single-use artifacts? It is certainly possible for someone to invent a contraption for a particular purpose, then use it perhaps for this or that purpose, without any larger community involved in the process. But then we would not have a concept for that thing, it would be just a one-off tool. We can call it an artifact if we want, but nothing of importance hangs on this, I believe.

This is somewhat rough, admittedly; reality is a bit more subtle. Different populations may use one and the same artifact somewhat differently. Semantics is a good example (or analogue, if you doubt that meanings are artifacts); a natural language tends to have idiolects, allowing for some variations of meaning relative to populations. Similarly, there might be variations of use in the artifacts we have without necessarily affecting the essential nature of the artifact in question. Popular legends, for example, are used somewhat differently in different cultures, but they are still, by and large, the same kind of artifact. And as is the case with linguistic idiolects, the demarcation of populations is often a bit rough and vague, and differences are often subtle.

One has to admit, however, that there are some difficult questions here. Consider, for example, ancient Greek mythology. Presumably we would now regard stories about the Olympic gods and other mythological creatures as pure fiction. For the ancient Greeks, however, they were as real as the rest of the world they could perceive. Can we still say that, despite these differences in beliefs about the relevant ontology, we are talking about the same objects, the same artifacts? I'm inclined to say yes, but I don't have a clear argument to support this intuition. In any case, and this is important, we have to allow for the possibility that people, even as a community, may entertain false beliefs about the ontology of the artifacts they have created. Religion is a prime example, but there may be others. A legend may erroneously be thought to be a true story; a national foundation myth often fools people to believe that things happened, perhaps roughly, the way the myth has it. Or some population may believe that the laws they have descended from heaven. People, including entire communities, can be wrong about such things, though not about others. More on this later.

Let us assume, then, that we can divide our world into the things we find or discover, and the things we create. We, meaning human beings, of course. Rough as this distinction is, it bears on an important and famous distinction concerning the directionality between meaning and reference. Many words in our natural language (or concepts if you prefer), identified by Putnam as "natural kinds," aim to designate things we find in the world, whatever their true nature may turn out to be.[10] What we, collectively as language users, intend to pick out or designate by natural kind words, is the way things are, regardless of us, so to speak. And then, of course, it is always possible that we don't quite know how things really are, and whatever hypothesis about it we entertain, can turn out to be false. Let me call this: the possibility of fundamental error. With natural kinds, fundamental errors about the true features of their reference are always possible.

[10] Hilary Putnam, *Mind, Language and Reality, Vol. 2* (Cambridge University Press 1975).

Not so, by and large, with the reference of words designating artifacts, whether tangible or intangible. If something is created by us, and its nature as the kind of object it is, is constituted by our use of it, then we cannot have fundamental errors about its essential features. An artifact's nature is what we make of it. Assuming that meaning captures what we make of things, what we—collectively as language users—think them to be, words designating artifacts are such that their meaning is constitutive of their reference. It is simply not possible to conceive of a situation in which we might discover that chairs, for example, are not really the kind of objects people sit on, or that books are cooked in the oven, not written, and so on and so forth. Our use of chairs, making them and sitting on them and all that, is constitutive of what chairs, qua artifacts, really are. There's nothing more to it that we can have a fundamental error about.

Well, with the one caveat I have mentioned above: people can be mistaken about ontology. They may think that something created by humans is not really an artifact but something out there that they somehow discovered. That is a fairly common mistake, if you think, for example, about the number of deities cultures have created over the millennia.[11] But notice that even when people erroneously think that an artifact is an entity that exists independently of their own creation, they cannot be fundamentally mistaken about the essential features of the artifact in question. Zeus did not exist, ontologically speaking, even when ancient Greeks thought that he is very real; but it makes very little sense to suggest that Zeus (for the Greeks, at least) was not really the chief Olympian deity. The features of the artifact Zeus are those, and only those, which are told by the stories depicting him. There is nothing more to it. The main features of products of our culture and imagination cannot be discovered to have features previously hidden from us, as it were, waiting to be discovered.[12] There is something very similar, and not unrelated, about possibilities of errors concerning social conventions. People, by which I mean communities or populations, can be mistaken about the conventional nature of some norms they follow; they may think that the norms are not conventional, where in fact they are. But they cannot be mistaken about the content of their conventions.[13]

[11] Ontological mistakes in the other direction seem to be much rarer. It is difficult to think of an example where natural kinds are mistakenly thought to be artifacts. (Perhaps some realists about mathematics may attribute such a mistake to their opponents. I am not sure.)

[12] We may come to discover things about ourselves, that is, the human mind and psychology etc., by learning more about our cultural creations, but that is something else entirely. Then we are talking about natural objects, not artifacts.

[13] See Andrei Marmor, *Social Conventions: From Language to Law* (Princeton University Press 2009) 5–6.

There are a few more qualifications I have to insert here. For one thing, as Kripke famously showed, proper names behave, in some respects, very much like natural kinds. They designate rigidly the object (person or thing) named.[14] Proper names, however, would seem to be paradigmatic examples of artifacts. Things don't come into the world carrying their labels; naming things is something that we do. Names are artifacts. And yet they designate rigidly, and thus, errors are possible and many interesting examples of that are discussed in the literature. For our purposes, however, we can grant that proper names (and perhaps also partially descriptive names) are *sui generis*. If there is an element of rigid designation in the meaning of names, then the possibility of fundamental error cannot be ruled out.[15]

Another difference between proper names and words designating artifacts is that the latter have a type-token distinction: we can talk about chairs as a type (or, concept if you prefer) and this or that particular object as a chair. Errors about the identification or classification of tokens is always possible. Suppose I say: "This chair I'm sitting on is very uncomfortable." Someone can respond to my assertion by saying "Oh, but what you are sitting on is not a chair, actually," and that might be true. The impossibility of fundamental errors about reference of artifacts concerns the type, not the tokens. More precisely, it concerns the essential properties of the type. We cannot be mistaken about what kind of things chairs, generally, are and about what makes them, essentially, chairs. Artifacts are what we make of them. In this sense, the reference of words designating artifacts (as a type) is in our minds, not something we discover.

Saying that the reference of artifact concepts/words is "in our minds" is a very imprecise way of putting things. So let me try to be a bit more careful here. Artifacts, tangible and intangible alike, often have some physical reality instantiated by them. There are things out there, in the world, occurring or being, irrespective of our minds, that artifact words pick out, so to speak. There are chairs, as physical objects, and there are stories told by people or poems recited, and there are guns that kill people. None of this is just in our minds, it's all about stuff out there in the world. What is in our minds, however, is the relevant type or category, and its essential properties. If *a* is an object of an artifact type F, the answer to the question of What makes an *a* an

[14] Saul A. Kripke, *Naming and Necessity* (Harvard University Press 1980). I should clarify, as an historical point, that Kripke's analysis of proper names precedes Putnam's theory of natural kinds; Putnam was influenced by Kripke's work on rigid designation, not vice versa.

[15] E.g., we can name something that doesn't really exist. There are some differences between rigid designation *á la* Kripke, in case of proper names, and rigid designation in Putnam's theory of natural kinds. See Scott Soames, *Philosophical Essays, Vol 2* (Princeton University Press 2009) ch. 7.

F?, is what is fully determined by ways in which we use a typical F in a purposeful manner, ways in which we think about it, categorize it, refer to it, etc.

Some philosophers might resist the idea that artifacts have essential properties.[16] If what makes an artifact is what we make of it and ways in which we employ it, then there is no room for a distinction between properties that are essential and those that are accidental or inessential. Perhaps in some deep ontological sense this might be true, I am not sure. But at a commonsense level, the distinction is clear enough. Color is not an essential property of a chair; being able to sit on it, is. Why is that? Simply because chairs just are the kind of artifacts made and used for sitting, regardless of color or particular shape, etc.[17] Similarly, we can say that it is essential to what fiction is that it requires and presupposes suspension of belief; the length of the story is not essential. Some fiction is short, other is long. But if a story purports to tell us the truth about how things really are, it is not fiction.[18] At least in this shallow sense, if you will, I will continue to assume that artifacts have some essential properties. And then again, my claim is that we cannot be fundamentally mistaken about what those essential properties are.

3. Compound Artifacts and Conventions

Many of the artifacts we encounter are compound, by which I mean that they are artifacts within artifacts or enabled by other artifacts. A book, for example, say, a novel, conveys contents, as an intangible artifact, by means of writing, which is itself compound of linguistic artifacts (semantics, syntax, etc.), conventions of script, and of course, the physical object of the book itself. Several layers of artifacts are compound here. Or think about a painting exhibited in an art museum. The painting is an artifact, of course, but so is the museum. Thus a painting exhibited in a museum is an artifact within an artifact, but not only in a spatial sense. An art museum is an institution with certain features created by humans for certain purposes, serving various functions. When a painting is exhibited in a museum, the exhibition, in the context of a museum, gives the painting certain context and function that it might not otherwise have. In some cases, the differences are subtle, in others,

[16] I suspect that van Inwagen would be inclined to resist it, but I am not sure.

[17] Needless to say, I do not mean to rule out deviant and borderline cases; a broken chair might still be a chair, and a chair made of thin paper exhibited in a gallery is, presumably, a borderline case of chair. Vagueness is ubiquitous.

[18] Though of course it may become to be regarded as fiction later, as the example of Greek mythology I mentioned earlier would demonstrate.

quite profound. The exhibit of a few sticks on a pile of sand in MOMA may contribute to the artistic nature of the object a great deal. It may not even be a work of art without the institutional support it gets by being positioned where it is. Putting an artifact in a certain context often changes the quality of the artifact.[19]

There is a particular kind of compound artifact, however, that is relevant to law. There are many instances in which social conventions shape the ways of creating artifacts of a certain kind. There are conventions, for example, about what counts as a novel, or as an epic poem, and those conventions would shape and guide ways in which authors create a new novel or write an epic poem and of course, the ways in which we read them. There are conventions about symbolism that would shape the ways in which road-signs are made or directions indicated in a given location. In previous work I argued that there are conventions about what counts as a structured competitive game, and they would shape ways in which we invent and play structured competitive games, how we react to them, etc.[20] If conventions are also artifacts, as I think they are, then these would all be examples of compound artifacts. A novel, for example, would instantiate both original creation by the author, which would make it a paradigmatic example of an intangible artifact, but also some conventional norms and guidance in the background, contributing something, perhaps tacitly, to what the novel as an artifact is. And this makes, essentially, every novel a compound artifact. Novels, in this respect, are very much like paintings in an art museum, obviously in a more intangible manner.[21]

I hope that it is sufficiently evident that conventions are (intangible) artifacts. Conventions meet all the conditions about artifacts we mentioned above; they are created by humans for particular purposes, their existence and character depends on the ways in which they are actually used, that is, followed and practiced, and metaphysically speaking, their existence is a function of what we make of them, they exist in our minds, as it were. Now it is true, of course, that conventions are rarely created in a deliberate manner to serve as conventions; conventions tend to emerge in an organic, often slow and invisible manner, evolving in ways that are sometimes difficult to trace

[19] Here is another similar example: consider the difference between exhibiting an artifact, say an African mask, in an art museum and exhibiting it in an anthropology museum. The same object is likely to be seen in different light depending on the kind of museum in which it is exhibited.

[20] Marmor, *Social Conventions* (n. 13).

[21] In Marmor, "Law as Authoritative Fiction" (n. 2) I expand on this topic, explaining in greater detail how works of art and other intangible artifacts are of an expressive kind, constituted by means of communication.

with any great accuracy, even in retrospect. But as I mentioned before, this is often true about artifacts, even tangible ones.

4. Compound Artifacts and Prefixed Contexts

Suppose you have read a few of Agatha Christie's Poirot mysteries, and therefore know a thing or two about the protagonist. You know that he is private detective, very smart and yet rather arrogant, that he is a Belgian who lives and works in London, he is very proud of his carefully groomed moustache, and things like that. How do you know any of this? Well, the books say so. It's what the stories tell us about Poirot. If Christie portrayed Poirot as a Frenchman, he would be French and not Belgian. If she portrayed him as humble and meek, he would be humble and meek, and not arrogant. In short, Christie's *saying so makes it so*. Poirot is not a natural person of course, but a fictional character. In other words, Poirot is an artifact, an intangible one, of course. Now you would think that there is no mystery in the fact that Poirot's attributes as a fictional character, as an artifact, are entirely due to the author's saying so. It's the nature of fiction that they create their plots and characters by their saying so.

But now consider a different kind of assertions we can express about the fictional character of Poirot that might be true or false, but not in virtue of the author's saying so. One can say, for example, that the character of Poirot is too flat and shallow, devoid of human complexities; or that Poirot's infallibility is incredulous and somewhat irritating. And things like that. These are not the kind of assertions which are rendered true or false by virtue of Christie's saying so. On the contrary, in a way they are critical of the character she created and ways she depicted him. So it seems that we can have two kinds of assertions about fictional characters: some that are true (or false) simply by virtue of what the story says or implicates, and others, whose truth value is not entirely a function of the author's saying so, at least not directly.[22] Following David Lewis's terminology, I will call them prefixed and non-prefixed statements.[23] The statement that Poirot is a Belgian is prefixed, it is true *in the fiction*, and in virtue of the story's say so. The statement that Poirot's character is flat and shallow is not prefixed. It is a statement *on* some aspect of the prefixed context, but from the outside, as it were.

[22] See Thomasson, *Fiction and Metaphysics* (n. 7) 105–6.

[23] David Lewis, "Truth in Fiction" in David Lewis, *Philosophical Papers, Vol. 1* (Oxford University Press 1983) 261–75.

Lewis was interested in cautioning us about ways of mixing prefixed with non-prefixed statements in an argument. His famous example is the following non-sequitur:

(1) Sherlock Holmes lived in 221B Baker Street.
(2) The house on 221B Baker Street is a Bank.
(3) Therefore, Sherlock Holmes lived in a Bank.

Quite obviously, what goes wrong here is that we combine in a syllogism a premise that is prefixed by "In fiction ... X," which is premise (1) above, with premise (2), describing some state of affairs in the world, which is not prefixed. But this logical fallacy is not what I am interested in. I want to focus for a bit on what enables prefixed contexts and distinguishes them from non-prefixed ones. Fiction is just one example. In earlier work I suggested a distinction between two kinds of prefixed contexts: open and closed.[24] Open prefixes are those that can range over non-prefixed statements to yield valid arguments. Modal operators might qualify, as well as prefixes like "According to the laws of physics ... ," or "According to X logic ... ." It is probably embedded in the semantics of such prefixes that they range over ordinary non-prefixed statements without yielding logical mishaps. They are meant to be true irrespective of the prefix, as it were. The kind of problems Lewis saw in prefixed statements, and rightly so I think, is with contexts that are closed. "According to fiction X ..." or "In the Agatha Christie mysteries ..." are closed prefixes. And this is not just about semantics. Closed prefixes are such that they presuppose a constitutive relation between a designated context and the truth values of statements asserted within that context. In other words, closed prefixes are those in which *the saying so makes it so*. If the fiction *says* that Poirot is Belgian, he *is* Belgian, but only in the story.[25]

You may wonder what other prefixes are closed, besides fiction. Quite a few, actually. When the umpire in a soccer game orders a player "out," the expression gains its game-related significance by virtue of the umpire's saying so. (It is now true, in the game, that the player has to exit the game, and it is true by virtue of the umpire's saying so.) Games, generally, are prefixed contexts, closed ones.

[24] Andrei Marmor, *The Language of Law* (Oxford University Press 2014) 77–84; Marmor, "Law as Authoritative Fiction" (n. 2).

[25] There are, of course, limits to how much the saying so can make it so, even in fiction. The saying so cannot make it that we think of a square circle or perhaps even something like a "lovely torture" of an innocent child. These limits and how to account for them are extensively discussed in the literature on fiction; see, e.g., Richard Moran, "The Expression of Feeling in Imagination" (1994) 103(1) *The Philosophical Review* 75. For a good account of the contemporary controversy, see: Nils-Hennes Stear, "Imaginative and Fictionality Failure: A Normative Approach" (2015) 15(34) *Philosopher's Imprint* 1.

And then, countless institutional settings provide for closed prefixed contexts. When the chair of a committee says that the meeting is adjourned, the meeting is adjourned, officially, and by virtue of her saying so; it is a closed prefix. And notice that the meeting can be officially adjourned by her saying so, even if nothing really happens and people hang around, keep talking, etc. Like with fiction, the prefixed statements can be true even if reality is different. A story that depicts the moon as pink makes the moon pink, but only in the story.

Now you might suspect that I overplay the extent to which closed prefixes are closed; after all, even fiction can incorporate, tacitly, an indefinite number of un-prefixed propositions. For example, we can safely assume that Poirot had a nose, and only one, by virtue of being human, that is, even if his nose is never mentioned in the stories. And we can assume that the city of London where his escapades unfold has streets and houses and shops, etc., etc. Fiction typically incorporates, by implication, an indefinite number of facts or factual assumptions. And sometimes it is not easy to determine whether an implicated factual assumption is really incorporated in the story, whether it can be taken to be true in the fiction, or not. Elsewhere I explained this in greater detail, but those details will not matter here.[26] Nothing in the argument that follows depends on ways in which prefixed contexts of various kinds, including the law, can incorporate by implication non-prefixed propositions. It is safe to assume, however, that incorporation of un-prefixed propositions into a prefixed context depends on the nature of the context and its underlying rationale. Fiction incorporates by implication all sorts of premises that can be assumed to be *common knowledge* between author and readers, the kind of presuppositions that are taken for granted, given the genre, the relevant time frame, the relevant state of knowledge at the time, and things like that.

For our purposes, what matters is that closed prefixed statements have to be enabled by something; there has to be something that creates contexts in which the saying so, in that context or prefix, makes it so (in the context). Though not in these terms, John Searle argued, a long time ago, that what I call closed prefixed contexts are necessarily enabled by rules or conventions.[27] There has to be some normative setting in the background that creates this constitutive relation between the context and the truth values of statements in that context. By and large, I think that Searle was right. Closed prefixed contexts are constituted by rules or conventions.[28] After all, think about the

[26] Marmor, "Law as Authoritative Fiction" (n. 2).

[27] John Searle, "How Performatives Work" (1989) 12 *Linguistics and Philosophy* 535. See also John Searle, *Speech Acts* (Cambridge University Press 1969).

[28] Contra Searle, I don't think that this is true of performative speech acts generally; see Marmor, *Social Conventions* (n. 13) 118–30.

question of why is it only the chairperson who can adjourn the meeting, why her saying so makes it so. Surely that is the case only because and in so far as the relevant institutional rules set things up that way. Similarly, only the umpire, thus defined by the rules of the game, can order a player "out," not another player or somebody from the audience. And more intricately, perhaps, there are certain conventions that guide ways of telling stories of this or that genre, conventions that are partly constitutive of what makes it true, in the fiction, that so and so. But there are two possible versions of what this constitutive relation might be, and it's important to draw the distinction.

Some constitutive relations in this context are strong and others are weak. A strong constitutive relation between rules or conventions and the prefixed context obtains when the rules actually create the relevant context. For example, the constitutive relations between the rules of a game and the meaning of the moves in it is a strong one. Without the rules there would be no game and no moves to make in it. Or if the rules were significantly different, we would get a different game with different moves. The truths of statements prefixed in a game context are constituted by the rules; without the rules we would not have the context itself. But the constitutive relation between rules or conventions and the context of fiction, for example, is not quite as strong. Fiction does not seem to require rules or conventions to take off the grounds, so to speak. As long as you can tell a story and people understand what you say and get it as a story, you have created an intangible artifact, which is the story you told. There does not seem to be a need for rules or conventions to constitute what you can do by telling a story.

But this last point is not entirely accurate. Not every story is fiction. (In a sense I am telling you a story here, but I certainly hope that it's not fiction.) We do need some conventional background for fiction to exist, as a particular kind of context that we can make moves in, and understand the moves as the kind of moves they are. The convention about suspension of belief is a prime example; without it there is no fiction. But there are many other conventions, though they tend to be more genre specific. There are conventions that distinguish novels from other genres of literature or fiction; there are conventions about what makes a certain type of fictional narrative have the requisite structure; and so and so forth.[29] The context of fiction is partly constituted by conventions. But again, the relation of constitution here is not as strong as in the case of games. Some aspects of fiction are constituted by conventions, others not so. The relation between the conventions and the context in the

[29] Worth keeping in mind that those conventions were very different in antiquity; there were times when the only conventional way of telling a story was by way of poetry. Prose was not available.

case of fiction is partly constitutive; conventions do not constitute the entire context, only part or some important aspects of it.

5. Law as a Prefixed Compound Artifact

With these observations on hand, we can turn to law. The legal domain is much more complex than any of the examples mentioned above, and therefore some simplifying assumptions will be needed as we go along. But a few essential connections we can make at the outset. Given the main features of intangible artifacts we identified in preceding sections, it should be fairly obvious that the law, by and large, is an artifact. It is a compound artifact, operating at various levels within other artifacts, often themselves compound. In previous work I have argued that the foundations of law are conventional: there are some deep conventions that constitute ways of making law, instantiated by surface conventions of different legal systems determining how law is made and identified within that particular system. I happen to think that the constitutive relation between the conventions and the legal domain is a strong one; in this respect, law is more like a game than like fiction.[30] Either way, if conventions are at the foundations of law, law is, fundamentally, an artifact. And it is a compound artifact because the conventions themselves do not determine what the law is, they just determine how to make law, modify it, annul it, apply it, etc. Only actions in accordance with the conventions would make this or that law, or have this or that legal impact in a given context. Conventions and subsequent rules give those actions and events the legal meaning they have. So making law is very much like creating fiction or playing a game; somebody, though not necessarily a single person of course, has to make some moves, that is, act in certain ways, to create this or that legal impact. Which is to say that laws are compound artifacts; they are artifacts created within artificial frameworks that are themselves intangible artifacts.

The law, however, is also a prefixed context; the saying so of legal authorities makes it so, in the law; the law is what various authorities say that it is.[31] And notice that we would never say that the law is such and such, period. We would say that the law in the Germany is such and such, or that from the point of view of Canadian law one ought to so and so, and things like that. Laws are always relative to jurisdictions. The legal point of view is a

[30] See Marmor, *Social Conventions* (n. 13), particularly ch. 7.

[31] I explained this in greater detail in Marmor, "Law as Authoritative Fiction" (n. 2). See also Marmor, *The Language of Law* (n. 24) chs. 1 and 3. (Notice that both Kelsen and Hart would have definitely agreed, though they expressed the same idea in different terms.)

closed prefix, and it's closed within particular systems of law, that is, within particular jurisdictions. By "jurisdiction" I mean a spatiotemporal artifact; jurisdictions are not natural entities, existing as it were, irrespective of human invention. Jurisdictions are created by humans, alas, sometimes with brute force, as zones of authority and sovereignty. Their identity and scope are path dependent. This, I submit, is a rather unique feature of law, as a closed prefix, that its domain is jurisdiction dependent, which means that it is, essentially, spatiotemporal.[32] Other closed prefixes, such as games, artistic genres, etc., are not tied to space and time. At least not essentially so. But the law is. And this should not be all that surprising, actually. After all, the law, unlike fiction and games and such, has something essential to do with power and authority, and those tend to be local, contained within space and time.[33]

Let me tie some strands together. I have been talking about two aspects of artifacts in tandem: many artifacts are compound, and some compound artifacts are such that they create closed prefixed contexts. The law, like games and artistic genres, are both. They are compound artifacts, partly constituted by conventional rules, that create closed prefixed contexts. What is unique to law is that its closed prefixed context is tied to the idea of a jurisdiction which has a spatiotemporal aspect.

To what extent is it true, then, that the law is fundamentally in our minds? To answer this question we need a distinction between legal contents that can figure in our practical reasoning, and actions and events in the world that follow from applying such reasoning. When we say that "the law is such and such" or that "the law requires so and so," we refer to legal contents, to the kind of thing that functions as a premise in practical reasoning. But we can also think about the law in terms of its impact in the world, as the kind of things that happen to people, or ways in which they conduct themselves, as a consequence of applying the law to this or that. People are sent to jail, their money is transferred, objects replace hands, things like that; things that happen in accordance with or, as a consequence of, some legal reasoning. Clearly the latter is not in our minds. Just as a chair, qua physical object, is not in our minds, so is the action or event that happens in accordance with law; being locked up in jail is as real as it gets for people. It is only law, as the kind of fact that we employ in our practical reasoning, that is the intangible

[32] Some religions have a similar jurisdictional aspect. Interestingly, historians and archeologists suggest that all the gods in the ancient near-east (around the first millennium BC) were believed to have territorial jurisdiction, quite literally as if they were sovereigns of particular geographical areas.

[33] On the essential relations between authoritative power and jurisdiction I have elaborated in Andrei Marmor, "An Institutional Conception of Authority" (2011) 39(3) *Philosophy & Public Affairs* 274. See also Marmor, "Law as Authoritative Fiction" (n. 2).

artifact, and as such, in our minds. Legal content, as a fact that figures in practical reasoning, is the artifact we call "the law," not the things that happen as a result from this reasoning. And then, I hope it's easy to see that law as the kind of fact that forms part of practical reason, is, indeed, entirely in our minds. The law is a compound intangible artifact, enabling a closed prefix that makes things true, in the law, by saying so.

The importance of this last point should become evident when we recall the idea that we cannot possibly entertain fundamental errors about the essential features of artifacts. If artifacts are the kind of things we, humans, make of them, then their essential properties cannot be misidentified; we cannot come to discover that things are not quite as we had thought that they are. Our thoughts, collectively shared, constitute what they are. And this clearly applies to law as well.[34] We cannot be fundamentally mistaken about what the law, as the kind of content that figures in our practical reasoning, is. Once again, however, bear in mind that people can be mistaken about the artifact nature of law; they can think that law is God's command, or long gone aliens' gift to humanity, or anything of the sort. (It may be worth remembering that people thought something like that about the Egyptian pyramids too.) Nothing of what I say here precludes the possibility that people, entire communities even, entertain false believes about the fact that law is an intangible artifact. The kind of error that is precluded by the artifact nature of law is about the essential features that make something the law in their communities.[35] If there is a community that regards the directives or their Grand Shaman as their law, then the directives of the Grand Shaman are the law, in that community. They just cannot be wrong about that.

Now again, we need to be careful with the type-token distinction: we can always be mistaken about identification or characterization of particular tokens of law. Just as I can mistakenly think that something is a chair when it's not, I can be mistaken about what the law on this or that particular thing is. Arguments and controversies about such things are commonplace. It is what enables attorneys to earn a living. But lawyers and judges cannot be mistaken about what law is, in general, as a type, at least in their own communities. Which would seem to entail that Dworkin's famous idea about what he called *theoretical disagreements* in law is not a real possibility. Dworkin famously

[34] This is something I had argued for, albeit on different grounds, a long time ago in Andrei Marmor, *Interpretation and Legal Theory* (Oxford University Press 1992; 2nd rev. edn., Hart Publishing 2005) ch. 5.

[35] Needless to say, people can be mistaken about features of artifacts of other cultures due to ignorance or misinterpretation. But those are standard epistemic problems we face whenever we seek to understand an alien culture.

suggested that lawyers and judges can have fundamental disagreements about what law, as a type, really is.[36] They can have an intelligible and sensible argument about what constitutes the legal domain and what conditions have to be met for something to be law, as a type, in their own legal community. But if I am right to argue that the essential features of an artifact cannot be mistaken by the community that uses it, then the essential properties of law, as a type, as the kind of fact that figures in our practical reason, cannot be misidentified. We cannot have the kind of disagreement Dworkin labeled "theoretical."

Now, I think that this critical conclusion follows, indeed, but with a caveat. The caveat has to do with the compound nature of the artificiality of law. When we have a compound artifact, especially with some intangible features, the various contributions of its elements may not be as clear as to rule out the possibility of serious disagreement. Think about the example I gave about a pile of sticks in the sand exhibited as contemporary art in MOMA. One can see an argument about the potential contribution of different elements here: is it a work of art, at least partly, because it is exhibited in MOMA or is it exhibited in MOMA because it is a work of art? I hope you can recall cases in which you looked at a piece of contemporary art and thought that the former option is more realistic. And we can certainly have an argument about this. Similar arguments we can have about the contribution of various aspects of the legal domain. Perhaps some of the age old arguments between legal positivism and its critics about the relations between legal validity and morality may have this character; these arguments end up with different views about what exactly is the contribution of different artifacts in creating the compound artifact we call law. And some level of disagreement about this complex composition is certainly possible. So in this respect, theoretical disagreements in law are sensible. But what makes no sense is to assume that we can come to learn something new about the essential features of our laws that we had not known before. The law is what we invent and what we make of it. Fundamental errors about what the law is, are just not metaphysically possible.

[36] Ronald Dworkin, *Law's Empire* (Harvard University Press 1986) ch. 1.

4

Law, Morality, Art, the Works

*Kevin Toh**

1.

Consider the following questions:

($Q1_L$) What is the law on such-and-such?

($Q2_L$) What is (the content of) the most fundamental law of this legal system?

($Q3_L$) In virtue of what is a certain rule the most fundamental law of a particular legal system?

($Q4_L$) What facts amount to or constitute a community of people having laws or a legal system?

($Q1_L$) and ($Q2_L$) are first-order or substantive legal questions. These are the questions that lawyers are supposed to answer for their clients, and that judges are supposed to answer in deciding cases brought before them. On the other hand, ($Q3_L$) and ($Q4_L$) are not really questions that lawyers and judges are familiar with. Instead, we might think, they are second-order or philosophical questions that legal philosophers deal with.

* Earlier versions of this chapter were presented at the European University Institute in Florence, University of Bologna, a BAFFLE meeting at U.C. Berkeley, Yale Law School, Institute of Advanced Studies in the Humanities (IASH) at University of Edinburgh, and University of Edinburgh Law School, on the last occasion as the keynote address of the first annual Oxford-Edinburgh Legal Philosophy Graduate Colloquium. I am grateful for the instructive feedback I received on these occasions. I also thank the students in my aesthetics seminar at San Francisco State University in Spring 2015 in which some of the ideas in the second half of the chapter were tried out. Finally, I thank the editors of this volume for their helpful comments. Despite these many opportunities for presentation and the excellent feedback I received from many people, the chapter remains very much a work in progress.

Law as an Artifact. First Edition. Edited by Luka Burazin, Kenneth Einar Himma, and Corrado Roversi. Chapter 4 © Kevin Toh 2018. Published 2018 by Oxford University Press.

I want to question the conception of the relation among these four questions that is the orthodoxy among contemporary legal philosophers. The orthodox position provides a "vertically integrated" set of answers to the four questions, so that in order to justify answers to ($Q1_L$)-questions, we need to have answers to ($Q2_L$), ($Q3_L$), and ultimately ($Q4_L$). In other words, answers to ($Q1_L$)-questions are supposed ultimately to bottom out with the facts that the correct answer to ($Q4_L$) would enumerate. Here is a recent articulation of that orthodoxy:

> [A] great deal *does* turn on the question of "What is Law?" ... In order to prove conclusively that the law is thus-and-so in a particular jurisdiction, ... [o]ne must ... know a general philosophical truth, namely, how legal authority and proper interpretive methodology are established in general. In other words, one must know which facts *ultimately* determine the existence and content of legal systems.... In short, if one wants to demonstrate conclusively that the law is thus-and-so in any particular case, one must know certain philosophical truths about the nature of law in general—precisely the information that analytic jurisprudence seeks to provide.[1]

Like statements abound in the current legal philosophical literature.[2]

I want to question this orthodox position in the first half of this chapter. I will first provide a fuller picture of the orthodoxy by using H.L.A. Hart's theory of the nature of law. If any legal philosophical theory deserves to be considered the orthodox or benchmark position in contemporary Anglophone legal philosophy, it is Hart's theory, or more accurately—*and this is very important for my purposes*—the common understanding of Hart's theory. Many currently prominent theories of the nature of law can be considered variations on Hart's theory, as that theory is commonly understood; and my subsequent arguments would be applicable to those theories with little or no adjustment. After fleshing out the orthodox position with the help of the common understanding of Hart's theory, I will set out an alternative understanding of Hart's theory, and use it to argue that contemporary legal philosophers overlook a very credible and promising conception of the nature of law, and furthermore that they overlook a conception of the relation between legal philosophy and first-order legal questions that is a credible and attractive alternative to the orthodox conception.

[1] Scott J. Shapiro, *Legality* (Harvard University Press 2011) 25.

[2] See e.g., Liam Murphy, *What Makes Law* (Cambridge University Press 2014) ch. 2, esp. 14, 21. I should note that Shapiro himself no longer seems to adhere to the orthodox position that he espouses in the passage quoted in the text, and more generally in *Legality*. He now apparently endorses something very much like the alternative position that I will go on to sketch subsequently. See David Plunkett and Scott Shapiro, "Law, Morality, and Everything Else: General Jurisprudence as a Branch of Metanormative Inquiry" (forthcoming) *Ethics*.

I should mention at the outset that I am not the only one who questions the orthodox conception of the relation among the four questions. At least from 1986 on when *Law's Empire* appeared,[3] and more explicitly in the last two decades of his life,[4] Ronald Dworkin sought to discredit the idea that in moving from ($Q2_L$) to ($Q3_L$), we are switching theoretical gears, so to speak, and moving from first-order to second-order matters. In raising and answering ($Q3_L$), Dworkin argued, legal philosophers are in effect raising and answering nothing other than ($Q2_L$) in needlessly and misleadingly recondite ways. I believe that much of what Dworkin has said on this particular issue is correct. My disagreements with him lie elsewhere, and in the second half of this chapter, I will outline some considerations, by relying on which I will register, near the end (§ 9), my disagreements with Dworkin's conception of how we are to go about answering ($Q1_L$)-questions.

2.

Look again at ($Q4_L$):

($Q4_L$) What facts amount to or constitute a community of people having laws or a legal system?

It is likely that the facts that amount to any community's having laws would be broadly similar to, but also different in significant details from, the facts that amount to a community's having other kinds of rules or norms—e.g. those of morality, scientific inquiry, etiquette, games, etc.

Pursuing this line of thinking, Hart argued that laws (or *legal* rules) come in hierarchically structured packages, with some specific kinds of second-order rules, or rules governing the operation of the rules within the package.[5] These second-order rules, which Hart calls "secondary rules"—to distinguish them from "primary rules" that directly govern conduct—include: *rules of change* which regulate any modification in the rules of the system; *rules of adjudication* which regulate settling of disputes about the content and application of the rules of the system; and the *rule of recognition* which regulates the identification of the rules of the system. A legal system exists or prevails in a community if some powerful subset of the members of the community—call them the "officials" of that community—*accept* the secondary rules (in the

[3] Ronald Dworkin, *Law's Empire* (Harvard University Press 1986).

[4] See esp. Ronald Dworkin, "Objectivity and Truth: You'd Better Believe It" (1996) 25 *Philosophy and Public Affairs* 87; Ronald Dworkin, *Justice for Hedgehogs* (Harvard University Press 2011).

[5] H.L.A. Hart, *The Concept of Law* (2nd edn., Oxford University Press 1994) ch. 5.

sense to be specified presently) and follow them as the result, and the rest of the community at least follow the rules that are valid according to the rule of recognition prevailing in that community. A person accepts a rule, or takes an "internal point of view" toward that rule, according to Hart, when he believes there to be reasons to follow it. Such acceptance is constituted by the person's dispositions to regulate his own conduct in accordance with the rule, to justify his own and others' conduct by appeals to that rule, and to criticize his own and others' deviance by appeals to that rule. Presumably, to treat a rule of recognition as reason-giving is to treat generally the rules that are valid according to that rule of recognition as reason-giving. Hart does not go into how thoroughly a person must be disposed to treat each valid law as reason-giving to count as accepting a rule of recognition, but we can assume that some general tendency must be there. In effect, according to Hart, a community has laws if certain behavioral and psychological facts obtain among the members of that community. That is his answer to ($Q4_L$).

We can sum up that answer as follows:

(H) A community is governed by laws when its members regulate their behavior and practical thought by a set of rules, which set includes some higher-order rules governing the following types of operations of the rules of the set: (i) revision of the rules of the set; (ii) resolution of disputes about the rules of the set; and (iii) identification of the rules that belong to the set.

Now, what is the relation between (H) and ($Q1_L$)–($Q3_L$)? As I indicated above, the orthodox position envisions a vertically integrated set of answers to the four questions. According to the orthodox position, the behavioral and psychological facts that (H) enumerates are the facts in virtue of which a particular rule is the rule of recognition of a particular community's legal system. Since (H) names only behavioral and psychological facts, and no moral or normative considerations, (H) motivates a legal positivist answer to ($Q3_L$). And the rule of recognition that the members of the relevant community, or more specifically their officials, accept in common is the most fundamental law of that community's legal system. Thus we would have an answer to ($Q2_L$). And that answer can be applied to vindicate answers to ($Q1_L$)-questions.

We can see many legal philosophers tracing out or assuming the implications of (H) as I have just outlined them. Here are a few:

> [I]f Hart is correct, and social practices explain how legal systems are possible, then legal reasoning must always be traceable to a social rule of recognition. Arguments about who has authority to do what, what rights individuals have, which legal texts

are authoritative, and the proper way to interpret them must ultimately be resolved by reference to the sociological facts of official practice.[6]

[T]he Rule of Recognition, on Hart's view, is a social rule, meaning its content—that is, the criteria of legal validity—is fixed by a complex empirical fact, namely, the *actual practice* of officials (and the attitude they evince towards the practice). So it looks like the only dispute about the criteria of legal validity that is possible, on Hart's view, is an empirical or "heads count" dispute: namely, a dispute about what judges are doing, and how many of them are doing it, since it is the actual practice of officials and their attitudes towards that practice that fixes the criteria of legal validity according to the positivist.[7]

Especially, but not only where a legal system has no canonical text, it is common to say that ultimate constitutional questions are questions of practice (or *realpolitik*), not questions of law. Hart exposed this as a false contrast. That a question is one of practice does not mean that it is not one of law. For some law is made by what people do ....[8]

3.

This common understanding of (H)'s implications, and the resulting conception of the relation among ($Q1_L$)–($Q4_L$) are, however, based on what I believe is an optional reading of Hart's legal theory. To bring that out, consider the following moral analogues of the four legal questions:

($Q1_M$) What is morally called for in such-and-such situation?

($Q2_M$) What is (the content of) the most fundamental principle of morality?

($Q3_M$) In virtue of what is a certain principle the most fundamental principle of morality?

($Q4_M$) What facts amount to or constitute a community of people having mores or a morality?

As the transition from ($Q1_L$)–($Q2_L$) to ($Q3_L$)–($Q4_L$) is usually thought to mark a transition from first-order or substantive legal questions to second-order or legal philosophical questions, so the transition from ($Q1_M$)–($Q2_M$) to ($Q3_M$)–($Q4_M$) could be thought to amount to a transition from first-order moral questions to second-order philosophical questions about morality. In

[6] Shapiro, *Legality* (n. 1) 102.

[7] Brian Leiter, "Explaining Theoretical Disagreements" (2009) 76 *University of Chicago Law Review* 1222.

[8] John Gardner, "Some Types of Law" (2008) repr. in John Gardner, *Law as a Leap of Faith* (Oxford University Press 2012) 69–70.

fact, however, we can think of philosophy as involved in both sides of the transition when it comes to morality. Normative ethics is concerned with ($Q1_M$) and ($Q2_M$), whereas metaethics is concerned with ($Q3_M$) and ($Q4_M$).

Would the facts specified by answering ($Q4_M$) have any implications for specifying the most fundamental moral principle, and in answering other first-order moral questions—that is, for answering ($Q2_M$) and ($Q1_M$)-questions? What is important to notice is that different answers to ($Q4_M$) would vary greatly in their first-order implications, not just in the contents of the answers that they would provide, but also in the degrees to which they determine or constrain answers to ($Q2_M$) and ($Q1_M$). It may be that the best answer to ($Q4_M$) would name the properties that constitute, or otherwise subvene under or ground, the properties of moral goodness or rightness.[9] It may even be the case that the sentences making up the best answer to ($Q4_M$) are analytically related to the sentences making up the best answer to ($Q2_M$) and ($Q1_M$).[10] In either case, we would have an affirmation of a moral analogue of the orthodox conception of the relation among the answers to the four legal questions that we began with. In answering ($Q4_M$), we would have gotten the answer to ($Q3_M$), which in turn would have furnished answers to ($Q2_M$) and ($Q1_M$)-questions. On the other hand, the best answer to ($Q4_M$) may have neither metaphysical nor analytical implications for answering ($Q2_M$) and ($Q1_M$). Compare:

(F) A community is governed by mores or a morality when its members regulate their behavior and practical thought by the goal of furthering human welfare [where this last notion is naturalistically or nonmorally defined].

and

(G) A community is governed by mores or a morality when its members regulate their emotions of guilt and resentment by a set of rules, and those emotions of guilt and resentment in turn regulate the members' behavior and practical thought.

[9] See e.g., Nicholas L. Sturgeon, "Moral Explanations" in David Copp and David Zimmerman (eds.), *Morality, Reason and Truth* (Rowman & Allanheld 1985); Peter Railton, "Moral Realism" (1986) repr. in Peter Railton, *Facts, Values, and Norms* (Cambridge University Press 2003); Richard N. Boyd, "How to be a Moral Realist" in Geoffrey Sayre-McCord (ed.), *Essays on Moral Realism* (Cornell University Press 1988); Michael Smith, *The Moral Problem* (Blackwell Publishers 1994).

[10] See e.g., Frank Jackson, *From Metaphysics to Ethics* (Clarendon Press 1998); Frank Jackson, "Cognitivism, A Priori Deduction, and Moore" (2003) 113 *Ethics* 557; David Lewis, "How to Define Theoretical Terms" (1970) repr. in David Lewis, *Philosophical Papers*, vol. 1 (Oxford University Press 1983); David Lewis, "Dispositional Theories of Value" (1989) repr. in David Lewis, *Papers in Ethics and Social Philosophy* (Cambridge University Press 2000).

These are approximations of the two influential answers to ($Q4_M$) that could be inferred from the early Philippa Foot and Allan Gibbard, respectively, and are labeled accordingly.[11] Notice that (F) would have metaphysical or even analytical implications for answering ($Q2_M$) and ($Q1_M$) by way of answering ($Q3_M$). On the other hand, (G) would not.

It may be tempting to think that (G) does have an implication for answering ($Q2_M$), and in particular to think that a commitment to (G) carries with it a commitment to something like:

> (C_M) The most fundamental principle of morality is the one that the members of the relevant community accept in common as the most fundamental principle governing their emotions of guilt and resentment.

(C_M) is a principle of moral conventionalism. It says in effect that what is morally right or wrong depends on what the locally prevalent norms say are right or wrong. It is an implausible moral thesis, to say the least, and it does a very poor job of competing against many other hypotheses about the most fundamental principle of morality, especially the standard utilitarian and Kantian hypotheses. But more important than the sheer implausibility of (C_M) for my purposes is the fact that one can accept (G) without committing oneself to (C_M) as well. (G) is in fact neutral among many different possible answers to ($Q2_M$). Gibbard for one happens to be a utilitarian.[12] He accepts (G), but rejects (C_M). And so can we.

The crucial question for us is whether we should read (H) as analogous to (F) or to (G) in its implications for answering ($Q1_L$)–($Q3_L$). Clearly, (H) could be read as a proposal analogous to (F), so that it is read as enumerating the behavioral and psychological facts that constitute, or otherwise subvene under or ground, the properties of legality or legal validity. And this is the reading that conforms to the orthodox conception of the relation among ($Q1_L$)–($Q4_L$), as shown by the words of some leading legal philosophers that I quoted at the

[11] See Philippa Foot, "Moral Beliefs" (1958–1959) repr. in Philippa Foot, *Virtues and Vices* (University of California Press 1978); Allan Gibbard, *Wise Choices, Apt Feelings* (Harvard University Press 1990). Note that although Gibbard is an expressivist about the meaning of ethical terms, his conception of morality, as summarized by (G), is detachable from expressivism. For conceptions of morality similar to (G), see Richard B. Brandt, *A Theory of the Good and the Right* (Oxford University Press 1979); Bernard Williams, *Ethics and the Limits of Philosophy* (Harvard University Press 1985); John Skorupski, "The Definition of Morality" (1993) repr. in John Skorupski, *Moral Explorations* (Oxford University Press 1999). A less developed conception along the same line can be found in Hart, *The Concept of Law* (n. 5) ch. 8.

[12] See Allan Gibbard, *Reconciling Our Aims* (Barry Stroud ed., Oxford University Press 2008) for an overview of how Gibbard combines his metaethical commitments with his substantive or first-order utilitarianism.

end of the preceding section. In effect, these legal philosophers have thought that (H) implies the following legal analogue of (C_M):

(C_L) The most fundamental law of the legal system of a community is the one that the members or officials of the community accept in common as the most fundamental rule governing the identification of the rules of the legal system.

But as the discussion in the preceding two paragraphs help us to see, this is an optional reading of (H). We can read (H) as more analogous to (G) than to (F). And read that way, (H) would underdetermine answers to ($Q1_M$)–($Q3_M$), and more specifically would not imply (C_L). We would thereby sidestep the orthodox conception of the relation among answers to ($Q1_L$)–($Q4_L$).

So which reading of (H) is better? I am not here concerned with the issue of fidelity to Hart's actual position, though I will have some things to say on that issue in the next section. Instead, I am concerned with which of the two readings renders (H) more credible as a thesis about the nature of law. A plausible line to take is that the contest between the two readings is an explanatory one. Whichever reading does a better job of accounting for the central noncontingent features of law is the one that we should go for. I am not here in a position to adjudicate that contest.[13] But let me offer the following observations. First, we should not start with a presumption that the best answer to ($Q4_L$) will also furnish answers to ($Q1_L$)–($Q3_L$). Second, as a matter of fact, it would be quite surprising and a lucky coincidence if the best answer to ($Q4_L$) we can muster were to line up closely with our best answers to ($Q2_L$) and ($Q1_L$)-questions.[14] There is a very significant chance of certain behavioral and psychological facts constituting or amounting to the facts of legal practice, including legal judgments that partly make up that practice, without those behavioral and psychological facts making their ways into the contents of legal judgments.

4.

I have so far focused mostly on the relation between (H) on the one hand and ($Q2_L$) and ($Q1_L$) on the other. Let me now turn more to ($Q3_L$), which once again asks:

[13] For Gibbard's own arguments for favoring his own conception of morality over conceptions like Foot's, see Allan Gibbard, "Moral Concepts: Substance and Sentiment" (1992) 6 *Philosophical Perspectives* 199.

[14] On the ethical analogue of this last point, see a fascinating and suggestive discussion in Williams, *Ethics and the Limits of Philosophy* (n. 11) 51–3. Cf. Bernard Williams, "Philosophy as a Humanistic Discipline" (2000) 75 *Philosophy* 477.

($Q3_L$) In virtue of what is a certain rule the most fundamental law of a particular legal system?

In recent years, this has been deemed *the* central question in legal philosophy, and the perennially warring factions in legal philosophy have been thought to provide competing answers to this question.[15] According to legal positivism, supposedly, it is in virtue only of behavioral and psychological facts (or "social facts," as many call them) that a certain rule is the most fundamental law of a particular legal system. According to natural law theories, on the other hand, it is in virtue of certain moral or normative considerations, in addition to some psychological and behavioral facts, that a certain rule is the most fundamental law of a legal system. That is the recently orthodox conception of the ongoing philosophical debate about the nature of law.

If my foregoing line of reasoning is on the right track, however, the orthodox conception of this debate is suspect, or at least optional. Hart's legal theory, as summed up by (H), is supposed to be the paradigmatic legal positivist theory of recent times. But as I have just argued, (H) need not be read as picking out or identifying the most fundamental law of any legal system; (H) can be construed as neutral among many different possible hypotheses about the most fundamental laws of legal systems. According to this alternative construal, the behavioral and psychological facts that (H) enumerates are *not* the facts in virtue of which a particular rule is the most fundamental law of any legal system. The situation can be seen as quite analogous to (G) and its upshot for ($Q3_M$). (G) does not help us to identify the facts in virtue of which a particular principle is the most fundamental moral principle. Analogously, we can read (H) as not helping us to identify the facts in virtue of which a particular rule is the most fundamental law of a particular jurisdiction.

Given that most contemporary legal philosophers have thought or assumed that (H) does in fact enumerate the facts in virtue of which a particular rule is the most fundamental law of that legal system, there arises a suspicion that ($Q3_L$) suffers from an ambiguity that have vitiated most legal philosophers' reasoning. This is indeed the case, I strongly suspect. ($Q3_L$) in fact could be construed in the following two different ways:

($Q3_L$') In virtue of what (facts) does a community's treatment of a particular rule as the most fundamental law of its legal system obtain or exist?

($Q3_L$") In virtue of what is the most fundamental law of a particular legal system legally valid?

[15] See in particular Mark Greenberg, "How Facts Make Law" (2004) 10 *Legal Theory* 157; Shapiro, *Legality* (n. 1); Murphy, *What Makes Law* (n. 2).

If ($Q3_L$) is read as ($Q3_L$'), then (H) does actually help us with this question. The facts we would name in answering the question would then be the same behavioral and psychological facts, or a subset of the same facts, that (H) refers to. But notice that both legal positivists and natural law theorists can think that behavioral and psychological facts, and only such facts, amount to a community's use or treatment of a particular rule as the most fundamental law of its legal system.

What about ($Q3_L$")? According to the orthodox conception, legal positivists are supposed to say that questions of legal validity are answered with finality by referring only to behavioral and psychological facts. As the legal philosophers I quoted above say, Hart is supposed to have shown us that questions of legal validity are answered ultimately by discerning certain behavioral and psychological facts. It is instructive to compare this reading with what Hart actually says at one point:

> There are, indeed, many questions which we can raise about [a rule of recognition]. We can ask whether it is the practice of courts, legislatures, officials, or private citizens in England actually to use this rule as an ultimate rule of recognition .... We can ask whether it is a satisfactory form of legal system which has such a rule at its root. Does it produce more good than evil? Are there prudential reasons for supporting it? These are plainly very important questions; but, equally plainly, when we ask them about the rule of recognition, we are no longer attempting to answer [the question of legal validity] ... which we answered about other rules with its aid. When we move from saying that a particular enactment is valid, because it satisfies the rule that what the Queen in Parliament enacts is law, to saying that in England this last rule is used by courts, officials, and private persons as the ultimate rule of recognition, we have moved from an internal statement of law asserting the validity of a rule of the system to an external statement of fact which an observer of the system might make even if he did not accept it. So too when we move from the statement that a particular enactment is valid, to the statement that the rule of recognition of the system is an excellent one and the system based on it is one worthy of support, we have moved from a statement of legal validity to a statement of value.[16]

Here, Hart in effect eschews the view that legal questions are ultimately answered by appeals to the behavioral and psychological facts of the sort that (H) enumerates. He is very far from equating "questions of law" to "questions of practice," as John Gardner for one has characterized him in a passage quoted at the end of Section 2 above. What lawyers and judges appeal to ultimately, to answer first-order legal questions, is a rule of recognition, and not the facts that amount to people or officials' common acceptance of such a rule.

[16] Hart, *The Concept of Law* (n. 5) 107–8.

It is possible to suspect here that the way that ($Q3_L$) is usually taken as *the* central question of legal philosophy in contemporary literature obscures from view a particular way of conceiving the implications of (H) and like answers for ($Q4_L$). This particular (often obscured) way is to think that the task of answering ($Q4_L$) should be clearly distinguished from the tasks of answering ($Q2_L$) and ($Q1_L$)-questions. And once these questions have been raised and answered, there is no distinct task of answering ($Q3_L$). The tendency to think that there is an outstanding question that can be formulated as ($Q3_L$) may actually tempt us to a misunderstanding of (H). A rule of recognition, as Hart sees it, is supposed to be the consideration in virtue of which other legal rules are legally valid; but there is no further consideration in virtue of which that rule of recognition is legally valid.[17] Insofar as ($Q3_L$) asks for a set of facts or considerations in virtue of which a particular rule of recognition is legally valid, it, according to the alternative conception of the relation among ($Q1_L$)–($Q4_L$) that I am delineating, is a pseudo-question that has no logical room to stand on after ($Q2_L$) is raised and answered. We here have grounds for sympathizing with Dworkin's diagnosis—that in raising and answering ($Q3_L$), most legal philosophers are doing nothing more than raising and answering ($Q2_L$) in needlessly and misleadingly recondite ways. We can agree with Dworkin's diagnosis of contemporary legal philosophy with the following proviso: we should exempt Hart himself from Dworkin's charge, as (H) is an answer to ($Q4_L$) rather than ($Q2_L$); and we should recognize ($Q4_L$) as a genuine philosophical question, whereas Dworkin does not.

The considerations I have discussed in this section and the last, I believe, provide sufficient reasons to be suspicious of the orthodox conception of the relation among ($Q1_L$)–($Q4_L$). At the very least, they should encourage us to explore the alternative conception of the relation that I have been delineating. And that is what I propose to do for the balance of this chapter.

5.

Let us sum up. Everyone—not just legal positivists, but also natural law theorists—can accept (H) or at least some variation on it that enumerates the

[17] This is not to deny that there could be further considerations in virtue of which our belief that some norm is the rule of recognition of our community can be epistemically justified or warranted. For example, we may be able to bring up paradigms of laws (in the relevant jurisdiction), and show that the norm we identify as the rule of recognition fits better with those paradigms than does any other norm. The point here is that legality and epistemic warrant can obtain in virtue of two different sets of considerations, and that the fact that there are further grounds for the latter fact would not necessarily mean that there are further grounds for the former.

behavioral and psychological facts that amount to a community's having laws or a legal system. And if we think of Hart as a paradigmatic legal positivist, then we can think of legal positivists, and not just natural law theorists, as being able to think that the most fundamental legal considerations are rules or norms, and not behavioral and psychological facts.

Where does this leave the distinction between legal positivism and natural law theories, and the longstanding contest between them? Sometimes, I wonder whether this is an interesting question. We should be after a theory about the nature of law that does the best job of explaining important noncontingent features of law. Which term we use to label such a theory appears unimportant. But at other times, I surmise that the traditional distinction between legal positivism and natural law is getting at something important.

So here is a conjecture that I want to work with, although I am not in a position here to defend it fully. Both legal positivists and natural law theorists should say that the most fundamental legal considerations are rules or norms, and not merely behavioral and psychological facts. But there is a difference between the kinds of rules or norms that the two legal philosophical schools would identify as the most fundamental laws. One way of drawing the crucial distinction is to say that according to natural law theorists, the rules or norms that make up the most fundamental laws need to pass a certain moral threshold; whereas legal positivists would say that the rules or norms that make up the most fundamental laws need not do so. This strikes me as quite right, but here I want to approach the crucial distinction from a different direction. According to legal positivism, laws, including the most fundamental ones, are *artificial* rules or norms; whereas according to natural law theories, the most fundamental laws consist at least partly of non-artificial rules or norms.

How should we draw the distinction between artificial and non-artificial rules or norms? This, I have found, is a surprisingly difficult and delicate question to answer satisfactorily, and I want to postpone a treatment of it for another day. I want here to merely gesture at some rules or norms that appear artificial and some that do not. So here goes: game rules, rules of etiquette, and laws appear artificial; whereas fundamental moral and epistemic norms appear non-artificial.[18] Without argument, let us assume that laws are

[18] Non-fundamental moral and epistemic norms could be considered artificial. T.M. Scanlon says at one point: "If it is important for us to have some duty of a given kind (some duty of fidelity to agreements, or some duty of mutual aid) of which there are many morally acceptable forms, then one of these forms needs to be established by convention. In a setting in which one of these forms is conventionally established, acts disallowed by it will be wrong.... For given the need for such conventions, one thing that could not be generally agreed to would be a set of principles allowing one to disregard conventionally established (and morally acceptable) definitions of important duties." T.M. Scanlon, "Contractualism and Utilitarianism" (1982), repr. in T.M. Scanlon,

artificial rules or norms, and let us see how much headway we can make with that assumption. I believe that quite a lot can be gained by thinking of laws as artificial rules or norms, and by drawing an analogy between laws and another kind of artificial rules or norms. To that task, I now turn.

6.

It seems safe to believe that works of art, and among them works of fiction, are artificial. Artists and authors (or perhaps artists and authors together with their audiences) create or manufacture works of art. The points I want to make subsequently do not apply just to works of fiction, or even just to works of representational art, but instead I believe to all works of art. But it will make my exposition easier if I stick mostly to fictions, and I will.

We can think of the propositions that make up works of fiction—i.e. fictional truths—as norms or rules. This is what Kendall Walton has suggested: "a fictional truth consists in there being a prescription or mandate in some context to imagine something. Fictional propositions are propositions that are *to be* imagined – whether or not they are in fact imagined."[19] When Arthur Conan Doyle tells us that Sherlock Holmes lived on Baker Street in London, we are to imagine that there was a man of Holmes's description who lived on Baker Street in the late nineteenth-century London. Given that works of fiction are artificial, and the propositions that make them up can be conceived as norms, we can further conceive these propositions as artificial norms. Laws (or legal truths) and fictional truths are then alike in being both artificial norms.

The similarity could be thought to run deeper, actually. Fictional truths, as Walton suggests, are norms meant to regulate our imagination. And Walton has recently conceived imagination in terms of mental simulation or something quite like it.[20] On the law side, Joseph Raz has repeatedly observed, following Hans Kelsen, that legal assertions are best conceived as

The Difficulty of Toleration (Cambridge University Press 2003) 133–4. Similarly, the correctness of some epistemic norms—e.g., a testimony norm that says something along the lines of "Believe what others tell me, and tell others what I believe"—appears sensitive to local practices. The norm should not be accepted if one is living in a community of dissemblers.

[19] Kendall Walton, *Mimesis as Make-Believe* (Harvard University Press 1990) 39.

[20] See Kendall Walton, "Spelunking, Simulation, and Slime: On Being Moved by Fiction" in Mette Hjort and Sue Laver (eds.), *Emotion and the Arts* (Oxford University Press 1997); Kendall Walton, "Projectivism, Empathy, and Musical Tension" (1999) 26 *Philosophical Topics* 407.

pretended or simulated normative assertions.[21] These are assertions—which Raz calls "detached statements"—by which speakers, who are not necessarily committed, pretend or simulate their commitments to the norms that they avow. Both fictions and the law, in other words, could be conceived as sets of norms calling for and regulating imagination or mental simulation. Of course, the law consists of prescriptions not just to simulate certain psychological attitudes; they also call for certain behavior. But we can be "moved" by fictions in a literal sense as well, and we should recognize that many simulated thoughts have behavioral outputs as well as simulated psychological outputs.[22]

Given these (to my mind) striking similarities between legal and fictional truths, there is a distinct possibility that we would learn things about first-order legal reasoning—the kind of reasoning we would use to answer ($Q1_L$) and ($Q2_L$)—by examining the way we reason about fictional truths.

7.

With that end in view, consider the following question:

(Q5) Did Sherlock Holmes live closer to Paddington Station or to Waterloo Station?[23]

In trying to answer questions like (Q5), we are after fictional truths, or what are true in works of fiction, that go beyond what the relevant fictions explicitly specify. Some hypotheses about such unspecified or implied fictional truths strike us as plausible or even correct, whereas some others seem implausible or incorrect. Since Conan Doyle tells us that Holmes lived on Baker Street, and Baker Street is closer to Paddington Station than to Waterloo Station in the actual London, we can conclude that Holmes lived closer to Paddington Station than to Waterloo Station. That seems obvious.

[21] Or this is how I have reconstructed Raz's discussion in various places. See e.g., Joseph Raz, *Practical Reason and Norms* (2nd edn., Princeton University Press 1990) 170–7; Joseph Raz, "Legal Validity" (1977) repr. in Joseph Raz, *The Authority of Law* (Clarendon Press 1979); Joseph Raz, "Sources, Normativity, and Individuation" in Joseph Raz, *The Concept of a Legal System* (2nd edn., Oxford University Press 1980); Joseph Raz, "The Purity of the Pure Theory" (1981) 35 *Revue International de Philosophie* 441. See also Kevin Toh, "Raz on Detachment, Acceptance and Describability" (2007) 27 *Oxford Journal of Legal Studies* 403.

[22] See Walton, "Spelunking, Simulation, and Slime" (n. 20); J. David Velleman, "On the Aim of Belief" in J. David Velleman, *The Possibility of Practical Reason* (Oxford University Press 2000); Ted Cohen, *Thinking of Others* (Princeton University Press 2008) ch. 4.

[23] This example is taken from David Lewis, "Truth in Fiction" (1978) repr. in David Lewis, *Philosophical Papers*, vol. 1 (Oxford University Press 1983).

Now, consider the following more difficult question:

(Q6) What motivated Iago?[24]

Iago does all kinds of horrible things to Othello and Desdemona, and at considerable risks to himself to boot. But Shakespeare does not really tell us why Iago acts as he does. There is an initial indication that Iago feels slighted by Othello for being passed over for promotion in favor of Cassio. But the magnitude of his eventual actions seems to go well beyond what such a motivation alone would prompt. So, we may wonder, what is *really* motivating him? Why does he do such terrible things? What is in it for him? Here are some possible answers:

(6.1) Iago was motivated by a felt slight in being passed over for promotion.
(6.2) Iago was just evil, and he was motivated by his evil nature.
(6.3) Iago suffers from an unrequited and unrecognized love for Othello, and he was motivated by an intense jealousy.[25]

Unlike in the case of (Q5), there is no obvious answer to (Q6). Hypotheses like (6.1) and (6.2) strike us as quite implausible, whereas some others, perhaps (6.3) among them, seem to do somewhat better.

Here is a point that I consider very important: even when a question concerns an implied fictional truth, or a truth not explicitly specified by an author or artist, it is *not* always pointless or idle to try to answer the question. To be sure, some such questions are entirely pointless and idle. Here is an example:

(Q7) Did Hamlet shave on the day he uttered his famous soliloquy?

This question appears inapt, and it seems pointless to try to answer it. And not so much because no profit or benefit could be gotten from answering it, nor because we have no epistemic access to the correct answer, but because there does not seem to be an answer to be accessed. My point is that not all questions of implied fictional truths are like (Q7). Some are like (Q6), and it can make sense to try to answer them. Of course, how much sense it makes to delve into such a question depends on the quality of the relevant fiction. In case (Q6) in particular does not work for the reader, consider the following:

[24] This is a question that Marjorie Garber posed in her class on Shakespeare's later plays at Harvard University some time in Spring 1991.

[25] If my memory serves me, this is a hypothesis that Garber entertained at one point in her lecture on *Othello*.

(Q8) Is Mona Lisa's smile "innocent" or "inviting"?

(Q9) Do Henry Higgins and Eliza Doolittle get romantically involved after the end of *Pygmalion*?[26]

(Q10) Is Rick Deckard in the film *Blade Runner* a replicant?[27]

(Q11) Is Tony Soprano shot dead at the end of the final episode of *The Sopranos*?[28]

The nature of our engagements with works of fiction (and with works of art more generally) would be quite a bit different than it is, different enough to be unrecognizable, if all questions like these were considered pointless and idle. The works that we find most compelling are the ones that enable and stimulate questions of implied fictional truths like these; and the poor works that we find boring and wasteful are those that do not allow for such inquiries.[29] We may go so far as to say that someone who thinks that all such speculations about implied fictional truths are pointless and idle, and hence uniformly like (Q7), is someone who does not understand the point of works of fiction.

8.

I want to generalize. Not all questions of implied *normative* truths, including implied *legal* truths, are idle and pointless. Even when a question concerns implied legal truth, or a truth not explicitly specified by legislators and other officials, it is *not* always pointless and idle to try to answer the question.

Here is a question of implied legal truth that is analogous to (Q6) and (Q8)–(Q11). Imagine a criminal defendant who is accused of defrauding an insurance company by submitting to it copies of falsified U.S. federal tax returns that were meant to show injury-induced income reduction. Consider:

(Q12) Does a court order requiring a criminal defendant to sign an Internal Revenue Service (IRS) form requesting that the IRS

[26] George Bernard Shaw was sufficiently irritated by the audience and directors' desire for a happy ending to the play to add a postscript to a later edition explaining why the two characters could not marry.

[27] By adding some additional scenes, the final cut of the film answers this question in the affirmative. Many fans of the film do not consider this particular aspect of the final cut an improvement.

[28] Thanks to Mitch Berman for this example.

[29] See Michael Fried, *Absorption and Theatricality* (University of Chicago Press 1980). As the discussion by Fried shows, Diderot influentially celebrated and advocated those works of art (e.g., plays, paintings) that enabled audience members to simulate intense participation in the goings-on depicted in the works.

> release his tax records to the state attorney general's office violate the defendant's privilege against self-incrimination under the Fifth Amendment of the U.S. Constitution?[30]

The Fifth Amendment merely states that no one "shall be compelled in any criminal case to be a witness against himself." And in interpreting this provision, the U.S. Supreme Court has over the years taken the position that the privilege against self-incrimination does not proscribe compelled production of every sort of incriminating evidence. Only when a defendant is compelled to "testify" against himself, the Court has said, is the privilege infringed.[31] Compelling defendants to undergo a field sobriety test, to stand in a lineup, to furnish a voice exemplar or blood sample, etc. have not been considered violations of the privilege; whereas compelling defendants to furnish a variety of subpoenaed documents such as diary entries and personal financial papers have been. On which side of this distinction would a court order of (Q12) fall?

There is one sort of answer to questions like this that the foregoing considerations discredit. That is the answer according to which questions about implied legal truths like (Q12) are uniformly pointless and idle because there are no answers to be gotten for such questions. Brian Leiter has in effect recently advocated such a position. Leiter's thesis is specifically about questions about the contents of the most fundamental laws of legal systems—what Hart calls "rules of recognition"—but it can be translated into a more general thesis. Here, once again, is a passage I quoted near the end of Section 2 above:

> [T]he Rule of Recognition, on Hart's view, is a social rule, meaning its content—that is, the criteria of legal validity—is fixed by a complex empirical fact, namely, the *actual practice* of officials (and the attitude they evince towards the practice). So it looks like the only dispute about the criteria of legal validity that is possible, on Hart's view, is an empirical or "heads count" dispute: namely, a dispute about what judges are doing, and how many of them are doing it, since it is the actual practice of officials and their attitudes towards that practice that fixes the criteria of legal validity according to the positivist.[32]

Leiter's position here results from his understanding of Hart's legal theory, and more specifically his view that (H) implies (C_L), so that the only genuine disagreements about the content of the most fundamental law of

[30] See *Commonwealth v. Burgess*, 426 Mass. 206 (1997).

[31] *Fisher v. United States*, 425 U.S. 391, 408 (1976).

[32] Leiter, "Explaining Theoretical Disagreements" (n. 7) 1222.

a community's legal system are invariably disagreements about what the community's members or officials accept in common—a "heads count dispute," as Leiter puts it. If there were no commonly accepted rule of recognition, the thinking goes, then there is no "fact of the matter" as to what the rule of recognition is, and judges and lawyers would dispute about the content of their most fundamental law only if they were either confused, or disingenuously dressing up their disagreements about what the law should be as disagreements about what the law is. Presumably, Leiter would give the same kind of diagnosis of the disputes about questions of implied legal truths that are not clear consequents of the legal rules that officials commonly accept. Any apparent disagreements about such legal matters, he would think, are instances in which judges and lawyers are confused or disingenuous.

There are two problems with Leiter's position (or the position that I am attributing to him). First, the theoretical motivation for his diagnosis is undermined once we see that his understanding of (H) and its relation to (C_L) are not forced upon us, as I have argued in the first half of this chapter. Second, more important, as (Q6) and like examples suggest, even when questions concern implied normative truths about which there is no clear consensus as to what the answers are, we act as if there are answers to be discerned, that there are "facts of the matter" as to what the answers are. We could discount all such appearances, or "phenomenology" as we might call it,[33] but that seems to involve very high costs in terms of our ability to maintain a significant practice. I opined above that a person who thinks that all questions about implied fictional truths are pointless and idle would be missing the point of works of fiction. A like diagnosis would be appropriate for someone like Leiter who thinks that questions about implied legal truths for which there is no clear official consensus are uniformly pointless and idle.

There is a position that, though much like Leiter's, appears to come nearer the truth, but that I believe is still off the mark. John Gardner classifies laws into three kinds—legislated law, customary law, and case law—and argues that all three are positive or man-made law. He warns against reaching a different conclusion based on the fact that the latter two types are not always made expressly or intentionally. Ronald Dworkin is a culprit that he singles out:

> Dworkin ... relied on these features of case law in arguing that at least some of it exists without anyone's ever having made it. The implicit law to be found in the cases

[33] Dworkin for one treats such phenomenology as important data to explain, and I believe he is right to do so. See Ronald Dworkin, "The Model of Rules II" (1972) repr. in Ronald Dworkin, *Taking Rights Seriously* (Harvard University Press 1977) 86; Ronald Dworkin, *Law's Empire* (n. 3) viii.

> exists, according to Dworkin, in virtue of the fact that it provides a sound moral justification for whatever explicit law there might be in those same (and other?) cases.... [T]his is a mistake. It is true that case law is implicit law in the sense that it is not made by being expressed. Nor is it always made intentionally. The rule in the case has to be worked out by examining the judge's argument, to see what rule he implicitly, and maybe accidentally, relied upon. Nevertheless, the judge brings the rule into existence by relying on it. So implicit law, like explicit law, is still brought into existence by someone. It is still positive law. For there is no such thing as non-positive law. There are no legal norms that come into existence without being brought into existence by someone.[34]

Even setting aside the fact that Gardner is motivated by what I consider an optional understanding of (H) and its implications, it matters here what he means by "rely" when he speaks here of judges relying on rules. It is doubtful that Gardner would require judges' reliance on rules to be actual psychological events. A significant part of case law is inferring general rules from lines of decisions, and the inferred general rules need not be any that judges were actually guided by, even implicitly.[35] Also important to notice is the fact that for any single judicial decision or line of decisions, there are likely to be multiple rules that fit the decision(s) equally well. If a judge or judges were to infer from a line of cases one such rule, and to identify it as the applicable law in a particular decision, it is difficult to maintain, as Gardner does, that judges must invariably think that that rule was relied upon by them in the past.

My criticism can be strengthened by an analogy between laws and works of art. Monroe Beardsley long ago warned against conflating works of art with artists' intentions, even implicit ones, and argued that philosophers who treat artists' intentions as finally authoritative in interpreting works of art are guilty of what he called "the intentional fallacy."[36] Many philosophers of art have subsequently faulted Beardsley for his categorical denial, and have provided some compelling arguments to show that artists' intentions may be partly constitutive of works of art, and that appeals to such intentions hence

[34] Gardner, "Some Types of Law" (n. 8) 85–6.

[35] Law school education consists in good part of reading judicial opinions that do exactly this. One of the more striking examples is provided by the opinion in *United States v. Carroll Towing Co.*, 159 F.2d 169 (2d Cir. 1947), in which Judge Learned Hand introduced the famous Hand formula for determining the standard of care for negligence cases.

[36] See William K. Wimsatt and Monroe Beardsley, "The Intentional Fallacy" (1946) 54 *Sewanee Review* 468; William K. Wimsatt and Monroe Beardsley, "The Affective Fallacy" (1949) 57 *Sewanee Review* 31; Monroe Beardsley, *Aesthetics: Problems in the Philosophy of Criticism* (2nd edn., Hackett Publishing Co. 1981) ch. 1.

may be legitimate ways to interpret many works.[37] But even these critics of Beardsley concede that the nature of individual works of art may diverge from respective artists' intentions. Consequently, the answer to (Q6) should not be thought to be determined necessarily by what Shakespeare thought, even implicitly. And likewise for (Q8)–(Q11). And if this is actually the case for questions about implied fictional truths, one suspects that analogous things could be said about implied legal truths that are products of legislation or even customs. Even when certain legal conclusions are not clearly implied by the rules that legislators and other officials have relied on, even implicitly, those legal conclusions may still be legal truths, and they may be legitimate queries of our legal investigations.

The bottom line is that our attempts to answer legal questions like (Q12) are not made pointless and idle by the absence of judicial or official consensus about what the law is, or about the content of the most fundamental law of their jurisdiction. Nor are they vitiated by the absence of any prior judicial or official reliance on the rules or principles that clearly answer such questions. In our debates about and our attempts to discern implied fictional truths, we do not let the absence of such behavioral and psychological facts foreclose the possibility of there being real answers. And this, despite the fact that such fictional truths are artificial norms. I do not see any reasons to think that the artificial norms that make up the law are any different in these regards.

9.

Both Leiter and Gardner were in large measures reacting to Dworkin's arguments. In criticizing Leiter and Gardner, however, I am not endorsing Dworkin's position. Like Dworkin, I reject the view that the most fundamental laws of legal systems consist of or are fixed by behavioral and psychological facts, and the accompanying view that our legal investigations are ultimately empirical investigations meant to discern certain behavioral and psychological facts. But I do not endorse Dworkin's motivation for that rejection—namely, his view that moral principles necessarily constitute those fundamental laws. Like Leiter and Gardner, and unlike Dworkin, I surmise

[37] See e.g., Kendall Walton, "Categories of Art" (1979) repr. in Kendall Walton, *Marvelous Images: On Values and the Arts* (Oxford University Press 2008); Richard Wollheim "Criticism as Retrieval" in Richard Wollheim, *Art and its Objects* (2nd edn., Cambridge University Press 1980); Jerrold Levinson, "Intention and Interpretation in Literature" (1992) repr. in Jerrold Levinson, *The Pleasures of Aesthetics* (Cornell University Press 1996); Stephen Davies, "Beardsley and the Autonomy of the Work of Art" (2005) 63 *The Journal of Aesthetics and Art Criticism* 179.

that even the most fundamental laws are artificial rules or norms, and my preceding arguments against Leiter and Gardner were premised on that surmise. The conception of laws as artificial norms, and the analogy between implied legal and implied fictional truths can help us to see what exactly is wrong with Dworkin's position.

As our reactions to (6.1)–(6.3) above indicate, we are disposed to discriminate between different hypotheses about implied fictional truths. Some strike us better than others. And given these dispositions to discriminate, we may think that there are principles that we rely on in doing so. David Lewis and Nicholas Wolterstorff suggest that we think of fictional truths as analogous to counterfactual truths, and argue that in determining unspecified fictional truths we should determine what would be the case if the explicitly specified fictional truths were the case.[38] But this proposal leaves open the possibilities of employing many different kinds of principles in generating such counterfactual truths—i.e. different possibilities as to what kind of world should be conceived as the actual world, nearest to which the counterfactual world obtains. Consider the following list of possibilities, which is not meant to be exhaustive:

(R_F) *The Reality Principle*: The fictional world should approximate as much as possible the real world as the specified fictional truths allow.[39]

(B_F) *The Belief Principle*: The fictional world should approximate as much as possible the author's contemporaries' beliefs about the real world as the specified fictional truths allow.[40]

(O_F) *The Optimality Principle*: The fictional world should approximate as much as possible the world that would make the relevant art work as aesthetically satisfying as the specified fictional truths allow.[41]

These are just the principles that we *usually* apply in generating implied fictional truths. As both Wolterstorff and Walton say, little industry would be needed to uncover yet more principles of generation that we rely on. And it

[38] See Lewis, "Truth in Fiction" (n. 23); Nicholas Wolterstorff, *Works and Worlds of Art* (Clarendon Press 1980).

[39] The term is Walton's. See Lewis, "Truth in Fiction" (n. 23) 270; Wolterstorff, *Works and Worlds of Art* (n. 38) 120–2; Walton, *Mimesis as Make-Believe* (n. 19) 144–50.

[40] The term again is Walton's. See Lewis, "Truth in Fiction" (n. 23) 273; Wolterstorff, *Works and Worlds of Art* (n. 38) 122–4; Walton, *Mimesis as Make-Believe* (n. 19) 150–61.

[41] The term is mine. Stevenson is often cited for this principle or the idea behind the principle, but I am not sure that that is an apt reading. See Charles L. Stevenson, "Interpretation and Evaluation in Aesthetics" in M. Black (ed.), *Philosophical Analysis* (Cornell University Press 1950). A related idea can be found in Walton, "Categories of Art" (n. 37) 212.

seems that we rely on some combinations of these and other principles, some of which are specific to particular genres, to discriminate between plausible implied fictional truths and implausible ones. Arguably, in choosing (6.3) as the best of the three above-listed hypotheses about Iago's motive, I was relying on a combination of the Reality Principle and the Optimality Principle. The thought that Iago was motivated to do such horrible things merely for being passed over for promotion strikes us as psychologically implausible, thus violating the Reality Principle. The hypothesis that Iago was just motivated by his evil nature seems uninteresting and ad hoc, and hence seems to violate the Optimality Principle.

What principles of generation to apply depends *partly* on what principles are "in play" or "in force" in the relevant community. Walton explains as follows:

> I do not assume that principles of generation are, in general or even normally, "conventional" or "arbitrary," nor that they must be learned. Nevertheless, what principles of generation there are depends on which ones people accept in various contexts. The principles that are in force are those that are understood, at least implicitly, to be in force.[42]

Some principles like (R_F), (B_F), and (O_F) seem to be always in play in varying degrees, and they may in some sense even be biologically programmed into us.[43] Some other principles may actually be "conventional" and "arbitrary" in the sense that artists and their audiences have reached certain specific, and oftentimes genre-specific, understandings as to how the relevant works are to be interpreted. In some cases, charismatic artists seem able to legislate the applicable principles of generation that are novel or against the grain. And even when the determinative principles are (R_F), (B_F), and (O_F), and not much else, the exact mixture and weights assigned may be partly conventional and arbitrary. People, both creators and consumers of representational art, accept certain principles of generation. Walton seems to think that their commitments to the principles are conditional on others being committed to the same principles. By creating a new work of representational art, an artist prompts the relevant audience to imagine certain things. A skillful artist is one who is sensitive to the principles of generation that prevail among his audience, and exploits (implicitly, more often than not) those principles to prompt them to imagine unexpected propositions. Similar things could be

[42] Walton, *Mimesis as Make-Believe* (n. 19) 38.

[43] For some fascinating related discussion, see John Tooby and Leda Cosmides, "Does Beauty Build Adapted Minds? Toward an Evolutionary Theory of Aesthetics, Fiction, and the Arts" (2001) 30 *SubStance* 6.

said of what the audience does. An audience member would explicitly or (more likely) implicitly rely on the prevailing principles of generation to appreciate or engage with a work of representational art. His imaginings would be functions of the prevailing principles of generation, and he is likely to adjust his imaginings should he come to realize that the principles that actually prevail are different from what he had initially thought they were.

What is plain is that the applicability of principles of generation—i.e., which is applicable when, in what combination, and in what weights—is something that often cannot be figured out easily or even with difficulty. Walton observes at one point:

> Implications seem not to be governed by any simple or systematic principle or set of principles, but by a complicated and shifting and often competing array of understandings, precedents, local conventions, saliences. Sharply divergent principles, answering to different needs, are at work in different cases, and it seems unlikely that there are any very general or systematic meta-principles for determining which is applicable when. Experience and knowledge of the arts, of society, and of the world will sharpen the critic's skills. But in the end he must feel his way.[44]

This picture contrasts sharply with Dworkin's conception of how implied legal truths are to be generated. According to him, the correct implied legal propositions are those that would be implied by the set of moral principles that would best fit and justify the explicitly stipulated laws, as well as the relevant community's mores, traditions, and social practices. In other words, Dworkin sees an analogue of (O_F) as invariably the sole correct principle of generation for implied legal truths. That analogue could be formulated as:

(O_L) *The Optimality Principle*: The legal system should approximate as much as possible the system that would make the relevant community as morally optimal as the explicit laws, mores, traditions, and societal practices of that community allow.

If generation of implied legal truths is anything like generation of implied fictional truths, then this is a wildly simplifying and ultimately distorting picture. As Walton and others point out, generation of fictional truths cannot proceed on such a simple and algorithmic way; it is a much messier and system-resistant affair. And I do not see a reason to conceive generation of implied legal truths to be that different in this regard.

My position is borne out by the problems that Dworkin's conception of adjudication encounters. The initial attraction of Dworkin's proposal stemmed

[44] Walton, *Mimesis as Make-Believe* (n. 19) 169.

much from the impression that the Optimality Principle works quite plausibly in generating implied legal truths in cases like *Riggs v. Palmer*[45] and *Henningsen v. Bloomfield Motors, Inc.*[46] In these cases, the implications of the moral principles that best fit and justify the explicit law and societal practices generally seem to yield the implied legal conclusions that we find compelling. Dworkin often speaks as if these and similar cases he appeals to were chosen casually and almost randomly from law school textbooks, and that there is nothing really atypical about them. But there is a reason that he returned to these specific ones repeatedly. For the Optimality Principle does not yield such compelling outputs in many other cases. This is spectacularly illustrated in the line of antebellum cases involving the Fugitive Slave Acts that Robert Cover's *Justice Accused* discussed.[47] Cover's book chronicles the story of judges sitting in the Northern states who had to decide cases involving the Fugitive Slave Acts. Almost without exception, despite their very strong ethical objections to what the Fugitive Slave Acts required of them, and in some cases at considerable political costs to themselves, these judges decided to return the runaway slaves caught in the Northern states to the slave-owners in the South. In his review, Dworkin puzzles over these cases, and eventually concludes that the judges behaved as they did because they made the mistake of overlooking a plausible legal theory—namely, one that relies on the Optimality Principle for generation of implied legal truths—that would have enabled them to be true to both their moral convictions and their legal scruples.[48] This is less than compelling, and the mere fact that the judges involved almost uniformly decided the cases contrary to what the Optimality Principle anticipates, and the fact that most lawyers who read Cover's account agree with these judges' legal assessments, illustrate the problem with relying exclusively on that principle to generate implied legal truths.

10.

Let us take stock for the last time. To be sure, there is something quite appealing and even seductive about the orthodox conception of the relation among $(Q1_L)$–$(Q4_L)$. If the correct answer to $(Q4_L)$ had the ramifying implications for the answers to the other three questions, as the orthodox

[45] 115 N.Y. 506 (1889). [46] 32 N.J. 358 (1960).

[47] Robert Cover, *Justice Accused* (Yale University Press 1975).

[48] See Ronald Dworkin, "The Law of the Slave-Catchers" *The Times Literary Supplement* (London, December 15, 1975).

position would have it, then there would be an immediate and significant first-order legal payoffs for our second-order or philosophical labors. Arguably, no better apology for legal philosophy could be offered. But once we delink ($Q4_L$) from ($Q1_L$)–($Q2_L$) as I have suggested, then the payoffs for our legal philosophical investigations are not as obvious. Nevertheless, they are real and significant, I believe. For one thing, we would no longer be misled or tempted to think that first-order legal questions ultimately bottom out with answers delineating behavioral and psychological facts. Instead, we leave open the possibility that legal questions are ultimately to be resolved in terms of normative considerations. And once we take this last possibility seriously, also take into account the possibility that laws including the most fundamental ones are artificial norms or rules, and also investigate how implied normative truths are generated in contexts involving other kinds of artificial norms, then we would no longer think that the only alternative to thinking that the law ultimately consists of behavioral and psychological facts is to think that they consist of moral principles. As some philosophers of art have argued in detail, generation of implied fictional truths is a complicated, messy, and algorithm-resistant affair. There is no reason to think that generation of implied legal truths is any different. The appeal and seduction of simplicity or instant first-order legal gratification should not make us blind to that likelihood. Legal philosophy, rightly done, can help us to see more clearly.

PART II

ONTOLOGY

5

On the Artifactual—and Natural—Character of Legal Institutions

*Corrado Roversi**

1. Which Theory of Artifacts for an Artifact Theory of Law?

An artifact theory of law proposes to describe the structure of legal institutions by looking at them through the features of ordinary artifacts. However, this is not going to be a fruitful theoretical move if we do not have an acceptable theory of artifacts, and it is quite striking to find that, as much as we may have a working familiarity with tools through our everyday use of them, this does not make it any easier to *explain* them. One could say that the laptop computer I have in front of me is what it is because it has certain physical features—a black-colored case containing a definite set of pieces of hardware. Let me call this the *physical model* of artifacts and show why it cannot work. There is a problem in saying that this assemblage of piece of hardware *is* my laptop, at least in the identity sense of *is*. In fact, I can certainly replace several pieces of my laptop's hardware—in the long run I could even replace all of them: the collection of pieces is different, but it is still my laptop. This is the classic problem of the persistence conditions of artifacts, one that has been discussed in the history of philosophy through the puzzle of the "Ship of Theseus" (see, e.g., Hobbes, *De Corpore*, II, 11).

Another and similar puzzle can be drawn from Alan Gibbard's famous discussion of the relation between the statue called *Goliath*, which is an artifact, and the piece of clay of which it is made, which Gibbard calls *Lumpl*. Gibbard

* I am grateful to Luka Burazin, Pierluigi Chiassoni, Kenneth Ehrenberg, Kenneth Einar Himma, Veronica Rodriguez Blanco, Giovanni Tuzet, and Giovanni Battista Ratti for their helpful comments on previous versions of this chapter.

Law as an Artifact. First Edition. Edited by Luka Burazin, Kenneth Einar Himma, and Corrado Roversi. Chapter 5 Published 2018 by Oxford University Press.

notes that if we were to say that *Goliath* is identical with *Lumpl*—as the identity thesis states—then this identity could be seen as violating Leibniz's law, in the sense that not all properties of Goliath can be attributed to Lumpl *salva veritate*:

> [S]uppose I had brought Lumpl in existence as *Goliath*, just as I actually did, but before the clay had a chance to dry, I squeezed it into a ball. At that point ... the statue Goliath would have ceasen to exist, but the piece of clay Lumpl would still exist in a new shape. Hence Lumpl would not be Goliath, even though both existed.[1]

In discussing Gibbard's puzzle, Lynne Baker notes that it cannot hold for objects whose essential properties are relational:

> [S]omething is a statue in virtue of its relational properties. But it is obviously false that, if *x* is an *F*, in virtue of its relational properties, and *y* is intrinsically like *x*, then *y* is an *F*. Anything defined in terms of relational properties—a planet, a U.S. dollar bill, a passport—provides counterexample to [this principle]. Specifically, artworks like statues are counterexamples [to this principle].[2]

What Baker states for artworks applies to artifacts in general. Artifacts are essentially relational objects, such that there is no intrinsic material structure they consist of that can also be an explanation of what they are. What an artifact is depends on its relation to us, and not simply on its physical features. This is true even of simple material artifacts such as screwdrivers: screwdrivers are not simply metal objects shaped like screwdrivers. The physical model therefore does not work. It does not for artifacts in general, and of course it does not for law: no one would say that a parliament, for example, is simply the place where members of parliament meet—the building and its furnishings or its street address.

In what sense are artifacts relational objects? A simple answer could be that this relationality consists in their necessarily being the product of human action. This, however, would not be sufficient, because many things that depend on human action cannot properly be conceived as artifacts. Think, for example, of waste and pollution. One might then say that artifacts are only the *intended* results of human action. But, as Risto Hilpinen explains, if I carve a sculpture out of a block of wood, I am intentionally producing something (a statue), and even though I know full well that many woodchips will fall off the block, I will not count them as artifacts even though they result from my productive intention.[3] This means that if artifacts are supposed

[1] Alan Gibbard, *Contingent Identity* (1975) repr. in M.C. Rea (ed.), *Material Constitution* (Rowman & Littlefield 1997) 93–125, 97.

[2] Lynne Rudder Baker, "Why Constitution Is Not Identity" (1997) 94 *The Journal of Philosophy* 599, 603–4.

[3] See Risto Hilpinen, "Authors and Artefacts" (1993) 93 *Proceedings of the Aristotelian Society* 155, 159–60.

to depend on human productive intention, their relation to these intentions must be stricter than simple dependence, in the sense that the maker of an artifact must *specifically* intend to produce something of that kind.

Hilpinen identifies a set of conditions under which the existence of artifacts may be said to depend strictly on the intentions of their makers or authors.[4] In a somewhat simplified version of his view, something is an artifact of a given kind iff (a) it has an author, (b) the author *wants* to produce something of that kind (i.e., the author's intentions include a sortal description corresponding to that kind of artifact), and (c) the artifact's existence and features depend on the author's intention to produce something of that kind. Let me call this the *author model* of artifacts. But even this view has its shortcomings, because if we apply it too narrowly, we will wind up with too restrictive a conception of artifacts. Many artifacts come out of routine-like or habitual actions, that is, actions lacking an explicit and conscious intentional creative content. Think, for example, of the products of expert craftspersons and artists, who "often work at great speed and with remarkably little conscious thought (apparently) at the time of creation."[5] Moreover, there are phenomena that do not straightforwardly meet the "conscious authorship" criterion that seem to be at least borderline cases of artifacts. Consider a wall surrounding a town and acting as a defensive perimeter that comes into being by accretion, simply as a result of the townspeople fortifying their own dwellings with walls that over time bunch up against one another. Here, nobody intended to build a wall around the entire town, but everybody wanted to create something to defend their houses. Hence, the wall surrounding the town did in fact come into shape through creative intentions having as their content a sortal description of walls, but that sortal description did not, strictly speaking, refer to the wall serving as a defense perimeter for the entire town: it referred to the walls surrounding the houses.

When it comes to the law, phenomena of this kind are particularly relevant. Of course there are many legal institutions that are created through a sort of authorial intention by an act of institutional design, but many others are customary in nature. Custom therefore offers itself as a significant legal counterexample to an artifact theory of law based on the author model.[6] But consider another problem with this model: If I intend to build a screwdriver and build an oddly shaped object which I consider a realization of my intention,

[4] See ibid. 156ff.

[5] Randall R. Dipert, *Artefacts, Art Works, and Agency* (Temple University Press 1993) 49.

[6] See also, in this regard, Luka Burazin, "Can There Be an Artifact Theory of Law?" (2016) 29 *Ratio Juris* 385, 395; Jonathan Crowe, "Law as an Artefact Kind" (2014) 40 *Monash University Law Review* 737, 739.

does all of this suffice to qualify that object as a screwdriver? Of course not. As Hilpinen himself concedes, what is crucial in assessing whether something is an artifact is to determine which kind it belongs to, that is, whether it satisfies the sortal description the author has in mind. Now the question is: How should we describe the identity conditions for the sortal descriptions of artifacts? Hilpinen introduces here the concept of function:

> The type-description which determines the identity of an artefact is normally associated with the intended function of the artefact (for example, a bridge) or it can be simply a description of its intended function (e.g., a hammer).[7]

This functional element in determining the identity conditions for the sortal descriptions of artifacts is widely acknowledged. In addressing the puzzle of the Ship of Theseus, for example, Lowe ends up saying that "with ordinary artefacts ... we are likely to be ... concerned with the object's utility."[8] In the same vein, David Wiggins states that "artefacts are collected up not by reference to a theoretically hypothesized common constitution but under functional descriptions."[9] In Hilpinen's model, however, the role of function in accounting for the ontology of artifacts is exclusively mediated by an author's acceptance.[10] This is where the problem comes in: the author model seems to give too much importance to the author's arbitrary judgment. As Wybo Houkes and Pieter E. Vermaas have noted with regard to technical artifacts, this model is too "intentionalistic" because, on the one hand, if all we need for something to be a technical artifact is the author's acceptance, then all kinds of intended and imaginary artifacts should count as genuine technical artifacts, and on the other hand, the author's acceptance could give place to a proliferation of intended functions for a single artifact.[11] With some qualifications, the same could be said of institutions that are legal by design: Italian legislatures are notorious for their intended reforms of the labor market that are unable to reform the labor market in any way.

Thus, it is not sufficient that the function and purposes intended and conceived by authors figure among the criteria for establishing the identity of an artifactual kind. It is also necessary that, at least to some extent, artifacts of that kind *be able to actually serve* the stated function and purpose, because the domain of artifacts is not simply the domain of their authors' arbitrary attributions of functions. The importance of functional elements in

[7] Hilpinen, "Authors and Artefacts" (n. 3) 161.

[8] Edward J. Lowe, "On the Identity of Artefacts" (1983) 80 *The Journal of Philosophy* 220, 231.

[9] David Wiggins, *Sameness and Substance Renewed* (Cambridge University Press 2001) 87.

[10] Hilpinen, "Authors and Artefacts" (n. 3) 161.

[11] Wybo Houkes and Pieter E. Vermaas, *Technical Functions: On the Use and Design of Artefacts* (Springer 2010) 51.

the ontology of artifacts has led some authors to formulate a *function model* of artifacts. This model can be cast in purely evolutionary terms or in a way that also takes into account the insights of the author model. An example of the first approach is Beth Preston's theory of artifacts. According to Preston, evolutionary success is the key criterion for ascribing functions to artifacts, while the designers' intentions have no substantial role in this process.[12] For an example of the "hybrid" author-function approach we can instead turn to Lynne Rudder Baker's theory, which she developed in working to solve the problem of material constitution: objects have primary-kind properties—i.e., properties they cannot lose without ceasing to exist as such—and there cannot be relations of identity between objects belonging to different primary kinds (Baker interprets Gibbard's example above in the sense that Goliath and Lumpl have different primary-kind properties and thus are not identical).[13] Artifacts, in this view, are objects whose primary-kind property is a function. This primary function—here is where the model becomes hybrid—is determined by the author's intentions but also (so as to avoid the problem of "imaginary" functions) by the actual "execution of those intentions."[14]

Both the "pure" function model and the "hybrid" author-function model in turn have some problems. For one thing, the pure function model has problems explaining how malfunctioning artifacts can still, in some sense, be artifacts of a given kind, however much defective. If the ability to perform their proper function is the only ground for their belonging to a given artifactual kind, it would simply be meaningless to speak of broken screwdrivers or rickety chairs: these objects would simply be non-screwdrivers or non-chairs. Instead, a theory of artifacts should explain how, despite their malfunctioning, objects belonging to a given artifactual kind can still be categorized in terms of defective instances of that kind.

Moreover, and more importantly, there is a direct counterexample to the pure function model, namely, artifacts without an evolutionary history: artifacts of new design. This is the core of Ruth Millikan's criticism of Preston's model.[15] Millikan distinguishes between *direct* proper functions and *derived* proper functions. Basically, a "device" *m* has a direct proper function *F* if it belongs to a "reproductively established family" whose members have a

[12] See esp. Beth Preston, "Why is a Wing Like a Spoon? A Pluralist Theory of Function" (1998) 95 *The Journal of Philosophy* 215, 243ff.; Beth Preston, "Philosophical Theories of Artefact Function" in A. Meijers (ed.), *Philosophy of Technology and Engineering Sciences* (Elsevier 2009), 226–7.

[13] See Lynne R. Baker, "The Ontology of Artefacts" (2004) 7 *Philosophical Explorations* 99.

[14] Ibid. 101–3.

[15] Others have noted that Preston's "pure" function model can be circular, for on the one hand artifacts would be reproduced in virtue of the evolutionary success of their "ancestors," but at the same time it seems impossible to identify those ancestors without already having a notion of the artifactual kind in question. See Amie Thomasson, "Artefacts in Metaphysics" in A. Meijers (ed.), *Philosophy of Technology and Engineering Sciences* (Elsevier 2009) 205. In this connection, it has

character *C* that historically has correlated positively with *F* and this positive correlation explains why *m* exists: the members of this family are reproduced with specific features because through these features they can perform a given function.[16] A device instead has a *derived* proper function if it is an "adapted device," namely, if it has no evolutionary history but is produced by a device with a direct proper function.[17] Now, according to Millikan, artifacts can have both direct proper functions, if they have been selected and reproduced in virtue of their capacity to fulfill that function, or derived proper functions, in case they have simply been created and derive their function from the intentions of their designers: innovative artifacts can have only derived proper functions.[18] Of course Millikan's criticism about artifacts of new design is relevant for law as well, because there can certainly be legal institutions built from scratch for a specific function, and hence institutions without an evolutionary history.

Even more significant for legal theory is a possible counterexample to a hybrid author-function model. This has to do with the phenomenon of repurposing, by which an artifact takes on new functions over the course of its history, or these functions are modified, in a process where old essential functions evolve into new ones (this kind of functional addition or modification applies, for example, to many technical artifacts). But if we follow Baker in considering functions to be ontologically essential to artifactual objects, then it seems that when functions change or stack, new objects arise, and it becomes difficult to assess the relation between the old artifacts and the newborn ones—among other reasons because the two can very well coincide spatially. Houkes and Vermaas explain the problem by referring to the example of Aspirin, having "attracted the attention of pharmacologists because of its beneficial properties other than alleviating pain and reducing fever."[19]

Of course this repurposing phenomenon is crucial to understanding how legal institutions develop. To indulge in metaphor, legal institutions—particularly the most important ones, those entrenched in a legal community—are more similar to Gothic churches than to screwdrivers. They have been reinterpreted several times, their project has been modified

been argued that in selecting what qualify as "real" proper functions we may have to look at social institutions, leading not to the conclusion that social institutions are artifacts, as I am arguing here, but to the inverse conclusion that artifacts require social institutions. See Marcel Scheele, "Function and Use of Technical Artefacts: Social Conditions of Function Ascription" (2006) 37 *Studies in History and Philosophy of Science* 23.

16 See Ruth Garrett Millikan, *Language, Thought, and Other Biological Categories* (The MIT Press 1984) 25–8.

17 Ibid. 39ff.

18 Ibid. 48–9.

19 Houkes and Vermaas, *Technical Functions* (n. 11) 146–7.

and overlaid by other projects throughout their history, and in the end they can very well wind up being functionally incomplete. Hence, if we want to explain legal institutions as artifacts, we should certainly take account of authorial intentions set in functionalistic terms, just as we would on the author-function model, but we should also look to the "pure" function model, borrowing from it a specific focus on the artifact's history, that is, on the way in which the artifact's function and content has been intended and interpreted over time, and so how it has changed.

I think this can be achieved through a *historico-intentional model*,[20] and here I am mainly thinking of Randall Dipert's theory. Dipert can be seen to combine a history model and an author model into a unified perspective. On this perspective, an artifact is by definition an object with a *deliberative* history, that is, a history of conscious intentions and actions that traces back to an author with creative intentions having a corresponding sortal description as their content. We can also incorporate the role of function if we include it among the criteria of identity of the authorial sortal description, as on the author-function model. However, in Dipert's view an artifact's deliberative history includes not only the original authorial intention but also the modifications and interpretation made of that intention over time.[21] Hence, for example, deliberative history is a relevant element of the artifact's criteria of identity both synchronically and diachronically: two ships are the same ship if they can be traced to the same deliberative history, that is, a history consisting in a "means-ends ordering of the relevant intentions," but also consisting in

> the other means considered for each end and rejected, beliefs about the means-ends connections, and the various other beliefs and cognitive processes that were used in any of the steps leading to an intention and the production of an artefactual feature.[22]

A historico-intentional model seems to be well-suited for an explanation of legal institutions. It can account for institutions of new design by reconstructing their deliberative history in terms of purely authorial intentions. It can also account for institutions of long tradition, reinterpreted and repurposed several times over the course of their history, precisely by tracing the artifact's criteria of identity to that history and not simply to a set of original authorial

[20] The expression "historico-intentional model" is being used here in a way that differs from Paul Bloom's (1996) "intentional-historical hypothesis," which is instead concerned with the categorization of artifacts. See Paul Bloom, "Intention, History, and Artefact Concepts" (1996) 60 *Cognition* 1.

[21] See Dipert, *Artefacts, Art Works, and Agency* (n. 5) 121, 125.

[22] Ibid. 55.

intentions. In a sense, it can also account for customs, because even though customs do not have authors, they may very well have a deliberative history of relevant intentions and actions. Hence, in what follows I will adopt this model. My characterization of an artifact is defined by the following "formula," which for the sake of simplicity I will be calling "ART": to be an artifact is to be the outcome of (1) a *deliberative history* tracing back to (2) an *intention-rooted creation process* whose content is (3) an *interaction plan* that works only if (4) its *mechanism* actually exists.

Let me expand on this brief statement. First, ART states that something's being an artifact is a historical property, for it consists in having a distinctive kind of history that traces back to a creation process rooted in human intentions. The term *process* is meant to capture the fact that the creation of an artifact can very well extend over time and involve several acts of different persons. This is also why the expression *intention-rooted* is used here in distinction from *intended*. In an assembly line, for example, the entire process is guided by a creative intention to produce something according to a design plan, but this intention may very well differ from the real content of the workers' intentional actions. And the same holds for the complex process of enacting laws—or, again, for the emergence of normative customs.

The intention-rooted creative process has a more or less definite content which I am calling an interaction plan. This is a modified version of Houkes and Vermaas's concept of a "use plan," which they use as a substitute for the concept of function because, while it can be difficult to understand the essential function of some artifacts, it is usually clearer how the artifact is supposed to work, namely, how we are supposed to interact with it.[23] While Houkes and Vermaas's use plan consists of an ordered set of actions geared toward a given goal, an interaction plan in my sense consists of a conditional statement through which an interaction between humans and an artifact is connected to a typical result relevant to those humans (a result that may be either enabling or disabling). As should be clear, disabling artifacts, like defensive walls, are particularly important in an artifact theory of law.

It is an *essential* property of an artifact that it is indeed able to carry out its interaction plan: an object *X* cannot be an artifact *A*, or at least it is a defective instance of A, if it cannot carry out the interaction plan typical of *A*s. This means that if *X*, for example, does not make it possible to turn screws after the correct kind of interaction, then *X* is not really a screwdriver, or at least it is a defective screwdriver, despite its author's intentions or its shape. Artifacts therefore have a dual ontological root: on the one hand is an intentional

[23] See Houkes and Vermaas, *Technical Functions* (n. 11) 20–1.

creative process, on the other is the actual ability of its interaction plan to be carried into execution. I will call the first root *historical* and the second *permanent*. An artifact with a historical root that does not also have a permanent root cannot fulfill its function and so is no longer a proper, non-defective artifact of that kind.[24] This distinction, as we will see, is crucial in assessing the explanatory power of an artifact theory of law.

The last element of the ART formula is its mechanism, consisting of the actual grounds on which an artifact's interaction plan rests. As we saw in criticizing the author model of artifacts, authors typically believe that the world backs up the artifact's intended interaction plan, but their beliefs are not sufficient for a mechanism to exist: if these beliefs turn out to be ungrounded and the interaction plan cannot achieve its results, the created object will wind up being nothing but an arbitrary and idiosyncratic realization. This shows that artifacts are essentially reason-based objects. They are so in two different senses. For one thing, they are built for a reason, and for another there must be good reasons for believing that results can follow from the envisaged interaction with them. I will call the first kind of rationality *teleological* and the second *technical*: an artifact's *teleological* rationality lies in the objective reasons for believing that the artifact's interaction plan answers our real needs; its *technical* rationality lies in the objective reasons for believing that its interaction plan can in fact achieve the intended results, independently of how we evaluate their relevance.

I will now describe how ART can be applied to legal institutions. I assume here a specific description of their emergence: proto-legal institutions began to emerge in the Middle Stone Age, when the temporal lobe of the human brain grew larger and became sufficiently developed to use recursive "meta-representations," namely, representations about the meaning of other representations.[25] Among these meta-representations were the rules defining the proto-legal roles necessary to organize social sanctions and regulate other kinds of social exchanges: here we had proto-legal institutions, which included secondary rules in Hart's sense, and hence basically power-conferring rules connected with a given social role.[26] Given that these representations were creative of other representations, these rules were constitutive: they defined

[24] The distinction between a historical and a permanent ontological root draws inspiration from Thomasson's distinction between historical and constant dependence: see Amie Thomasson, *Fiction and Metaphysics* (Cambridge University Press 1999) ch. 2.

[25] Benoît Dubreuil, *Human Evolution and the Origins of Hierarchies: The State of Nature* (Cambridge University Press 2010) 123–5.

[26] Ibid. 166–7.

a given kind of social fact by imposing on it a "status function" defined in normative terms.[27]

Now, if from an evolutionary point of view legal institutions emerged when the human brain developed the ability to produce meta-representations in the form of constitutive rules, it seems reasonable to conclude that legal institutions are grounded in the first place in these meta-representations. This seems to be confirmed by empirical research that connects the emergence of institutional facts in the consciousness of children with an ability to play games of make-believe, namely, cooperative games based on the attribution of statuses and on principles under which fictional truths are generated in the form of constitutive rules.[28] The central role that meta-representations have for legal artifacts has three consequences. First, legal institutions are to be conceived as abstract, immaterial artifacts consisting of representations. Second, legal institutions are linguistic constructs, because they consist of *meta*-representations, and so consist in the semantic operation of giving meaning to other representations. Third, a legal institution's interaction plan must be based precisely on the constitutive rules expressed in this semantic operation. This is therefore how the ART formula applies to legal institutions: what it is for something to be a *legal institution* is to be an *immaterial rule-based artifact*, that is, the outcome of (1) a *deliberative history* tracing back to (2) an *intention-rooted linguistic creation process* whose content is (3) a *system of constitutive rules defining interaction plans* that work only if (4) their *mechanism, that of shared acceptance* within the community, actually exists.

According to this description, legal institutions in the first place have an immaterial, semantic aspect: they consist of a set of concepts specifically created by linguistic declarations to organize, define, empower, and limit human behavior in a complex social setting. These concepts are defined through meta-representations in the form of constitutive rules, and they entail interaction plans allowing individuals to deal with the relevant organizations and social structures by means of a normative framework that empowers or limits them. But this organization of social life cannot work if there is no supporting mechanism, and what this mechanism consists in comes down to the fact of shared acceptance and compliance, meaning that the system of constitutive

[27] See John R. Searle, *The Construction of Social Reality* (Penguin 1996) 27ff., 100ff.

[28] See Hannes Rakoczy, "Play, Games, and the Development of Collective Intentionality" (2007) 115 *New Directions for Child and Adolescent Development* 53; Hannes Rakoczy and Michael Tomasello, "The Ontogeny of Social Ontology: Steps to Shared Intentionality and Status Functions" in S.L. Tsohatzidis (ed.), *Intentional Acts and Institutional Facts* (Springer 2007). On the generation of "fictional truths" on the basis of principles of generation, see Kendall Walton, *Mimesis as Make-Believe* (Harvard University Press 1990).

rules the institution consists of is widely accepted and people actually abide by those rules.[29]

As mentioned, the concept of a creative process is framed in a deliberately broad way in the ART formula, and the same goes for the concept of a *linguistic* creative process. In the legal domain, the paradigmatic cases of linguistic creative processes are authoritative speech acts enacting the constitutive rules of a given institution. But it is important to note that even customs can be explained in these terms. People simply behave in a certain way; then, in time, they begin to refer to this habit of behavior as a custom; the custom then becomes an institution and is referred to as such. This is a typical case of an intention-rooted creation process in which the original intentions did not include the artifact's sortal as part of their conceptual content. That sortal is a byproduct of a given community's legal discourse: here we indeed have a linguistic creative process, but one that differs from the example of authoritative speech acts.[30]

2. Why an Artifact Theory of Law?

I have provided a description of legal institutions in terms of artifacts. Now the question is: Can we really have any explanatory gain from it? I submit that we can, and in fact that the gain can be significant. In particular, an artifact theory of law can explain and solve the dialectics between legal positivism and legal realism, thus accommodating some of their respective theoretical insights in a coherent way. However, I also submit that an artifact theory cannot encompass all these insights: from legal positivism and legal realism it must draw crucial elements that it cannot provide on its own. In this sense, an artifact theory of law is a crucial link in the chain of explanation of legal ontology, but it cannot form the whole substance of that chain.

[29] On shared acceptance as a part of a legal artifact's mechanism, compare also Jonathan Crowe's conclusion that collective acceptance is part of an institutional artifact's success conditions. See Crowe, "Law as an Artefact Kind" (n. 6) 747ff. The claim can be weakened depending on the specific features of the legal system in which the legal institution at issue is embedded. It could be maintained, as Hart does, that in developed legal systems citizens must simply abide by the relevant legal institutions without actually accepting them, and that in these systems it suffices that legal officials accept a rule of recognition from which the formal validity of other rules can be derived.

[30] It seems to me that this explanation of a legal artifact's linguistic creation process is consistent both with Jonathan Crowe's explanation of customs proceeding from the example of a fallen tree used as a bench and with Luka Burazin's concept of informal institutional artifacts, where "the true authors ... are the participants themselves." See Crowe, "Law as an Artefact Kind" (n. 6) 740; Burazin, "Can There Be an Artifact Theory of Law?" (n. 6) 396.

In order to explain how an artifact theory of law can provide the common ground on which to hold together the insights of legal positivism and legal realism, I will proceed from the assumption that legal ontology is characterized by a tension between objectivity and acceptance: both objectivity and acceptance, that is, play a crucial role in our conceptualization of law. On the one hand, given the crucial role that legal institutions play in society and the important and possibly tragic consequences they can have on our lives, their content and their actual existence must be objective to the greatest extent possible. On the other hand, given that legal institutions are aimed at regulating behavior, the rules framing these institutions must be accepted or at least recognized as such. I describe this as a tension because, given the contingent, fuzzy, and wavering character of human intentional states, if legal institutions were to fully depend on such states, their outcomes would not be predictable, and people would thus not be able to really regulate their behavior on that basis; but, on the other hand, if legal institutions were completely objective to the point of being detached from human intentional states, their existence could in principle be independent of people' behavior and recognition, which is absurd.

This tension between objectivity and acceptance in legal ontology can be described in more familiar terms as a tension between legal certainty and legal effectiveness. Legal certainty is the idea that legal institutions must be open to public knowledge and predictable in their outcomes—indeed that they must be "objective" to the greatest extent possible. Legal effectiveness is a situation where legal institutions are in fact followed and applied, and hence play the role they are supposed to in our concrete life. Indeed, the historical dialectics between legal positivism and legal realism show that an explanation of legal institutions must account for both certainty, on the one hand, and effectiveness, on the other hand. Let me briefly summarize the main passages of these dialectics.

At the outset of the nineteenth century, legal objectivity was perceived as the main problem in legal science, and formalistic legal positivism sought to solve it against the relativity which was typical of natural law theories. In order to ensure legal certainty, the scholars of the French exegetical school argued on the one hand for a rigidly statualistic conception of law, according to which the only source of legally valid norms can be the creative activity of the legislator, and on the other hand for a strictly cognitivist conception of adjudication, according to which the application of law amounts to nothing more than a strict deduction from the text of statutory law, which expresses the legislator's will. This and similar perspectives sought to account for the ontology of law in terms of its objective contents, independently of the variability of the intentional states that members of a given community, or even judges applying the law, can have.

These tenets of formalistic legal positivism show that the tension between objectivity and acceptance in legal ontology can be further analyzed into two different relations. On the one hand, there is the relation and possible tension between legal institutions as designed by the legislator and legal institutions such as the citizen actually accepts, practices, and adapts to them. On the other hand, this relation holds between the legislator's will and the way in which this will is applied and interpreted by judges in deciding concrete cases. The twofold nature of effectiveness (the rule-abiding behavior of citizens and rule-applying behavior of officials) translates into two possible sources of tension, and positivistic legal formalism solves both problems in the same way, namely, by stating that formal validity and direct deduction from what is formally valid is the law. Here, objectivity holds sway in legal ontology.

But this stance soon came to be perceived as oversimple. The equivalence between the existence of legal institutions and formal validity of the rules by which such institutions are constituted was harshly criticized by antiformalistic movements and by legal realism, both Continental and American. In all its variants—from the free law movement to the jurisprudence of interests, from the legal-sociological approach to institutionalism and the realisms—antiformalism challenged the statualistic approach of formalistic legal positivism by arguing that legal institutions exist not in virtue of the semantic content of legal texts, however much validly enacted, but in virtue of their social rootedness and of the interests they serve.

This approach resulted in at least two conceptions of legal ontology that are directly opposite to that proposed by formalistic legal positivism: the pluralistic conceptions maintained by French and Italian institutionalism, on the one hand, and the psychologistic conceptions typical of Scandinavian and Polish-Russian legal realism, on the other. Moreover, among the outcomes of the antiformalistic conception of legal ontology was a noncognitivist conception of judicial decision-making according to which judges play a norm-creating role in deciding cases, and in so doing must take into account not only the relevant statutes but also the complex intertwining of social factors that form the backdrop to the case at hand—and American legal realism is of course paradigmatic in this regard. On all these views, the legal-positivistic insistence on objectivity and certainty at the expense of actual social recognition was out of the picture: it is actual acceptance, actual recognition, actual application rooted in social factors that makes the law, and legal certainty is nothing but an ideological illusion. As Leon Petrażycki writes, the existence of norms comes down to "the existence and operation in our psyche of immediate combinations of actions representations and emotions (rejecting or encouraging the corresponding conduct . . .)."[31]

The two main variants of twentieth-century legal positivism—Hans Kelsen's and H.L.A. Hart's—tried to steer a middle course between the quest for absolute legal certainty typical of nineteenth-century formalistic legal positivism and the reduction of law to actual, social effectiveness that we find in antiformalism and legal realism. In fact, both Kelsen and Hart trace the existence of legal institutions to the formal validity of the norms that constitute them. In Kelsen, legal norms exist objectively (they are objective *Sollen*) so long as they belong to a legal system grounded in a *Grundnorm* presupposed as valid.[32] Similarly, in Hart, the existence of a norm in developed legal systems "depends on whether it satisfies certain criteria provided by the rule of recognition," and in this sense the existence of a norm means that the norm is "valid given the system's criteria of validity."[33]

The objectivity and certainty of the existence of legal institutions, in the sense of the formal validity of the corresponding norms, is therefore a crucial element for both Kelsen and Hart. But in several respects both also acknowledge the crucial role that recognition and actual acceptance play in legal ontology. In Kelsen, a basic norm conceived as the ultimate foundation of formal validity can be presupposed only at the root of a legal system which is effective overall.[34] In Hart, the existence of a legal institution conceived as the satisfaction of the criteria of validity set forth in a rule of recognition rests on the officials' actual acceptance and internal point of view toward that rule of recognition, and the existence of a legal system must be grounded in general obedience.[35] This middle course that both Kelsen and Hart try to find between the problem of certainty and objectivity, on the one hand, and the problem of recognition and effectiveness, on the other hand, also comes through in their conception of judicial reasoning. In fact, both Kelsen and Hart hold that legal certainty as an outcome of legal decisions is an illusion, at least in hard cases. And, in Hart's view, it is also something we should not aim for.[36]

[31] Leon Petrażycki, *Law and Morality* (N.S. Timasheff ed., Harvard University Press 1955) 30; cf. also Edoardo Fittipaldi, "Leon Petrażycki's Theory of Law" in E. Pattaro and C. Roversi (eds.), *Legal Philosophy in the Twentieth Century: The Civil Law World. Tome 2: Main Orientations and Topics* (Springer 2016).

[32] See, e.g., Hans Kelsen, *Introduction to the Problems of Legal Theory* (S. Paulson and B.L. Paulson tr., Clarendon Press 1992) 12, 55.

[33] H.L.A. Hart, *The Concept of Law* (2nd edn., Clarendon Press 1994) 110.

[34] See, e.g., Kelsen, *Introduction to the Problems of Legal Theory* (n. 32) 59, 62.

[35] See Hart, *The Concept of Law* (n. 33) 114.

[36] See, e.g., ibid. 251–2; Kelsen, *Introduction to the Problems of Legal Theory* (n. 32) 83–4.

Dworkin's criticism of Hart's conception of judicial discretion can be interpreted as a new emergence of the need for objectivity in law, and thus as a restatement of formalism, though of course on entirely new grounds.[37] When, for example, Dworkin claims that "it remains the judge's duty, even in hard cases, to discover what the rights of the parties are, not to invent new rights retrospectively,"[38] or later, when he claims that the "propositions of law are true if they figure in or follow from the principles of justice, fairness, and procedural due process that provide the best constructive interpretation of the community's legal practice,"[39] his aim is to reframe the idea of legal objectivity in terms of the best moral justification that fits with a statute and its institutional background rather than in terms of that statute's literal meaning or of the corresponding speaker's intention: "The model for Dworkinian legal reasoning, therefore, is not geometry but morality."[40] However, it was still his aim to find a new way to make a case for legal objectivity, albeit "avoiding the mechanism of the older 'law is law' view as well as the cynicism of the newer 'realism'."[41]

This is where an artifact theory of law becomes relevant. I think an artifact theory of law framed along the lines described in the previous section can explain the tension between objectivity and actual acceptance, thus serving as a sort of bridge between the main tenets of formalistic legal positivism and those of antiformalistic legal realisms. In fact, the ART formula applied to legal institutions explains that tension *as the mutual ontological interdependence between the creative process of legal artifacts and their mechanism*. As noted, artifacts have both a historical and a permanent ontological root: they must be created in accordance with a given intentional design, but they must also be able to fulfill the interaction plan envisaged in that design. In light of that fact, where legal institutions are concerned, the mechanism that enables them to fulfill the interaction plan is that of actual shared acceptance, without which the artifact ceases to be what it is meant to be—and here ART hews to legal realism, because it implies that every legal institution needs shared acceptance if it is to exist and be deemed nondefective. This does not mean, however, that shared acceptance is all that matters, to the point of being the *only* relevant element defining an institution's nature and content. Shared acceptance is necessary as a mechanism but is not in itself constitutive of what

[37] See Scott Shapiro, *Legality* (Harvard University Press 2011) ch. 9.

[38] Ronald Dworkin, *Taking Rights Seriously* (Harvard University Press 1977) 81.

[39] Ronald Dworkin, *Law's Empire* (Harvard University Press 1986) 225. Cf. also Ronald Dworkin, "Is There Really No Right Answer in Hard Cases?" in R. Dworkin, *A Matter of Principle* (Harvard University Press 1985).

[40] Shapiro, *Legality* (n. 37) 264.

[41] Dworkin, *Law's Empire* (n. 39) 228.

a legal artifact is. This, according to ART, is instead determined by a given deliberative history consisting of creative processes, subsequent modifications, intended repurposing, adjustments, and emergent features: the whole of this history is an objective fact. It can be fuzzy, vague, and difficult to ascertain. But it is nonetheless objective, and *therein* lies what a legal artifact is.[42] Hence, in interacting with a legal institution at a given time T_x, I have to take into account the extent to which the artifact is accepted within the community. But statements and theoretical discussions about the nature of that institution are not simply statements about the content of actual, shared intentional states, in the same way that statements about a Gothic church are not simply statements about what we believe about that church. We could, for example, all believe that our Gothic church was built from scratch, and thus that its structure is completely original, and if this view were to gain sufficient shared acceptance, it could be taught in schools and become the mainstream view about our Gothic church. But someone could always turn up and show that the church was built on top of a preexisting Roman temple with a similar structure, and hence that the mainstream view is false. The same holds for legal institutions. To understand what a legal institution is within a legal system, we try to reconstruct the legislator's intention, the institution's legislative and judicial history, and how its function and structure have been understood and have changed over time in the broader framework of the legal system. This explains what the institution is, its role and rationale in our legal culture. Of course, these are not facts that can be empirically ascertained in the same way that we would be able to do with Roman ruins hidden beneath a Gothic church. But this does not mean that they are not facts. If we all lapsed into a collective amnesia and started to think, for example, that property can be protected only by private means, without any intervention of the state, it would be perfectly appropriate to discuss whether this makes sense, legally speaking, given the objective development of our legal culture.[43] Of course, an institution's deliberative history can evolve, and good

[42] On the relation between the mechanism of shared acceptance of a legal artifact and the artifact's deliberative history (and so, in the first place, its original authorial process), cf. Burazin, "Can There Be an Artifact Theory of Law?" (n. 6) 396. Burazin writes in particular that "our collective concept of what a Kx (institutional artefact) is, is what determines, at the first level only, the nature of that Kx," but he also writes that "the final real nature ... of a produced institutional artefact is, at the second level, nevertheless shaped by its author's intentions ...." Also, the dialectic between shared acceptance and deliberative history in legal artifacts can be interpreted as a way to merge the dependence principles of institutional entities with those of artifactual kinds, as discussed by Amie Thomasson. See Amie Thomasson, "Realism and Human Kinds" (2003) 68 *Philosophy and Phenomenological Research* 580, 587–8, 600.

[43] An argument "from amnesia" can also be found in Kenneth Ehrenberg, *The Functions of Law* (Oxford University Press 2016) ch. 5, sec. C, where it is deployed to show that an institution's

constitutional arguments can perhaps be found to support the need for a new understanding of property. But this, again, would not be a discussion about the content of shared intentional states of acceptance. Hence my conclusion: as immaterial artifacts, legal institutions cannot be what they are if there is no shared acceptance behind them, but the content of any actual shared acceptance can be criticized and discussed in light of the artifact's objective deliberative history.

As mentioned, however, the artifact theory cannot explain everything about legal institutions. The ART formula cannot, for example, explain the specific features that distinguish legal artifacts from other kinds of immaterial, rule-based artifacts, such as games and rituals. Hence, it can explain the anthropological proximity of these phenomena—they all unfold in domains where immaterial artifacts play a relevant role—but not the specific features that distinguish them. Legal positivism and legal realism, by contrast, have insisted on at least two peculiar features of legal artifacts. First, legal artifacts are created by political authority, and so are binding in a specific sense having to do with social coercion. Second, legal artifacts are made to adapt to contextual circumstances by means of authoritative interpretations of the original creative process and of its technical and teleological rationality. Thus, without either of these two elements—the legal-positivistic focus on authority and the legal-realistic focus on judicial interpretation—the artifact theory of law would be incomplete, at least as I have framed it, because it cannot on its own explain those two peculiarities of legal artifacts.

This is where context comes into play. Given their symbolic, linguistic nature, immaterial artifacts are in fact dependent on the social practices in which they are embedded.[44] An artifact consisting of a system of rules cannot determine its own practical import: it constitutes, on a "surface" level, an indefinite number of technical, institutional concepts, but it cannot constitute the overall meaning of that system of concepts, which depends on the "deeper" practice for which those concepts are created.[45] The same system

existence depends on shared acceptance. Ehrenberg, however, argues that the existence of legal artifacts over time cannot be reduced to the existence of actual psychological states, and this is precisely what I am trying to capture with the idea of deliberative history. To this end, Ehrenberg instead appeals to Searle's concept of an institution, and in particular to the entrenchment of institutional frameworks in background assumptions.

[44] On the relation between legal institutions as artifacts and law as a kind of artifact and as a broader practice of using such artifacts, see John Gardner, "The Legality of Law" (2004) 17 *Ratio Juris* 168, 171, 174.

[45] See Andrei Marmor, *Social Conventions: From Language to Law* (Princeton University Press 2009) ch. 3; Corrado Roversi, "Constitutive Rules in Context" (2010) 96 *Archiv für Rechts- und Sozialphilosophie* 223.

of rules can amount to a *game* of chess or a *ritual* of chess or perhaps a *legal procedure* called chess, depending on the background needs and values for which that system has been built.[46] That authority and interpretation have such a central role in the legal domain, and that they apply to immaterial artifacts—these are facts that need to be located in the deeper context, having to do with the deeper practices rather than with the surface artifacts created within those practices: we are dealing here with the deeper, shared concept of law rather than with the specific artifacts created within that context.[47] This is why a theory of how those artifacts are structured cannot explain everything about law—nor, I submit, could it explain everything about any context in which immaterial artifacts are relevant. Even for the legal domain, then, we may need a deeper treatment of the possible ethnological contexts in which artifacts are used and categorized: we may need what Beth Preston calls an "ethnotechnology."[48]

One could object at this point that if a theory of law cannot explain the specific features of legal institutions as distinguished from other normative phenomena, it is not a theory of law at all. I will concede this point: we would not have a comprehensive theory of law, but it would still be able to explain some features of legal institutions that any legal theory should take into account.

3. Can the Artifact Theory of Law also Be Connected with Natural Law Theory? Institutional Mimesis

The discussion has so far been aimed at explaining how an artifact theory of law can act as an explanatory bridge between legal positivism and legal realism. The question that comes up at this point concerns natural law theory.

Considered ideal-typically, natural law theory maintains that the existence and content of legal institutions (at least the most basic ones) is determined by factors that are at least in part objectively valid, such that it then becomes the task of human beings to figure out what those requirements are and to mould their institutions accordingly. Whether an artifact theory of law is consistent with this view depends on what the natural lawyer identifies as the objective factors serving as criteria for determining whether something exists as

[46] See Hubert Schwyzer, "Rules and Practices" (1969) 78 *The Philosophical Review* 451.

[47] See also, in this regard, Luka Burazin, "Practical Concepts of Law as an Artefact Kind" (2015) 31 *Pravni vjesnik* 70–2.

[48] See Beth Preston, "Ethnotechnology: A Manifesto" in M. Franssen, P. Kroes, T.A.C. Reydon, and P.E. Vermaas (eds.), *Artefact Kinds: Ontology and the Human-Made World* (Springer 2014) 157–8.

law and what contents it needs to have to that end. In the rationalistic version of natural law theory—the one that has been historically dominant—these objective factors are determined by objective reasons that humans should be able to recognize as correct. Framed in terms of the artifact theory of law, this tenet can be interpreted as one of either teleological or technical rationality. In the first case, the claim is that in order for legal artifacts to be paradigmatic and nondefective, they must ultimately serve an objectively rational *purpose*; in the second case, the claim is that, whatever purpose they serve, they must pursue it in an objectively rational *way*. If we assume that what contemporary natural lawyers by and large subscribe to is the first thesis,[49] we would see a contrast with the historico-intentionalistic theory of artifacts presented here, which instead subscribes to the *second* thesis. But in so doing it does not rule out the first one: nothing in this theory prevents the teleological reasons behind legal artifacts from being objective. In fact this is a *liberal* theory, envisioning a whole range of possibilities for these reasons: these could be determined by our evolution as members of the human species, for example, or by objective moral standards. So the artifact theory of law here advanced neither *rules out* the possibility of these reasons being objective nor *requires* them to be objective. What it does assume is rather that *deliberative histories* are objective, and that they form the criteria of objectivity for legal discourse. Hence, if these deliberative histories are grounded in objective teleological reasons, then rationalistic natural law theory and this artifact theory of law will arrive at similar conclusions, showing that essential to legal artifacts is the emergence of objective functions: the artifact theory would in this case take a distinctively functionalist stance. But if the deliberative histories behind legal institutions are not grounded in objective teleological reasons, then on the historico-intentional theory of law they will still exist: they will not lose their legal character, nor will they for that reason be deemed defective. In this case, the artifact theory and natural law theory would lead to different conclusions.

[49] This assumption can very well be simplistic. Indeed, while John Finnis and Michael Moore can be seen to espouse the first view, it is unclear to me whether Mark Murphy's concept of "decisive reasons for action" should be interpreted in teleological or technical terms, even though his discussion of the "common good" suggests that he inclines to the first view. See in particular John Finnis, *Natural Law and Natural Rights* (Clarendon Press 1980) 11–19; Michael Moore, "Law as a Functional Kind" in R.P. George (ed.), *Natural Law Theory: Contemporary Essays* (Oxford University Press 1992); Mark Murphy, *Natural Law in Jurisprudence and Politics* (Cambridge University Press 2006) 32 and ch. 3; cf. also Jonathan Crowe, "Clarifying the Natural Law Thesis" (2012) 37 *Australian Journal of Legal Philosophy* 159. For a deeper and critical discussion of contemporary natural law theory from the standpoint of an artifact theory of law, see Ehrenberg, *The Functions of Law* (n. 43) ch. 4.

However, even if a historico-intentionalist artifact theory of law can be inconsistent with natural law theory, and in most cases it will be, there is a way in which it can explain how legal artifacts can *appear* to be natural—a way in which it can explain how legal relations can be conceived as derived from nature, thus at least accounting for the original view of classic natural law theory.[50] This requires a further assumption, namely, that conceptions of nature can play a role in the deliberative history of legal artifacts, thus influencing the way in which they are framed. This phenomenon I call "institutional mimesis," which more specifically takes place when one or more rules constitutive of a legal artifact imitate or at least are structurally homologous to some descriptions of a natural reality which is supposed to exist before and independently of the construction of that artifact. There are several examples in the history of law that can be interpreted as mimetic constructions of legal artifacts.[51] Here, I will provide one.

It is a traditional view in legal and political history that the modern concept of the state emerged in seventeenth-century Europe, progressively transforming the multi-centered, pluralistic legal arrangements typical of the Middle Ages into a single, hierarchical organization governed by its own logic. Now, according to Stephen Toulmin, the rise of such a new and unified political framework, organized according to an internal rationality and in a sense universal, should be viewed as inextricably intertwined with a specific conception of the natural world: the conception encapsulated in the new mathematical science that emerged in the same period and whose foremost champion was Isaac Newton.[52] According to Toulmin, from the beginning of the eighteenth century, the hierarchical structure associated with the modern state could be seen to "mirror" the structure of nature (on a specific conception of the physical world) and could thus be justified through this analogy. And, conversely, the scientific conception of nature that underpinned this analogy was in its own turn strengthened from its very inception by its justificatory power.[53] This is precisely an example of institutional mimesis, because the constitutive rules defining the mutual relations of hierarchy within the state's structure, and hence the corresponding interaction plans connected

[50] Admittedly, this argument depends a lot on how we describe the "classic" version of natural law theory. Here I am assuming that the rooting of justice in a natural framework is extremely important for understanding the development of natural law theory in Ancient Greek philosophy.

[51] For a fuller discussion, see Corrado Roversi, "Legal Metaphoric Artefacts" in J. Stelmach, B. Brozek, and Ł. Kurek (eds.), *The Emergence of Normative Orders* (Copernicus Center Press 2016) 240ff.

[52] Stephen Toulmin, *Cosmopolis: The Hidden Agenda of Modernity* (University of Chicago Press 1990).

[53] Ibid. 128.

with those roles, imitated relations of dependence among natural entities described through nomological scientific statements.

An example of how institutional mimesis may have guided the development of legal conceptions about the state can also be found in Kelsen. Kelsen devotes some attention to a variant of the kind of institutional mimesis I am considering in regard to the state, namely, the idea typical of organicism, traceable to Thomas Hobbes and later defended by Otto von Gierke, that the state can be seen as a "macro-anthropos," or natural organism. In Kelsen's view, this idea was "ideological" and highly problematic, because its primary effect was to bring into the picture the conception, common in public law, that the state is something that *precedes* law and can be justified through law.[54] Although this example is not equivalent to that advocated by Toulmin (the state is described by Kelsen to be mimetic of an organism, and not of cosmic order), it is interesting to note that, in doing so, Kelsen tacitly presupposes precisely the kind of institutional mimesis indicated by Toulmin, namely, that of the state as a hierarchic order in which everything "has its place," as Toulmin says.

One could say that these examples of mimetic legal institutions are simply a curiosity, something which may be significant for the concept of the state but not for law overall. But I want to conjecture that this kind of institutional mimesis is not simply a byproduct of contingencies: it is rather something that has had a more profound impact on the creation of legal institutions. Consider the very genesis of the concept of corporation in Western legal thought, namely, the Roman idea that a *universitas* can be endowed with a legal personality separate from that of its members, as in Ulpian's famous passage, "If a debt is owed to the *universitas*, it is not owed to the individual members, and what is owed by the *universitas* is not owed by the individual members" (*Digest* 3, 4, 7, I). In his 1928 essay "Corporations as *universitates*," Karl Olivecrona maintains that, in Roman legal thought, the very idea of a corporation having a legal personality separate from that of its individual members depended on its being considered a separate entity, something that can exist in its own right, and not simply as a collection of parts. This was possible in light of a specific distinction between three kinds of natural *corpora*, a distinction which can be found in the Stoic philosophers and which was accepted by the Roman jurists. According to this distinction, there are three kinds of *corpora* to be found in nature: homogeneous objects of a given species whose parts are melted together and have no separate standing, for example, a statue; objects of a given species whose parts have their own separate species but are connected in a coherent way, for example, a ship (*corpus*

[54] Kelsen, *Introduction to the Problems of Legal Theory* (n. 32) 97.

ex cohaerentibus); and, finally, objects of a given species whose parts have their own separate species and are also physically independent, for example, a herd of sheep (*corpus ex distantibus*). In Olivecrona's view, the *universitates* discussed by the Roman jurists were to be conceived as *corpora ex distantibus*, and

> [th]e fundamental rules concerning their rights and duties are only applications of the general theory of *corpora*. The essential thing is that the entity is a *corpus*, distinct from the parts, with an individuality that remains unchanged despite changes in the parts. The rules are inferences drawn from these assumptions.[55]

As in the case of Toulmin's hypothesis on the rise of the modern state, here a legal organization is created in such a way that it mirrors natural reality according to a common conception of it, or what we would call a "scientific" conception (scientific according to the standards of the period).

If Olivecrona's and Toulmin's theses are correct, institutional mimesis has played a role both in giving rise to the very concept of a legal organization in ancient Western legal thought and in the development of the paradigmatic case of a legal organization—the state—in the Western public law of the modern era. The question is whether it is possible to find some independent ground for this conjecture. Now, if we consider the kind of conceptual transformation that moves from the universe to the state, or from a kind of "body" to a legal corporation, it seems that there are a couple of important metaphors involved: one revolving around the idea of an overall order, another revolving around the idea of physical unity. And this is where we can find backing for the overall idea of institutional mimesis. In fact, theories about "conceptual metaphors," prominent in the current debate in cognitive linguistics, show that abstract concepts can be created through the use of metaphors that can very well originate in the physical domain.[56] Other authors have elaborated on the idea of conceptual metaphors by showing, more in general, how conceptual structures can result from a "blend" between different conceptual domains.[57] In this kind of conceptual "blending," two or more different "mental spaces" are connected in virtue of a structural similarity by way of a more or less arbitrary correspondence relation which can very well be metaphorical. This relation gives rise to an "integration network" in which elements are connected by way of their common features, and in

[55] Karl Olivecrona, "Corporations as *universitates*" in K. Olivecrona, *Three Essays in Roman Law* (Ejnar Munksgaard 1949) 35.

[56] George Lakoff, *Moral Politics: How Liberals and Conservatives Think* (The University of Chicago Press 1996); George Lakoff and Mark Johnson, *Metaphors We Live By* (2nd edn., University of Chicago Press 2003); Mark Johnson, "Mind, Metaphor, Law" (2007) 58 *Mercer Law Review* 845.

[57] See Gilles Fauconnier and Mark Turner, *The Way We Think: Conceptual Blending and the Mind's Hidden Complexities* (Basic Books 2002) ch. 3.

which the resulting connections are projected onto a new integrated conceptual construct having an "emergent structure," that is, new features that were not present as such in the original input mental spaces. This idea of emergent structures, along with that of a metaphorical correspondence relation, seems to support the hypothesis that legal artifacts can be created by taking into account an underlying conception of nature and transforming it metaphorically into a normative structure.

This, of course, is a conjecture, but not one constructed out of thin air. In fact, if we assume that legal institutions are immaterial artifacts whose deliberative history is based on linguistic creative processes and whose mechanism is based on actual acceptance, conceptual blends of this kind could have a role to play in the conceptualization of basic legal institutions, and this can be tested experimentally.[58] In this way, by assuming an artifact theory of law and reframing within it one of the original ideas behind natural law, we arrive at a totally new way of considering natural law theory: a sort of *descriptive* natural law theory aimed at studying the way in which natural or physical patterns can shape our conceptualization of institutions. And this, too, can work as an original contribution which an artifact theory of law can make to legal philosophy.

[58] See Corrado Roversi, Leonardo Pasqui, and Anna M. Borghi, "Institutional Mimesis: An Experimental Study on the Grounding of Legal Concepts" in J. Stelmach, B. Brożek, and Ł. Kurek (eds.), *Reason and Emotions in Law and Morality* (Wolters Kluwer 2017). Cf. also Corrado Roversi, Anna Borghi, and Luca Tummolini, "A Marriage is an Artefact and not a Walk that We Take Together: An Experimental Study on the Categorization of Artefacts" (2013) 4 *Review of Philosophy and Psychology* 527.

6

Legal Systems as Abstract Institutional Artifacts

*Luka Burazin**

1. Introduction

To say that a legal system is an artifact can have at least two meanings. On a very broad reading often found in jurisprudential literature, it means that legal systems as systems of positive (human) law are human-made, non-natural entities, in the sense that they are causally created by humans. Even natural lawyers do not deny the fact that systems of positive law are human creations and, thus, artifacts.[1] This is, in fact, what is meant when one uses the expression "positive law," the law posited by the intentional actions of some human authority.[2] The second reading is an ontological thesis which uses the conceptual apparatus of the dominant general philosophical theories of artifacts in order to explicate what kind of an entity a legal system (or law) is and what its specific mode of existence amounts to.[3] The basic idea rests on an antirealist ontological position,[4] according to which artifacts (and thus, per hypothesis, legal systems

* I am grateful to Francesco Ferraro, Michael Giudice, Kenneth Einar Himma, Corrado Roversi, and Tomasz Gizbert-Studnicki for comments on an earlier draft.

[1] See, e.g., John Finnis, "The Truth in Legal Positivism" in Robert P. George (ed.), *The Autonomy of Law* (Clarendon Press 1996) 195.

[2] See, e.g., Neil MacCormick, *Institutions of Law: An Essay in Legal Theory* (Oxford University Press 2007) 243–6.

[3] See, e.g., Jonathan Crowe, "Law as an Artifact Kind" (2014) 40 *Monash University Law Review* 737; Corrado Roversi, "Legal Metaphoric Artifacts" in Bartosz Brożek, Jerzy Stelmach and Łukas Kurek (eds.), *The Emergence of Normative Orders* (Copernicus Center Press 2015) 215; Mark C. Murphy, "Two Unhappy Dilemmas for Natural Law Jurisprudence" (2015) 60 *The American Journal of Jurisprudence* 121, at 124–7; Luka Burazin, "Can There Be an Artifact Theory of Law?" (2016) 29 *Ratio Juris* 385; Kenneth M. Ehrenberg, *Functions of Law* (Oxford University Press 2016).

[4] See, however, for a realist position with regards to artifacts (a position according to which artifacts are mind-independent entities) e.g., Jonathan Lowe, "How Real Are Artefacts and Artefact Kinds?" in Maarten Franssen, Peter Kroes, Thomas A.C. Reydon, and Pieter E. Vermaas (eds.),

Law as an Artifact. First Edition. Edited by Luka Burazin, Kenneth Einar Himma, and Corrado Roversi. Published 2018 by Oxford University Press.

as well) depend on the human mind (i.e., they are mind-dependent entities), in the sense that the mental states of the authors of artifacts and the concepts on which these states are based are (at least partly) constitutive of their existence. In other words, in the sense that artifacts not only causally, but also existentially or ontologically depend on their authors' mental states and concepts.

This chapter deals precisely with the second reading of the claim that legal systems are artifacts. Its aim is to explain what kind of an entity a legal system is and what its mode of existence amounts to. Thus, the present inquiry is clearly an ontological one. The main method used in giving the attempted explanation is conceptual analysis. Even though I shall sometimes use such notions as "emergence" and "creation" (of a legal system) and present things as if there were some sort of an ordered sequence between the ontological building-blocks of the analyzed entity, the explanation provided in the chapter is not to be confused with a historical explanation seeking to identify the causes of the emergence of legal systems. On the contrary, I shall strive to show, in an analytical and conceptual manner, what it is that constitutes legal systems as social phenomena, i.e., in virtue of what a legal system can be said to exist.

I have already given the initial answer to the question about what kind of an entity a legal system is (reflected in the title of this chapter) in my "Can There Be an Artifact Theory of Law?" paper.[5] In it, I have claimed that legal systems should best be understood to be abstract institutional artifacts and have outlined what the so-called artifact theory of law might look like.[6] Roughly, I have claimed that legal systems are: 1) artifacts since they are created by human "authors" who have relevant mental states based on authors' concept of a legal system, under the condition that these mental states are largely successfully realized; 2) institutional since they are norm-based and require collective intentionality for their existence (meaning that they can initially be created only if there is collective recognition or acceptance of relevant constitutive norms which confer this institutional status accompanied with relevant deontic powers and can continue to exist only for as long as this recognition is maintained); and 3) abstract since they are not created by imposing the status of legal system to any existing physical object or person, but by making it the case that they exist provided that certain conditions are fulfilled and are, thus, ontologically immaterial (in the sense that a legal system would not cease to exist if, for example, all the original normative texts of a system

Artefact Kinds: Ontology and the Human-Made World (Springer 2014) 17; Crawford L. Elder, "Artifacts and Mind-Independence" in Maarten Franssen, Peter Kroes, Thomas A.C. Reydon, and Pieter E. Vermaas (eds.), *Artefact Kinds: Ontology and the Human-Made World* (Springer 2014) 27.

[5] Burazin, "Can There Be an Artifact Theory of Law?" (n. 3).

[6] Ibid. 397–9.

were destroyed). However, I have also suggested that a more elaborate analysis should be provided so as to grasp the full potential of this view and assess its explanatory adequacy. An analysis which should provide, e.g., a more detailed account of who can be considered to be an author of a legal system, what kind of and whose mental states are constitutive of the existence of a legal system, what degree of understanding of what a legal system is forms the basis of authors' mental states, what kind of norms confer the institutional status of legal system, and whether mental states should be socially validated in order for a legal system to exist, and if yes, to what degree. This is, of course, the main task of the present chapter.

In order to avoid any confusion about the object of my present inquiry, a brief preliminary remark on the notion of "legal system" that I use here is needed. A legal system (or "legal order") is here understood to be a dynamic (or diachronic) sequence of static (or synchronic) sets of norms forming a system on the basis of some unifying criteria or features, which is by and large socially efficacious. Accordingly, my analysis will mostly focus on structured (or institutionalized), "more-than-one-tier,"[7] "mature," or "developed" legal systems (e.g., national legal systems), which include norm-creating and norm-applying organs (hereinafter called officials). However, I shall sometimes also use, as an example, unstructured (or non-institutionalized), "primitive" legal systems (e.g., a system of customary law in a primitive community or a preinstitutionalized system of international law) which do not include officials in order to explain some distinctive features of structured legal systems.

2. Collective We-Mode Recognition

As has been said in the Introduction, legal systems existentially or ontologically depend on collective intentionality. The basic idea is the following. A relevant group of people (at least the majority of group members) collectively recognizes that a legal system exists. This recognition, as a social practice accompanied with its participants' particular attitude toward it, in fact constitutes a (constitutive) social norm, on the basis of which members of the relevant group make it the case that there exists something with the institutional status of legal system. By making it the case that there exists an institutional entity of legal system, members of the relevant group also attach corresponding deontic powers (powers, rights, duties, liabilities, etc.) to the people involved in the practice which includes the use of the legal system

[7] I here use MacCormick's terminology. See MacCormick, *Institutions of Law* (n. 2) 23.

(hereinafter called legal practice). While in unstructured legal systems only the general population is engaged in the collective recognition of the existence of their legal system, in structured legal systems there is a division of labor regarding collective recognition, so that both citizens and officials take part in making their legal system exist.

The form of collective intentionality required for the creation and existence of a legal system, I argue, is collective recognition (or acceptance). According to Searle, collective recognition can go "all the way from enthusiastic endorsement to grudging acknowledgment, even the acknowledgment that one is simply helpless to do anything about, or reject, the institutions in which one finds oneself."[8] Collective recognition does not necessarily imply moral approval. It might consist only in a "technical approval"[9] or even only "going along with the structure."[10] Legal systems, per hypothesis, exist if and only if they are collectively recognized or represented as existing.[11] Of course, this does not mean that the content of collective recognition is not constrained in any way. It can be constrained, e.g., by the criteria of rationality, physical laws, and even human culture.[12]

To get an initial sense of a possible way of how recognizing or representing a legal system as existing can be constitutive of its existence, let me quote an illustrative example provided by the description of how the "new" legal order of the European Union (EU) emerged:

> In two cases from the 1960s—*Van Gend en Loos* and *Costa v ENEL*—the European Court suggested a different view of the European legal order. The word 'suggested' is used deliberately, since the European Court does not have at its disposal any mechanism to force member states to accept its view of law. Thus, the fact that today European law is no longer international law, but an autonomous legal order, is the result not only of the European Court's opinion, but also of this opinion being accepted by member states. One of the 'proofs' that the states have accepted the existence of a new legal order and its relationship with their internal legal systems is

[8] John R. Searle, *Making the Social World: The Structure of Human Civilization* (Oxford University Press 2010) 8.

[9] Raimo Tuomela, *The Philosophy of Social Practices: A Collective Acceptance View* (Cambridge University Press 2002) 151.

[10] Searle, *Making the Social World* (n. 8) 57.

[11] Cf. Raimo Tuomela, *Social Ontology: Collective Intentionality and Group Agents* (Oxford University Press 2013) 228, who claims that "only group items that are represented (thus accepted in my acceptance-as-true sense) as existing by the group are institutional."

[12] Tuomela, *The Philosophy of Social Practices* (n. 9) 148 and 253–4 at n. 14; Tuomela, *Social Ontology* (n. 11) 8.

the fact that, during the numerous later revisions of the Founding Treaties, they have never tried to change this.[13]

The kind of collective recognition which is necessary for the creation and maintenance of a legal system is intentionality in the "aboutness" sense of intentionality, i.e., in the sense that members of a relevant group have particular collective attitudes (i.e., we-attitudes) which are about or refer to the existence of their legal system and in this way constitute their recognition. It is "that capacity of the mind by which it is directed at, or about, objects and states of affairs in the world."[14] Thus, it is sufficient that members of a relevant group collectively recognize (or accept) that their legal system exists. This, of course, does not exclude the possibility of collective intentionality in the "conduct" sense of intentionality, i.e., in the sense that members of a group, e.g., officials, recognize collectively the sources of law in their legal system on purpose and jointly control this recognition, which presupposes some pre-existing collective plan.[15] However, this type of collective intentionality is conceptually not necessary.

Although collective intentionality can, in principle, be in either an I-mode or a we-mode, the one required for the creation and maintenance of a legal system has to be in a we-mode. Unlike in an I-mode, where a group member acts as a private person and is privately committed to a certain attitude at least in part for herself, in a we-mode a group member acts for the group and is collectively committed to a certain (we-)attitude at least in part for the group.[16] According to Tuomela, the members of group g "share a we-attitude A if and only if (a) the members of g have the attitude A, (b) the members of g believe that the members of g have A, and (c) they also believe (or are disposed to believe) that it is mutually believed in g that the members of g have A."[17]

In the case of legal systems, a we-mode collective recognition which involves sharing a we-attitude is (conceptually) necessary for several reasons. Just like money, government, or language, a legal system is a group, social,

[13] Tamara Ćapeta and Siniša Rodin, *Osnove prava Europske unije* [The Basics of European Law] (*Narodne novine* 2010) 47 (my translation from Croatian). One could, however, object that the practice of some member state courts and the failed attempt at an EU constitution could count as proof against the creation of a new legal order as the European Court of Justice (ECJ) conceives it. I am indebted to Michael Giudice for this point.

[14] Searle, *Making the Social World* (n. 8) 25.

[15] On the general distinction between the "aboutness" and "conduct" sense of collective intentionality, see Tuomela, *The Philosophy of Social Practices* (n. 9) 79.

[16] See ibid. 36–7.

[17] Ibid. 152.

and public phenomenon.[18] It is always for a group, and exists only in a group and public context. There can be no "private" legal system, just as there can be no private language, government, or money. Thus, roughly, those who recognize a legal system as existing and by doing so make it existing must be taken to recognize it as members of the group[19] (or a community) and as existing for the group and within the group.

Furthermore, it intuitively seems impossible that each member of a group acting as a private person separately recognizes a legal system as an institution and that this purported legal system exists as an institution on the basis of the sum of individual I-mode attitudes of the same content. The norms of a legal system create legal positions (claim-rights, powers, duties, immunities, liabilities, liberties, etc.) for the members of a relevant community. There is no member of a community who holds a certain legal position and who is simultaneously not, with respect to this position, in some legal relationship with at least one more member of the community (or the state, in the case of, e.g., criminal or tax law) who is, again, at the same time a holder of a (correlative) legal position. Each legal relationship includes at least two subjects. Legal relationships would be impossible if each member of the community recognized, on the basis of her I-mode private attitude, the existence of a legal system separately. If that were the case, members of the community would not be collectively aware of the normative structure necessary for the functioning of a legal system as an institution. They could not, as individuals, rationally demand of others to respect the "rules of the game" common to all the members of the community when they, e.g., want to enforce some of their legal rights if they lack the belief that others believe that a legal system in their community exists. It would simply not be rational for members of a legal system to, e.g., conclude contracts, enter marriages or sell their property.[20] (The web of legal institutions depends on the existence of the institution of legal system.) This could, in turn, lead to the inefficaciousness of the purported legal system itself (the "legal system" could, for example, entirely lose, or not have from the beginning, its primary efficaciousness, i.e., compliance with norms), which, according to the dominant view in legal philosophy,[21] would deprive this "system" of its existence. Thus, the content of

[18] Cf. Eerik Lagerspetz, *The Opposite Mirrors: An Essay on the Conventionalist Theory of Institutions* (Kluwer Academic Publishers 1995) 7; Tuomela, *The Philosophy of Social Practices* (n. 9) 153 and 177; Searle, *Making the Social World* (n. 8) 59–60; Tuomela, *Social Ontology* (n. 11) 37–8.

[19] Cf. Tuomela, *The Philosophy of Social Practices* (n. 9) 153.

[20] On the rationality argument see ibid. 176–7 and 185.

[21] See Hans Kelsen, *Reine Rechtslehre* (1st edn., Mohr Siebeck 2008) 78–84; Herbert L.A. Hart, *The Concept of Law* (Oxford University Press 1994) 116.

a member's recognition has to be that a legal system (and its norms) relates not only to her, but also to all the other members of the relevant community.

This content, of course, can only be the content of a we-mode recognition. If a member of the relevant community were not to believe that other members of her community recognize the existence of their legal system and if the belief that members of a community recognize the existence of their legal system were not mutually believed within a community, this member could not meaningfully recognize that a legal system existed in the first place.[22] A set of unmeaningful recognitions is not sufficient to constitute an institutional fact that a legal system exists. In order for our recognition of the existence of a *legal system* to be the basis of the creation and existence of a *legal system*, which implies the existence of a community of people toward whom it is directed governing their mutual relationships, the recognition by each member of the community has to include, amongst other things, this feature of legal systems, i.e., the existence of a community to whom the system relates, whose members by their recognition make it the case that a legal system exists. Thus, each member of the community has to have the belief that other members of the community recognize a legal system and that there also exists a mutual belief that members of the community recognize the existence of their legal system.

In fact, there is no conceptual possibility that members of a community recognize the existence of a legal system without, at the same time, having the belief that the other members to which this legal system should relate recognize the system as well, and without there existing the mutual belief within the community that their members recognize the existence of their legal system. The group of people who were to recognize the existence of a "legal system" without it being mutually believed within the group that the members recognize the existence of a legal system would not constitute a legal system, but something different from it, since what they purportedly constitute does not imply the existence of a community whose members have mutual we-beliefs that they all (or the majority) recognize the existence of their legal system. Since it is in the nature of the legal system to be a group phenomenon, this implies that the concept of legal system (at least a rudimentary one), on the basis of which members of a relevant community recognize the existence of a legal system, includes the legal system's "groupness" feature. Thus, members of a community recognize the existence of a legal system as the existence of something that is "for the group," and it is to this extent that their recognition is necessarily a we-mode recognition (constituted by the we-mode attitude).

[22] Cf. Lagerspetz, *The Opposite Mirrors* (n. 18) 209.

Additionally, recognition of a legal system by an individual member without the individual believing that others also recognize it cannot be a meaningful recognition. The norms of a legal system regulate mutual relationships between individuals (property law, family law, labor law, law of obligations, etc.) or between individuals and the state (e.g., criminal law, tax law). Thus, if an individual recognizes the existence of a legal system (the totality of its norms), then she must recognize that its norms apply not only to her, but also to other members of the community and that these norms regulate their mutual relationships. If a member of a community were to know that others do not recognize the existence of a legal system (but also if he were not to have any knowledge about whether others recognize its existence or not), she would not be able to meaningfully recognize the existence of a legal system, since she would not have any reason to believe that her recognition of a legal system would really constitute a legal system, that others would comply with its norms and that her relationships with others would effectively be regulated and governed by the norms of the system.

Finally, that the recognition of a legal system cannot be individual, but collective and in the we-mode also follows from the fact that an individual, a member of a community that collectively recognizes the existence of a legal system, cannot, independently of others, withdraw her recognition and rescind her obligations that derive from the recognized (institutional, deontic) status of legal system.[23] One can rescind such obligations only when members of a relevant community withhold their prior recognition of a legal system collectively, in a we-mode.

3. Constitutive Norms of Recognition

Collective recognition of a legal system is the practice of having collective we-attitudes in the sense of collectively recognizing that a legal system exists. It is a social practice since it is performed (at least in part) for social reasons. Participants' social reasons to collectively recognize that their legal system exists consist in the fact that other participants recognize it too and are expected to do so.[24] This acting on the attitudes and actions of other participants creates for each participant the feeling of being bound to recognize a legal system and all the deontic powers (e.g., the duty to comply with the norms of the

[23] For a similar argument, although concerning "joint commitment," cf. Margaret Gilbert, "Social Rules as Plural Subject Phenomena" in Eerik Lagerspetz, Heikki Ikäheimo, and Jussi Kotkavirta (eds.), *On the Nature of Social and Institutional Reality* (SoPhi 2001) 52.

[24] On social reasons see Tuomela, *The Philosophy of Social Practices* (n. 9) 79.

system) that follow from its institutional status. Since participants have (social) reasons to recognize the existence of a legal system and expect others to do so, we can say that the practice of collective recognition constitutes a social norm of recognition.[25] It seems that in cases of unstructured legal systems (those lacking officials), such a norm is sufficient to constitute a system out of a theretofore unconnected set of norms. Members of a relevant community collectively recognize that customary norms which apply to them (and which are, in fact, created by them) form a system of norms and, thus, by their practice of collective recognition, make it the case that their legal system exists. Of course, as we shall see shortly, this is a necessary, but not a sufficient condition for the (effective) existence of a legal system.[26] Thus, apart from being a social and regulative norm, as it generates (social) reasons for actions (i.e., reasons for recognizing a legal system), it is also a constitutive norm, as it constitutes the institutional status of legal system.

Things are slightly different in cases of structured legal systems, although the basic conceptual building blocks (i.e., collective recognition and constitutive norms) remain the same. In structured legal systems, which regulate the production and application of their norms, besides citizens, there are also officials (i.e., organs that create and apply the norms of a system) as a subgroup of "operative members"[27] of the whole population affected by a given legal system. As operative members, officials are (in a sense yet to be explained) authorized by citizens (non-operative members of a group) to authoritatively say what the norms of their legal system are (to be). As we know from Hart, officials carry out their own social practice of identifying legally valid rules of their system, constituting the social rule of recognition which sets the criteria of legal validity.[28] However, besides this constitutive role with respect to the rules of a system, the rule of recognition is also a rule in virtue of which a system of these rules *is* a legal system. Since the necessary feature of a legal system is that it is a system rather than a set of rules, and since it is the rule of recognition that provides for this unity of rules, one can say that the rule of recognition constitutes not only each of the rules of a legal system, but also the system as such. The rule of recognition can, thus, be said

[25] I deliberately use the expression "norms" rather than rules. Norms can be both individual and general (which will show to be important when introducing a distinction between individual and general norms of recognition), while rules can only be general. I use the expression "rule" only when referring to Hart's rule of recognition.

[26] See Section 5 of this chapter for the social validation requirement.

[27] I here use Tuomela's distinction between operative and non-operative members of a group. See Tuomela, *The Philosophy of Social Practices* (n. 9) 144; Tuomela, *Social Ontology* (n. 11) 129.

[28] See Hart, *The Concept of Law* (n. 21) 100–10 and 256.

to confer on the system its (institutional) *status* as a legal system.[29] Since the rule of recognition is constituted by the social practice of collective recognition by officials, officials can be said to be the primary authors of a particular instantiation of a legal system. Thus, by collectively recognizing the rule of recognition (i.e., that some set of validity criteria is a public standard to be followed), officials (operative members of a relevant community) make it the case that their legal system exists.

However, unlike in cases of unstructured legal systems, here the institutional status of legal system created by the operative members of a relevant community has to be (in some sense) additionally supported by the community's non-operative members, i.e., citizens. Citizens are those who, by their collective recognition, impose the institutional status of officials to certain people.[30] Although certain people can define themselves as "officials" by agreeing on some criteria for having this status, they do not have the said institutional status unless collectively recognized as such by a relevant community (a community in respect to which they carry out their deontic powers which follow from their status as officials).[31] Citizens' collective recognition of officials represents their social practice of regarding certain people as their officials. As a social practice resting on social reasons for action (recognizing certain people as officials since others recognize them as such and are expected to do so), it constitutes a social norm of recognition. Apart from being a social norm, it is also a double constitutive norm as it constitutes the institutional status of officials and makes the conceptual framework for an instantiation of their legal system, which, on the basis of the division of labor, is carried out by officials setting the criteria of identification of the sources of law in a relevant community.

So, basically, the existence of a legal system is (indirectly) supported by citizens' collective recognition of a social norm of recognition (i.e., that certain people should be counted as officials), since citizens, by their collective recognition, impose the status of officials to certain people, and thus also attach to them the corresponding powers of identifying, creating, and applying law, i.e., that in regard to which they have the corresponding duty to comply with. Hence, by collectively recognizing the status of officials, citizens recognize that the object of their powers is law (a legal system) and, by doing so,

[29] See Luka Burazin, "The Rule of Recognition and the Emergence of a Legal System" (2015) 27 *Revus—Journal for Constitutional Theory and Philosophy of Law* 115, at 117–19.

[30] This is in contrast to both Kelsen's view according to which first officials (i.e., the founding fathers) are authorized by a presupposed *Grundnorm*, and Hart's view according to which officials are authorized by the rule of recognition.

[31] Cf. Lagerspetz, *The Opposite Mirrors* (n. 18) 15.

they also recognize the fact that a legal system exists. Of course, this recognition may be merely tacit, "involving the possibility of at least some degree of dissent and opposition," since officials presumably "have the authority to collectively accept institutions for the collective and ... also have the power to coerce and pressure the other members to accept what has been instituted."[32] Even if there were some external power which imposed certain people as legal officials on a subjugated community forcefully, and members of this community collectively recognized these people as their legal officials, these people would have the institutional status of officials in respect to the community.[33] This recognition, of course, would amount to a rather weak recognition and would consist in merely going along with the fact that there are officials in (and for) the community.[34] Again, as we shall see shortly, collective recognition (that of both officials and citizens) is a necessary, but not a sufficient condition for the (effective) existence of a legal system.[35]

The abovementioned social norms constituted by the practice of collective recognition are constitutive by their nature in yet another sense. The norms in question create the possibility of the very conduct they regulate.[36] There would be no *legal* practice were there not both a social norm of recognition by which certain people are attached the institutional status of legal officials, and a rule of recognition by which particular norms are identified as legal norms which form a legal system. Only in virtue of these norms can one say that the practice of officials, which consists in identifying, creating, changing, and applying legal norms, and the practice of citizens, which consists in complying with the norms of their legal system and using them so as to regulate their mutual relationships, are *legal* practices. Thus, legal practices do not exist detached from the norms which constitute them as legal. These norms are constitutive of legal practices since they create the possibility for such practices, which, as institutional practices (since they are norm-based practices) make a legal system an institution.

[32] Tuomela, *The Philosophy of Social Practices* (n. 9) 161.

[33] As Nannini says: "Recognizing the authority of certain people is, of course, quite different from submitting willingly to them or from deeming as morally just the fact that they have a certain power. A tyrant, too, is as a matter of fact recognized by his subjects as an authority (i.e., recognized such that his orders are *legally* binding), unless and until they are in a position to rebel, notwithstanding the fact that their wish to rebel has been strong and morally justified from the beginning." Sandro Nannini, "Legal Validity and Conformity to Law" in Letizia Gianformaggio and Stanley L. Paulson (eds.), *Cognition and Interpretation of Law* (G. Giappichelli editore 1995) 239, at note 18.

[34] Cf. Tuomela, *Social Ontology* (n. 11) 30–1.

[35] See Section 5 of this chapter for the social validation requirement.

[36] See Leo Zaibert and Barry Smith, "The Varieties of Normativity: An Essay on Social Ontology" in Savas L. Tsohatzidis (ed.), *Intentional Acts and Institutional Facts: Essays on John Searle's Social Ontology* (Springer 2007) 157, at 165; Searle, *Making the Social World* (n. 8) 10.

It is here useful to introduce a distinction between different types of (constitutive) norms by which a group of people collectively imposes a certain institutional status (such as that of officials) or make it the case that a certain institutional status (such as that of a legal system) exist. A distinction can be drawn between codified or explicit and uncodified or implicit norms of recognition, and between general and individual norms of recognition. Codified or explicit norms of recognition are those norms that are explicitly posited and formulated by some human authority. Uncodified or implicit norms of recognition are those norms that are constituted by the social practice of collective recognition (which can be the practice of either ordinary citizens or some authority). Uncodified or implicit norms of recognition are, in fact, social norms. General norms of recognition are those norms that constitute (or set the grounding criteria for[37]) a type-institutional artifact. Individual norms of recognition are those norms that constitute (or set the grounding criteria for) a token-institutional artifact (or an instantiation of a type-institutional artifact).

Let us now turn to the application of these norms to particular cases of officials and legal systems, which will require some modifications to the general description given at the beginning of this section. The historically first officials (including "revolutionary" officials) of a certain legal system are constituted by collective recognition of an uncodified or implicit individual constitutive norm.[38] A relevant community collectively recognizes a certain group of people as their legal officials, thus imposing on them the institutional status of officials with the corresponding deontic powers of identifying, creating, changing, and applying law. All subsequent officials are (in principle) constituted by the codified or explicit general constitutive norm (e.g., a constitutional norm) posited by the historically first officials. However, even in this case, there necessarily has to be at least an informal, uncodified, or implicit collective recognition by citizens, which ensues from their initial recognition of the status of the first or original officials and their corresponding deontic powers (including the power to codify the norms on the basis of which subsequent officials are elected or appointed). This is so since codification

[37] See Brian Epstein, *The Ant Trap: Rebuilding the Foundations of the Social Sciences* (Oxford University Press 2015) 76.

[38] According to Searle, this would be a case where no constitutive rule exists and, thus, a pre-institutional example of the same logical structure as constitutive rules. It is merely an *ad hoc* collective recognition that something has a certain status and a step toward codification in the form of rules. See Searle, *Making the Social World* (n. 8) 19–21. See also Amie L. Thomasson, "Social Entities" in R. Le Poidevin et al. (eds.), *Routledge Companion to Metaphysics* (Routledge 2009) 548. According to her typology of constitutive rules, in these cases one is dealing with a singular constitutive rule, on the basis of which institutional objects are created on a token-by-token basis.

cannot be socially efficacious if a legal system as a whole lacks a certain degree of informal collective recognition by a relevant community.[39]

Legal systems are, in principle, constituted by uncodified or implicit constitutive norms. First, the conceptual framework within which an instantiation of a legal system can emerge is created by a social norm of recognition, on the basis of which citizens collectively impose the institutional status of officials to a certain group of people, thereby also collectively recognizing the type-institution of law. Second, a particular instantiation of a legal system is created by a social rule of recognition, on the basis of which officials collectively recognize the criteria of validity in their legal system, thereby unifying a set of norms into a system of norms. This is so, of course, in cases where historically first legal systems emerge in a particular community and in cases of revolution-based emergences of legal systems. However, there is also the possibility for legal systems to be constituted by a codified or explicit general constitutive norm (e.g., in cases of secession of federal states on the basis of federal constitutional norms). In such cases, collective recognition by citizens is implied by their collective recognition of a given legal system which contains the said codified norm. Nevertheless, officials of the newly formed legal system might call a referendum where citizens would be given the opportunity to express their implied collective recognition explicitly. However, this explicitly expressed collective attitude is conceptually not necessary for the new legal system to exist. What is conceptually necessary is only that the relevant community does not withdraw their prior collective recognition.

4. Preceding Practices and Concepts

It is conceptually possible for collective recognition to be preceded by a joint plan. One can imagine members of a community reaching an (implicit or explicit) agreement on who should be their leader or, in our case, their legal officials. One can also imagine officials making an (implicit or explicit) agreement on what the criteria of legal validity in their legal system should be. However, even though this is conceptually possible and perhaps there are some (albeit presumably never ideal) examples of such plan-based or agreement-based creations of legal systems, it is conceptually not necessary.

According to Tuomela, collective recognition is often preceded by and emerges from some existing rudimentary practices.[40] Hence, even before a

[39] Cf. Tuomela, *The Philosophy of Social Practices* (n. 9) 159.

[40] Ibid. 126. According to Tuomela, this leads to a diachronic chicken-or-egg problem, i.e., the what-came-first problem. However, it seems that the "temporal" problem does not really exist if we

norm-based collective recognition of a legal system comes to be within a relevant community (including here recognition by both citizens and officials), it is possible (and highly likely) that some "legal" practice which is involved in the genesis of collective recognition already exists. One might even take this practice to be the inceptive core of a particular instantiation of a legal system. After a certain practice has existed for some time, e.g., the practice of creating and applying certain norms by certain people or the practice of complying with these norms and using them to regulate interpersonal relationships, members of a relevant community come to have and hold particular we-attitudes. Namely, collective intentionality in the sense of collective recognition that certain people are their officials having the corresponding deontic powers of identifying, creating, and applying law, thereby also collectively recognizing the type-institution of law.

The said preceding practice may be said to create the context or the background in which constitutive social norms of recognition can emerge. Thus, for example, a line of stones which has the status of border "has acquired this status against the background of the context C, which is constituted by the tribes' collective practice of trying to get along with each other, etc."[41] Hence, a particular collective practice comes first and then comes collective recognition of the institutional status. One might thus imagine, in the case of law, for example, over time, the practice of complying with norms created and applied by certain people becoming so entrenched that these people come to be counted as legal officials in and for a relevant community. They acquire their status of legal officials against the context which is created by the collective practice of members of a relevant community, a context in which (at least the majority of) members of a relevant community come to have and hold a we-attitude in the form of a we-recognition that these people are their legal officials and that that which they identify, create, and apply as law is law. We-recognitions do not have to be performed at the same time and at the same place.[42] In the case of law (but also other such institutions), they are usually performed over a (long or longer) period of time and at different

distinguish between different types of relations between the two, i.e., between collective recognition and the rudimentary practices preceding it. Collective recognition *constitutes* the preceding practices as social or institutional practices (it imposes on them the institutional status). On the other hand, the preceding practices lead to or *cause* (in the sense that they take part in the psychological genesis of) collective recognition by which they acquire their institutional status.

[41] Hannes Rakoczy and Michael Tomasello, "Ontogeny of Social Ontology: Steps to Shared Intentionality and Status Functions" in Savas L. Tsohatzidis (ed.), *Intentional Acts and Institutional Facts: Essays on John Searle's Social Ontology* (Springer 2007) 126.

[42] Seumas Miller, "Joint Action: The Individual Strikes Back" in ibid. 78–9.

places.[43] This is so because what makes individual we-recognitions be part of a collective recognition is neither time nor space, but a shared social reason.[44]

Claiming that collective recognition is conceptually necessary for a legal system to exist might imply that the participants in the practice of collective recognition are conscious agents completely aware of the structure of the institutional reality they create. However, institutional reality is often created unconsciously (at least to some degree), in the sense that people might not be aware of the institutional structure of the entity they have created, and might even have false beliefs about what constitutes a particular institution.[45] Thus, members of a relevant community might have false beliefs about what makes certain people be their officials or what renders a certain system of norms a *legal* system. They might believe that their legal system is a legal system because it was created by God or some supernatural power, or since its norms derive from natural law or moral norms. They do not have to believe that their legal system is constituted by both their and their officials' collective recognition that it exists. However, this does not change the fact that a legal system exists only in virtue of the relevant collective recognition of its existence. Hence, even if citizens have false beliefs about that which constitutes the institutional status of their officials or the existence of their legal system, in order for officials and a legal system to exist, they collectively have to recognize that these "things" exist, i.e., they have to recognize that there exists something that amounts to a set of norms which regulate their behavior and mutual relations, and provides for sanctions of the violations of these norms.

Here, however, a question arises about whether, and, if yes, to what extent, participants in the practice of collective recognition have to have a concept or conceptual understanding of the object that they recognize as existing. Institutional artifacts, as has already been pointed out, can exist only if represented as existing. In order to represent something as existing, it is necessary to have at least some degree of (conceptual) understanding of that which is being represented as existing, which, of course, does not presuppose

[43] Of course, when we speak of national legal systems, we might perhaps speak of collective recognition being performed on the territory of a particular legal system and, in that sense, figuratively speaking, at the same place. However, what is meant to come to the fore is that there does not have to be (although this is conceptually possible) some gathering of people who make a plan and reach a decision on collectively recognizing certain people as their legal officials and on recognizing as their law that which these officials recognize as law.

[44] Tuomela, *The Philosophy of Social Practices* (n. 9) 96.

[45] See John R. Searle, "Social Ontology and the Philosophy of Society" in Eerik Lagerspetz, Heikki Ikäheimo, and Jussi Kotkavirta (eds.), *On the Nature of Social and Institutional Reality* (SoPhi 2001) 37–8.

that there also has to be a word denoting the concept in question.[46] However, participants have to have a conceptual understanding of the "thing" they collectively recognize as existing which is rich enough to make its existence possible. What really matters is how participants actually treat and use the institutional artifact in question and what deontic powers they attach to this institutional artifact or, more specifically, to its users, i.e., all those participating in the practice based on the fact that the institutional artifact in question exists.[47]

Thus, members of a relevant community do not have to collectively recognize that a "legal system" or "law" exists in order for a legal system or law to exist. It is sufficient that they collectively recognize that there is some entity X with regard to which certain people have deontic powers which are otherwise regarded as distinctive of legal systems.[48] It is crucial that citizens, in the case of structured legal systems, collectively recognize that there exists a group of people (officials) who have the deontic powers to identify, create, change, and abrogate norms which regulate their behavior, and that they have, e.g., a duty to comply with these norms and a power to use them when regulating their mutual relationships. Thus, there cannot exist *legal officials* without members of a relevant community having at least some conceptual understanding of what makes someone a legal official (which is most clearly manifested in the deontic powers she has and uses), on the basis of the understanding of which members of a relevant community collectively recognize certain people as legal officials. Members of a relevant community cannot, in turn, collectively recognize a certain group of people as *legal* officials unless they also have at least some conceptual understanding of what law or a legal system is.

Citizens do not necessarily have to know what the distinctive features of legal officials are, but they have to necessarily have at least some conception of what the people that they count as officials "can or cannot do, and when and how far they should be obeyed."[49] It is also not necessary that the content of citizens' representations overlap with the content of the logical structure of particular deontic powers. The constitutive norm of the form "X counts as Y in context C" constituted by the practice of collective recognition is only a rational reconstruction of the content of citizens' representations or, better

[46] Ibid. 34; Tuomela, *The Philosophy of Social Practices* (n. 9) 146 and 249, at note 3; Searle, *Making the Social World* (n. 8) 95–6; Tuomela, *Social Ontology* (n. 11) 225.

[47] Cf. Searle, *Making the Social World* (n. 8) 118.

[48] This is what makes it possible for anthropologists to, e.g., discover that some ancient society had that which we today call "legal system" or "law."

[49] Lagerspetz, *The Opposite Mirrors* (n. 18) 160.

still, of the implicit norm which follows from the "overlapping consensus, or broad commonality of attitude"[50] amongst members of a relevant community.

Thus, citizens do not have to have a full-blown concept of officials or a legal system. However, since the status of officials imposed by collective recognition goes beyond the physical nature of the people counted as officials,[51] citizens have to be able to symbolically represent the status of officials, and since they impose this status collectively, they have to be able to communicate it.[52] Therefore, in order to symbolically represent and communicate the status of legal officials and the deontic powers that follow from it, citizens must have and share at least some rudimentary concept or conceptual understanding of "officials" and "legal system."

In the case of legal officials and their collective recognition of the validity criteria constituting the rule of recognition, the question about whether they have to have and share some concept of a legal system seems to have an even more straightforward answer. Since a legal system acquires its main feature (i.e., that of being a system of legal rules) through the rule of recognition, that is, a rule constituted by the practices of legal officials, legal officials are arguably the primary authors of a particular instantiation or token of a legal system. If legal officials are the authors of a legal system collectively recognized by a relevant community as having the status of legal officials (a status which implies the corresponding deontic powers of identifying, creating, modifying, and applying law), it seems justified to assume that their practices also include their collective recognition that what they produce is to belong to the kind "legal system" and not some other system of rules. Hence, in order to collectively recognize that what they produce forms a *legal* system, they have to have and share some concept of "legal system." In contrast to the case of citizens, sharing only a rudimentary concept of "legal system" here does not seem to be sufficient. According to Hart's theory, the concept of "legal system" that officials would presumably have and share would include at least the following two features: that the legal system is a system of valid legal rules, i.e., rules that are members of one and the same system of rules, and that the legal system is structured as a union of primary and secondary legal rules. The requirement that officials have to share a concept of "legal system" richer than that of citizens follows naturally from the fact that officials are the so-called

[50] See MacCormick, *Institutions of Law* (n. 2) 18.

[51] Amie L. Thomasson, "Foundations for a Social Ontology" (2003) in *Understanding the Social II: Philosophy of Sociality*, 18–19 *Protosociology: An International Journal of Interdisciplinary Research* 269, at 271.

[52] Anthonie Meijers, "Collective Speech Acts" in Savas L. Tsohatzidis (ed.), *Intentional Acts and Institutional Facts: Essays on John Searle's Social Ontology* (Springer 2007) 93, at 108.

operative members of a relevant community authorized by the non-operative members to fulfill their official role.

Note that the concept of law or legal system that citizens collectively recognize while collectively imposing the institutional status of officials to a certain group of people (and attach to them the corresponding authority regarding the identification and creation of law) is, in fact, a type-institution of law or legal system. This way, citizens can be said to create a conceptual framework for the emergence of a token-institution of law. A token-institution of a legal system, which depends on its type-institution (i.e., a kind to which it belongs), is created by officials since their social practice (i.e., collective recognition of the criteria of identification of legal norms) constitutes a unifying criterion (i.e., the criteria of identification) of the dynamic sequence of static sets of norms in virtue of which these norms form a system of norms.

5. Social Validation Requirement

The thus far presented account of that which constitutes the existence of a legal system relies solely on the mental states of members of a relevant community (both citizens and officials). Such a mental states-based ontology of institutions might imply that, e.g., citizens determine what law is and what its essential features are on the basis of their folk classifications, and this seems unrealistic. According to Guala, "[f]olk classificatory practices are in principle quite irrelevant. What matters is not what type of beliefs people have about a certain class of entities (the conditions they think the entities ought to satisfy to belong to that class), but what they do with them in the course of social interaction."[53] This view seems right to some extent. Let me explain.

General philosophical theories of (ordinary) artifacts say that artifacts have both an intended and an actual character (or nature). The intended character is determined by the concept or description involved in the mental states of the author of an artifact (which, in the case of ordinary artifacts, are authors' intentions).[54] However, in order for an artifact to be created and to acquire its *actual* nature, it is also necessary that the author's intention indeed be realized in practice. From this it follows that the author's *concept* alone is not sufficient to determine the actual nature or properties of an artifact. What matters is whether this concept or description is successfully realized. Although the

[53] Francesco Guala, *Understanding Institutions: The Science and Philosophy of Living Together* (Princeton University Press 2016) 170.

[54] Risto Hilpinen, "Artifact" in E.N. Zalta (ed.), *The Stanford Encyclopedia of Philosophy* (Winter 2011 edn.) ch. 1.

relevant intention need not be realized in its entirety, some degree of success is necessary.[55] It has been suggested that the author's intention should at least be "largely successfully realized."[56] For, as it has rightly been noted, "if an author fails in every respect, he does not produce a genuine artifact, but only 'scrap'."[57] Thus, in order for an ordinary artifact to be said to exist, it is necessary that its intended character (i.e., the content of the mental states of its author) be realized. The same goes for institutional artifacts. Collective recognition in the "aboutness" (or attitude) sense, which purportedly determines some features of the potential institutional artifact (i.e., which "defines" it), determines only the "intended" character of the institutional artifact in question. However, the actual existence of the institutional artifact (and its actual character) depends on whether the content of collective recognition (collective attitudes) was largely successfully realized. This realization is manifested precisely in people actually using the institutional artifact, i.e., in their social practices which are based on the collective recognition that the institutional artifact in question exists.

Hence, collective recognition that a legal system exists is not sufficient for the creation of an instantiation of a legal system. In addition, some cognitively more full-blown legal practice has to be in place in order to "define" a legal system for a relevant community.[58] Collective recognition (or acceptance), according to Tuomela, "involves acceptance action, viz., acting in the right way concerning the accepted content in order to 'validate' this content."[59] One can, thus, say that social validation, consisting in carrying out and maintaining a shared we-attitude from collective recognition, is the realization of or the bringing about of the institutional artifact in question. For example, a newly created language collectively recognized as language by members of a relevant community would not really be language if members of the relevant community never used it for their interpersonal communication. Or, something collectively recognized as money would not really be money if it were never actually used as money. If attitudes were sufficient, and no deontic power following from the imposed institutional status were ever carried out, the institutional artifact in question would not really exist since it would not fulfill its function. It fulfills its function through the practices of

[55] Risto Hilpinen, "Authors and Artifacts" (1993) New Series 93 *Proceedings of the Aristotelian Society* 155, at 160–1.

[56] Amie L. Thomasson, "Realism and Human Kinds" (2003) 67(3) *Philosophy and Phenomenological Research* 580, at 598; Amie L. Thomasson, "Artifacts and Human Concepts" in Eric Margolis and Stephen Laurence (eds.), *Creations of the Mind* (Oxford University Press 2007) 59.

[57] Hilpinen, "Authors and Artifacts" (n. 55) 161.

[58] Cf. Tuomela, *The Philosophy of Social Practices* (n. 9) 126.

[59] Tuomela, *Social Ontology* (n. 11) 16.

those who hold the corresponding deontic powers in relation to its institutional status, i.e., practices which manifest themselves as carrying out those powers. This implies that function is a conceptually necessary feature of institutional artifacts. Of course, this does not mean that artifacts cannot fulfill their function poorly. However, in order for something to be an artifact, it has to fulfill its function at least to a certain degree.

By collectively recognizing certain people as officials, members of a relevant community create public deontology, i.e., "public reasons for action that are desire-independent."[60] In contrast to social institutions in the sense of imposing a new conceptual status to an entity (e.g., the Saturday sauna in parts of Finland),[61] officials and legal systems are social institutions in the sense of creating a *deontic* (institutional) status, i.e., an institutional status from which the corresponding deontic powers follow. By collectively recognizing certain people as their legal officials, members of a relevant community ascribe the relevant deontic powers to people recognized as having the institutional status of officials. These powers consist in the power of officials to identify, create, change, and apply law. However, since citizens have collectively recognized that certain people are their legal officials, and have thereby collectively recognized that that which officials identify as law is law, they are committed to the fact that certain people are their officials and that that which they identify as law is the law of their community. They are thereby also committed to participating in a legal practice conceptually made possible by the practice of officials. That is, once identified as legal norms by the officials of a legal system, citizens are committed to complying with these norms and to using them when regulating their mutual relationships.[62] These deontic powers of citizens follow directly from the institutional status of their legal system.

If collective recognition were not supported by the social efficacy of the deontic powers ensuing from the statuses of officials and a legal system, constituted by collective recognition (i.e., if collective recognition were not "socially in force"[63]), only the concepts or conceptual features of officials and the legal system would at best be created.[64] If, for example, purported officials

[60] Searle, *Making the Social World* (n. 8) 85.

[61] Tuomela, *The Philosophy of Social Practices* (n. 9) 174.

[62] This shows why a separate recognition of the institutional facts or the institutions created within an existing institution is not necessary. By collectively recognizing the institution of officials and (indirectly) a legal system, I have already committed myself to recognizing particular norms created by these officials as the legally valid norms of my legal system. This explains why the social efficacy of legal norms is not a condition of their validity. Social efficacy can indicate that citizens do recognize norms as legally valid norms. However, this indication is not necessary since collective recognition of officials already implies collective recognition of the norms they create as legal norms.

[63] Tuomela, *Social Ontology* (n. 11) 129.

[64] Cf. ibid. 234–5.

were never to identify any norm as a legally valid norm of their system, it would be counterintuitive to say that these purported officials are indeed officials. This would be so, since identifying norms as legally valid norms of a system is a conceptually necessary function of legal officials. Furthermore, it is only by the practice of officials of identifying legally valid norms that an instantiation of a (structured) legal system and thereby a new institutional status with corresponding deontic powers is created. Thus, if there is no practice of norm-identification, then there is neither a legal system nor deontic powers following from its institutional status. Hence, it follows that, as a matter of conceptual truth, in order for a legal system to exist, the social practice of officials has to be in place.

But, what about citizens? Do they have to effectively comply with the norms of their system and use them to regulate their relationships, thereby socially validating their collective recognition, in order for a legal system to exist? It seems that the answer is again yes. The function of officials is not merely to identify legally valid norms, but also to identify legally valid norms which will be socially efficacious. If the purported officials merely identified legally valid norms which no one ever complied with, we could at best say that some people put forward a proposal that something be a legal system. It would be counterintuitive to claim that a set of norms which no one has ever complied with represents a legal system. Hence, it is necessary that citizens use the norms of their legal system in order for the system to exist.

In addition to this, a lack of at least some degree of social validation might indicate a lack of the "correct" collective recognition. If it is commonly understood by people that legal norms provide them with reasons for action, then legal norms necessarily take part in their practical reasoning. If no member of a relevant community in which there was a purported collective recognition of the existence of a legal system were to ever act on the reasons generated by the norms of that "system," then the purported norms of the system would not in fact be norms. This, in turn, would mean that that which members of a relevant community collectively recognized as law is in fact not law at all, but something else, i.e., that the "correct" collective recognition was not in place in the first place.

Furthermore, a lack of at least some degree of social validation might even indicate a complete lack of collective recognition. If no member of a relevant community acted according to that which (at least the majority of) members of a community (indirectly) collectively recognized as law through the recognition of the status of legal officials and their deontic powers, then this would be a strong indication that members of the community have collectively withdrawn their collective recognition. Since collective recognition has to be (at least implicitly) maintained in order for a legal system to exist, one might claim that such a legal system ceased to exist. The tacit assumption underlying this argument is that there has to be at least some degree of consistency between what people collectively recognize and how they collectively behave. When this consistency completely vanishes, it is reasonable to assume that what they collectively recognized as law has simply changed.[65]

Of course, the non-compliance of members of a community with that which was collectively recognized as law could, from the members' internal point of view, be interpreted as a violation of the norms of their legal system. However, widespread violation of legal norms does not necessarily mean that there is no collective recognition in place. If I do not comply with a rule, and interpret my non-compliance as a violation of the rule, then I, in fact, recognize the rule as a legal rule, but a rule that I do not wish to comply with. Thus, it is possible for a legal system to exist even if there is widespread (but, as has been pointed out, not total) violation of its norms (i.e., even if primary social inefficacy exists).[66] Of course, this is possible so long as the official law-enforcement mechanisms are efficient enough to maintain the general (secondary) social efficacy of a legal system,[67] since, as has been said, some degree of the successful realization of relevant collective recognition is necessary for a legal system to exist.

Of course, all of the above does not mean that citizens necessarily comply with the norms voluntarily. In order for an institutional artifact to be able to perform its deontic powers, support of the powers by organized force or coercion is sometimes needed.[68] This is evidently so in the case of structured institutional artifacts, where the operative members of a group, although existing in virtue of being collectively recognized by the non-operative members of the group, set the rules for these non-operative members. Since, in the case of structured legal systems, legal norms are created by officials and are to be applied to citizens, and since these norms are only indirectly and implicitly collectively recognized through the collective recognition of certain members of the group as officials, in order for these norms to be socially efficacious (and to eventually constitute a legal system), formal sanctions and permanent threat of the use of force is required. In the case of unstructured legal systems,

[65] I am indebted to Corrado Roversi for this point and clarification of the tacit assumption underlying the argument.

[66] We can contrast this case with the case of a successful revolution, which is often referred to as an example of an existing legal system being replaced by a new legal system. In this case, it is not the case that members of a relevant community violate the norms of the pre-revolutionary legal system. They simply no longer recognize it as their legal system. The system they now collectively recognize as theirs is a new, "revolutionary" legal system.

[67] Secondary social efficacy consists in the efficacy of the sanctions of a legal system.

[68] Searle, *Making the Social World* (n. 8) 106–7.

where members of a community constitute the existence of their legal system by their own social practice of collective recognition, social pressure and informal social sanctions (e.g., social disapproval) are sufficient to maintain the collective recognition and the functioning of the relevant deontic powers.

Tuomela puts the point this way: "some degree of social 'functionality' is necessary for an institution. For instance, when we take money to be a social institution, we imply that the use of money (e.g., in contexts of exchange) is an institutional social practice."[69] Thus, "one can say even that a social institution ultimately amounts to a special kind of norm-governed social practice (or set of practices)."[70] Hence, to say that a legal system is an institution (institutional artifact) is in fact to say that the use of a legal system, i.e., legal practice (e.g., identifying, creating, changing, applying, or complying with law), is an institutional social practice. Of course, to be an institutional social practice means that, besides being collectively recognized as such, it has to be actually performed by members of a relevant community for it to exist.

6. Conclusion

In this chapter I analyzed the claim that legal systems should best be understood to be abstract institutional artifacts and sought to provide a more detailed account of some of the questions arising from such a claim. In Section 2, I argued that legal systems existentially or ontologically depend on collective intentionality and that it is conceptually sufficient that it be in the form of (a we-mode) collective recognition (or acceptance), where this is understood in the sense that members of a relevant group have particular collective attitudes (i.e., we-attitudes) which are about or refer to the existence of their legal system and in this way constitute their recognition. In Section 3, I claimed that this recognition, as a social practice accompanied with its participants' particular attitude toward it, in fact constitutes a (constitutive) social norm, and distinguished between different types of (constitutive) norms by which a group of people collectively imposes a certain institutional status (like that of officials) or make it the case that a certain institutional status (like that of a legal system) exists. In Section 4, I claimed that legal systems often emerge gradually from a standing practice since collective recognition is often preceded by and emerges from some existing rudimentary pre-legal practices which may be said to create the context or the background in which

[69] Tuomela, *The Philosophy of Social Practices* (n. 9) 161. [70] Ibid.

constitutive social norms of recognition can emerge. I also argued that those who collectively recognize that someone is a legal official or that a legal system exists do not have to have a full-blown concept of what they recognize but only some degree of conceptual understanding and that what really matters is how participants actually treat and use the institutional artifact in question and what deontic powers they attach to it or its users. Finally, in Section 5, I argued that the actual existence of a legal system (and its actual character) depends on whether or not the content of collective recognition was largely successfully realized, which is manifested precisely in people actually using a legal system, i.e., in their social (legal) practices.

7

The Conceptual Function of Law

Law, Coercion, and Keeping the Peace

*Kenneth Einar Himma**

1. Introduction: The Concepts of Law and Artifact

Although there might be many positions in the conceptual theory of artifacts that are contested, this much is not: artifacts are contrived and constructed by human beings. Risto Hilpinen provides what I take to be a canonical definition in the first sentence of his *Stanford Encyclopedia of Philosophy* article on the topic. According to Hilpinen, "An artifact may be defined as an object that has been intentionally made or produced for a certain purpose."[1] As he subsequently explains:

> Aristotle makes here a distinction between natural objects and artifacts ('artificial products' …), and describes the latter as products of the art of making things. The art of making something involves intentional agency; thus an artifact may be defined as an object that has been intentionally made for some purpose …. An artifact has necessarily a maker or an author; thus *artifact* and *author* can be regarded as correlative concepts: … An object is an artifact if and only if it has an author. The concept of authorship is here assumed to involve the same kind and degree of intentionality as the concept of an artifact.[2]

Here it should be noted that Hilpinen is not making any claims about the conceptual function of any particular artifact or artifacts as such; he is merely

* I am indebted to Luka Burazin and Corrado Roversi for comments on an earlier draft.

[1] Risto Hilpinen, "Artifacts," *Stanford Encyclopedia of Philosophy* (Winter edn., 2011) <http://plato.stanford.edu/archives/win2011/entries/artifact/> accessed August 7, 2017. I cite the *Stanford Encyclopedia of Philosophy* because what is reproduced there may be presumed to enjoy a consensus among the relevant community. It should be noted that there are no page numbers for *Stanford Encyclopedia* articles.

[2] Ibid.

indicating that artifacts are not naturally occurring objects that have uses or purposes—and hence are "artificial products."

Nevertheless, the conceptual relationship between the terms "artificial" and "artifact" should be obvious. As Oxford Online Dictionary defines it, "artificial" means "[m]ade or produced by human beings rather than occurring naturally."[3] Similarly, *Black's Law Dictionary* defines the term "artificial" as follows: "Made or produced by a human or human intervention rather than by nature."[4] It should be clear that the terms "artificial" and "artifact" are conceptually linked since both pick out objects that are contrived and manufactured by human beings.

Nevertheless, the conceptual relationship between the two notions is not one of logical equivalence. While it is certainly true, as a conceptual matter, that all artifacts are artificial, it is not true that all artificial objects are artifacts. Certain forms of air pollution, for example, are artificial because not naturally occurring, but are not properly characterized as "artifactual" since these types of pollution are not invented and manufactured for a purpose. Similarly, if I take a few Legos and connect them together in a random way, it is true that I have constructed something that is both an object and artificial; however, in the absence of some sort of purpose it is not properly conceived as an artifact. An artifact must, according to Hilpinen's definition, have some kind of use—although what that use is and who determines it is somewhat contentious.[5]

In any event, it is taken for granted that laws and legal systems are artificial in the sense that they are human contrivances and not naturally occurring objects. Indeed, on all accounts of *positive* or *posited* law, the existence and content of legal systems and law can be explained wholly in terms of social facts.

Legal positivism, of course, is robustly committed to the view that law is artificial in character. To begin, the existence and content of a rule of recognition is explained in terms of a social convention among officials, which is a social fact and hence *artificial* in character in the sense of being a non-naturally occurring object. Likewise, the existence and content of valid legal norms is explained by officials' conformity to the rule of recognition in their lawmaking and adjudicating activities; such norms are also artificial in the

[3] Oxford Online Dictionary <http://www.oxforddictionaries.com/definition/english/artificial> accessed August 7, 2017.

[4] "Artificial," *Black's Law Dictionary* (West Publishing 2014).

[5] E.g., the purpose of an art object is for presentation, on one influential contemporary theory, to an audience for the purpose of creating an aesthetic experience. See George Dickie, *Art and the Aesthetic: An Institutional Analysis* (Cornell University Press 1974).

same sense. Both the rule of recognition and the laws valid under it, then, are artificial in relevant sense.

By itself, as we saw above, the claim that law is artificial does not imply that law is an artifact; however, given that law is characteristically used, at a minimum, to guide behavior (which is a purpose), law is properly thought of as an artifact. Every law is a non-natural occurring object that is used for some purpose, and is hence not only *artificial* but also an *artifact*. As the existence of a legal system, on a positivist view, requires merely the existence of a rule of recognition and general citizen conformity to valid legal norms, it seems clear that, on the positivist view, law is an artifact all the way down.[6]

The most currently influential theory of natural law ("neoclassical natural law theory"), like positivism, takes law to be wholly artifactual in character.[7] This contemporary natural law theory of positive law has two pieces. The first is a metaethical theory, according to which the natural law consists of principles of *objective* morality that have the content they do in virtue of the nature of things in the universe, including human beings. The second is a theory of the positive law that holds that legal systems and laws are social artifacts in the sense of being manufactured by human beings, but holds, further, that it is in the nature of these things that their content *ought* to be just, and thereby that their content *ought* to conform to the relevant natural laws.

This view does not, on the surface, differ much from legal positivism with respect to the social and artifactual nature of law and legal systems. As far as I can tell, the only real disagreement here is whether there is something in law's nature that gestures in the direction of law's aspiring to be objectively just as a conceptual requirement of being a legal system. Since merely *aspiring* to be objectively just but failing to do so would not entail that a norm was legally invalid, this particular difference does not have any implications that would distinguish the views with respect to their artifactual character. It seems perfectly reasonable to think that, on this view, laws and legal systems are artifactual all the way down.

One might think that the strongest of natural law theories (or "classical law theories") implies that law is not wholly artifactual since there are necessary moral constraints on the content of valid law. But the existence of moral constraints on what a structured group of people might do does not imply

[6] The term "law" is ambiguous as between referring to a legal system and referring to individual norms of a legal system. The thesis of this paper is concerned with the conceptual function of a legal system, as the conceptual function of legal norms presents comparatively few puzzles of theoretical interest. Norms guide behaviors in particular directions.

[7] See, e.g., Mark Murphy, *Natural Law in Jurisprudence and Politics* (Cambridge University Press 2006).

that the institution constituted by that structure is not an institution of "justice" that is wholly artifactual in character.

Regardless of whether it is a conceptual truth that there are objective moral constraints on legal validity, laws and legal systems are obviously not naturally occurring objects (even if it makes sense to think of morality as naturally occurring). The claim that an objective morality is not artifactual does not imply that a non-naturally occurring institution constructed, in part, out of a non-artifactual moral piece is *not artifactual.* Material artifacts are usually composed out of naturally occurring physical entities—and that does not entail those entities are not wholly artifactual.

Consider the simple example of a boundary between two countries that coincides with the path of a river.[8] The river is, of course, a natural occurring object that might define the location of the boundary for various geopolitical reasons; however, it would be a mistake to think of the boundary as not being wholly artifactual in nature. Although the boundary is defined by the river and might be used by people to recognize where the boundary line is, it is implausible to think of a boundary as even partly naturally occurring. Boundaries are artifactual.

As a general matter, it is worth noting that the fact that the operations of something considered artifactual are limited by certain features of the world, whether normative or not, does not play a role in determining whether or to what extent that thing is artifactual. That there are physical laws that limit what rockets are capable of does not make a rocket any less artifactual. That there are such constraints casts no doubt, nor should it, on the claim that a rocket is wholly artifactual—assuming that it is plausible to think of artifactuality as a property that admits of degrees.

The general point here is that the mere fact that a human contrivance is constrained with respect to its design, structure, or purpose by descriptive laws of nature or normative objective moral norms does not bear on whether the contrivance is an artifact. As Raimo Tuomela puts the point:

> Collective construction is conventional in the sense that one can imagine alternative constructions that could be taken to be true. However, collective construction is not unconstrained as to its content, because, e.g., causality and the physical laws of the universe and also *human culture* underlie what can be feasibly rationally constructed, and also determine much of what social constructions such as institutions will ontologically lead to in the social world.[9]

[8] I am indebted to Luka Burazin for this helpful example.

[9] Raimo Tuomela, *Social Ontology* (Cambridge University Press 2007) 8 (emphasis added).

Accordingly, something can be artifactual even when its constitution or existence conditions are constrained by physical laws or laws of "human culture," which would include norms of morality.

This would seem to imply that social institutions, such as law, can be wholly artifactual despite any such constraints.[10] Indeed, as Tuomela puts it, "[s]ocial artifacts such as social institutions are created (not always intentionally) and maintained by 'us' (the group members) for us" because "[i]n a world without human beings or human-like beings and their conceptual activities, there would be no institutional facts."[11] Since law is created and maintained by us for us, law is an artifact, on any plausible conceptual theory of artifacts—no matter what conceptual theory of law one chooses. In the next section, I will discuss legal theory and the conceptual function of law.

2. The Idea of a Conceptual Function of Law

As mentioned above, artifacts are taken to have a use or purpose; an artificial object that has no use or purpose remains artificial but it is not an artifact. Artifacts are characterized as having uses or purposes, and these uses or purposes are fairly characterized as conceptual functions, although this notion is not always well explained. The intuitive idea is that any object contrived and constructed by human beings for a use that meets certain standards has a primary purpose, and this purpose constitutes its conceptual function. This is surely true of material artifacts, and the idea that material artifacts have a function of this sort is uncontested among theorists specializing in the conceptual theory of artifacts.[12]

The question of whether artifacts like legal systems and norms have conceptual functions is not one that has attracted a great deal of theoretical attention; however, it seems to be a commonplace that law has a conceptual function. John Austin defined the notion of a legal norm, as opposed to a legal system, in terms of its conceptual function: "A law ... may be defined as a rule laid down *for the guidance of an intelligent being by an intelligent being having power over him.*"[13] As Lon Fuller conceived it, "[t]he only formula

[10] Ibid. 38. [11] Ibid. 214.

[12] Although art-objects might be taken to be an exception to that thesis, conceptual accounts of art nearly always include some kind of conceptual function; one commonly accepted account, for example, explains the nature of art as an artifact that is presented to an audience for an aesthetic experience. See (n. 5).

[13] John Austin, *Lectures on Jurisprudence or the Philosophy of Positive Law* (Scholarly Press 1977) 5 (emphasis added).

that might be called a definition of law offered in these writings is by now thoroughly familiar: law is the enterprise of subjecting human conduct to the governance of rules."[14]

H.L.A. Hart is commonly assumed to hold that law has a conceptual function, but a closer look at his remarks indicates some skepticism about the idea. As Hart states it, "it is quite vain to seek any more specific purpose which law as such serves beyond providing guides to human conduct and standards of criticism of such conduct."[15] Although this would seem to indicate a commitment to the idea that law *qua* legal system has a conceptual function, the entire passage in which these remarks appear evinces a more skeptical attitude:

> [W]hereas Dworkin's interpretive legal theory in all its forms rests on the presupposition that the point or purpose of law and legal practice is to justify coercion, it certainly is not and never has been my view that law has this as its point or purpose. Like other forms of positivism my theory makes no claim to identify the point or purpose of law and legal practices as such; so there is nothing in my theory to support Dworkin's view, which I certainly do not share, that the purpose of law is to justify the use of coercion. In fact, I think it quite vain to seek any more specific purpose which law as such serves beyond providing guides to human conduct and standards of criticism of such conduct.[16]

What is striking about this passage is the apparent skepticism Hart displays for the project of finding a conceptual function for law, as well as for the idea that it is necessary that an account of the concept of law include reference to such a function. Skepticism for the project of *identifying* a conceptual function of law can be seen in the very last sentence of the text quoted immediately above; he begins that sentence with the idea that it is "quite vain to seek any more specific purpose" of law than that it guides conduct. Skepticism for the idea that it is *necessary* to specify a conceptual function of law to fully articulate the nature of law is expressed in the second sentence of that quoted text: "Like other forms of positivism my theory makes no claim to identify the point or purpose of law and legal practices *as such*."[17]

These remarks—coupled with the facts that they are the only remarks Hart seems to have made on the subject and that these remarks were made in the Postscript, and not in the body of his book *The Concept of Law*—indicate some skepticism about the project of identifying a conceptual function of

[14] Lon Fuller, *The Morality of Law* (Yale University Press 1964) 106.
[15] H.L.A. Hart, *The Concept of Law* (2nd edn., Oxford University Press 1994) 248–9.
[16] Ibid. [17] Ibid. 248 (emphasis added).

law. I see little reason to accept Hart's skepticism given the artifactual character of law. As was seen above, what distinguishes the artifactual from the merely artificial is that the former has some kind of use. As will be seen below, it is uncontroversial among conceptual theories of *artifacts* (of which law is one type) that artifacts have conceptual functions—although theorists might disagree as to how best to characterize the notion of a conceptual function.

3. The Concept of an Artifactual Function

The issue of how to flesh out the concept of an artifactual function is a contested one in the literature on the nature of artifacts. Accounts of artifactual function include so-called intentionalist accounts, which conceive of artifact function as "directly and *exhaustively determined* by individual and/or collective human intentions,"[18] and non-intentionalist (or reproduction) accounts, which conceive artifact function as the function "that they have been historically reproduced to serve."[19]

The difference between the two accounts has to do with the prominence of the role human intentions serve. In the intentionalist accounts, human intentions directly determine the relevant function. In the reproductive accounts, which accord a primary role in determining artifactual function to "ancestry or system context,"[20] human intentions play a secondary role insofar as "they are necessary for the histories and reproductions of social systems."[21] The difference, on Beth Preston's view, is that the relevant human intentions are necessary *and* sufficient to determine an artifact's conceptual function on an intentionalist account, while on a reproduction account the relevant human intentions are necessary but *not* sufficient, to determine an artifact's conceptual function.

Although of obvious theoretical interest, this difference is not particularly relevant here inasmuch as whatever intentions might be behind the creation and maintenance of a functioning legal system will likely coincide with the reasons for the history of reproduction of legal systems and the underlying intentions that explain that history and reproduction. Either way, the assessment of the conceptual function of a legal system will focus on the intentions regarding the purposes that a legal system is created to serve or historically has served. It is doubtful, as far as I can see, that the content of

[18] Beth Preston, "Philosophical Theories of Artifact Function" in Anthonie Meijers, Dov M. Gabbay, Paul Thagard, and John Woods (eds.), *Philosophy of Technology and Engineering Sciences* (North Holland 2009) 218.

[19] Ibid. 226. [20] Ibid. [21] Ibid.

the relevant intentions will turn on whether those intentions play a primary or secondary role in the manner described above. In either case, the relevant intentions will gesture, I argue, in the direction of law being used to keep the peace.

A second distinction that should be mentioned here pertains to whether a conceptual function is *multiply realizable* in the sense that the relevant function can be performed by distinct kinds of artifacts. Chopsticks might be an example of something that can be used to perform the same function as a fork. The argument in this chapter is agnostic with respect to whether the conceptual function of law is unique to law or multiply realizable.

Another distinction pertains to whether an artifact is *multiply utilizable* in the sense that it can be used to perform more than one function. As Preston points out, a uniform can be used for different functions, such as to keep one warm, distinguish friends from foes, and display rank, among other things. There is little reason to doubt that laws and legal systems can be used to do different things. For example, laws and legal systems can be used, in some more or less casual sense, to oppress some, enrich others, etc. The list of things that can be done with a legal system might be quite long, as human beings are quite ingenious in adapting tools to serve different purposes.

But in order to do any of these things, there is one thing that a law or a legal system must be able to do—and that is to coherently guide behavior. Legal systems and laws are capable of oppressing some or enriching others only insofar as at least *some* of these norms *sometimes* succeed in guiding behavior. As Hart rightly points out, the minimum conditions for the existence of a legal system include that valid legal norms are efficacious in guiding behavior.[22] As Hart put the matter:

> There are therefore two minimum conditions necessary and sufficient for the existence of a legal system. On the one hand, *those rules of behaviour which are valid according to the system's ultimate criteria of validity must be generally obeyed*, and, on the other hand, its rules of recognition specifying the criteria of legal validity and its rules of change and adjudication must be effectively accepted as common public standards of official behaviour by its officials.[23]

Hart's use of "obey" suggests that he believes that conforming behavior must be motivated by a desire to conform to the law; however, this is not a charitable construction of his remarks. The fact that the vast majority of people do not commit murder likely has little, if anything, to do with the fact that it is illegal. No minimally decent person would be tempted to kill

[22] Hart, *The Concept of Law* (n. 15) 116.

[23] Ibid. (emphasis added).

an innocent person; morality and empathy are far more likely to explain such compunctions than legal prohibitions.

It is true, of course, that there are many people who lack such compunctions or who misinterpret the requirements of morality in a particular case and would attempt to do what is legally prohibited as murder if not for the law. Although it is clear that the criminal law does not always deter people from committing murder, it surely does in some cases. In these cases, the overarching point of the law is to keep the peace—a point that I will argue for in more detail below. For now, it suffices to observe that whether or not the law is multiply utilizable in the relevant sense, there are certain functions that law must perform in order to accomplish the vast majority of these purposes—and keeping the peace by efficaciously guiding behavior in some cases is one of those purposes.

This suggests that there are different general types of functions that artifacts might perform. The possibility of law being multiply utilizable suggests that there are basic functions and derived functions.[24] The derived functions of law would be those that law could not perform without its being able to perform some basic function which is not derived from other functions. Again, one candidate for a basic function of a legal system would be to guide citizen behavior in such a manner as to keep the peace.

Further, this suggests the familiar but related distinction between law's conceptual and accidental functions. There are certain functions that any artifact of some kind must be capable of performing to count as a thing of that kind; this is its conceptual function. That is, a conceptual function is a function that something of a certain kind must be capable of performing in virtue of the *nature* of things of its kind. To count as a "hammer," something must be capable of whacking a nail into some extended material object. Of course, this is not to deny that some artifacts characterized as hammers are unable to perform that function; a broken hammer will not work. A television might malfunction for some unexpected reason yet still be correctly characterized as a "television"; that it is correctly characterized as "malfunctioning" makes sense only insofar as televisions have some conceptual function.

Likewise, there are certain functions of an artifact that are accidental in the sense that they can be performed only in virtue of having certain characteristics that enable the artifact to perform its conceptual function. One accidental function of a hammer is that it can perform the function of killing another person by bludgeoning that person to death; this it can do only in virtue of

[24] It should be noted that the function of an object can evolve throughout history so that what was once basic is now derivative. For example, a sword, once considered a weapon, is now more commonly used as an honorific object; its use as a weapon is hence now derivative, rather than basic. I am indebted to Corrado Roversi for this point and distinction.

the design features that make it possible to drive a nail into an extended substance. Insofar as the head of a hammer is hard and heavy enough to drive a metal nail into another hard, extended surface, it is hard and heavy enough to cause fatal injury to a person using the same motions used to drive a nail into a wall. A hammer that is broken in virtue of the head being irreparably detached from its handle might be able to cause fatal injury (e.g., by throwing it at someone's head), but the cause of that fatal injury will not be a matter of the victim's being "hammered" to death.

As is readily evident, the two distinctions are logically related. While the concepts of a conceptual and a basic function seem clearly different in *intensions* or propositional meanings, they do seem to have the same extensions or reference classes. The class of functions picked out, referred to, or denoted by the term "basic" would seem to be the same class as those picked out, referred to, or denoted by the term "conceptual." Nevertheless, nothing of importance for purposes of this paper turns on this; it is just helpful to understand the various distinctions that might be used to identify the functions of a legal system. What is relevant with respect to the thesis of this paper is the notion of a conceptual function, as this paper is concerned to identify the conceptual function of a legal system.

The project of identifying the conceptual function of an artifact is not as simple as it might first appear. Identifying that function is more than a matter of simply specifying some primary function, *f*, that it is intended to perform. It is also a matter of determining why that artifact is needed to do *f*; that is to say, it is also a matter of determining what *problem that artifact is needed or used to solve*. Although that latter task might be obvious depending on the artifact, it need not always be so. Clearly, the fact that a hammer can drive nails through hard surfaces is a function that is needed because human beings have many reasons to join one hard surface with another using an object like a nail, and that is something that cannot be done without artifacts that can accomplish that in one way or another. We are vulnerable to the elements, so we need shelter that is constructed out of hard, durable substances that can protect us against those elements. It is obvious that a hammer can address that problem by joining large surfaces of wood together to shelter us from natural forces that can cause us harm. The reason that there is little reason to make much noise about this in the case of a hammer is that: (1) it is obvious; and (2) the philosophical project of specifying the nature of a hammer is just not that important.

Identifying the conceptual function of law presents a different problem of much greater philosophical importance. Indeed, the philosophical project of specifying the nature of law is of substantial theoretical interest because of what law does in our lives—namely, constrains our freedom by limiting what acts can legally be performed. This, of course, implicates a variety of normative and descriptive philosophical issues of importance.

At first glance, it might not be obvious what problem law is needed to solve. Consider, for example, the issue of identifying the conceptual function of a rule of recognition. Clearly, the function is to guide the behavior of officials in making, changing, and adjudicating law. But it might not be obvious what problem the rule of recognition is needed to solve. Anticipating an important but underappreciated issue, Jules Coleman argued that the rule of recognition was needed to solve a coordination problem if law was to be possible; however, he later abandoned the view that the rule should be regarded as a coordination convention, in essence, because he realized that it matters a great deal, morally and politically, how a rule of recognition provides for the legislative and adjudicative function.[25] As Andrei Marmor persuasively argued, people are not comparatively indifferent to how a rule of recognition coordinates such activities as long it succeeds in doing so.[26] As he puts the point, "it does matter to us who makes the law in our society, and how it is done."[27] What problem a rule of recognition solves is, clearly, of a very different nature than the problem of which side of the road people should drive on.

Nevertheless, Coleman makes an important observation about law in the same discussion. In particular, he notices that there must be some problem that *law* is contrived to solve (the rule of recognition being needed, on his view, to enable officials to solve that problem)—and one that, on my view, is largely correct and gestures in the direction of the problem that a *legal system* is needed to solve by subjecting human conduct to regulation by legal norms:

> If Hobbes is right, then the state of nature is a situation that may best be modeled game theoretically as a prisoners' dilemma. Law provides a potential solution to the prisoners' dilemma. But law can solve this problem only if legal authority is possible; and legal authority is possible, on Hart's view, only if there is a rule of recognition that sets out criteria of legality and imposes a duty on officials to apply the norms that satisfy those criteria. *The rule of recognition does not solve the prisoners' dilemma. Law solves that problem.* Instead, the rule of recognition solves a coordination problem that must be solved if law is to be possible.[28]

[25] Jules Coleman, *The Practice of Principle* (Oxford University Press 2001) 92–5.

[26] Andrei Marmor, *Social Conventions: From Language to Law* (Princeton University Press 2009) 169–71.

[27] Ibid. 171.

[28] Coleman, *The Practice of Principle* (n. 25) 93. Coleman goes on to suggest that law need not be viewed as the solution to any problem: "[W]e need not regard law as a solution to any sort of problem at all—let alone one that can be modeled game-theoretically. Law may exist in order to make more determinate the requirements of a shared political morality, or to organize society in a way that enables individuals to be responsible for the lives they lead. Or law can create an efficient scheme of production and distribution." Coleman, ibid. It seems clear that all these other uses are intended to solve some kind of problem—if not one that can be modeled game-theoretically.

Although Coleman goes on to reject the claim that law solves a prisoners' dilemma problem, I argue below that the problem a legal system solves is something like the problem posed by the so-called state of nature (though I have nothing to say about whether it is best described or modeled as a prisoners' dilemma), and that this must be taken into account in specifying the conceptual function of a legal system.

4. The Conceptual Function of a Legal System

As already noted, this chapter is concerned with the conceptual function of law *qua* legal system, and not law *qua* norm, but the reference class of the term "legal system" depends on the breadth of the relevant concept of law that underlies it. "Law" can be used in a broad sense that would encompass the rules of a chess association. Thus construed, a chess association would count as a "legal system."

This is not the sense of "law" that is the subject of jurisprudence, conceptual or otherwise. The concept of law of interest to legal theorists, lawyers, and law students concerns institutional entities that exercise broad authority to regulate the behavior of citizens. These institutional entities enact norms that contain what Hart calls the minimum content of the natural law, which include norms that prohibit violence and that regulate property in an orderly way. As Hart puts it, the relevant notion of law applies to municipal entities, which should be construed broadly enough to include international law.

Accordingly, the issue is to determine what human problems give rise to a need for institutional normative systems like legal systems. One promising place to start, if somewhat unusual for a conceptual account of a legal system, would be with normative political theory. In particular, it would be helpful to look to normative theories of state legitimacy (i.e., theories intended to state the conditions a legal system must satisfy to be morally justified in regulating behavior) for a sense of what purposes legal systems are intended to serve.

As we saw above, Coleman argues that law should be conceived as solving a problem that arises in a Hobbesian state of nature. Although the problem of surviving in a state of nature as Thomas Hobbes describes it might be an example of a prisoners' dilemma, that characterization seems to understate the problems that arise in the state of nature. The state of nature, as Hobbes and others conceive it, is a pre-social condition of anarchy—one that arises prior to any successful communal living in society and is hence a condition utterly bereft of the benefits of social cooperation. As Hobbes pessimistically describes this condition:

> Hereby it is manifest, that during the time men live without a common Power to keep them all in awe, they are in that condition which is called Warre; and such a warre, as is of every man, against every man .... In such condition, there is no place for Industry; because the fruit thereof is uncertain; and consequently no Culture of the Earth; no Navigation, nor use of the commodities that may be imported by Sea; no commodious Building; no Instruments of moving, and removing such things as require much force; no Knowledge of the face of the Earth; no account of Time; no Arts; no Letters; no Society; and which is worst of all, continuall feare, and danger of violent death; And the life of man, solitary, poore, nasty, brutish, and short.[29]

This terrible state of war of all against all arises, on Hobbes's view, because human beings of roughly equal abilities must compete to survive in a world in which there are not enough material resources to satisfy human needs, much less wants. The war of all against all arises because, whether capable of altruistic motivation or not, human beings are primarily motivated by self-interest and, if pressed, will frequently place their needs above those of others.

Hobbes, of course, utilizes the state of nature to argue that human beings would contract with one another to submit to an absolute sovereign in order to keep the peace among human beings. Keeping the peace is a necessary precondition for being able to engage in the socially cooperative activities that enable us to increase the quantity and quality of material resources available for human sustenance and comfort. Since human beings are conceived to be rationally self-interested, Hobbes argues that pre-societal schemes of cooperation are not possible because human beings cannot trust each other not to defect on such schemes, leading to more conflict. This is why, as Coleman points out, the state of nature can be conceived as presenting a prisoners' dilemma—indeed, of the worst imaginable type.

Although Hobbes utilizes this anarchic condition as a way of arguing that an absolute monarchy is morally legitimate (i.e., morally justified) on hypothetically consensual grounds, the social-contract strategy he employs gestures in the direction of identifying the conceptual function of a legal system. The point of the agreement, on Hobbes's theory, is to solve a problem that arises in the pre-social anarchic condition—namely, how to keep the peace among self-interested beings likely to resort to violence to solve conflicts over resources in a world of material scarcity.

[29] Thomas Hobbes, *Leviathan* (first published 1651, Classic Books 2017) 84, 85; available online at <http://www.gutenberg.org/files/3207/3207-h/3207-h.htm#link2HCH0013> accessed August 7, 2017.

It is important to note here that such conflicts are not limited to the usual items needed to feed, water, and shelter persons in a fashion they find acceptable. Such conflicts can arise over mates, as people frequently find themselves competing for the same male or female for sexual companionship. Murder is an all-too-common, if utterly counterproductive and unhelpful, response to a person's (nearly always a heterosexual man) not getting or being able to retain the companionship of someone whose companionship he wants. In an anarchic condition with people being what they are, the probability of violent conflicts is quite high. On Hobbes's view, what justifies the state in asserting coercive authority over subjects is that they would consent to such authority as a means of keeping the peace between them—and this suggests that the very point of a legal system is to keep the peace by creating norms that guide behavior in a way that succeeds minimally in keeping the peace.

Hobbes's conception of the state of nature is somewhat problematic for my purposes in two respects. First, he assumes that human beings in the state of nature are incapable of altruistic motivations. Second, the state of nature is utterly pre-societal in character and hence lacks all the benefits of social cooperation that we have at our disposal today—including all the technological advancements that have enabled us to grow the stock of material resources to quantities that Hobbes likely could not have predicted.

More contemporary versions of social contract theories of legitimacy modify these unrealistic conceptions of an anarchic social condition. Robert Nozick begins from more plausible assumptions about human motivations and about the anarchic condition in order to identify the legitimizing purpose or point of the state. On his view:

> If one could show that the state would be superior even to this most favored situation of anarchy, the best that realistically can be hoped for, or would arise by a process involving no morally impermissible steps, or would be an improvement if it arose, this would provide a rationale for the state's existence; it would justify the state.[30]

Notice that, as Nozick describes it, his argument is intended to provide a moral justification by identifying a "rationale" for the state's existence, which would presumably be the problem that it is contrived to solve.

In this favored situation of anarchy, Nozick rejects the Hobbesian assumption that social cooperation and moral behavior among human beings is impossible. Nozick's conception of the state of nature conceives it as one in which "people generally satisfy moral constraints and generally act as they should."[31] Although Nozick says little about the other conditions of the state

[30] Robert Nozick, *Anarchy, State, and Utopia* (Reprint edn., Basic Books 2013) 5.

[31] Ibid. 4.

of nature, he seems to be defining a condition that is as much like ours as is possible given the absence of a legal system to do the things that legal systems characteristically do.

Even at this early stage in Nozick's discussion, it becomes clear what the point or purpose of a legal system is ("legitimizing rationale," as he might put it)—namely, to keep the peace among self-interested beings in conditions of material scarcity. Nozick's argument proceeds by describing a series of morally permissible steps that people would take, given plausible assumptions about human psychology, that would culminate in the acceptance of the "minimal state"—a state with laws that protect only the natural moral rights to life, liberty, and property, as Locke conceived them. The very limits that Nozick believes morally constrain what the state can do indicate that, on his view, the point of the state is to keep the peace.

Nozick's discussion proceeds in terms of persons voluntarily forming a series of associations ("protective associations") designed to protect them from attacks on their persons or property. Insofar as the protective associations are intended to protect from assaults originating outside the group, they are intended to promote a peaceful life within the group. One of the problems, however, with the simplest association is that it lacks a means to resolve conflicts among members of the association. While it promotes peace among members of the resulting society by protecting them from assaults by non-members, it is not fully successful in keeping the peace because it lacks effective mechanisms for resolving potentially violent conflicts among members of the group. Accordingly, these associations evolve in scope and sophistication until the result is an institutional normative system that is morally constrained to limit interference with freedom by laws that protect only the natural rights to life, liberty, and property.

Accordingly, Nozick's view assumes the basic rationale or function of the state is to keep the peace. The state's performance of this conceptual function, however, is limited by considerations of political morality, on Nozick's view, to promulgating laws that protect the natural moral rights to life, liberty, and property. Any coercive taxation for the purpose of redistributing the scarce material resources of a society, which is a frequent cause of conflict in our world, is morally illegitimate. Thus, while Nozick is clear in taking the rationale or function of a state to be keeping the peace, it is likewise clear that he believes that there are only so many things that can legitimately be done to achieve this.

This is not an implausible idea. A totalitarian regime with a police presence capable of monitoring all communications and actions would do a better job of keeping the peace than a legitimate state that protects privacy rights. If one knows that the state is effectively monitoring all one's communications and actions, one is less likely to attempt a violent crime. That is one reason that convenience stores have hard-to-miss cameras recording what happens in the store. It is also one reason that people favor the use of video cameras on the streets to monitor the actions of citizens.[32] Indeed, such results seem to suggest that people are willing to trade some protected rights for increased security. Once again, it appears that the primary function of the state is best conceived as the enterprise of keeping the peace.

This would also appear to be true of systems of international law—even if the relevant institutions are not properly characterized as a "state," strictly speaking. International law differs from paradigmatic cases of municipal law in that the subjects of first-order legal norms are nations, rather than citizens. But the idea that the point of international law is to keep the peace among nations, rather than to keep the peace among citizens of a nation, is equally plausible. After all, ordinary crime in a municipality is nowhere near as socially disruptive as wars between nations. It seems eminently plausible to think that systems of international law are intended to guide nations so as to minimize conflicts that might lead to war.

A similar idea of the conceptual function of a legal system emerges in utilitarian theories of legitimacy. John Stuart Mill, for example, argued that the only purpose for which liberty can legitimately be restricted is to protect harm to others. In a justly famous passage, he asserts:

> The object of this Essay is to assert one very simple principle, as entitled to govern absolutely the dealings of society with the individual in the way of compulsion and control, whether the means used be physical force in the form of legal penalties, or the moral coercion of public opinion. That principle is, that the sole end for which mankind are warranted, individually or collectively, in interfering with the liberty of action of any of their number, is self-protection. That the only purpose for which power can be rightfully exercised over any member of a civilised community, against his will, is to prevent harm to others. His own good, either physical or moral, is not a sufficient warrant. He cannot rightfully be compelled to do or forbear because it will be better for him to do so, because it will make him happier, because, in the opinions of others, to do so would be wise, or even right. These are good reasons for remonstrating with him, or reasoning with him, or persuading him, or entreating him, but not for compelling him, or visiting him with any evil in case he do otherwise. To justify that, the conduct from which it is desired to deter him must be calculated to produce evil to someone else. The only part of the conduct of any one, for which he is amenable to society, is that which concerns others. In the part which merely concerns himself, his independence is, of right, absolute. Over himself, over his own body and mind, the individual is sovereign.[33]

[32] In a recent poll, 78 percent of people in the US favor the use of such cameras. Mark Landler and Dalia Sussman, "Poll finds strong acceptance of public surveillance," *New York Times* (April 30, 2013) <http://www.nytimes.com/2013/05/01/us/poll-finds-strong-acceptance-for-public-surveillance.html?_r=0> accessed August 7, 2017.

[33] John Stuart Mill, *On Liberty* (Ticknor and Fields 1863) 23.

As is readily evident, the very point of the state is to keep the peace by exercising "power" to enact laws that protect people from harming one another in attempts to solve conflicts.

Intriguingly, Lord Patrick Devlin's view that the state may legitimately enact laws to protect society's shared morality presupposes that the state's function is to keep the peace.[34] Devlin believes that such enactments are justified because what binds a society as a whole is a shared morality so vital to society that any threats to it are threats to the very existence of the society itself. Protecting the shared morality is simply another mechanism for protecting against conflicts that might breach the peace.

As an exhaustive survey of theories of legitimacy is neither needed nor possible here, two more brief examples should be sufficient to secure the point. If one takes a more expansive utilitarian view, as Henry Sidgwick did,[35] one might think that the state's legitimate authority permits the state to enact any laws that have the effect of maximizing utility, which might, depending on the circumstances, allow for the use of redistributional mechanisms that Nozick rejects on principle. Similarly, one might argue, as Robert George does, that the state need not, as a matter of morality, confine itself to merely protecting citizens from being harmed by others; it may legitimately enact laws that serve to improve the character of citizens. But one clear benefit of maximizing utility or improving the character of citizens is to reduce the likelihood of self-help recourse to violent means of resolving conflicts. In every such case, the function of the legal system is defined in terms that include keeping the peace.

As far as normative political philosophy is concerned, the problem of legitimacy arises in connection with how a legal system may *permissibly* do what it is characteristically used to do—namely, keep the peace. Different theories might disagree on what steps are morally justified in doing so, but all presuppose that the basic function of the state, regardless of whether the state-of-nature device is used, is to prevent self-interested human beings from resorting to violence, as we are frequently prone to do, to resolve conflicts. In a world like ours with beings like us, violent conflicts are nearly inevitable—and those conflicts have significant effects on others who are nearby. And, as noted above, the same analysis seems applicable to the institutions of international law.

[34] Lord Patrick Devlin, *The Enforcement of Morals* (Oxford University Press 1970).
[35] Henry Sidgwick, *The Methods of Ethics* (MacMillan 1874).

Notably, a legal system is needed in Joseph Raz's society of angels for the same reason. As Raz describes them, the angels are "rational beings (. . .) who have, and who would acknowledge that they have, more than enough reasons to obey the law regardless of sanctions"[36]—although they are neither morally perfect nor morally impeccable. Indeed, the "angels," on Raz's characterization, are not really angels at all, as that notion is traditionally conceived:

> We should not think of the imagined society as a community of self-denying saints. Its members pursue their self-interest when they think they are right to do so, and they may be wrong.[37]

The angels, thus, instantiate two characteristics that are likely to lead to conflicts that might breach the peace: self-interest and moral imperfection.

In the society of angels, law is needed, on Raz's view, because conflicts can arise among the angels that require resolution by an authority that all angels, by assumption, are disposed to obey. As Raz observes, "its members may pursue many different and conflicting goals and they may share our difficulties in settling disputes and resolving conflicts by mutual agreements."[38] To coordinate the behavior of angels, Raz holds that "they have, therefore, all the reasons that we have for having legislative authorities and an *executive.*"[39] Further, to resolve conflicts of interests and the disputes that inevitably arise because of them, the angels will also need courts.

While Raz believes that sanctions will not be needed because the angels will be motivated always to obey law (a psychological characteristic that distinguishes them so much from human beings one can legitimately deny the relevance of the example to conceptual jurisprudence[40]), the example, as he describes it, seems to presuppose that *law is needed to keep the peace*. After all, why would an authoritative resolution of a conflict be needed if the angels were unlikely to resort to some socially undesirable self-help means to settle the conflict in the absence of an authority they can trust? The mere fact that sanctions are not needed given the angels' motivations does not entail that the otherwise self-interested angels are incapable of socially disruptive conflicts.

Indeed, it is not clear why an *executive* agency would be needed if the angels are not disposed to such behavior because the function of the executive agency is enforcement of the laws. In any event, the point is not that Raz fails to describe the example in a way that rules out the possibility of socially

[36] Joseph Raz, *Practical Reason and Norms* (Oxford University Press 1999) 159.

[37] Ibid. 160. [38] Ibid. 159. [39] Ibid. (emphasis added).

[40] See, e.g., Kenneth Einar Himma, "Can There be Law in a Society of Angels?"; first draft available online at <https://papers.ssrn.com/sol3/papers.cfm?abstract_id=2839942> accessed August 7, 2017.

disruptive behavior; it is rather that it is hard to see how a need for authoritative resolution of conflicts could be needed among a society of beings utterly *dis*inclined to resort to socially disruptive means of resolving conflict. Even in Raz's society of angels, the problem that law is needed to solve, which defines its conceptual function, seems to be how to keep the angels from breaching the peace.

If one is concerned by the reliance here on normative political theory to derive a conceptual function, it should suffice to note that the views of these theories on the purpose of law conform to ordinary experience. Although, as a contingent practical matter, legal systems can be used to serve a variety of differing purposes from one legal system to the next, it seems clear that the basic purpose in every existing legal system is to keep the peace. One cannot use, for example, a legal system to consolidate one's power or to keep a minority oppressed unless it succeeds in keeping the peace. Further, given what we know about human beings, such as we are at this point in time, a total suspension of law is likely to result in a coast-to-coast violent free-for-all.

Accordingly, it is reasonable to conclude that the problem that a legal system is contrived to solve is how to keep the peace among self-interested beings likely to breach that peace and hence that the conceptual function of a legal system is to prevent such breaches. Of course, the characteristic means by which legal systems do so is through the regulation of behavior by promulgating and applying norms. Thus, the conceptual function of a legal system—which it must have in virtue of its being artifactual in character—is most plausibly thought to be to keep the peace among self-interested beings—or entities like states, in the case of international law—likely to resort to socially disruptive means of resolving conflicts by subjecting their conduct to the governance of rules.

5. Keeping the Peace and Authorized Coercion

In the last section, I argued that the conceptual function of a legal system (as opposed to a legal norm) is to regulate behavior as a means of keeping the peace—i.e., to minimize potential violent conflicts among self-interested beings. As it turns out, this conception of law's conceptual function can be made more specific by considering how, conceived as a distinctively human institution, law characteristically functions to keep the peace. In particular, I argue that, thus conceived, law can efficaciously keep the peace only by backing some legal norms with authorized coercive enforcement mechanisms.

In this connection, it would be quite helpful to consider Ronald Dworkin's view on the conceptual function of a legal system. On Dworkin's view, the point of a *legal system* is to provide a moral justification for the use of a society's coercive enforcement mechanisms, but that justification is holistic in the sense that it depends on the moral quality of a society's legal practices considered as a whole.[41] As Dworkin defines "law," "[t]he law of a community ... is the scheme of rights and responsibilities that meet that complex standard [namely, providing a moral justification for use of society's coercive force]: they license coercion because they flow from the past decisions of the right sort."[42] Law's conceptual function is, thus, an irreducibly moral one, on his view.[43]

As is readily evident, Dworkin's view of the conceptual function of law presupposes that it is a conceptually necessary feature of a legal system that it includes authorized coercive enforcement mechanisms for some violations of law. The conceptual function of a legal system could not be to provide a moral justification for use of the state's coercive mechanisms unless it is a conceptually necessary feature of a legal system that it authorizes coercive enforcement mechanisms for some violations of law. After all, coercive enforcement mechanisms cannot be *legally applied* unless they are legally authorized. Thus, Dworkin's view of law's conceptual function presupposes that it is a conceptually necessary feature of a legal system that coercive enforcement mechanisms are legally authorized for some violations of law.

On any plausible methodology for conceptual jurisprudence, that is a reasonable position to take. After all, we know of no existing legal system, past or present, that lacks authorized coercive enforcement mechanisms for some violations of law. Whether one adopts a purely descriptive or normative conceptual methodology, an analysis of *our* concept of law will have to be grounded in empirical observations of paradigmatic instances of *our* legal practices. The content of *our* concepts is constructed by our social practices, which include, in this case, legal and linguistic practices. Accordingly, the content of our concepts is determined by intersubjective practices, which entails that the relevant content is determined by mind-dependent considerations pertaining to language and legal usage. It is thus a mistake to think that the content of our concepts is *objective* in the sense that the content is wholly

[41] Ronald Dworkin, *Law's Empire* (Harvard University Press 1986) 93, 109, 127.

[42] Ibid. 93.

[43] Similarly, Larry Alexander believes that the conceptual function of law is a moral one; as he puts it, "the role of law is to make moral requirements more determinate." Larry Alexander, "All or Nothing at All?" in Andrei Marmor (ed.), *Law and Interpretation: Essays in Legal Philosophy* (Clarendon Press 1995) 360.

fixed or determined by mind-independent considerations and hence those that have nothing to do with what human beings believe, desire, or do.

Indeed, the idea that we could have reliable intuitive access to the content of wholly objective concepts is as implausible as the idea that we could have reliable intuitive access to objective laws of morality; intuitionism as a conceptual epistemology is as implausible as intuitionism as a moral epistemology. Whether or not one holds the view that there is, or should be, a normative element to conceptual methodology, no such methodology could be plausible without being grounded in observations and explications of the relevant intersubjective practices. In the case of law, no such methodology could be plausible without being grounded in observations of what *we* take to be paradigmatic features of law as those features are expressed in *our* legal (and corresponding linguistic) practices, which, as Raz points out, construct the content of our legal concepts.

If this is correct, then Dworkin's view of the conceptual function of law is vulnerable to objection. The problem arises because Dworkin's view presupposes that the officials who make, adjudicate, and enforce law *necessarily* believe it to be morally legitimate and act so as to ensure the law's legitimacy; otherwise, the conceptual purpose of law could not be to legitimate the use of coercion. Although it is surely true that, as an empirical matter, officials and subjects tend to view their legal systems as legitimate, this need not be so. As Hart points out, it would be implausible to think it is a conceptually necessary feature of law either that officials accept the rule of recognition for moral reasons or that citizens view the legal system as legitimate. If that were true, then a system resembling the U.S. legal system in every respect compatible with: (1) officials accepting the rule of recognition for purely personal reasons; and (2) citizens merely acquiescing to the legal system would be conceptually disqualified as counting as a "legal system." Such a result is a *reductio* of any view that logically implies it.

But, for our purposes, the more important question is this. Assuming authorized coercive enforcement mechanisms are a conceptually necessary feature of law, as Dworkin plausibly assumes given the prominence of such mechanisms in every existing legal system, the question is what reason we have to think *we* need an institutional normative system that includes authorized coercive enforcement mechanisms. Why couldn't beings like us simply make do with an institutional normative system that resembles the institution that Raz believes is sufficient to regulate behavior in the society of angels?

The answer to that question has to do with the conspicuous difficulties of bringing beings like us together (or nations) in communities that enable them to reap the benefits of cooperative social living (or cooperative co-existence). Unlike the self-interested angels who are conclusively motivated to obey law, self-interested human beings are not conclusively motivated to do so. It is not just the Holmesian bad man that causes the problem, here, although the existence of such persons is probably inevitable until all root causes of social conflict can be eliminated. It is also that good people are frequently motivated to disobey laws they believe are unjust or unfair—either for moral reasons or for prudential reasons. The supposition that Raz's self-interested angels are not willing to disobey either wicked laws for moral reasons or good laws for prudential reasons calls into question whether the needs of such theoretically alien beings can tell us anything of significance about the concept of a legal system that is, on his view, constructed by *our* legal practices.[44]

The reason beings like *us* need legal systems to keep the peace in a world like ours, as suggested in the last section, is that beings like us are likely to resolve conflicts of self-interest by recourse to violent self-help methods that breach the very peace necessary to achieve the benefits of social living, which provides the motivation for living together in the first place. It is probably true that every person gets angry when he or she feels wronged. It is probably also true that most people tend to think that moral complaints against them are false, and they respond with anger when they are charged with a moral offense. The likely result of such conflicts is mutual anger, and mutual anger tends to exacerbate social conflicts, rather than resolve them.

This is not to say that every conflict that leads to anger is likely to lead to violence. But once parties to a conflict become angry, that conflict gets worse and frequently leads to acts that all parties come to regret. It is surely true that the vast majority of angry conflicts remain non-violent and simply lead to hurt feelings that must be repaired for the relationship to continue.

But there can be no question that beings like us easily find cause for acts that can breach the peace in various ways. Here are four of many germane statistics, compiled by the Peace Alliance, about our propensity for violence that creates the need for law to keep the peace by sometimes utilizing authorized coercive enforcement mechanisms:

[1] Violence causes more than 1.6 million deaths worldwide every year. Violence is one of the leading causes of death in all parts of the world for persons ages 15 to 44. [Krug EG et al., eds. World report on violence and health. Geneva, World Health Organization, 2002. Via CDC] ....

[2] 35 percent of women worldwide—more than one in three—said they had experienced violence in their lifetime, whether physical, sexual, or

[44] See Himma, "Can There be Law in a Society of Angels?" (n. 40) for further development of this line of criticism.

both. One in 10 girls under the age of 18 was forced to have sex. [UN Report on violence against women worldwide, 2015] ....

[3] The world spends just $1 on conflict prevention for every $1,885 it spends on military budgets. Here in the U.S., less than 2 percent of income tax goes to civilian foreign affairs agencies; meanwhile, 39 percent goes to the military. And though taxpayers provide almost $1 billion per year for military academies, they pay only about $40 million for the United States Institute of Peace—the only U.S. agency dedicated to conflict prevention and peacebuilding. [Friends Committee on National Legislation report, *Prevention is 60:1 Cost Effective*, 2011] ....

[4] The 20th century was one of the most violent periods in human history. An estimated 191 million people lost their lives directly or indirectly as a result of conflict, and well over half of them were civilians ....[45]

And all this in a world *already* carved up into separate legal systems that *have* authorized coercive mechanisms in a variety of forms, including armies and police agencies. Although it is true that many of these legal systems are themselves wickedly violent, it is reasonable to surmise that these statistics would be much worse without legal systems providing for mechanisms of conflict resolution backed by authorized coercive enforcement mechanisms.[46]

As normative political philosophers have realized, the problem of violent conflict among self-interest beings like us is the problem that legal systems with authorized coercive enforcement mechanisms are intended to solve. There is no reason to think that much about whether the institutional normative system in Raz's society of angels is morally legitimate because we are not like beings like that. Our world is very different, and it is the practices of *our* legal systems that pose the moral problem of justification—as well as determine the content of *our* legal concepts.

[45] "Statistics on Violence and Peace," *The Peace Alliance*; available at <http://peacealliance.org/tools-education/statistics-on-violence/> accessed August 7, 2017.

[46] The norms of international law authorize coercive enforcement mechanisms, such as economic sanctions, for some violations of norms of international law. See, e.g., Frederic Kirgis, "Enforcing International Law" 1 (January 22, 1996) *ASIL Insights*; available at <https://www.asil.org/insights/volume/1/issue/1/enforcing-international-law> accessed August 7, 2017. As Kirgis points out, international law contains such mechanisms, which include "sanctions [that] may be economic (such as a trade embargo against a country threatening the peace), diplomatic (such as severance of diplomatic relations) or military (the use of armed force to maintain or restore international peace)." Indeed, the very first sentence of this chapter asks the common question (which seems to presuppose the intuition that law is essentially coercive in the sense in which I explicate it), "Nearly always, the first question asked about international law is, [']How can it be law if it cannot be enforced[']?" The second sentence states his answer: "To experienced international lawyers it is an old and rather tiresome question, not only because it is asked so often, but also because of the crucial assumption it contains. The assumption, of course, is that international law cannot be enforced."

In this connection, it should be noted that the problem of moral legitimacy either does not arise in a system without coercion or is of little practical importance. Without authorized coercive enforcement mechanisms, law merely issues commands or directives that are, so to speak, hollow. It might be rude for you to (try to) direct (or command) me to do *p*. But, without a threat of violence, there is no moral problem of any import that requires a solution. As far as I can see, regardless of the content of *p*, merely commanding or directing me to do *p* poses a problem of little moral interest or significance. Once the command is backed by coercion, however, the scope and significance of the problem change dramatically.

It is when those directives are backed by authorized coercive enforcement mechanisms that the content of those directives make some moral difference with respect to what is legitimately demanded. It is clearly worse for you to point a gun at me and say, "give me your money," than it is to point a gun at me and say, "wipe your nose"—although both are clearly problematic from a moral point of view. The problem of the *limits* of what law can justifiably dictate by way of behavior becomes a problem of content when that content is backed by authorized coercive enforcement mechanisms. Indeed, that is what all non-skeptical theories of political legitimacy do—i.e., identify the limits of what legal content may justifiably be backed by authorized coercive enforcement mechanisms.

The problems of legality and legitimacy are, of course, distinct problems. But it is hard to justify the idea that the concept of law that gives rise to the normative problems of political philosophy should be so far removed from the obvious facts about us and our world that create the problem that legal systems are needed to solve. While the problematizing case of international law once called into doubt whether it is a conceptually necessary feature of law that legal systems authorize coercive enforcement mechanisms for some violations of law, it is hard to see how anything in the legal practices that construct our concept of law would suggest that there are legal systems in the society of angels.

The conceptual explication of law that most coheres with: (1) the facts of the human reality that gives rise to the need for law; (2) the concerns of officials, law students, and citizens; and (3) the problem of moral legitimacy to which legality gives rise is one that views the conceptual function of a legal system as keeping the peace by enacting norms that are, at least in part, backed by authorized coercive enforcement mechanisms. Law, as we conceive and practice it, is a distinctively human enterprise that responds to problems that arise only in connection with beings like us who live in circumstances, like we do, of material scarcity. And that distinctively human enterprise, as a matter of conceptual necessity, requires the authorization of coercive enforcement mechanisms to achieve its purpose of keeping the peace.

PART III

NORMATIVITY

8

Obligations from Artifacts

*Brian H. Bix**

1. Introduction

A persistent question in modern legal philosophy is whether or how (human-created) legal rules and legal systems can produce moral obligations for citizens. As a threshold matter, this is an issue that derives from the "is-ought" ("fact/value") distinction: How can *the fact* that legal officials have acted in a certain way change our *moral* reasons for action?[1] Contemporary theorists have sought answers to this problem in the ideas of conventions,[2] coordination problems,[3] and plans.[4] Some theorists argue that the law—that all legal rules—create general and at-least-presumptive moral obligations; others argue that the law, at best, occasionally triggers pre-existing moral obligations—some legal rules creating moral obligations for some people. This chapter will explore the issue of how and when law creates moral obligations, and will also consider a more recent approach to the nature of law which has raised doubts regarding whether the law is in fact artifactual in the way most theorists (and most citizens) believe.

* I am grateful for the comments and suggestions of Kenneth Einar Himma and Luka Burazin.

[1] Facts can create other sorts of reasons in a straightforward way: for example, (the fact of) a threat (including a legal threat of sanction for non-compliance) can create *prudential* reasons for acting in compliance; and (the fact of) an offer to help us achieve our goals (including power-conferring legal norms relating to wills, trusts, and contracts) can give us *instrumental* reasons to act.

[2] See Jules Coleman, "Negative and Positive Positivism" (1982) 11 *Journal of Legal Studies* 139; Gerald J. Postema, "The Normativity of Law" in Ruth Gavison (ed.), *Issues in Contemporary Legal Philosophy* (Clarendon Press 1987) 81–104; Andrei Marmor, "The Conventional Foundations of Law" in Stefano Bertea and George Pavlakos (eds.), *New Essays on the Normativity of Law* (Hart Publishing, 2011) 143–57 (analysis that relies on distinctions between coordination and constitutive conventions, and between deep and surface conventions).

[3] See John M. Finnis, "Law as Co-ordination" (1989) 2 *Ratio Juris* 97.

[4] See Scott J. Shapiro, *Legality* (Harvard University Press 2011).

Law as an Artifact. First Edition. Edited by Luka Burazin, Kenneth Einar Himma, and Corrado Roversi. Chapter 8 © Brian H. Bix 2018. Published 2018 by Oxford University Press.

Section 2 looks at the general issue of normativity and the fact/value distinction. Section 3 surveys the views of important legal philosophers on the normativity of law, including M.B.E. Smith, Joseph Raz, and John Finnis. Section 4 considers some more recent views, which offer a different understanding of the normativity of law, while complicating the view of law as an artifact.

2. Artifacts and Normativity

By "artifact," I mean an intended human product: not something found in nature, independent of human efforts, and not an accidental by-product of some other intended action or production.[5] Legal systems are (or are primarily[6]) artifacts, in the sense that they are social standards and social practices created by human beings for a purpose, or a variety of purposes—order, control, guidance, promoting the good, facilitating autonomy and cooperation, etc.

There is, to be sure, significant variety among the ways law is understood and how it is characterized: e.g., law as a set or system of norms (a view associated with Hans Kelsen,[7] among others), law as commands of a sovereign to its subjects (a view associated with John Austin),[8] and law as a form of practical reasoning (a view associated, to some degree, with both John Finnis and Joseph Raz[9]). However, all of these views of law converge in seeing the norms or reasons for action created by law as deriving from the purposive (or mostly purposive[10]) actions of officials, acting within established social structures and social practices.[11]

[5] See Luka Burazin, "Can There Be an Artifact Theory of Law" (2016) 29 *Ratio Juris* 385, 388; Kenneth M. Ehrenberg, *The Functions of Law* (Oxford University Press 2016) 150.

[6] With law, there is also the question of how to treat customary law (in those legal systems that recognize customary law), as it is not a form of law that seems to have an author. Jonathan Crowe, "Law as an Artifact Kind" (2014) 40 *Monash University Law Review* 737, 739. Though some might argue that customary legal rules still are artifactual, in the sense that the customs are only treated as (legal) rules at the point where a person in authority recognizes them as such. Cf. Burazin, "Can There Be an Artifact Theory of Law" (n. 5) 395.

[7] See Hans Kelsen, *Pure Theory of Law* (University of California Press 1967); Hans Kelsen, *Introduction to the Problems of Legal Theory* (B.L. Paulson and S.L. Paulson, trans., Clarendon Press 1992).

[8] See John Austin, *The Province of Jurisprudence Determined* (Wilfried E. Rumble ed., Cambridge University Press 1995).

[9] See, e.g., John Finnis, *Natural Law and Natural Rights* (2nd edn., Oxford University Press 2011); John Finnis, *Philosophy of Law (Collected Essays: Vol. IV)* (Oxford University Press 2011); Joseph Raz, *Ethics in the Public Domain* (Clarendon Press 1994).

[10] The possible exceptions are customary law (see n. 6 above), and certain basic moral norms that some legal theorists claim are part of law even without any social source. See Section 3.5, below.

[11] Cf. Burazin, "Can There Be an Artifact Theory of Law" (n. 5) 385–6.

The question is how one can go from the social facts that ground the existence of a legal system and the validity of individual legal norms, to conclusions about what individuals should do (as a matter of morality). The inquiry is motivated in part by the claim (often associated with David Hume[12]) that there is a sharp division between "is" and "ought," that one cannot derive any conclusion about what should be done based *solely* on premises stating what is the case. To put the same point a different way, under this analysis, one cannot reach a normative conclusion—a conclusion about what ought to be done, or what state of affairs ought to be brought about—without there being a normative premise.

If we do not always see the need for a normative premise in our own reasoning, it may be because our normative premises are often unstated—and not expressly argued for—because they seem too obvious or uncontroversial. For example, from the premise that "doing X will create no benefit, but will cause suffering to innocent babies," it is *not* sufficient to conclude: "one should not do X." One needs also the uncontroversial (we hope) premise: "do not cause the innocent to suffer, at least without there being some significant benefit achieved." Comparably, it does not follow from any of the following premises alone—"the creator-God commanded that one not do X" or "X is (statistically?) 'abnormal' " or "everyone thinks that doing X is wrong"—that one ought not to do X. One would need a normative premise, stating that one ought to do whatever the creator-God commands,[13] that one ought to follow the (statistical) norm, and that one ought to act in accordance to the

[12] Hume wrote: "In every system of morality, which I have hitherto met with, I have always remark'd, that the author proceeds for some time in the ordinary way of reasoning, and establishes the being of a God, or makes observations concerning human affairs; when of a sudden I am surpriz'd to find, that instead of the usual copulations of propositions, is, and is not, I meet with no proposition that is not connected with an ought, or an ought not. This change is imperceptible; but is, however, of the last consequence. For as this ought, or ought not, expresses some new relation or affirmation, 'tis necessary that it shou'd be observ'd and explain'd; and at the same time that a reason should be given, for what seems altogether inconceivable, how this new relation can be a deduction from others, which are entirely different from it . . . [I] am persuaded, that a small attention [to this point] wou'd subvert all the vulgar systems of morality, and let us see, that the distinction of vice and virtue is not founded merely on the relations of objects, nor is perceiv'd by reason." David Hume, *A Treatise of Human Nature* (2nd edn., P.H. Nidditch, ed., Clarendon Press 1978) § 3.1.1 at 469–70. For the different readings of this paragraph, see Rachel Cohon, "Hume's Moral Philosophy" (2010) § 5, in Edward N. Zalta (ed), *The Stanford Encyclopedia of Philosophy* <https://plato.stanford.edu/entries/hume-moral/> accessed August 12, 2017.

[13] Some would think it obvious that one ought to do what God says, given that God (under some theological traditions) is threatening eternal punishment for disobedience. However, thinking of the matter this way makes the "ought" in following divine command a prudential one (one ought to avoid eternal pain and suffering) rather than a moral one.

consensus views of one's community. (How controversial these premises are varies across communities and individuals.)

With law, we have the actions of legal officials who create constitutions, promulgate statutes, and resolve disputes. These are facts; when, if ever, can we draw normative conclusions from them? For some people, the claim that one ought to do what the law requires is no more controversial than the propositions that one ought to do what God commands and that one ought to act the way most people do. However, for others—and for most contemporary philosophers—these are propositions that, at the least, are in need of further argument.

3. Law and Normativity: Some Views

3.1 M.B.E. Smith and Joseph Raz

As M.B.E. Smith reported,[14] until quite recently the consensus among philosophers (not to mention politicians and the general public) had been that there is a general moral obligation to obey the law—or at least a presumptive obligation that could be overridden in the case of significantly unjust laws or some other significant countervailing moral reason to disobey (e.g., going faster than the speed limit to get a dying friend to the hospital).

However, as Smith showed, the arguments offered to support such a general obligation—arguments grounded on consequentialism, consent, gratitude, and fair play/reciprocity—all fell short of justifying such a general obligation (even for generally just legal systems). Much of the time, the arguments would falter in contexts where violating the law had no apparent negative consequences for other citizens or for society in general. In retrospect, it is not surprising that one has moral reasons to obey the law where obedience helps the common good or particular individuals in some significant way, or when disobedience harms the common good or particular individuals in significant ways. It is all those acts of obedience and disobedience when little else is at stake where, perhaps predictably, a moral obligation to do as the law prescribes is harder to prove.

Additionally, Smith offered creative arguments to show that even if there were a general obligation to obey the law, that obligation carries little normative weight.[15] That is, to the extent that there is a general moral obligation

[14] M.B.E. Smith, "Is There a Prima Facie Obligation to Obey the Law?" (1973) 82 *Yale Law Journal* 950, 950.

[15] Ibid. 969–73.

to obey the law, it adds little weight to the existing, independent moral obligations we already have—actions which are morally wrong do not become significantly worse morally if they are also illegal (or significantly *less* wrong if found *not* to violate the law[16]).

Joseph Raz's analysis was similar: showing that while we might have an obligation to obey individual legal rules—because, for example, they were grounded on expertise we lacked or because they solved important coordination problems—there was no basis for asserting that we had a *general* obligation to obey the law.[17] Raz, like Smith, argues that the analysis of the obligation to obey the law must be made, as it were, on a retail basis, rather than wholesale:

> [T]he extent of the duty to obey the law in a relatively just country varies from person to person and from one range of cases to another .... [And] the extent of the obligation depends on factors other than whether the law is just and sensible. It may depend on the expertise of the individual citizen ... or on the circumstances of the occasion for the violation ....[18]

Raz, like Smith, argues that there is no obligation to be found *generally* from legal systems; obligations are to be found, if at all, only from individual legal norms, in particular circumstances, and from the perspective of individual potential rule-followers. In response to an argument made by John Finnis,[19] Raz observed that one should not speak (for example) in the abstract about responses to coordination problems, because in determining whether (say) a legal rule gives us reasons for action *as* a coordination of behavior to tackle a social problem, it matters whether it currently is, or is likely to become, a *successful* basis for coordination. A legal rule responding to pollution that requires the cooperation of most people probably does not create moral obligations for us to act if almost no one else is currently acting as the rule requires. And whether a rule gives a citizen a reason for action based on the scientific evidence on which it was grounded depends on (among other things) the scientific expertise of that citizen. A non-expert in the area may

[16] The example I give to my classes is of those bankers and mortgage brokers who defrauded families of their life savings, but where there were significant questions as to whether the sharp practices in question in fact violated the law. I do not think that the moral culpability of those bad actors varied much depending on what the court ultimately concluded regarding the actions' legality.

[17] Raz, *Ethics in the Public Domain* (n. 9) 325–53; see also Joseph Raz, *The Morality of Freedom* (Clarendon Press 1986) 70–105.

[18] Raz, *Ethics in the Public Domain* (n. 9) 334.

[19] John Finnis, "The Authority of Law in the Predicament of Contemporary Social Theory" (1984) 1 *Notre Dame Journal of Law, Ethics and Public Policy* 115.

have reason to defer, while someone who is expert in the area may have no reason (or less reason) to defer.

For both Smith and Raz, social facts are the ground of *legal* validity for rules. These social facts include matters that are more clearly designated as artifacts (e.g., legislation and judicial decisions) and also matters that are artifactual only in a penumbral or metaphorical sense (e.g., shared attitudes or beliefs[20]). The social fact basis of legal validity is clearer with Raz, who writes at length about his "Sources Thesis"—that the content of law is discernible entirely from social sources.[21] With Smith, the social nature of law is more assumed than argued for. In both cases, however, whatever social facts (or other facts) create the law (valid legal rules), these are not sufficient to automatically or universally create moral facts (that we should obey).

Kenneth Ehrenberg has recently argued that an obligation to obey arises from the collective acceptance of an institution.[22] While I would agree that acceptance of an institution by a sufficient portion of the population affected by it goes to the moral legitimacy of its exercising coercive power over that population, I do not think that it is conclusive as to individuals' obligations to obey. (I thus agree with Raz and Smith[23] that we should reject the classical equation of legitimacy to rule with moral obligation to obey.)

3.2 Shortcuts to Normativity—Conventions and Plans

A number of theorists have offered what one might call "quick fixes" to the question of how law creates moral obligations. However, like most solutions that seem too good to be true, defects or the need for further substantial argument become more evident when these solutions are considered carefully.

3.2.1 Jules Coleman and Brian Leiter

Jules Coleman and Brian Leiter, in a work summarizing and defending the legal positivist approach to law, offer an explanation for "the authority of law" in "convergent behavior." They write:

[20] As with the shared beliefs that ground or constitute Hart's "Rule of Recognition." H.L.A. Hart, *The Concept of Law* (3rd edn., Oxford University Press 2012) ch. 5.

[21] Raz, *Ethics in the Public Domain* (n. 9) 210–11.

[22] See Kenneth Ehrenberg, "Law's Artifactual Nature: How Legal Institutions Generate Normativity" in George Pavlakos and Veronica Rodriguez-Blanco (eds.), *Reasons and Intentions in Law and Practical Agency* (Cambridge University Press 2015) 247–66.

[23] Raz, *Ethics in the Public Domain* (n. 9); Smith, "Is There a Prima Facie Obligation to Obey the Law?" (n. 14).

The authority of the rule of recognition depends ultimately on considerations of coordination and knowledge. The same is true with respect to the authority of rules subordinate to the rule of recognition. With respect to the rule of recognition, officials have reason to coordinate their behavior with what others do, or if they believe that the behavior of others reflects an understanding of what the appropriate standards of validity are.... [With subordinate rules,] the line is between the reasons that already apply to agents and the agents' ground for believing that the law's reasons provide a better avenue for complying with them than they otherwise would have.[24]

The last part of the analysis (as the authors expressly note[25]) follows Raz's argument. However, as discussed above, Raz's argument denies a general obligation to obey the law, holding that moral obligations need to be proven on a case-by-case basis, and whether there is such an obligation is likely to differ significantly from one rule to the next and from one citizen to the next. Additionally, the legal rules cause (or "trigger") moral obligations—when they do—primarily based on pre-existing moral obligations (e.g., moral obligations to further the common good, where this requires social coordination and law is the salient coordinator).

As for the behavior of officials, Coleman and Leiter give two justifications: that legal officials have reason to coordinate their behavior (to avoid "confusion and mayhem"[26]), and that one should follow what others are doing if one thinks that the others are probably getting it right.[27] Officials likely do have obligations to do what their role entails—not a general obligation, like that of citizens, but an obligation arising from a role undertaken. Additionally, though, the reasons for action here would, one would think, be overridden if going along with the other officials meant being complicit with significant injustice.[28]

[24] Jules L. Coleman and Brian Leiter, "Legal Positivism" in Dennis Patterson (ed.), *A Companion to Philosophy of Law and Legal Theory* (2nd edn., Wiley-Blackwell 2010) 228–48, at 244–5.

[25] Coleman and Leiter, "Legal Positivism" (n. 24) 240–1.

[26] Coleman and Leiter, "Legal Positivism" (n. 24) 234.

[27] There are hints here of the Cordorcet Jury Theorem: where individuals have a greater than 50 percent chance of being correct, the greater the number of voters the more likely the majority vote will be correct. See Brian H. Bix, *A Dictionary of Legal Theory* (Oxford University Press 2004) 38 (defining "Condorcet jury theorem"); Coleman and Leiter, "Legal Positivism" (n. 24) 234 (following what others do is instrumental to doing the right thing if one thinks that general agreement on action is a good indication that the action is the right thing to do).

[28] John Finnis argues that convergent official behavior may offer reasons for the officials, but little or no reason for a citizen or advocate, particularly in the case of an unjust law. Finnis writes: "How does this fact of convergent official behavior (...) make the law not merely *accepted as* legally authoritative but actually *authoritative* for [the advocate] or anyone else who recognizes its injustice?" John Finnis, "Natural Law: The Classical Tradition" in Jules Coleman and Scott Shapiro (eds.), *The Oxford Handbook of Jurisprudence and Philosophy of Law* (Oxford University Press 2002) 1–60, at 21 (emphasis in original).

3.2.2 Scott Shapiro

In his recent influential work, *Legality*,[29] Scott Shapiro offered a new and distinctive response to the problems of how law can give us reasons and how the chasm between the "is" of official actions and the "ought" of obligation can be crossed—seeing law as planning. Shapiro (following Michael Bratman) observed that when people create plans—whether plans for the evening or plans for their career—they give themselves reasons for action. And according to Shapiro, law should be seen as planning: not merely that law is *like* planning; but legislation *is*—really, not just metaphorically—planning; statutes are plans.[30]

The idea that one has reasons created by one's plans is already, arguably, a provocative tie between "is" and "ought" and between artifact and obligation: I have made a plan (a human product, a statement of what is the case), and now I ought to do those things consistent with the plan (and avoid those things inconsistent with the plan). Defenders of this plan-focused approach to traverse "is" and "ought" would note that plans here play the same role that "promising" does—promising as another sort of bootstrap method of creating obligations, or at least reasons for action, seemingly out of thin air. If I have made a promise, I have a reason to do those things necessary to keep my promise (and avoid those things that would get in the way).

On first glance, though, promising seems like an easier case for creating obligations or reasons for action: promises are usually thought of as a commitment, a more significant act of will; and, in any event, the norm-creating capacity of promises can be connected to a social practice which authorizes legal or social sanctions for those who invoke that practice (to both respect and encourage reliance on promises). A plan is the merest act of will, and usually involves no third-party reliance; why should one need a special reason to change one's mind about some (perhaps trivial) plan? Of course, the plans Shapiro discusses are not mere casual ideas about how to spend the afternoon: they are detailed, multi-layered, shared plans, often involving "planning about planning," incremental development, and the delegation of further development of the shared plan to other people (officials).

Still, even if one concedes that plans create reasons, one might ask about the *nature* and *weight* of those reasons. Shapiro himself is careful regarding the normative claims that come from plans: he writes that those who have made or "accepted" an individual or shared plan are "bound to heed the plan" "*from the point of view of instrumental rationality*," but not necessarily "from the moral point of view."[31] As with Kelsen's approach (discussed in the next

[29] Scott J. Shapiro, *Legality* (Harvard University Press 2011).
[30] E.g., ibid. 225.
[31] Ibid. 142–3 (emphasis added).

section), there is no need to "accept" the plan of one's legal system, and the question of whether to do so involves the application of moral standards. And even then, the plan-based reasons for action may be relatively weak—a matter of mere instrumental rationality rather than morality.

3.3 Hans Kelsen

Hans Kelsen's influential works[32] on the nature of law are grounded on the division between "is" and "ought." For Kelsen, law is essentially normative, and the mystery is one that is now familiar: How could legal norms be grounded on the social facts of officials' actions? According to his analysis, there is also a second complication and a second barrier to overcome: the difference between what an official may ("subjectively") intend through her actions and its ("objective") normative significance within the legal normative system.[33] There is thus a gap—or perhaps two—between the observable facts of officials acting in certain ways and the legal norms. Looking at the perspective of the "legal scientist," Kelsen argues when people view officials' actions in a normative way, those people have thereby "presupposed" the Basic Norm (*Grundnorm*) of that legal system.

To retrace the argument: according to Kelsen, no artifact—no human action, practice, institution—on its own could ground normativity, without the addition of a higher normative premise. Within a legal system, each legal norm is authorized by a higher or more general legal norm.[34] As one moves from specific norms to more general norms, and from norms to the institutions authorized to create them, and the norms that authorize *those* institutions, the process ultimately ends with the foundational norm of the legal system. And one ought to act consistently with the most specific norm, only if one ought to act consistently with the higher and more basic norm, etc. Thus, Kelsen argues that when one (citizen or legal scientist) views the actions of legal officials normatively, one is implicitly endorsing the Basic Norm.[35] The Basic Norm is the foundational norm of a normative system, the norm that is both logically and chronologically prior to other norms of the system. So the Basic Norm of a religious system might be "do whatever is commanded by the Creator God" and the Basic Norm of a legal system may be "act in accordance with the historically first constitution."

[32] Kelsen, *Pure Theory of Law* (n. 7); Kelsen, *Introductions to the Problems of Legal Theory* (n. 7).

[33] E.g., Kelsen, *Introductions to the Problems of Legal Theory* (n. 7) 8–10.

[34] There are both static and dynamic aspects to the authorization of legal norms, dynamic in that there are norms that authorize law-making bodies to create new legal norms.

[35] Kelsen, *Pure Theory of Law* (n. 7); Kelsen, *Introductions to the Problems of Legal Theory* (n. 7).

In summary, Kelsen's theory is built around the question of how artifacts can lead to obligations, and his intricate and controversial theory displays (if it does not necessarily solve) the problems involved.

3.4 David Enoch

David Enoch's recent writings[36] put forward a view that in many ways overlaps that of Smith and Raz, discussed above. He frames the general question much as this chapter has done:

> [L]aw is at least partially a social matter, its content at least partially determined by social practices.... [H]ow can something social and descriptive in this down-to-earth kind of way be normative?[37]

Enoch's ultimate answer is that the normativity comes not from legal norms, at least not directly. The normativity instead comes from the moral norms that already apply to us. The acts of legal officials still play an important role in determining what moral obligations we have, but the role is as a "trigger," operating at the same level as other facts (e.g., increases in the price of groceries or dangerous weather conditions) that can "trigger" our moral obligations.[38] The path to the moral obligation via law might be various: by creating a sanction, by solving a coordination problem, by creating an expectation, by offering mechanisms for enforcing promises and exchanges, and so on.[39] Legal rules are artifacts that do not *create* our obligations, but only occasion particular duties that arise from the general moral obligations that already apply to us.

3.5 Natural Law Theory and John Finnis

Under Thomas Aquinas's view of law and morality, the rules promulgated by legal officials create a moral obligation ("bind in conscience") if they are just.[40] They are just when they are consistent with the Natural Law, are within

[36] E.g., David Enoch, "Reason-Giving and the Law" in Leslie Green and Brian Leiter (eds.), *Oxford Studies in Philosophy of Law, vol. 1* (Oxford University Press 2011) 1–38.

[37] Ibid. 1 (footnote omitted).

[38] Here and elsewhere in this chapter, I am assuming, for the sake of simplicity in the analysis, that there are objective moral truths and moral duties that apply to us. Obviously, the analysis becomes much different if one's starting point is some version of moral relativism, moral skepticism, or moral nihilism.

[39] Enoch, "Reason-Giving and the Law" (n. 36) 28.

[40] Thomas Aquinas, *The Treatise on Law: St. Thomas Aquinas Summa Theologiae I-II; qq. 90–97* (R.J. Henle, trans., Notre Dame University Press 1993) Question 96, *corpus*. Aquinas states that in the case of a law that does not meet these standards (that is unjust), citizens may disobey if this can be done "without scandal or greater harm." Ibid.

the authority of the official who promulgated them, and do not impose undue burdens.[41] In the Thomistic tradition (as interpreted by John Finnis[42]), law can—but does not always or necessarily—add to our moral reasons for action. For Finnis, the connections between law, fact, and (moral and non-moral) reasons are necessarily complicated:

> To consider law (whether in general or as the law, our law) precisely as reasons rather than as facts involves paying full attention to many facts relevant to judging that one's law-related actions (as legislator, judge, or other subject) are based on sound reasons for action.[43]

For Finnis, as for Aquinas, law slots into our practical reasoning, but not all the time, only contingently, in a way that directly creates moral reasons for action.

One can find another interesting theme about law and artifact in Finnis' work. He argues that there are certain moral norms that are part of law even if never promulgated by a social source, and, indeed, even if there are socially promulgated norms that purport to be contrary.[44] Briefly put, this is the problem of the Nuremberg Trials: Are certain norms (e.g., prohibitions of genocide and other "laws against humanity") part of a legal system—all legal systems—even if the legal system in question does not expressly promulgate them, and even if the system seems to have promulgated norms that authorize their violation? Finnis replies:

> [T]he moral rules applied [at the Nuremberg Trials] were also rules of the 'higher law' applicable in all times and places (and thus in Germany and its territories, before as after the Charter) as a source of argumentation and judgment 'according to law' when the social-fact sources which are the normally dominant and quasi-exclusive source of law are, in justice, inadequate and insufficient guides to fulfilling obligations such as the judicial obligation to do justice according to law, or everyone's obligation to behave with elementary humanity even when under orders not to—even if those orders have intra-systemic legal validity according to the formal or social-fact criteria of some existing legal system.[45]

[41] Ibid.

[42] E.g., Finnis, *Natural Law and Natural Rights* (n. 9); Finnis, *Philosophy of Law* (n. 9). Finnis reading of Aquinas and the Thomistic tradition owes much to the work of German Grisez. See Germain G. Grisez, "The First Principle of Practical Reason: A Commentary on the Summa Theologiae, 1–2, Question 94, Article 2" (1965) 10 *Natural Law Forum* 168.

[43] John Finnis, "Law as Fact and as Reason for Acton: A Response to Robert Alexy on Law's 'Ideal Dimension'" (2014) 59 *American Journal of Jurisprudence* 85, 96.

[44] John Finnis, "Natural Law Theories" (2015) § 3.1.1, in Edward N. Zalta (ed.), *The Stanford Encyclopedia of Philosophy* <https://plato.stanford.edu/entries/natural-law-theories/> accessed August 12, 2017.

[45] Ibid.

This view is clearly controversial, but we need not fully evaluate its merits here. The controversial part of the view is whether certain moral norms can also be considered *legal* norms, despite the absence of any social act. Our concern is the opposite: how and when the social acts that ground and constitute (most) law create moral obligations.[46]

4. Views that Law Is Not an Artifact

A number of articles have been published in recent years putting forward a very different picture of the nature of law, one in which it could well be said that law is not really an artifact at all. In this new approach, associated primarily with Mark Greenberg,[47] law is not a set of norms promulgated by legislatures, administrative agencies, judges, and other lawmakers. Rather, "legal obligations are a certain subset of moral obligations.... [L]aw is the moral impact of the relevant actions of legal institutions."[48]

Under this approach, what legislatures do is not the creation of law, but, at most, the creation of factors that go into the mix, into the process, from which law is a product. One might hear an echo here of the American legal realist, John Chipman Gray, who argued that legislation is not law, but, at most, a *source* of law.[49] Gray's point had been that it was only what judges did that was *really law*. Parallel to the perspective of Oliver Wendell Holmes' "bad man,"[50] Gray is arguing that all that is important to most people (*as law*) is what will be enforced by a court; everything else is irrelevant. However, the point Greenberg et al. are making is different. Greenberg is not trying to bring a more worldly or cynical perspective to the law, the way the American legal realists did. He is responding to the observation and conceptual point that the "standard picture" of law, with legislatures producing law in a direct way, is unsupportable.[51]

[46] Of course, there are those who doubt the existence of (all) moral obligations, or our ability to know of them. However, as noted earlier, debates about moral nihilism and skepticism are far beyond the scope of this chapter.

[47] Mark Greenberg, "The Standard Picture and Its Discontents" in Leslie Green and Brian Leiter (eds.), *Oxford Studies in Philosophy of Law, vol. 1* (Oxford University Press 2011) 39–106; Mark Greenberg, "The Moral Impact Theory of Law" (2014) 123 *Yale Law Journal* 1288; see also Scott Hershovitz, "The End of Jurisprudence" (2015) 124 *Yale Law Journal* 1160.

[48] Greenberg, "The Moral Impact Theory of Law" (n. 47) 1290 (footnotes omitted).

[49] John Chipman Gray, *The Nature and Sources of Law* (Columbia University Press 1909) § 191, at p. 82.

[50] Oliver Wendell Holmes, "The Path of the Law," (1997) 10 *Harvard Law Review* 457, 460–1.

[51] Greenberg, "The Standard Picture and Its Discontents" (n. 47).

This is partly a point that parallels many of Ronald Dworkin's discussions: that through the operation of interpretive norms, including the direct and indirect application of moral norms, what judges apply as "law" is often quite different from what legislatures promulgate.[52] Another part of the analysis is the effort to respond to the general problem discussed in this chapter: How do the actions of legal officials become binding (moral) norms?

There is in a sense a general parallel between the otherwise distinct views of David Enoch, Mark Greenberg, and John Finnis. Each of them focuses on the way that the actions of legal officials might *indirectly* (yet purposefully) create moral obligations, by invoking in some way the (preexisting) moral obligations that already apply to us. At the same time, there are distinct differences. For Finnis, law is primarily (if not exclusively[53]) a matter of human actions, and these human actions, if properly guided, can change our (moral) reasons for action. Law is an artifact that is an "input" into our practical and moral reasoning.[54] For Enoch, legal rules constitute facts that can (but need not) trigger our existing moral obligations.[55] For Greenberg, by contrast, law is *constituted by* the moral norms that are the product of many inputs, including the social sources (artifacts) of official actions.

The notion that law is an artifact is built on the "standard picture" that associates law with statutes and institutions. Other approaches might associate law more with its effects in the world, as Greenberg does in his theory, and as, in a quite different way, the American and Scandinavian legal realists did, when they focused primarily on the effects of purported norms on the behavior of both judges and citizens.[56]

5. Conclusion

In some ways, the most persistent mystery regarding the nature of law is how legal systems and legal rules (appear to) give us moral reasons for action we did not have before. This is mysterious, because we generally believe that there is a chasm between facts—including social facts and human artifacts—and morality. Focusing on law's status as (mostly and on most accounts) artifactual

[52] See, e.g., Ronald Dworkin, *Law's Empire* (Harvard University Press 1986).

[53] As per the issue of the norms for the Nuremberg Trials, discussed above.

[54] John Finnis, "Reflections and Responses" in John Keown and Robert P. George (eds.), *Reason, Morality, and Law: The Philosophy of John Finnis* (Oxford University Press 2013) 459–582, at 554–6.

[55] This is also largely the view of Smith and Raz, as discussed above.

[56] See, e.g., Brian H. Bix, "The American and Scandinavian Legal Realists on the Nature of Norms," (2009) *De Lege* 85.

emphasizes the issue. This mystery motivates most contemporary theoretical approaches to the nature of law—from the various legal positivisms (of Hans Kelsen, Jules Coleman, Brian Leiter, Joseph Raz, and Scott Shapiro) to the natural law theory of John Finnis to the non-artifactual theory of Mark Greenberg. The efforts to solve the mystery have been intricate and sophisticated, but none has, to date, resolved all doubts.

9

Law Is an Institution, an Artifact, and a Practice

Kenneth M. Ehrenberg

1. Introduction

I have recently argued that law is a genre of institutionalized abstract artifact, and that this ontological position suggests that law is best understood in terms of the social functions it performs.[1] (I prefer the term "institutionalized" to "institutional" to suggest that this is something done to the artifact to give it additional properties important to its creators and users.) One point of making this metaphysical claim was to shed light on precisely how social facts like laws can have normative implications. The reason this needed light shed upon it is that drawing such normative implications would generally violate Hume's caution that we not attempt to derive normative conclusions from merely descriptive premises. But the law is frequently described as a social "practice," so the question might arise how these two metaphysical positions can be reconciled. One might reasonably think that artifacts are not generally practices,[2] and wonder how law could be both at the same time. Perhaps more worrisome is the potential category mistake that Hume is warning us against: just as descriptive social facts and normative mandates belong to different ontological categories (preventing us from deriving the latter from the former), normative rules and descriptive practices appear to belong to distinct ontological categories. The aim of this chapter is to investigate the notion of a social practice a bit further and show how it can be reconciled with the idea that law is a genre of artifact. More specifically, we will see how

[1] Kenneth M. Ehrenberg, *The Functions of Law* (Oxford University Press 2016).

[2] Of course many practices involve extensive use of artifacts. See Raimo Tuomela, *The Philosophy of Social Practices: A Collective Acceptance View* (Cambridge University Press 2002) 98.

Law as an Artifact. First Edition. Edited by Luka Burazin, Kenneth Einar Himma, and Corrado Roversi. Chapter 9 © Kenneth M. Ehrenberg 2018. Published 2018 by Oxford University Press.

locating the law within the metaphysical genre of artifacts allows us to say that it is a set of (normative) rules that is also a (descriptive) practice.

2. Law: Social Practices and the Practice Theory of Rules

H.L.A. Hart gives us a practice theory of certain rules. The rules he was most concerned with explaining using this theory were basic validity rules (such as his "rule of recognition"), which set forth the conditions under which certain historical actions taken by certain people (given a special status by such rules) were to be deemed as creating valid legal norms within the legal system those rules validate. Under this view, the basic validity rule is a special rule that reflects a practice which is adopted as normative by a key set of "officials" (the status of these special people).[3] What makes a mere regularity of behavior that we can describe as a practice into a rule is that it is accepted from an "internal point of view" by those adopting it. That is, they see the regularity of behavior as normative, making it into a social rule.

Hart's practice theory is echoed elsewhere. In preparation for a move to London, I recently read a popular book by the prominent social anthropologist Kate Fox titled *Watching the English*. In it, she explains that the primary focus of social anthropologists is to reason backwards from observed social practices to the rules that govern them.[4] While she incorrectly believes that this undermines the Humean maxim that one cannot derive an "ought" from an "is,"[5] she helpfully explains that though some social rules may be based upon pre-existing beliefs in underlying principles, some also arise out of prescriptivizing a pre-existing practice. This is precisely what Hart meant (although the practice need not be pre-existing) in explaining how a practice theory rule develops when people internalize a rule the content of which is a description of the practice.

From here we can see that a practice is (among other things) a regularity of behavior or activities that comes under an identifiable description. It would

[3] H.L.A. Hart, *The Concept of Law* (Penelope A. Bulloch and Joseph Raz eds., 2nd edn., Clarendon Press 1994 (1961)) 110, 255.

[4] Kate Fox, *Watching the English: The Hidden Rules of English Behavior* (2nd revised and updated edn., Nicholas Brealey Publishing 2014 (2008)) 14–19.

[5] Ibid. 15, n. 3. It is instead merely evidence that we must search more deeply for the source of normativity within the descriptive premises. For further discussion on the use of law's artifactual nature to provide that source, see my paper, "Ontology and Reason Giving in Law" in Pawel Banas, Adam Dyrda, and Tomasz Gizbert-Studnicki (eds.), *Metaphilosophy of Law* (Hart Publishing 2016) 147–58, although we will also touch upon this here.

need to be identifiable in order for the practice to be capable of being prescribed. But even before any prescription, we would need to identify it in order to segregate it as a practice from other forms of repeated behavior. It doesn't have to get a unique description, since more than one description could be used for a given practice. But it must be an identifiable description, in that any multiple descriptions can only refer to the same practice when people can use the various descriptions to pick out the same practice. That is, whatever description we have for the practice must be capable of picking it out among other practices and other repeated or shared behaviors more generally.

While we can certainly have very idiosyncratic practices that we might develop as individuals, in considering law to be a kind of practice, we are seeing it as a social practice. Social practices, according to Raimo Tuomela, are "activities performed for social reasons of a certain broad kind" (i.e., with some shared attitudes of collective engagement).[6] He points out a distinction between a shared practice and mere group repetitive behavior is that social practices are done for a "shared social reason," which is "that others are doing it and expect everyone in the group to do it."[7] In other words, the thoughts and behaviors of others are at least part of the reason for behaving as one does when engaging in the practice (although one does not have to be consciously aware of this reason).[8]

While this analysis seems to capture Hart's practice theory of the basic validity rule quite well, it is not a very good description of other legal rules. We can all think of legal rules that are not well respected. If these rules are followed at all, it may be because of the threat of punishment rather than the expectations of others. (And those punishing or threatening us still might not have much expectation of compliance.) Hart was similarly clear that the practice theory was not meant to explain other legal rules within a legal system.[9] So perhaps this means that the common description of law itself as a social practice is misplaced.

I think that such a judgment is too quick. While the practice theory itself does not explain the vast majority of legal rules, those legal rules depend upon a wider system for their existence.[10] It is precisely the basic validity rules that individuate those wider systems necessary for the existence of more common

[6] Tuomela, *The Philosophy of Social Practices* (n. 2) 78. [7] Ibid. 92.

[8] Ibid. See also ibid. at 94: "the core sense of a social practice is a repeatedly performed collective social action ... because of a certain shared we-attitude, where the we-attitude must be a 'primary' reason for the repeated activity, one without which the agents would not take part in it."

[9] Hart, *Concept of Law* (n. 3) 256, noting that enacted legal rules exist as such before any practice regarding them has arisen.

[10] John Gardner, "The Legality of Law" (2004) 17 *Ratio Juris* 168, 169–70; see also Ehrenberg, *The Functions of Law* (n. 1) 16–18.

legal rules. Furthermore, they determine which rules are valid members of the system and which are not. (Indeed, that is their entire purpose.) Hence, while the practice theory does not describe most laws or legal norms, it describes the norms that are necessary existence conditions for legal systems (and are conceived of as the basis for those systems) which are, in turn, necessary existence conditions for those laws or legal norms not explainable by the practice theory. So it is not incorrect to say of the law as a whole, wherever it is found, that it is a practice insofar as it depends upon practice theory rules, and is describable as social practices in Tuomela's sense.[11]

3. Shapiro's Metaphysical Challenge

Echoing our Humean worry, Scott Shapiro claims Hart's practice theory commits a category mistake: "Social rules cannot be reduced to social practices because rules and practices belong to different metaphysical categories."[12] If he's right, Shapiro is identifying a metaphysical tension between seeing law as a system of rules and seeing it as a practice at the same time. If practices are regularities of behavior, then that would be entirely captured by descriptive explanatory data: which individuals are engaging in which behaviors with what regularity. Rules, on the other hand, could provide reasons for that behavior or its regularity, but they couldn't be identified with the behavior or its regularity. If they are in different metaphysical categories, then it would seem that law can't be both at the same time.

Even though the target of his attack is Hart's practice theory, which is only meant to supply an explanation for basic legal validity rules, if Shapiro's criticism has weight, it would have a much broader implication: if rules can never be reduced to practices then it becomes difficult to see what the relation is between them such that we can call law a system of rules and at the same time

[11] Another way in which law is sometimes described as a practice should be mentioned, if only to dispense with it. We also speak of "the practice of law," referring to the professional work of attorneys. Now, I think that there is an important way in which the law itself must be a social practice in order for this description of their professional work to be apt. But this sense of the term is more generally applied to any industry that is organized around professional norms. These norms are themselves institutionalized, generally with extra bars to entry into the profession such as additional educational attainments, tests, memberships in professional bodies, and behavioral standards usually articulated and enforced by a subset of such professionals given some kind of "official" status within the industry. Thus we speak also of the practice of medicine, of architecture, and of accounting, for example. This does not mean that we can't meaningfully speak of those operating outside the official norms in these industries as also engaging in the practice of that profession. But such people are generally deemed to be violating important norms (sometimes even legal ones) in doing so.

[12] Scott J. Shapiro, *Legality* (Harvard University Press 2011) 103.

a practice. Even if we might be able to say as a result of this claim that law has some sort of dual nature, perhaps it is merely a coincidence that law is both and the dual elements of its nature are not related.

Shapiro's main argument in favor of holding that it is a category mistake to say that rules can be practices is that each occupies a different metaphysical space. "Rules are *abstract objects*," while practices are "*concrete events*."[13] He claims that we don't really reduce one to the other anyway, saying instead "that practices *exemplify, embody, conform to, are structured by,* and *are grounds for* rules."[14] This can be added to the more obvious point that rules are normative and practices are generally descriptive, although they may come to have a normative element.

This metaphysical distinction is glossing over a more fundamental relation. While it is true that practices are instantiated in concrete events, the fact that practices are generally repeatable under a specific description makes me think that a practice cannot be identified with any one of those events. After all, if it happens only once it would be difficult to call it a practice. And if it happens more than once, the practice is not identical with its instances. Furthermore, the fact that there is a difference between a practice and merely repeated behavior suggests that a practice cannot be identical with the set of those events, since otherwise we would not be able to maintain that distinction between practices and merely repeated behavior. This is not to say that practices are abstract objects, but it does seem that the relation between a practice and an instantiating event is similar to the relation between a rule and an instance of its compliance. Also of apparent significance (as Shapiro points out) is the fact that rules can provide the basis for a practice of following them.

In a single paragraph, John Gardner and Timothy Macklem seek to dismantle Shapiro's argument against Hart, showing that it treats Hart's claim far too broadly.[15] They note that Hart was clear in thinking that the practice theory only applied to certain social practices, such as those that form the basis of basic validity rules, and not to social practices generally, which is what Shapiro clearly implies.[16] Even with those practices that are used within practice theory rules, the practice is not identified with the rule, but rather provides its content.[17] I disagree with their claim that "Shapiro says *nothing* to suggest that this is a category mistake,"[18] since he does note the different

[13] Ibid., emphases in original. [14] Ibid.

[15] John Gardner and Timothy Macklem, "Review of *Legality*" (2011) Notre Dame Philosophical Reviews <http://ndpr.nd.edu/news/27609-legality/> accessed March 5, 2015.

[16] Shapiro, *Legality* (n. 12) 103, speculating that Hart's reply to his criticism would still have Hart claiming "social practices necessarily generate social rules."

[17] Gardner and Macklem, "Review of *Legality*" (n. 15). [18] Ibid., emphasis added.

metaphysical categories to which rules and practices seem to belong. But they are correct that Shapiro seems to miss the distinction between rules and practices, on the one hand, and their content, on the other.

But it is not clear that this reply, as strong as it is, is enough to settle our difficulties with the relationship between social practices and rules. It allows that the rule and the practice may have the same content—the behavior that is expected and the occasions on which it is expected. That is enough to defend Hart against Shapiro's attack: the practice theory is merely an explanation of how the content of a practice comes to be seen as the content of a rule. However, it leaves intact the basic claim that rules and practices belong to different metaphysical categories and hence we still have the problem of how to get from one to the other. Officials might be content to observe a regularity of behavior and collectively prescriptivize that regularity by internalizing it as a reason for behavior in conformity with it. But we are left without an account of whether they have any good reasons for doing so. With Gardner and Macklem's reply in hand and contrary to Shapiro's claims, *we* (legal philosophers) might not be running afoul of Hume's caution, but we are certainly still making it look like these officials are doing so.

4. How Norms Are Embedded within Social Practices and Artifacts

Recall Tuomela's claim that social practices must be at least partially based upon the expectations of others. Those expectations were supposed to be at least one of the reasons for engaging in the practice. Hence, Tuomela's explanation embeds a norm within the understanding of social practices. It is not merely a regularity of behavior; it is a regularity of behavior engaged in for a specific kind of reason. (Remember that Tuomela mentioned that one need not be aware of that reason and hence we are not understanding these reasons to be merely psychological or motivating reasons, but rather potentially robust, normative reasons of the kind that we are worried about.) If this is correct then social practices are normative at their core. Hence there isn't really a problem with prescriptivizing them (especially if doing so is part and parcel with the practice itself) because they are regularities of behavior that come bundled with their own reasons. There is no problem deriving an "ought" from a merely descriptive "is" because the practice comes with its "oughts" already in place.

I think this is basically correct but calls for a bit more explanation. There could be a worry that bundling the norm into the practice this way is ad hoc. One might think that the practice, properly speaking, is still just the regularity of behavior and its occasions, while the reasons are still separate grounds for the practice, metaphysically distinct. The way out of that worry is to ask whether one might be able to say that the practice itself can be a reason for an instance of behavior in conformity with it. If, as I suspect, the answer is yes, then it makes sense to say that social practices are normative in both directions: both in that they have reasons for them and in that they can provide reasons. Bundling the reasons for the practice into the understanding of the practice itself is then not ad hoc since when citing the practice as a reason for behaving in conformity with it, one is thereby indirectly citing the reasons for the practice itself. One is showing that the practice is normative in its very nature. If the answer is no, we are saying that the reasons for the practice are separable from the practice itself. But in this case we are back to the problem of understanding the distinction between a practice and a mere regularity of behavior. If the reasons and the practice are separable, we have no obvious alternative on which to base the distinction between practices and mere regularities of behavior. This in itself is a good reason to reject the option of saying that practices cannot be reasons for behavior in conformity with them.

If we agree with Tuomela, we see that the practice is at least partially based upon the expectations of others, and that this lends it at least some of its normativity. But there is something that is still a bit opaque in the relation of the practice to its normativity that goes to the question of whether the mere expectations of others can ever be a good reason to engage with the practice. After all, the mere expectations of others is still just merely descriptive information. The answer to this is found in understanding law as a genre of artifacts, specifically institutionalized ones. Understanding more about artifacts helps to show exactly the metaphysical relation between norms and certain descriptive facts, at least in so far as to show how those descriptive facts can be reasons for action. Understanding institutions, as a subset of artifacts, helps to understand how certain descriptive facts can create a normative reality by creating and assigning statuses that carry deontic powers.

To call law a genre of artifact might appear to generate a concern similar to Shapiro's: artifacts are generally concrete particulars, while rules are abstract objects. But this shouldn't cause us too much of a problem when we realize that the general understanding of artifacts as a subset of tools allows them to be abstract objects as well. To see this, let us borrow Randal Dipert's taxonomy and say that artifacts are a subset of tools, which are themselves a subset of instruments. Anything used for a purpose would be an instrument; anything adapted to serve that purpose is a tool; and anything adapted to serve that purpose and communicate its usage is an artifact.[19] (To say that it is

[19] Randall R. Dipert, *Artifacts, Art Works, and Agency* (Temple University Press 1993) 23–8. See also Ehrenberg, *The Functions of Law* (n. 1) 10–12.

adapted to communicate its usage is to say that it has elements (usually structural) that are designed to be recognizable to a population of potential users, conveying to them the artifact's purpose or method of use.)

If an artifact is a tool that communicates its usage, then we might have a momentary worry that the medium of communication must be something concrete and therefore wish to shy away from saying that artifacts can be abstract objects. But we can dismiss that worry by distinguishing between a tool that communicates its usage and the medium of that communication. Sometimes they are certainly identical. With a chair, the shape of the chair communicates its usage to the viewer. But with institutions like hospitals, universities, and legal systems, the tool and the medium for communication can come apart.[20] In such cases, the medium is linguistic or other symbolic representations of the functions performed by the institution. A university is not identical to its buildings, students, faculties, or administration, although all of those concrete elements are institutionally important. The communication of the fact that a university is institutionally present (physically or in cyber-space) is done by using the word "university" or other symbolic representations such as pictures of students, books, graduation attire, etc.

Legal systems are institutions that are made up of members or elements, each of which are not themselves concrete particulars, although they come to exist as a result of concrete events and so have a history. Similarly, they apply in a jurisdiction, which is generally a physical area, although with artificial institutional boundaries. They are not concrete particulars since they are not identical to any instance of the words that create or report their existence. Consider that if every recording of a law were destroyed, the law itself would continue to exist so long as there were people who knew about it and accepted it. When a law is created, the language that is used is supposed to communicate the norm it thereby creates to those subject to the law. That is, the language is telling them the behavior that is expected of them or what behaviors will have what institutional results.

If artifacts communicate their usage, they thereby carry a very basic normativity of recognition. That is, the very fact that something is an artifact means that it is generally created to serve a purpose and to communicate that purpose.[21] When someone creates a token artifact of a certain kind, she

[20] In all of these examples, of course, the communication can fail, as with any communication. But to support the fact that it is the artifact's usage that is being communicated consider that when archeologists uncover a previously undiscovered ancient implement, they try to identify it by trying to understand its function.

[21] Amie L. Thomasson, "Public Artifacts, Intentions and Norms" in Maarten Franssen and others (eds.), *Artefact Kinds: Ontology and the Human-Made World* (Springer 2013) 45, at 49. Amie Thomasson does give a theory of artifacts in which not all artifacts are understood in terms of

thereby communicates an intention for the relevant audience to recognize it as an instance of that kind of artifact.[22] The artifact therefore comes bundled with a norm of recognition or identification.[23] Now of course one might fail to recognize it as a member of that kind. Also one can certainly repurpose the artifact for other uses than the one usually associated with its kind. So, I can use the chair to hold open a door and not for sitting. But it doesn't stop being a chair when I do so.

As a result of these considerations, one might think that the norms of artifact usage and of artifact identification are identical.[24] After all, if what distinguishes an artifact from other kinds of tools is that artifacts communicate their usage as a means of identifying them, to recognize an artifact as an example of its type is to understand its supposed usage. We generally recognize a created object as a carpenter claw hammer once we recognize that its intended usage is to drive and extract nails. If this is the complete story, then it might pose a problem for an artifactual theory of law, since in the case of law, the norms of recognition and of usage are a bit more distinguishable from each other. We recognize something as a law by seeing it as coming within the standards of legal validity for a certain legal system. But the norms of usage for the law are the more particular norms of behavior that it purports to impose, and perhaps any guidance it provides (generally for officials) about states of affairs that the law is aimed at achieving. So if the norms of usage and of identification are supposed to be identical, and that is not the case for law, then that might be seen as a reason against understanding law to be a kind of artifact.

We can dispel this worry by seeing that norms of usage and of recognition or identification can easily come apart with many different artifacts. The best way to show this is to see that I can violate one without violating the other. When I use the chair to prop open a door, I am not thereby failing

their functions in order to make space for works of art that might not have functions. But she acknowledges that for artifacts other than works of art (and perhaps religious artifacts), most types of artifacts are understood in terms of their functions. See ibid. 48. I'm using "function," "supposed usage," and "purpose" somewhat interchangeably here. I go into greater detail on this in Ehrenberg, *The Functions of Law* (n. 1) 20–9.

[22] Of course, differences between the token and other members of the set can serve to set it apart as a new kind, although generally this will be a variation of some previous kinds of artifacts. Beth Preston calls this "reproduction with variation." Beth Preston, "Philosophical Theories of Artifact Function" in Anthonie Meijers (ed.), *Philosophy of Technology and Engineering Sciences* (Elsevier 2009) 213, at 216–17.

[23] While I recognize there are differences between identification and recognition, when it comes to the class of norms by which artifacts are identified and recognized as belonging to a certain type or group, I will use these terms interchangeably.

[24] I thank an anonymous reviewer for suggesting that I dispel this misconception.

to recognize or identify the object as a chair; I'm only failing to *use* it as a chair. I may have violated a norm of usage,[25] but I have not thereby violated a norm of identification or recognition. While the norm of recognition of the object is *tied to* its function, it cannot be identical to it since other objects can generally perform the same function (so the function is not sufficient for identifying the object), and we can use the object in other ways than to perform its function without undermining its identity (so using the object to perform its function is not necessary for identifying the object).

There is therefore an interesting asymmetry between the norms of recognition and the norms of usage for artifacts. It seems that the norms of recognition are much stronger and more difficult to ignore than the norms of usage. Part of that might have to do with the fact that the artifact's identity, while strongly dependent upon its characteristic function,[26] does not depend upon it performing (or even attempting to perform) that function every (or even any) time we interact with it. While we understand what most artifacts are in terms of the functions they perform, they need not be performing those functions in order to be members of the class in which we recognize them. I suspect this has a lot to do with the way in which the norms of recognition and usage are addressed and how strong they are in relation to other reasons that addressees may have. When someone creates an artifact and thereby communicates its usage, it is similar to communicating a request: "I've taken the time and energy to fashion this X for your benefit, please treat it accordingly." Since it is for my benefit, my beneficial usage might not ultimately be the same as the function that the object is usually identified with. (Hence "treat it accordingly" may not require me to use the object in the way it was meant to be used.) But that identity is something that its creator endowed it with in making it an X and it is much harder to have a good reason not to see it as a member of that X class than it is to use it differently from how X's

[25] Some may reasonably question whether mundane objects like chairs really have norms of usage that are violated when using them in ways other than intended. While I think that there is a very weak norm of usage for such objects, it does not much matter since there are certainly some artifacts that have stronger norms of usage. National flags come to mind as an example here. If they didn't have norms of usage associated with them, then burning them or trampling them underfoot wouldn't be making much of a symbolic statement. Yet this is another example showing how the norms of usage and of identification come apart. By burning or trampling the flag, I am purposely violating the norms of usage but emphatically *not* violating the norms of identification, since my symbolic statement depends heavily upon myself and others continuing to identify the object as the flag of the country against which I am protesting.

[26] I have elsewhere argued that functions are essential to any complete explanation of a public artifact like law (as opposed to artworks), but that performance of those functions is neither a necessary nor a sufficient condition for a token artifact's membership in the class to which it belongs. See Ehrenberg, *The Functions of Law* (n. 1) 43–54.

are typically used. Hence the norm of recognition is much stronger than the norm of usage.

Additionally, the norm of recognition is addressed to the relevant audience generally and as a group, while the norms of usage are usually dependent upon each individual's interaction with the artifact (unless it is an artifact that can only be used communally, in which case the norm of usage is probably stronger than in the individual case). So there is a way in which the artifact's identity is dependent upon some form of mutually dependent recognition among the community of those who might interact with it. To go against that norm, while not impossible, is not simply to violate the wishes of the person who created the artifact, but to go against the shared communal understanding of what it is, likely established by the wider group who are generally respecting that recognition. To use the artifact differently than intended, on the other hand, is more likely to be an individual interaction with the artifact, in which my personal purposes are more important than those of the creator.

This helps us to see that a person or body creating a law is creating an artifact along the same lines. It also helps to explain why that person or body's intentions about how the law is to be understood or used are not as important as the recognition of the law as a valid member of the system of which it is supposed to be a part.[27] I think it is more than a happy coincidence that Hart called his notion of the basic validity rule, which is the paradigm example of his practice theory, the "rule of recognition."[28] It is a practice of officials, which they see as normative, about what features a putative law (or other legal norm) must have in order to be recognized as a member of that legal system. When the right people (as specified by the rule) engage in the right behavior in enacting such a law, they are conforming themselves to the details of that normative practice in order to create a law that will be recognized as a bona fide member of that system. Whether we use or apply the law in the way that they intended or envisioned is here less important than whether it is a valid member of the system. The norm of recognition of their artifact, so created by their undertaking the practice in the specified normative way, is to see their behavior as producing a new member of the system in which they are operating. The practice, a bundle of regular behaviors, is normative

[27] This makes no claims whatsoever about interpretive theories or their strengths. It is as consistent with interpretive theories that place a heavy emphasis on drafters' intentions as with those that discount or ignore those intentions. Artifactual understandings of law can still put a heavy emphasis on the role of those drafting and enacting the law for the law's membership in the relevant legal system without implying anything about the relevance of their intentions in favoring some interpretive theories over others.

[28] Hart, *The Concept of Law* (n. 3) 94.

in the sense that it is a shared set of expectations which form a key reason for engaging in it (following Tuomela). Engaging in the practice in the correct way creates an artifact that carries the norm of recognition associated with artifacts generally, that people recognize the artifact as a member of the kind to which it is supposed to belong.

5. Institutionality Addresses Lingering Concerns about Seeing Law as an Artifact and Practice

Now one might be bothered by a couple of dissimilarities between the description of artifacts generally, and the explanation of how the same thing happens with law. Most of the time, we only interact with artifacts if doing so is somehow to our benefit. (Of course, sometimes we interact with artifacts that others are using for their own benefit and such interactions may not be to our benefit.) After all, they are a subset of tools and there is generally no reason to interact with a tool unless doing so is useful in some way. One might worry that our interaction with law is very different; we often don't really have an option about whether to interact with it and it sometimes might require that we make sacrifices of our interests or benefits in doing so. Another worry is that there aren't generally any rules about how to make or use most artifacts. A created token is successfully a member of the kind just in case people can recognize it as such. The creator doesn't usually have to follow any set rules about the means of creation, what the artifact looks like, the materials used, etc. As long as people can recognize it as the thing he intends it to be, he's successfully made a new token of that kind of artifact. But the law doesn't work that way. Creation isn't open to everyone. Usually it's only open to some special group of people whose characteristics are set out in the basic validity rules. Those people also have to follow the other specifications in the basic validity rules successfully in order to make a new member of the legal system.

The answer to both of these concerns is the final piece of our puzzle. Law is a special kind of artifact, an institution. Institutions are a subclass of artifacts that have a special kind of purpose: to create and manipulate what John Searle calls "desire-independent reasons for action."[29] In other words, they carry the possibility of giving reasons for people to act in ways that are against their interests or desires, giving them duties—at least insofar as the institution is

[29] John R. Searle, *Making the Social World: The Structure of Human Civilization* (Oxford University Press 2010) 23, 99.

concerned. They do this by instituting and assigning special statuses to people, events, objects, or states of affairs. These statuses are generally creations of the institution itself through processes laid out in foundational rules, or other rules created according to those foundational rules. Those statuses carry "deontic powers" to alter the rights and responsibilities of those within the ambit of the institution.[30] Generally (at least for "formal institutions"[31]), to be valid instances of institutional action, the creation, assignment, or use of those statuses to manipulate people's reasons for action must take place according to the rules that create and govern the institution, its basic validity rules.

Understanding how law is a kind of institution and the nature of institutions helps to answer questions about the distinction between law and other kinds of artifacts. Where most artifacts that we are familiar with are only useful when using them is to our benefit (or someone else's), institutions, by creating desire-independent reasons for action, can impose obligations (at least for those legitimately subject to the institution), which carry the possibility of providing reasons to act against our interests and benefit. But the institution is still a kind of artifact and hence still a kind of tool. So we would expect that it only gets used when it's useful for someone. Of course, the law is only used when it is to someone's benefit. We hope that it is used only when it is to the benefit of the majority of those within the ambit of its institutional reach (its jurisdiction), or at least not to their detriment. But it can also be used in cases where it's useful only to the monarch, the governing elite, the wealthy and powerful, or (probably less often) only to the underclass. In such cases, those being asked to act against their interests may not really get any legitimate obligation to do so, even as the institution gives them reasons to do so within the institutional reality. The point here is to see that of the many people who interact with this particular kind of artifact, some may not be doing so by choice (although that may be true of many more mundane artifacts as well), but that in no way threatens seeing law as a kind of artifact.

The other worrisome supposed dissimilarity between law and artifacts is that there aren't generally any rules about the creation of mundane artifacts. Now one might point out against this worry that there are sometimes "official bodies" that do set down rules about which tokens are to be members of the class of those particular artifacts. We have "Denominazione di Origine Controllata" pizza and the idea that nothing is "real" champagne if it doesn't come from Champagne, France, "genuine" Toyota parts for your car, and

[30] Ibid. 8–9.

[31] On the distinction between formal and informal institutions see ibid. 23, 91; Ehrenberg *The Functions of Law* (n. 1) 35–6; as well as Ehrenberg, "Ontology and Reason Giving in Law" (n. 5) 156–7.

Herman Miller chairs. But these examples are actually ones of institutional realities laid on top of other more mundane artifacts (and many are themselves creations of law). So it is one of the main facets of (formal) institutions to set forth rules about which putative tokens, instances, or products of institutional action are bona fide and which are counterfeit and void, not to be given the deontic powers assigned to the bona fide members. One of the many ways they may do that is by limiting the creation of institutional instances, or uses of the institutional imprimatur, to a specified set of officials or to individuals following only specified procedures.

By seeing the institutional nature of law, we can see even more clearly that it is compatible to see law both as a practice and as an artifact. Institutions are kinds of artifacts, albeit with some special properties. They are still tools used to accomplish certain tasks and to communicate their usability for those tasks. Institutions are generally organized around certain central purposes such as research and education for universities, or healing for hospitals. Law's purposes are much more myriad, but it still accomplishes those tasks by assigning statuses that carry deontic powers. The fact that so much of institutional reality takes place in a linguistic medium makes the communication of institutions' usability that much more clear. But the created rules and norms of a legal system are still tools that are created in such a way as to communicate to people how they are to interact with them and, under them, with each other.

A practice is a pattern of behavior that is given some special status or significance by those engaging in it, beyond the mere immediate effects the behavior might have. As such, we can see that practices are the foundations of institutions, which are means of assigning statuses. But also, the engagement with and implementation of an institution is a kind of practice, a practice of creating and deploying those statuses through declarations, votes, and other behaviors that fulfill the prescriptions of the rules that constitute that institution in its basic validity rules.

Normativity is lurking within the social facts of calling something a social practice, an artifact, or an institution, so we make no category mistake in moving from those social facts to normative conclusions. Social practices have reasons for compliance in the expectations of others. Artifacts carry norms of recognition in the communicated desire of creators to have their artifacts recognized as members of the kinds of artifacts they aspired to make. Institutions have a much more complete set of norms governing their creation and application, but those norms are only valid within that institutional reality and it is a separate question whether those norms are legitimately obligating. That question is answered by whatever conditions determine whether one has good reasons to be subject to that institution.

It should not be surprising that the law is all of these things since they are all so intimately related.

6. Conclusion

In this chapter we've seen that there might be a concern about a clash between seeing law as a practice and seeing it as a kind of artifact, but that concern would be misplaced. Hart himself understood his "rule of recognition" (a basic rule about the norms of legal validity within a legal system) as a rule founded upon a practice. We saw that this fit nicely with Tuomela's understanding of social practices, but that Scott Shapiro thinks it shows that Hart is guilty of a category mistake. While Shapiro's particular worry about Hart's practice theory was easily addressed, there was a wider issue it raised about how something could be both a rule and a practice, calling into question the possibility of practices that are normative merely because they are practices. This led us to investigate how norms are embedded within practices on the basis of social expectations that create reasons. But there was a lingering worry that those social expectations are still just descriptive facts, leaving opaque how reasons are being created. The answer there was to see some of these social practices (law as a primary example) as artifacts, which come bundled with norms of usage and of recognition as a result of their being created to serve a purpose and to communicate that purpose. Finally, we saw that there might be some worries about dissimilarities between law and other kinds of artifacts in that usually artifacts are only used when beneficial to those using them and in that most artifacts can be made by anyone with enough skill to do so, neither of which is generally true for law. The answer to these worries was to see law as an institution, a special kind of artifact for altering people's rights and responsibilities by creating and assigning artificial statuses to do so. This allows law to create desire-independent reasons for action and allows that only people with special statuses defined by the institution can make and alter the law.

10

Processes and Artifacts

The Principles Are in the Author Herself

*Veronica Rodriguez-Blanco**

1. Introduction

It is much agreed that intentions can create artifacts, whose key feature is whether they perform the intended function and fall under the concept and predicates of their intended character. Additionally, artifacts are possible because there is agreement on what they are and therefore their existence is mind-dependent.[1] However, in contemporary philosophy of action and the metaphysics of artifacts, there are no explanations or only very sketchy and unsatisfactory views on *how* intentions can create artifacts, e.g., law, performing arts, works of art, or social institutions.[2] The explanations resort to speech acts, or intentions as mental states, or to beliefs that are materialized in agreements, conventions, or acceptances. However, I will argue that none of these instances can truly explain the diachronic process of effectively producing a state of affairs by human authorship. At some point within the discussion, there has been a particular focus on the ontology of artifacts to the detriment of reflecting on how authorship can create practically a certain state of affairs. My diagnosis is that this is due to a theoretical view on intention and action, in which the idea of will and intention tends to be reduced to an understanding, or to expressions of

* I am grateful to Ken Ehrenberg, Tria Gouvkas, and Andrej Kristan for comments on earlier drafts.

[1] John Searle, *The Construction of Social Reality* (The Free Press 1995) 1.

[2] There are some recent exceptions, see Kenneth Ehrenberg, *The Functions of Law* (Oxford University Press 2016). However, Ehrenberg takes as a starting point a different conception of intentional action than the one defended in this chapter. In his work, intentional action still is mainly a mental state.

Law as an Artifact. First Edition. Edited by Luka Burazin, Kenneth Einar Himma, and Corrado Roversi. Published 2018 by Oxford University Press.

our language. I will concentrate on two such accounts and show that they rely on an incomplete and at times defective conception of intention. I will then advance a different conception of intention which focuses on practical reason and powers and capacities with the aim of illuminating the character of artifacts. The key conclusion of the latter conception is that *artifacts belong to voluntary things and practical reason. Therefore the principles of the artifact are in the author herself.*

2. Intention as a Mental State and their Effects

Let us imagine the following two examples:

Tango choreography. A choreographer is creating a dance sequence based on the tango dance. There are a few basic steps, e.g. parallel walk, cross walk, weight change, and promenade, which he combines with some techniques and embellishments. In addition, he endeavours to insert an emotional understanding of the dance into its performance.

Making coffee with a stovetop coffee maker. You put the coffee grains and the hot water into the coffee maker then put on the stove and wait until the coffee is ready.

At first glance one might be reluctant to associate the performance of the tango by a dance group to an artifact and nor does the making of coffee seem to be an artifact. Typical examples of artifacts are "chairs," "pencils," "houses," "hammers," and so on. In these examples the focus is on the effects of the creation rather than on the process of creating the artifact. The mere observation of the physical properties of a chair, hammer, pencil, house, musical score, or coffee does not help us to understand that some things are created by human intentional acts as opposed to naturally occurring phenomena such as rocks, oceans, mountains, etc. Thus, it seems that we can expand our intuitive understanding of artifacts to the activity of producing an object or a state of affairs. The artifact is not only the cup of coffee, the stovetop coffee maker, or the dance sequence, but also the activity of producing it, e.g., the activity of making coffee and the activity of performing the tango.

Hilpinen asserts that artifacts have an author who intends to create an object or the state of affairs under a certain description.[3] Thus the author intends to make an artifact of a certain type or kind. The intention connects the object, Hilpinen tells us, with different properties and predicates which

[3] Hilpinen refers only to objects but I will extend his notion to states of affairs for reasons that will become clear later. Risto Hilpinen, "Belief Systems as Artefacts" (1995) 78 *The Monist* 136.

constitute the intended property of the newly created object or artifact.[4] These properties are called the Intended Character of an Object "IC (o)." By contrast, the Actual Character of an Object "AC (o)" is the resultant effect of the intention. "The success of the author's productive activity depends on the degree of fit or agreement between the intended and the actual character of o."[5] Additionally, Hilpinen tells us that an artifact is identified by a description which refers to its intended function. "I shall call the object made for a purpose F an F-object."[6] He asserts that the author's productive activity can be evaluated according to: (a) the degree of agreement or fit between the intended character and actual character of the object; (b) the degree of fit between the intended character of the object and the purpose F of the object; and (c) the degree of fit between the actual intended object and the purpose F.[7]

But this is puzzling and unsatisfactory. It cannot be right or at least there is something fundamentally missing. Let us think about the following example. A mathematical theorem has an author who intends to show that the theorem is true by means of a proof that has certain properties, i.e., consistency, simplicity, truthfulness, etc. Thus, the success of the proof is determined on the basis of the degree of fit or correspondence between the intended properties or intended concept of the proof and the actual properties or concept of the proof to the theorem. Its success will also be evaluated in terms of the degree of fit between the intended character of the proof and the purpose of the proof (b) and the degree of fit between the actual character of the proof and the purpose of the proof (c). Let us say that the purpose of the proof is to establish the truth of the theorem. The proof could be defective because it is too complicated and inelegant, and is contrary to the intention of the mathematician who wanted a simple and elegant solution. It might also be incoherent and this would contradict the intended character of the proof. Thus, we might also find that there is an inadequate fit between the actual intended character of the proof and its purpose, i.e., its truth. We see then that all the conditions of an artifact are fulfilled in the example of proving a mathematical theorem. However, we intuitively know that the proof of a mathematical theorem is *not* an artifact. What, hence, is the problem arising from the conditions placed on artifacts by Hilpinen? The problem lies in not taking sufficiently seriously the idea that for artifacts, as opposed to natural kinds (including mathematical kinds that involve theoretical knowledge), the author *determines* the character of the artifact. The tendency is to overlook the

[4] Ibid. 139. [5] Ibid. [6] Ibid. 140. [7] Ibid.

nature of the *determination* and to use the idea of intention in an ambiguous way. Intention might mean "expectation" or it might mean "directing" the will toward a purpose or end. Thus in the former case there is a reduction of the idea of intention to understanding in the form of "what we expect to obtain." In the latter case intention is an *active power* that aims to produce something or a state of affairs or object in the world. The problem of *how* intentions produce something in the world does not truly arise if we confine ourselves to the idea of intention as an expectation that obtains or does not obtain. What is left unexplained is *how* an intention can direct itself toward the production of the intended state of affairs.

You might argue that authors like Searle have focused on the idea of language, i.e., speech acts, to show how an intention can create artifacts. Thus, Searle argues that to move a brute fact, e.g., a piece of paper, into the status of an institutional fact, e.g., a piece of paper that has an exchange-value, we need language and thoughts. We learn that "X counts as Y in C" because of a series of conventions. They become symbols beyond themselves. We learn to treat the pieces of paper printed with an image of Darwin as being worth ten sterling pounds. This piece of paper now has a function in relation to exchange for goods. We have, according to Searle, a "precondition capacity to symbolize"[8] and this is the *condition of possibility* of the creation of artifacts as human institutions, i.e., games, law, property, money, etc. According to Searle the predication of truth or falsehood can equally apply to institutional facts as to propositions about natural kinds. The only difference is that we need to recognize that their truth-conditions depend, in the former case, on the representational conventions of the practice, e.g., the rules of the game, the rules of law, conventions on property, and the institutional rules of exchange in contemporary economies, and *nothing* beyond the convention. Whilst in the latter case the truth conditions of statements about natural kinds depend on something non-conventional and beyond our thoughts and language, e.g., the constitution of molecules, the nature of the universe and its objects.

But again, we have in Searle the collapse of the idea of intention or will into the idea of understanding. The convention involves an *acceptance or agreement* that creates institutional facts which, according to Searle, emerges with time and about which we are not fully aware. The collective intention gives institutional status to specific entities, e.g., money, law marriage, property, games, etc. But how can a collective intention create something that endures and unfolds with time? Searle resorts to the idea of "background abilities," which establishes that due to our dispositions we display a capacity

[8] Searle, *The Construction of Social Reality* (n. 1) 75.

to create institutional facts. He asserts that background abilities are prior to intentions. However, the problem that Searle faces is how intentions construed as mental states can be connected to our background abilities. The idea of background abilities is underdeveloped. He asserts that "background" is the "set of non-intentional or pre-intentional capacities that enable intentional states to function."[9] According to Searle "capacity" falls under causal neurophysiological causation about which we do not have sufficient knowledge, and that we therefore need to explain at higher order levels. Thus, to speak English is to exercise a capacity that is in my brain. Searle understands intentional states as mental states and asserts that we "know how" to interpret and recognize the adequate meaning of words that are used in different contexts. For example, we can easily recognize the use of the word "growing" in two different contexts such as when I assert "The American economy is growing" and you assert "My son is growing."

However, Searle argues that the causal role operates at the level of the "background." Thus, institutional facts demand the following of certain rules, e.g., rules of the game, rules of promises, rules for the exchange of goods, etc. and because of this demand, the individual develops a set of "background" habits, skills, and dispositions that enables her or him to follow the rules.[10] But this is puzzling and unclear. The question that arises is *how* collective intentionality creates the institutional structure. We cannot argue that it is *because* there is a "background" that enables the emergence of a specific kind of collective intentionality. On this view intentionality has no causal and creative role, it only establishes the pattern of conduct that we *expect* you to perform. But the performance is possible *because* of the background abilities. Again, will or intention seems to be reduced to understanding or expectation. Let me illustrate Searle's point with the previous example of choreographing a tango dance. The dancers perform the steps because they have the abilities and talents to dance according to the institution "dancing the tango." It is not that they are dancing the tango because they are following the rules of the tango. Additionally, they behave like tango dancers because they are conforming to the rules of tango dancing. The rules of tango dancing have been created by collective intentions that give them the status of institutional facts and for everyone who claims that he or she dances the tango, we say

[9] Ibid. 129.

[10] Ibid. 144. Searle asserts: "Instead of saying the person behaves the way he does because he is following the rules of the institution, we should just say, First (the causal level), the person behaves the way he does, because he has a structure that disposes him to behave that way; and second (the functional level) he has come to be disposed to behave that way, because that's the way that conforms to the rules of the institution."

that we "expect" them to conform to these rules. I repeat, intentions have no creative role in this model since they only establish a standard of conduct or institutional framework within which we assess what people are doing when they are acting. According to Searle, we acquire skills, dispositions, and habits that are responsive to an institutional structure, which is created by intentions as mental states. These skills, dispositions, and habits are pre-intentional.

Apart from reducing intention or will to understanding or expectation, Searle does not provide a satisfactory answer to the question of *how* we create institutional facts through our intentions. The question is left unanswered since the idea of creating institutional facts by intentions is already *given or granted as necessary to make sense of the actors in the social context.* Thus, in the previous example, it is *given or granted* that tango is a dance that was created by collective intentionality since dancers are responsive to the rules of tango. If it were not an institutional fact, Searle would assert, we could not have dancers following the rules and being responsive to the different steps and so on.

In his later work, Searle recognizes that he previously overstated the causal role of psychological antecedents and asserts that voluntary and rational action does not have causally sufficient psychological antecedents.[11] Thus reasons are neither causally sufficient nor causally efficient. For Searle, the only plausible causality is efficient causality, but reasons and intentions do not operate at the level of efficient causality. The question that then arises is how reasons and intentions create a state of affairs, including artifacts. According to Searle it is not possible to answer this question but we can use deductive reasoning to show that a non-Humean self needs to be presupposed to give an explanation of the phenomenon of reasons and intentions together with the phenomenon of free human rational and volitional action. Following Searle, the structure of the deductive argument is as follows. We have the experience of acting, which is the conscious intention-in action. We act for reasons and intentions that give order and intelligibility to the movements of our body. In the example given above, we dance tango according to choreographed movements and stylistic rules, and we follow these rules for different reasons, e.g., embellishment of our lives, entertainment, playfulness, friendship. According to Searle, these reasons neither sufficiently nor efficiently cause the bodily movements. Neither the intention nor reasons of embellishment, entertainment, playfulness, or friendship cause the creation of the choreographic and stylistic rules of tango. However, when we dance tango, we have the experience of dancing tango and of following the choreographic and stylistic rules of tango for specific intentions and reasons. There is therefore, according to

[11] John Searle, *Rationality in Action* (MIT Press 2001) 73.

Searle, an explanatory gap. To explain this experience of acting for reasons and specific intentions, we need to presuppose that there is a non-Humean self that advances reasons and intentions. This non-Humean self has certain key features. This self cannot be reduced to empirical properties, e.g., to a bundle of experiences. The self is a unity of apperception that transcends empirical conditions. All my experiences at any given point in time come to me as part of a unified conscious field.[12] The presupposition of a self with these features provides an intelligible explanation of my experience of freely, rationally, and volitionally dancing tango. Thus, I do not only have the sight of myself moving my body, the feeling of my arms and legs following the steps of tango, but I also have a unified conscious experience of dancing tango for the intentions and reasons that made me choose to dance tango.

But Searle's revised account does not provide an answer to our initial question, which is how intentions and reasons *determine* institutional facts, including artifacts. Searle takes for granted that there are institutional facts and artifacts, which are determined by reasons and intentions. He concentrates on advancing an explanation of the conditions of possibility of institutional facts and artifacts, but this is not an explanation of the conditions of creation of institutional facts and artifacts.

In the next section, I will advance a view of intention and an explanation of how intentions create institutional facts. Thus, in my account, the latter are not taken as *given or granted.* According to this view and in contrast to Searle, the dispositions, skills, and habits of the agent are actualizations of her intention. They are not pre-intentional. Unlike Searle and Hilpinen, this account does not reduce intentions to understanding or expectation.

3. Intentional Action as Diachronically Directed to an End

Imagine the following two examples:

> NEIGHBOR. You see your neighbor coming out of the supermarket and a few minutes later you see his well-known enemy (Mr. Enemy) driving his vehicle and running into him. Your neighbor is killed.
>
> OMELET. You are a cook and instruct a group of people who are attending your cooking workshop on how to make a good omelet.

[12] Ibid. 77.

In NEIGHBOR you can provide a description of the action in terms of mental states, i.e., the beliefs/desire pair that cause the bodily movements. The effect of this is to rationalize the action and make its description intelligible. You can, thus, say that Mr. Enemy had the desire to kill his enemy *and* the belief that driving his vehicle over him would kill him.

NEIGHBOR is a description of the action as a mental event, i.e., pair belief/desire and a consequential effect, which includes the bodily movements of Mr. Enemy, e.g., his pressing the pedal, controlling the wheel, and the *further* effect of killing the neighbor. However, this account faces the difficulty encountered by some counter-examples which is that there is no connection between the mental state, i.e., pair belief/desire, and the bodily movements. In other words, the agent has the appropriate mental state and the *further* effect has been obtained, nevertheless there is no intentional action. The description fails as a correct description of the action. Let us imagine the following alternative scenario:

> SWERVING THE WHEEL. You see your neighbor coming out of the supermarket and a few minutes later you see his well-known enemy (Mr. Enemy) driving his vehicle and running into him. Your neighbor is killed.

SWERVING THE WHEEL is exactly like NEIGHBOR but there is one key difference. What really happens is that Mr. Enemy has the relevant mental states, i.e., the desire to kill your neighbor and he believes that driving his vehicle into him will enable him to kill him, but he suffers an involuntary spasm that makes him swerve the vehicle toward your neighbor and kill him non-intentionally. All the elements of an intentional action as mental events are present, i.e., the relevant desire and belief, nevertheless there is no intentional action. Consequently, the model of belief/desire as a mental event causing the action does not really explain the action in SWERVING THE WHEEL. The key problem is that the model cannot ensure the causal connection between the mental event and the *further* effect.[13]

[13] This is called in the literature the deviant causation problem: see Roderick Chisholm, "Freedom and Action" in Keith Lehrer (ed.), *Freedom and Determinism* (Random House 1976). Surprisingly, there are some philosophers who assert that this is a problem for every theory of action: see David Enoch, "Reason-Giving and the Law" in Leslie Green and Brian Leiter (eds.), *Oxford Studies in Philosophy of Law* (Oxford University Press 2011); David Enoch, "Giving Practical Reasons" (2011) 11 *The Philosopher's Imprint*. This is incorrect. It is not a problem for accounts of action that do not rely on mental events. Furthermore, my diagnosis shows that something else is happening and that the idea that we can provide a pure description of actions is mistaken. Searle's idea of "background abilities" seems to bypass the deviant causation problem since the causal work is done at the background level and not at the intention level. However, an account of an intention as creator of a state of affairs is either left unexplained or the order of explanation is reversed, i.e., intention as authorship is given or necessarily presupposed.

In OMELET the cook is not telling the participants his beliefs and desires so that they can act upon them. It would be absurd and unintelligible if he were to say, "I desire to instruct you to make an omelet because I can charge a fee for this and I believe that giving you these instructions will enable you to make an omelet and pay me a fee." What about if the desire/belief pair is present in every single instruction on how to make an omelet? In the example, the cook would have to say, "I desire the eggs to be stirred and I believe that putting them in this bowl and moving the fork in this way will enable the eggs to be stirred." The participants will probably look perplexed. It does not say anything about *how to make an omelet*. Worse, it does not say anything about the next steps in the omelet making process or about *the know-how* required to follow these steps. It would presuppose an absurd sequence of randomly connected mental states (the pair belief/desire). There would be no answer to the questions, "Why should we *not* put the stirred eggs in the frying pan prior to the butter? Why shouldn't we begin the process with putting the frying pan on the heat, then taking the fork and stirring the eggs, then washing the frying pan, and finally pouring the eggs on the wet and unoiled frying pan?" By contrast, in order to ensure success in his instructions the cook needs to tell the participants the chain of reasons that are required to correctly perform the action, i.e., the making of the omelet. His "know-how" to make an omelet entails knowing the answers to the "Why?" questions involved in making an omelet, i.e., knowing why it is necessary to stir the eggs; knowing why there needs to be a knob of butter in the pan; knowing why the pan needs to be hot before you pour in the stirred eggs, and so on. He also needs to know "why" people make omelets and the good-making characteristics of omelets, i.e., that they are nutritious, delicious, and a quick and easy meal to make, etc. The cook presents the chain of reasons but the final end that unifies the series of actions is advanced by the agent who actually performs the action. It might be that the answer to the question "why?" is obvious in many circumstances due to the internal rationality of the activity or social practice, but perhaps in other circumstances it is required in order to explain "why" certain actions should follow others. The final end of "why" the participant aims to learn to make omelets can be various, e.g., for nutritional reasons, for reasons of practicality or expense, but this final end provides unity to the action *when* the participant executes the set of actions in order to make an omelet. Let us imagine that the participant goes home and starts to make an omelet as instructed; he will "know how" because he knows "why" certain actions follow other actions. In response to the final question "Why are you making an omelet?" he might reply in different ways, but always providing the end as a good-making characteristic, e.g., "because it is practical and easy," "because it is nutritious," "because it is delicious." If he responds "I do not know" we will probably suspect that his action is not intentional. I am not asserting that he constantly reminds himself of "why" he is making an omelet, but if the action is intentional he certainly knows "why" he is making it. In order to succeed in his action he is *only* looking forward; thinking about the next step in the series of actions and "knowing how" to make it and "why" there is a series of actions x, y, and z.

The diagnosis of SWERVING THE WHEEL is that action is conceived in its secondary conception, namely as a description of events, i.e., mental states, bodily movements, and further effects that happen in the world. But the primary conception of an action is the model of OMELET. If we ask Mr. Enemy "why" he deliberately moved the wheel in the direction of your neighbor he will respond that "he did not" and then understand that his action was not intentional.

The difficulty is that any correct description of an action must grasp the model of OMELET, including the action of creating institutional facts. In other words, it needs to grasp the deliberative mode of the agent and this is only possible if we begin and finish with the answers to the question "Why?." The correct interpretation is not that we "effectively" ask the agent "why" he did this and not that. It is rather that it is implicit because we ourselves are "knowers" of the "know-how" of the practice and tap into the good-making characteristics, values and principles of the intentional actions and resultant practices. We are all practical reasoners, we have acquired know-how and exercise this capacity. Therefore we can perceive this capacity in others.[14]

In her book *Intention*, Elizabeth Anscombe engages with the task of explaining intentional action along the lines of OMELET. Her explanation should be understood within the philosophical tradition of Aristotle and Aquinas. Anscombe identifies a number of key features that characterize intention and intentional action.[15] These features include:

(a) *The former stages of an intentional action are "swallowed up" by later stages.* Intentional action is composed of a number of stages or series of actions. For example, if I intend to make a cup of tea, I first put on the kettle *in order* to boil water, I boil water *in order* to pour it into a cup of tea. While I am making tea, however, there are many other things that I am doing that are irrelevant to my intentional action and to *what is happening as*

[14] This point requires a deeper analysis of perception and practical knowledge. This is, however, an under-researched area. The Aristotelian notion of "perception" is widely explored in ancient history of philosophy, but its connection to practical knowledge is almost absent in the secondary literature.

[15] To develop this section, I have relied on material that was published in Veronica Rodriguez-Blanco, *Law Under The Guise of the Good* (Hart Publishing 2014).

intentional. For example, I sneeze, I look through the window, I sing, and so on. Similarly, many other things are happening in the world that are irrelevant to what I do and that happen as a result of what I do intentionally. Thus, the kitchen has a specific location, the flowers in the garden are in bloom, the wind is blowing and blows open the window, and so on. Because my action of making tea is intentional, *I impose an order on the chaos of the world and this order is the order of reasons.* Thus I put on the kettle *in order* to boil water and I boil water *in order to* pour it into a cup. This is how I understand the sequence of happenings in the world that I, as an agent, *produce or make happen.* But, arguably, there could be an infinite number of series of actions; there could be a continuous infinite, or ceaseless, seamless web of actions. The question "Why?" can always be prompted: "Why are you making tea?" and the agent might reply, "Because it gives me comfort in the morning." There is, however, an end to the "Why?" series of questions and the end comes when the agent provides a characterization of the end or *telos* as a good-making characteristic. The action becomes intelligible and there is no need to ask "Why?" again. The end as the last stage of the "Why?" series of questions swallows up the former stages of the action and makes a complete unity of the action. Intentional actions are not fine-grained, they are not divisible into parts. Thus, parts of series of actions are only intelligible because they belong to an order that finds unity in the whole.

(b) *Intentional action is something actually done, brought about according to the order conceived or imagined by the agent.* Intentional action is not an action that is done in a certain way, mood or style.[16] Thus, it is not an action plus "something else," i.e., a will or desire that is directed toward an action. *Intention is not an additional element; e.g., an interior thought or state of mind,* it is rather something that is *done* or *brought about* according to the order of reasons that has been conceived by the agent. Consequently, if the question "Why?" has application to the action in question, we can assert that the action is intentional. The prompting of the question "Why?" is the mechanism that enables us to identify whether there is an intentional action. Intentional action is neither the mere movements of our body nor the simple result of transformations of the basic materials upon which agency is exercised, e.g., the tea leaves, kettle, boiling water. It is a doing or bringing about that is manifested by the expression of a future state of affairs and the fact that the agent is *actually* doing something or bringing

[16] Elizabeth Anscombe, *Intention* (2nd edn., Harvard University Press 2000) § 20.

it about according to the order of reasons as conceived or imagined by the agent.[17]

(c) *Intentional action involves knowledge that is non-observational, but it might be aided by observation.* If I am an agent that acts in an intentional way, I know that I am bringing about something and I know this without the need to observe every single step of my series of actions to verify that (effectively) I am acting.[18] In performing my action I might be aided by observation, but I know *what* is the order of the series of actions and *why*. This is the essence of practical knowledge. You do not need a theoretical stance toward yourself, a verification and observation of the movements of your body to know that you are performing an intentional action and bringing about *something*. Following the previous example, you do not need to observe that "you are making tea" to know that you intend to "make tea" and that you are bringing this about. You put on the kettle and boil the water, you do not ask yourself, "let me see what my body is up to, let me observe what I am doing," and then infer from the movements of your body that you are actually bringing about "making tea." Of course you can be aided by observation, you need your sight to put the kettle in the right position and to pour the boiling water without spilling it. But you do not use your observation and inferences from the observational data to know that you are making tea. On the contrary, the more you need this verification or theoretical stance toward yourself, the more likely it is that your action is not intentional, you are not controlling the action and you are not guided by the order of reasons. You are not an agent on this occasion, rather something is happening to you.

The state of affairs that you intend to bring about is at a distance, it might not be within your sight.[19] Imagine a painter who intends to make a painting. He has an idea about what the painting will look like, e.g., how the colors will be distributed across the canvas, and what topics and concepts will be at work in the painting. The painting is at a distance and the painter does not need to observe the movements of his body and the motion of the brushes to know *what* he is painting and *why* he is painting what he is painting. Certainly, his sight will help him to find the adequate color at the correct time and to shape the figures at the right angle, but his intentional action is not what he observes; it is not the result of his painting but what he is actually doing. We do what happens.

[17] Ibid. §§ 21–2. [18] Ibid. §§ 28–9. [19] Ibid. §§ 29–30.

(d) *In acting intentionally, we exercise our practical knowledge. We can understand practical knowledge if we understand the structure of practical reasoning.* Intentional action is not in the mind, it is not primarily a mental state, it is not an internal thought.[20] Rather it manifests itself publicly and within the public reasons that we share as creatures with certain constitutions and who belong to a particular time and place. For example, we eat healthy food because it is good to survive, we look after our family because we love them, we avoid harm because we aim to enjoy pleasant things and so on. Similarly, we know that to make a cake you need flour, sugar, eggs, and milk. If I see you mixing grass and earth and you tell me that you are making a cake, then I can assert, if I consider that you are in sound mind, that there might be a mistake in your performance or that you do not understand what it is "to make a cake."

According to Anscombe, Aristotle establishes a strong analogy between practical and theoretical syllogism and this has led to misinterpretations about what practical syllogism is.[21] Like theoretical syllogism, practical syllogism is often systematized by Aristotelian interpreters as having two premises, i.e., major and minor, and a conclusion. It is said that, as in the case of theoretical syllogism, the practical syllogism is a proof or demonstration. The typical form might be as follows:

Vitamin X is good for all men over sixty
Pig's tripes are full of vitamin X
I am a man over sixty
Here are pig's tripes

But in this case nothing seems to follow about doing anything. Furthermore, the practical syllogism is sometimes interpreted as having an ethical or moral character and establishing a way to prove what we ought to do. Following the previous example, the conclusion might be "I should eat pigs' tripes." Anscombe rejects this view since Aristotle's examples are not in ethical contexts, i.e., "dried food is healthy," "tasting things that are sweet" is pleasant. Additionally the word "should" (*dei*) as it appears in the Aristotelian texts has an unlimited number of applications and does not necessarily refer to the ethical or moral context.[22]

Aristotle insists that the starting point of any intentional action is the state of affairs or something that the agent wants and is wanted because it is presented to the agent as having good-making characteristics or as being valuable. For example, the man wants to have vitamin X because it is healthy.

[20] Ibid. §§ 21–2, 25, 27–8. [21] Ibid. § 33, §§ 33–4. [22] Ibid. § 35.

Furthermore, the practical syllogism is not limited to two premises and a conclusion, there can be many intermediate instances that are part of the syllogism. After a close analysis, the analogy between practical and theoretical syllogism breaks. Unlike theoretical syllogism, practical syllogism is not a proof or demonstration of a true proposition, nor is it a proof or demonstration of what ought to be done or what we ought to do. It is a form of *how* and *why* we are bringing something about when we are *actually* bringing it about.

Anscombe presents us with an alternative analysis to the practical syllogism and a different way to understand practical reasoning. Thus, the series of responses to the question "Why?" manifests or reveals the practical reasoning of the agent and enables us to identify whether the action that the agent is performing is intentional or not. However, she warns us, the why-question methodology is as "artificial" as the Aristotelian methodology of practical syllogism.[23] When we act intentionally, we are exercising a kind of reasoning which is not theoretical and which is grounded on a desire for that which seems to the agent to be constituted by good-making characteristics. You know the thing or state of affairs that you are bringing about because you desire the thing or state of affairs that you are bringing about, and you are able to desire the thing or state of affairs that you are bringing about because you know *practically* the state of affairs. Your desire arises because you represent the thing or the state of affairs to be brought about as valuable or good. Volition and knowledge do not fall apart.[24] For example, if you are a painter, you know how and why the shapes and colors on the canvass are what they are, it is because you desire and value the painting you will produce that it should be such and such a color and shape. But it is also true that because you desire and value *this* and *not that* arrangement of colors and shapes, that you are able to know it *practically*. Consequently, moral approbation is irrelevant for practical reasoning and for our practical engagement with the world.[25] This does not mean that there are no instances of objectively justified reasons for actions.

Whatever strategy we follow to show the structure of intentional action, whether we take the Aristotelian practical syllogism or the Anscombian series of actions revealed by the question "Why," we are able to grasp the mechanism of practical reasoning in its different manifestations.

In the following section, I will argue that if Anscombe is right and both strategies are "artificial" ways of understanding,[26] then a deeper and more "natural" way of understanding practical reasoning is by grasping the nature of the capacity that is exercised by the agent. *In other words, the answers to*

[23] Ibid. §§ 41–2. [24] Ibid. § 36. [25] Ibid. §§ 37–8. [26] Ibid. §§ 41–2.

the "Why?" questions show a capacity that the agent is exercising when acting. In the next section, I will show that the Aristotelian potentiality/actuality distinction sheds light on understanding the exercise and nature of our practical reasoning capacities. Furthermore, the potentiality/actuality distinction illuminates each of the key features of intentional action (a, b, c, and d) and their interplay as identified by Anscombe. This metaphysical distinction between potentiality and actuality is the key to understanding how human actions that are intentional can cause institutional facts and artifacts like law. We determine such artifacts through our intentions, but the correct way of thinking about this determination is, as Searle correctly points out, neither in terms of efficient causation, nor in terms of an exploration of the conditions of possibility of the experience of acting. The reason for this is because then we are not truly explaining how intentions *determine* artifacts. The distinction between potentiality and actuality enables us to understand how capacities work and how selves with practical capacities, such as practical reasoning and intentions, can create artifacts like law.

4. Aristotle's Distinction between Actuality and Potentiality

Contra Parmenides who has argued that motion is impossible since something cannot come from nothing, Aristotle advances the idea that motion or change is possible if there is an underlying nature or constant feature that does not change. To explain this, Aristotle resorts to the distinction between potentiality and actuality. In *Metaphysics*, book Θ, Aristotle uses the analogical method to show that particular instances of the scheme or idea of potentiality and actuality have a pattern.[27] Thus he begins with the particular instances of capacity/change and matter/form to explain the common patterns that will illuminate the general scheme of potentiality/actuality. However, since our purpose is to elucidate the character of practical reasoning which is a power or capacity, and I have argued that the general scheme of potentiality/actuality will help us to clarify the nature of practical reason, it is circular to resort now to the particular instance of capacity/change to explain potentiality/actuality. I will, therefore, amend the Aristotelian argumentative strategy and explain

[27] I follow the interpretation of Aristotle's *Metaphysics*, book Θ advanced by Stephen Makin and Michael Frede. See Aristotle, *Metaphysics Theta* (S. Makin tr. and ed., Clarendon Press 2006); Michael Frede, "Aristotle's Notion of Potentiality in Metaphysics" in Theodore Scaltas, David Charles, and Mary L. Gill (eds.), *Unity, Identity and Explanation in Metaphysics* (Clarendon Press 1994).

the general scheme of potentiality/actuality. I will then proceed to explain the particular instance of exercising our practical capacities as the actuality of a potentiality.

Capturing what "motion" is, is difficult and many definitions of "motion" tend to use terms that presuppose motion. For example, "a going-out from potency to act which is not sudden," but "going-out" presupposes motion and "sudden"[28] is defined in terms of time which is also defined in terms of motion. Therefore, this kind of definition is discarded by Aristotle for being circular and unhelpful. Nor can we define motion in terms of pure potency, because if we say that "bronze is potentially a statue," we are merely referring to the piece of bronze which has not yet been changed in which case there is no motion. You cannot refer to motion or to change as being "actual." (For instance, you cannot refer to what has been built or transformed, e.g., a building or statue, because it is not being moved but has *already* moved.) In the example of a building, the bricks, wood, clay, cement of the building have been already moved; and in the case of a statue, the bronze has already been transformed. Thus, Aristotle defines motion as a kind of actuality, which is hard to grasp. In other words, *the actuality of what exists potentially, in so far as it exists potentially.*[29] Motion is an actuality that is incomplete. It is hard to grasp and the tendency is to say that motion is the actuality. In the example of the house, it is the house that has been built. The other tendency is to say that motion is the privation of something, i.e., the going from nothing to something, from not being a house to being a house. Finally, the tendency is also to think that motion is what exists before potentiality, e.g., the bricks, steel, wood, cement, and so on. Contrary to these tendencies, Aristotle insists that motion is what happens exactly at the *midpoint*, neither *before* when nothing has been moved and is mere potentiality, and neither *after*, when something *has* been moved. Furthermore, motion is not privation, it is rather constitutive actuality. For example, if the baby has not learned to speak English, we say that the baby is potentially a speaker of English. If a man knows how to speak English and is in silence, he is also potentially a speaker of English. Finally when the man is speaking English, we say that he is actually an English speaker speaking English. However, the potentiality of the baby (p1) is different from the potentiality of the man in silence (p2), and motion is located in the second potentiality (p2), when the man is in silence, but begins to pronounce a sentence to speak English. Motion is midway and is not privative, but rather constitutive. We do not say that the man speaking

[28] Aristotle, *Physics Book III and IV* (E. Hussey tr., Clarendon Press 1983) 284.
[29] Ibid. III.1.201a9-11.

English went from being a non-speaker of English to a speaker of English, we say that he went from being in silence to speaking English (he knew how to speak English, but did not exercise his capacities).

The previous example locates us in the domain of the particular instance of capacity and change as exemplified by the potentiality/actuality distinction. Aristotle argues that there are many different types of capacity, i.e., active/passive, non-rational/rational, innate/acquired, acquired by learning/ acquired by practice, and one way/two way capacities. Two-way capacities are connected to rational capacities, whereas one-way capacities are linked to non-rational capacities. For example, bees have a natural capacity to pollinate a foxglove flower in normal circumstances[30] ("normal" circumstances might include a healthy bee in an adequate foxglove, and the absence of preventive circumstances). In the case of two-way capacities there ought to be an element of *choice or desire* to act, and the rational being can exercise her capacity by producing or bringing about "p." Furthermore, she also knows how to produce or bring about the absence of a state of affairs. The paradigmatic example used by Aristotle is medical skill. The doctor knows how to make the patient healthy and how to eliminate disease or illness. Therefore the doctor can bring about two opposite effects.[31] For Aristotle, to have a rational capacity is to have an intellectual understanding of the form that will be transmitted to the object of change or motion. Thus, the doctor will have an understanding of what it means to be healthy and without illness. Let us suppose that a chef is making a cake. He needs to understand the order of the series of actions that will result in a cake and he needs to possess knowledge about the necessary ingredients and temperature of the oven. The chef also needs to understand how to avoid producing non-cakes, e.g., crepes. His action will be directed to making a cake and to not making a non-cake.

In the exercise of practical reason we choose to act[32] and this choosing activates the action and directs the capacity toward the series of actions that will be performed. By contrast, a non-rational capacity is non self-activating, its acts are necessary. If the bee is in good health and there are no obstacles, it will pollinate the foxglove flower. By contrast, rational agents need to *choose or decide* to act to produce a result.

When we say that the medical doctor has the rational capacity to change the unwell patient into a healthy human being, Aristotle says that she has the "origin of change." She is curing the patient and therefore she is in motion because she actualizes her practical reasoning capacities to bring about the

[30] Aristotle, *Metaphysics Theta* (n. 27) 43.

[31] Ibid. 1046b4-5, 6-7.

[32] Ibid. 1048a10-11.

result as she understands it. She has an order of reasons that connects a series of actions and knowledge of how to produce changes.

She is the origin of change because her medical know-how explains why certain changes occur in situations involving that object, e.g., the patient who suffers chickenpox has fewer spots and less fever. For example, when a teacher intends to teach and starts to say some sentences on the topic of "Jurisprudence" to her pupils, we say that she is teaching. She is the origin of change in the pupils who are the objects of change. Thus, the students begin to understand the topic and have a grasp of the basic concepts.[33] Similarly, when legislators create the law and judges decide cases, they establish rules, directives and principles and these rules, directives and principles can be found in statutes and case reports. Can we say that legislators and judges have reached the end of the process? No, we cannot: statutes and case reports do not represent the end of the process since citizens need to comply with the legal rules and directives and perform the actions as intended by the legislators and judges. We say that legislators and judges are the origin of change because they know how and have an order of reasons that enables citizens to comply with legal rules and directives. The order or reasons as good-making characteristics ground the rules, decisions, and legal directives. In parallel to the situation of the teacher, I cannot say that I am teaching unless my pupils begin to understand the topic that I am teaching. Thus, the legislator cannot say that she is legislating and the judge cannot say that she is judging, in paradigmatic cases, unless there is some performance of their actions by the addressees as they intend.

The distinction between potentiality/actuality clarifies the structure of practical reason as a capacity that is actualized when we act intentionally. We can now understand that the features of an intentional action identified by Anscombe can be illuminated by the potentiality/actuality distinction. The idea that the former stages of an intentional action are swallowed up by the later stages is explained by the idea that motion is constitutive and not privative. It is not that when I begin to act I do so as an irrational or arational being, and that when I finish acting I am a rational being, or that I go from non-intentional to intentional action, but rather that I go from being a rational being and *potentially* intentional action to being a rational being and *actual* intentional action. Later stages begin to actualize something that was potentially there. My practical reason was always there *potentially* and the

[33] Makin argues that the teacher analogy is intended to show that the teleological perspective is equally appropriate for other-directed capacities and self-directed capacity: see Aristotle, *Metaphysics Theta* (n. 27) 198.

intentional action actualizes an order of ideas provided by my practical reason. For Anscombe, intentional action is something *actually* done, brought about according to the order conceived or imagined by the agent. If practical capacity is understood in the light of the general scheme of actuality/potentiality, then intentional action involves knowledge that is non-observational, but it might be aided by observation. In acting intentionally, I am exercising my practical reasoning capacity and this capacity is in motion. This motion is represented at the midpoint—*after* I potentially have an intention to act and *before* I have reached the result of my intentional action. It is not that the forming of an intention from nothing to something is a *magical* process. *It is rather that I potentially have the power to intend which in appropriate circumstances can be exercised.* As being in motion, I am the agent who knows *what* she is doing and *why* she is doing what she is doing, but if I observe myself doing the action, then I have stopped the action.[34] There is no action. There is no more motion and no exercise of my capacities. Finally, Anscombe asserts that in acting intentionally we exercise our practical knowledge. Because we are the kind of creatures that we are, we can *choose* or *decide to bring about* a state of affairs in the world. We choose according to our reasons and practical knowledge. Practical knowledge is potentially in all human beings and when we decide to bring about a situation or do a certain thing, then we actualize this potentiality. We can direct our actions to producing either of two opposing results (e.g., health or illness, ignorance or knowledge). By contrast, non-rational creatures can only produce one result under normal circumstances and with no impeding conditions (e.g., the bee pollinating the foxglove). It should be noted that to have an actual capacity, such as practical reasoning and the capacity to act intentionally, does not mean that A can Φ, nor that A will Φ if there are normal conditions and no impeding conditions. Instead it means that *A will Φ unless she is stopped or prevented.* Thus, once our practical reasoning capacity begins to be actualized, it will strive to produce or do what A has conceived. Once A decides or chooses to act then a certain state of affairs will be produced unless she is prevented or stopped. Intentional action and practical reasoning are not dispositions like being fragile or elastic, nor are they possibilities that something will be done. They are powers.

Now that we have grasped the idea of potentiality/actuality as the general scheme for explaining the structure of practical reason, we can turn to the problem of authorship of institutional facts.

We could say that within this conception of intention the process of practical reasoning runs parallel to the intention. The process is understood as the

[34] See J. David Velleman, *Practical Reflection* (Princeton University Press 1989).

order of reasons, including values, ends, and/or principles that the agent conceives he or she is bringing about. The *effect* (i.e., the *physical or empirical aspects* of an omelet, coffee, tango dance, law, games, a banknote, and so on) are unintelligible without an understanding of the process, i.e., intentions that run parallel to practical reasoning. The process is not something external or contingent to the effect. On the contrary, the process illuminates the effect and in some sense, the effect is swallowed up by the process. We can say, therefore, that the principles of the different artifacts, including the institutional facts are in the author since he or she knows *practically, i.e., in terms of an order of the reasons,* what he or she is producing. On this account the agent who exercises his or her intention as running in parallel to practical reasoning is genuinely a *producer.* Intention is not what is expected nor the standard against which we will assess the effect. Neither is it only a mere mental state that has a theoretical stance that randomly causes an effect which cannot clearly be connected to its cause, i.e., intention as mental state. On the contrary, it is the agent exercising her or his practical capacities that is truly the creator of the effect (i.e., the physical or empirical conditions of the artifact) which cannot become intelligible and be understood without looking carefully at the process. Under the appearance of a contingent assembly of empirical or physical conditions (which, in the case of a law for example, would be the relevant acts of parliament, the bodily movements of the citizens following the law, and the language of the law) lies an *order* that is provided by the agents. They are the origin of what they produce and the production is due to a specific process, i.e., practical reasoning. The process gives intelligibility to the effect.

If law is a specific kind of artifact, i.e., an institutional fact, then it is created under the OMELET type of reasoning. Legislators and judges engage in reasons, including principles, values, and ends, that they aim to bring about and imagine an *order* to produce it. Intention is neither granted nor given, and nor is the expected result against which we ought to interpret the law.

The "background abilities" advanced by Searle are actually part of intention as a process conceived as the structure of practical reasoning. They have both a causal and functional level *at the same time.*

This chapter began with the question of how intentions can create artifacts. The answer provided is that intentions create artifacts because intentions involve practical reason and practical knowledge. To adequately explain practical reason, the empirical model that reduces reason to a bundle of experiences and effective causation of prior mental states seems unsatisfactory. However, it is not sufficient to take intentions and practical reason for granted and to argue that they are a given phenomenon, whose conditions of possibility explain the given phenomenon. This solution avoids the question of how our intentions and practical reason create artifacts.

By contrast, we have argued that intentions create artifacts because intention as practical reason is a capacity. Like all capacities, e.g., speaking a language, practical reason can exist in two forms, i.e., potentially or actually. We have explained in detail the metaphysics of potentiality and actuality but we have also shown that this capacity is actualized to produce effects or ends. These ends are values or principles that are conceived and known by the agent.

Similarly, we argue that law is an artifact because its key feature is that it performs the intended function, but the question that then arises is how law as an artifact is created by intentions and practical reason.

Our argumentative strategy has been to bring attention to the dynamic structure of practical reason and to show that the underlying structure of complex artifacts, including legal systems, is the structure of practical reason. Law-makers create law as an artifact invoking good-making characteristics and making it possible for citizens to understand the reasons of the law as good-making characteristics. We have focused on the idea that law is an activity that unfolds within the structure or order of reasons as values and principles. However, law-makers can exercise their practical capacity in a defective way. If the citizens of a legal system, e.g., the European Union, feel *systematically* alienated from the laws imposed on them and cannot avow the ends as good-making characteristics that law-makers intend to produce, we confront, most likely, a marginal case of a legal system. I have explained elsewhere that marginal cases arise due to the inversion of values, the misunderstanding of good-making characteristics in law, and the defective realization of elements that constitute the Rule of Law, e.g., clarity, coherence, and so on.[35] One might object that the normal citizen cannot have access to the technicalities of certain laws in complex legal systems. If the law is excessively technical and there is no *logos* in terms of values that can connect to the practical reasoning of the citizen, then one might say that the practical reasoning of the law-maker has been defectively exercised. Law-makers can fail because of a defective exercise of practical reason.

Let us take a paradigmatic example of intentions and practical reason creating law as an artifact according to the principles and values of the law-maker. Let us take the EU Toy Safety Directive 2009/48/EC. Chapter 1 of the Directive establishes the subject matter, the scope of the Directive, and the definitions used by it, e.g., risk, harm, hazard. Chapter 2 establishes the obligations of economic operators. Chapter 3 describes the rules for conformity of toys, including warnings. Chapter 4 indicates how the conformity

[35] See Rodriguez-Blanco, *Law Under The Guise of the Good* (n. 15).

assessment will proceed. Chapter 5 describes the notification of conformity assessment bodies, and Chapter 6 considers the obligations and powers of the Member States. The final chapters concentrate on committee procedures, administrative provisions, and transitional provisions. Article 2(1) indicates: "This Directive shall apply to products designed or intended, whether or not exclusively, for use in play by children under 14 years of age." Economic operators are defined in the Directive as "the manufacturer," "the authorised representative," "the importer," and "the distributor." A "chemical toy" is defined as "a toy intended for the direct handling of chemical substances and mixture and which is used in a manner appropriate to a given age-group and under the supervisor of an adult." "Harm" is defined as "physical injury or any other damage to health, including long-term health effects." Article 10(2) establishes the essential safety requirements: "Toys, including the chemicals they contain, shall not jeopardise the safety or health of users or third parties when they are used as intended or in a foreseeable way, bearing in mind the behaviour of the children."

Despite the complexity of the Directive, the ends as good-making characteristics that the law-maker intended are clear. If I am a manufacturer, I am able to avow the ends of the Directive as ends with good-making characteristics. I manufacture toys with chemical substances and need to ensure that these substances do not cause harm to children. The law-maker has created the Directive as an artifact with an underlying *logos, which is that the health of children is a value or good.* Of course, it might be that as the owner of a toy manufacturing company I am completely insensitive to the health of children, but this only shows that I fall short of the good exercise of practical reason.

5. Conclusions

I have argued in favor of a model of intention as diachronically directed to an end. Thus, intention is conceived as an activity, process, or bringing about of an object or state of affairs. This model explains how we effectively produce artifacts and specific kinds of artifacts which are institutional facts. I have rejected the model of intention as a mental state since it cannot explain how mental states are effectively connected to its *intended* effects. We are tempted to add something such as "volition" to re-establish the causal connection between mental states and effects but the idea of "volition" as an entity that operates within us has been criticized by authors such as Wittgenstein and Ryle. The alternative solution advanced by the classical tradition and some contemporary authors, such as Anscombe, provides the idea of intention as a process of bringing about something. Intentions run parallel to our capacities for reasoning and this process creates an order to reasons that makes intelligible the product of the process. I have used this model to illuminate the idea of artifacts, including institutional facts. I have also rejected the idea that intentions should be reduced to theoretical explanations as expected results or should be understood as *given or presupposed.*

PART IV

SKEPTICISM

11

A Strange Kind of Artifact

Giovanni Tuzet

How does the real get into the made-up?
Ask me an easier one.

Seamus Heaney, *Electric Light*

1. Introduction

Law is a strange kind of artifact, for it has a set of properties that are significantly different from those of everyday artifacts such as tables and chairs. First, law is not a material artifact (as a table) but an intellectual one. Second, it is different from other intellectual artifacts (as poems) because it is normative. Third, it is different from an individual creation because it is social: it exists only in, and for, a society. And fourth, as a social artifact, it cannot be reduced to some authors' intentions, nor to some users': in fact, it is the interplay of different social actors (such as legislators, scholars, judges, etc.) that makes up the law, through interpretation in particular.

These points are not entirely new. They have been made in the literature, often under different terminologies. But I find it useful to make them together in order to discuss the idea of law as a kind of artifact. Notice that I won't deny that law is an artifact: once the claim that law is a natural kind is rejected, there is no reasonable alternative to conceive of it as a human and social creation. Nevertheless, law is different from other artifacts and it deserves a careful discussion to illustrate why it cannot be theoretically explicated by reference to standard artifacts such as tables and chairs, poems and symphonies, etc.

The chapter starts by making some preliminary claims on the ontology of law (Section 2). Mainly, I will distinguish process-ontology from product-ontology, so as to distinguish, from the creation itself, the conditions out of

Law as an Artifact. First Edition. Edited by Luka Burazin, Kenneth Einar Himma, and Corrado Roversi. Chapter 11 © Giovanni Tuzet 2018. Published 2018 by Oxford University Press.

which law is created. Then, assuming that law is a kind of artifact, the chapter explores the peculiar features it has (Section 3). The chapter concludes with a comment on the need to discuss the functions of law (as a kind of artifact) and argues on the interdependence of what-questions and why-questions about artifacts in general and law in particular (Section 4).

2. Some Ontological Preliminaries

There are two readings of the phrase "ontology of law." It can be taken to address the ontology of law as a kind of entity the status and properties of which must be scrutinized in philosophy. Alternatively, it can be taken to address the ontology of the entities the law is about or the law deals with.

The phrase is usually interpreted in the former way. In this sense, you find scholarly claims about law as a set of commands, a set of norms, a set of institutions, a set of decisions, and still other claims. Different theories of law (Imperativism, Normativism, Institutionalism, Realism, and so on) distinguish themselves in this respect. But the phrase above can be interpreted in the latter sense also, which is less usual and quite intriguing. The law deals with a great variety of entities ranging from natural ones such as hydric resources and natural gas, and from very concrete artifacts such as tables and chairs (the property of which may be discussed in a lawsuit), to very abstract things like constitutional values such as dignity, liberty, and equality. Surprisingly enough, law may also deal with imaginary things like poltergeists: if a certain house is reputed to be haunted and the seller does not inform the (non-local) buyer of this reputation, the buyer might have a remedy according to the law.[1]

A critical examination of the idea of law as a kind of artifact belongs to the realm defined by the former reading of the "ontology of law" phrase. It's about law itself, not about the things with which law is concerned. But further clarification is needed to fully comprehend the issue: the ontological distinction between the process out of which something is produced and the product itself must be made. Let me state that, for the sake of generality, I'll be using "process" in the broadest meaning it has, encompassing unintentional and intentional happenings, social practices and events (sometimes opaque to their participants) together with overt decisions and acts.

[1] [1991] *Stambovsky v. Ackley* 169 A.D.2d 254.

Now, as an entity, or better, a set of entities, law is ontologically different from the process that generates it. So, if we aim to inquire into the nature of law, we must distinguish *process-ontology* from *product-ontology*. Like a poem is different from the process of writing it, law is different from the process that generates it. But of course there is no product without production process, so we should not disregard where law comes from. It does not exist by itself out there, it's not like water. At the same time we should not erroneously identify the instances of law with the acts and processes that generate them. It would be a category mistake.

Many things that are much discussed and highly disputed in the recent literature, such as collective intentions, collective recognition or acceptance, shared cooperative activity, jointly intentional activity, and legal practice, belong to the realm of the first account, i.e. process-ontology. Legal rules and procedures belong to the second, i.e. product-ontology. Those who ask questions like "Is law grounded in a social practice?" or "Is law based on a shared cooperative activity?" wonder about the things law depends upon; strictly speaking they don't ask what law is, they assume instead that what we call "law" is a given kind of entity and then wonder about the process that generates it and sustains it. For one thing are the conditions out of which law is produced, and quite another is law itself, even though the two are strictly related by the simple fact that the former produces the latter.[2] Kelsen put it this way:

> Though a legal norm is not identical with any natural fact, the existence of a legal norm is dependent upon certain objectively verifiable facts.[3] The norm-creating act is a fact which exists in time and space and can be perceived by our senses. This fact can be described in an *is*-statement. But this fact is different from its meaning—that is, the norm—which is the object of jurisprudence, and which cannot be described in an *is*-statement, but only in an *ought*-statement.[4]

Similarly, the process of writing a poem is different from, but strictly related to, the poem itself. The process or act of creation has some spatiotemporal properties that its outcome has not, and vice versa the outcome has some aesthetic properties that the process has not. For instance, it would be improper to say that the act of writing a poem is sad because the poem is sad; and it would be incorrect to say that a poem is in Berlin because it is composed in Berlin.

[2] I have already stressed this point, discussing Marmor's conventionalism, in Giovanni Tuzet, "The Social Reality of Law" in Paolo Comanducci and Riccardo Guastini (eds.), *Analisi e diritto 2007* (Giappichelli 2007) 189, 194.

[3] Hans Kelsen, "Value Judgments in the Science of Law" (1942) 7 *Journal of Social Philosophy and Jurisprudence* 312, 330.

[4] Hans Kelsen, "What is the Pure Theory of Law" (1960) 34 *Tulane Law Review* 269, 271.

So artifacts and practices are different because they have different properties. But remember they have some important relations: for instance, some artifacts are made through practices (e.g., law as the outcome of social practices); and some practices depend on the possibility of using certain artifacts (e.g., hunting wild animals with traps, weapons of various sorts, etc.).

Returning to the subject of law, it can be said that our focus should be on the process of creating and maintaining a political society or community endowed with a legal system. Yet equally important is the focus on the results of that process and in particular on the rules and devices it establishes for the life of the society or community. What comes first from a conceptual viewpoint is hard to say. This is a form of the "chicken-egg" problem or paradox.[5] Chickens cannot exist without chicken eggs, and vice versa. Legal acts cannot exist without legal norms defining them as such, but legal norms cannot exist without acts that produce them. Legal institutions cannot exist without legal norms conferring upon them some legal powers, and vice versa legal norms cannot exist without legal institutions or authorities creating them. But from an explanatory viewpoint I assume that things are less troublesome in our case than with chickens: the social process generating law is explanatorily prior to the results it yields.

In other words, some collective intentionality is necessary to confer upon certain acts the status of legality and the capacity to produce instances of law.[6] And some kind of social force is necessary too.[7] The example may sound a bit extreme, but think of a self-proclaimed Emperor in the late Roman age, which was replete with intestine fights, barbarous challenges, and corruption: without the support of the legions in the first place, nothing legal followed from the self-proclamation.

Traditionally, legal theory has been concerned with product-ontology. The same will be true of our question about law as a kind of artifact, without neglecting however the material conditions of its generation.[8] Let me repeat it: we should not conflate the social process that generates it, nor the social conditions out of which law is produced and maintained, with the product itself and the features it has. But we should not forget that no product exists without a production.

[5] Scott Shapiro, *Legality* (Harvard University Press 2011) 39ff. Cf. Ota Weinberger, "Institutionalist Theories of Law" in Paul Amselek and Neil MacCormick (eds.), *Controversies About Law's Ontology* (Edinburgh University Press 1991).

[6] In Tuzet, "The Social Reality of Law" (n. 2) I suggest an account that combines philosophical ideas from Kripke and Searle, an act of "baptism" (the role of the authority) sustained by collective intentionality (the role of the relevant community).

[7] Cf. Frederick Schauer, *The Force of Law* (Harvard University Press 2015).

[8] See Amie L. Thomasson, "Realism and Human Kinds" (2003) 67 *Philosophy and Phenomenological Research* 580, 587.

Let me also add that the Hartian discussion on the "rule of recognition" has probably obscured the distinction I'm making: while Hartian primary rules and, among his secondary rules, rules of change and rules of adjudication are products of some law-making activity, his rule of recognition is ambiguous in this respect: you can take it either as the practice out of which the law is made or as the rule defining the criteria of legality.

3. Is Law a Kind of Artifact?

A positive answer to the question whether law is a kind of artifact is at variance with a natural law theory, of course. If you assume that there is some sense in which law is a natural kind, then in that sense there is no room for it being an artifact. If you assume that all law is natural, you would reject any claim about law being an artifact. The case would be different if you assume that some part of the law is natural and some artifactual, or that some laws are natural and some are not. Then an artifactual theory of law might have a point concerning that part of the law, or those laws, that are not natural. But of course a supporter of a positivist theory of law is more inclined to discuss and accept the idea of law as an artifact. Because for the positivist there are no instances of law but those that we create.

To give some examples, Eugenio Bulygin claims that for the positivist "all law is man-made: it is a human artefact";[9] John Gardner says that law is a "genre of artefacts" (laws are artifacts and law is the genre);[10] Brian Leiter claims that "law is an artefact concept";[11] Kenneth Ehrenberg says that law "as a genre is a type of institutionalized abstract artifact";[12] Luka Burazin states that "particular legal institutions are artifacts" and that the legal system can be "viewed as an artifact kind."[13]

Our preliminary discussion on process- and product-ontology is in tune with this: law comes out of social practices, acts, and events. There is no law apart from that, for the positivist. It may be good or bad, but that is a completely different issue: the positivist I am referring to talks from a theoretical

[9] Eugenio Bulygin, "Objectivity of Law in the View of Legal Positivism" in Paolo Comanducci and Riccardo Guastini (eds.), *Analisi e diritto 2004* (Giappichelli 2004) 219. See also Bruno Celano, "Giusnaturalismo, positivismo giuridico e pluralismo etico" (2005) 35 *Materiali per una storia della cultura giuridica* 161.

[10] John Gardner, "The Legality of Law" (2004) 17 *Ratio Juris* 168, 171.

[11] Brian Leiter, "The Demarcation Problem in Jurisprudence: A New Case for Scepticism" (2011) 31 *Oxford Journal of Legal Studies* 663, 666.

[12] Kenneth M. Ehrenberg, *The Functions of Law* (Oxford University Press 2016) 179.

[13] Luka Burazin, "Can There Be an Artifact Theory of Law?" (2016) 29 *Ratio Juris* 385, 386.

point of view, not from a moral or evaluative one. Positive law can be bad law. Being a positivist doesn't mean to endorse positive law.

Notice an additional aspect of this question that is somewhat intriguing: the positivist stance is usually associated with a scientific view or attitude toward human and social phenomena. Nowadays, in philosophy, having a scientific stance about a certain topic usually comes with being engaged in a project of "naturalization." Naturalizing the mind, consciousness, intentionality, morality, law, jurisprudence, etc.[14] Here it is quite the opposite. The positivist scholar inquiring into the "nature" of law as an artifact does not aim at reducing legal phenomena to natural ones. This is because such a positivist is committed to the idea that law is a human and social creation. Law is not the business of neurobiology, let alone chemistry or physics. It's rather the business of social ontology.

Moreover, if we look at the world around us we realize that it is more and more endowed with things we create. American pragmatist and sociologist George Mead had a nice way to put this: "We do not have to develop a new form with hairy covering to live in cold climates; we can simply produce clothes which enable the explorers to go to the North Pole."[15]

I'm writing this text in a library with a laptop, my sunglasses and cellphone on the table. I'm wearing a shirt, a pair of trousers, shoes, etc. The same is true of the people around me: they are not in a "natural" state, they have plenty of artifacts with them. From the window we see some trees, fortunately, but planted and grown by men between various buildings and other artifacts such as antennas and streetlights. Airplanes cross the sky while cars and other vehicles pass in the streets, canals, etc. The existence of all these things is regulated in some way or another by legal norms that define property rights, conditions of use, remedies for harm, sanctions for violation. It's definitely awkward to think that a natural science alone could make sense of all this.[16]

[14] See Brian Leiter, *Naturalizing Jurisprudence: Essays on American Legal Realism and Naturalism in Legal Philosophy* (Oxford University Press 2007), favoring in philosophy and jurisprudence the *method* of natural science (not the ontological reduction of everything to physics).

[15] George H. Mead, *Mind, Self, & Society: From the Standpoint of A Social Behaviorist* (first published 1934, Charles W. Morris ed., The University of Chicago Press 1967) 252.

[16] "What seems to me to be most fascinating in the legal and, more generally, ethical experience of men, is that it places us on the same level as the poetic dimension of our existence in the world (the term 'poetic' being understood with all its connotations—creative activity, addition to what is natural, supernatural).... From this point of view, the conception of our legal experience is not only distorted, but singularly impoverished when we localise law in Nature, outside its true, its real domain, which is the mind." (Paul Amselek, "Law in the Mind" in Amselek and MacCormick, *Controversies About Law's Ontology* (n. 5) 27.) Cf. Matthew H. Kramer, "Is Law's Conventionality Consistent with Law's Objectivity?" (2008) 14 *Res Publica* 241, for the claim that there can be no law without minds in general, but that individual minds and also communities can be in error about the law and its features; for a weaker point see Leiter, *Naturalizing Jurisprudence* (n. 14) 257ff.

Assuming that law is a kind of artifact (which is a reasonable assumption, when one excludes that it is a natural kind), it is interesting to inquire into the particular features of it.

3.1 An Intellectual Artifact

First, law is not a material artifact (as a table) but an intellectual one. I'm not claiming that it is nothing more than an intellectual (or mental) entity. In fact I will claim below that it is a social artifact too. Here I simply claim that it is not material. To fully appreciate this, consider our cognitive activity with respect to law.[17]

We do not perceive the law. We do not touch the rules, we do not smell the principles, we do not taste them either. It's true that in some sense we hear them when someone makes an oral legal statement in front of us. But that is loose talk: what we hear is an utterance having a legal content. We do not perceive the content, we perceive the signs that convey the content. We can hear someone stating what the law is on a certain topic, or a judge making a decision in a case. But we don't directly perceive the law: we hear some sounds that prompt an understanding and convey some legal content.

The same is true of the sight sense. We do not see the law, strictly speaking. Of course we can read legal documents, codes, written acts, and so on. But again we perceive some signs that convey a legal content. Everyone with a functioning sight system can see an approaching car, but no one can see the law in the same way. No one can understand what the law is if they don't understand the language it is expressed in, or if they are not able to interpret the relevant sentences.

It's true that we sometimes talk about "legal phenomena." But again it's loose talk. There are no legal phenomena in a strict sense, since there is nothing legal that can be perceived as such. "The very idea of phenomenality of norms is nonsensical," as French philosopher of law Paul Amselek put it.[18]

In this respect law is a peculiar artifact. The standard examples of artifacts are things like tables and chairs. They are material artifacts that can be perceived. We must admit that an individual without the concept of a table cannot perceive the table as a table: he or she will perceive some form made of wood or other material and will probably wonder about the use of it. Nevertheless they will perceive the artifact in its structure and materiality. Nothing of this kind happens with the law. You might use a chair even for

[17] Of course, as a reviewer has pointed out to me, being jailed is not an intellectual state of affairs. But I think it is a state of affairs motivated and possibly justified by intellectual (or abstract) things such as legal rules.

[18] Amselek, "Law in the Mind" (n. 16) 22.

uses that go beyond the standard one. For instance, you might use a chair as a weapon to hit someone and this person will experience the hardness of the chair. On the contrary, you cannot hit someone with a rule, apart from metaphorical talk.

In a nutshell, as I said, law is not a material artifact that can be perceived as all material things can. It's rather an intellectual artifact, a creation of the intellect that is similar to a poem in this respect. But again we should avoid a misunderstanding here: of course we read and hear poems, talking loosely; speaking literally, instead, what we read and hear are written or vocal signs whose meaning is the poem.

Other scholars make the point under a different terminology. Some say that law is a "mental" entity, something existing only in our minds.[19] Suppose we all disappear from this planet and some extraterrestrial explorers come down here after our extinction: they would not find any law. They would find buildings, cars, tables and chairs. But no law. They would likely find legal books and documents, but they would need to understand them and interpret them in order to have a grasp on what we call "law." They would perceive some written signs and would probably understand that they were creations of our mind put to some use. So they would make guesses about our minds and society.

Amselek made this point in a very convincing way, to my judgment, in a passage which is worth quoting at length:

> One may look at or touch an umbrella, since both this object and the ash-tray, by virtue of their composition, belong to the world of objectively perceivable things, whereas a rule is intangible and remains as a pure content of thought, within the closed intimacy of our mental circuits. It is impossible to hold a rule of conduct in one's hand. Of course, I can tear out a page of any legal code, the Civil Code for example, and I can brandish it. In doing this, I will only be waving a piece of paper, and certainly not rules of law, even if the piece of paper in question bears printed characters which represent the expression, in writing, of legal rules. These rules are not of themselves to be found in any of these materials, neither in the paper, nor in the ink printed on it, nor, besides, in the graphic characters which the ink produces on the paper. They belong to a universe quite different from that of objectively perceivable things.[20]

I have no deep troubles with labeling law as a "mental" entity. But I prefer the term "intellectual" as it better conveys the idea of something created by

[19] Ibid. 15. "Law cannot be observed amongst the objects of the external world, or in Nature: it is confined to a quite different place, and one from which it is impossible for it to escape—the minds of men."

[20] Ibid. 16.

our mind, not just present in it. In addition, I would like to avoid a solipsistic reading of what I've been saying: to say that law is in our mind is not to say that it's just in my mind, in yours, etc. As we shall see below, law is not only an intellectual but also a social artifact.

Other scholars say that law has an "abstract" nature, to differentiate it from concrete things like tables and chairs.[21] I have nothing against this label either, save the fact that also numbers and propositions are abstract entities. If we think it plausible to believe that there are abstract entities which are not our creations and have instead some independent status (such as numbers) we may prefer to characterize a poem or a law as an "intellectual" artifact.

I must also point out that some scholars differentiate artifacts from tools and instruments. Ehrenberg, referring to Randall Dipert, uses the following taxonomy: *instruments* constitute the broadest category, which includes "any object used purposely in an attempt to effect an intentional goal, and would include natural objects used by humans in an unmodified state"; *tools* are "instruments that are intentionally modified in some way to serve the purpose for which they are to be used"; and *artifacts* are "instruments that are intentionally modified in such a way so as to be recognizable by others as a certain kind of thing."[22]

This being said, not much changes for my purposes. To summarize the view I've been exposing, for the sake of ontology we must make a distinction between concrete or material artifacts (hammers, tables, chairs, cars) and abstract or intellectual ones (poems, symphonies, law, theories), since they have different properties and identity conditions. Notice that, once created, material artifacts continue to exist independently of us and continue to have their causal powers or dispositions even if no one uses them as such.[23] A looking glass maintains the disposition to reflect, even when no one is observing it. The causal powers and dispositions of such artifacts depend on their structure and material constitution. Now suppose that all human beings disappear from the universe: it makes sense to say that (what we call) a chair continues to exist on earth as a material thing, and it is equally clear that law, *qua* intellectual artifact, would disappear if all human beings were to disappear.[24] Of course those material objects that we call codes, legal books, and the like will

[21] Ehrenberg, *The Functions of Law* (n. 12) 11, 120. Cf. Burazin, "Can There Be an Artifact Theory of Law?" (n. 13) 387, 393, 397.

[22] Ehrenberg, *The Functions of Law* (n. 12) 10–11.

[23] Diego Marconi, "Artefatti e oggetti sociali" in Tiziana Andina and Carola Barbero (eds.), *Ermeneutica, estetica, ontologia* (il Mulino 2016).

[24] As a reviewer has observed, one reason that law would not continue to exist without people is that the existence of officials and citizens (or law-makers and law-subjects) is a necessary condition for the existence of a legal system.

continue to exist, but it makes no sense to claim that the law will continue to exist, for it is not identical with those objects themselves, being rather the semantic content of the marks printed in them.[25]

3.2 A Normative Artifact

Second, law is different from other intellectual artifacts (as poems) because it is normative. Perhaps this is a trivial point, for everyone agrees on the fact that law is normative. Nonetheless, it is important to see how this point contributes to the idea of law as a "strange kind of artifact."

Poems and symphonies are intellectual artifacts that serve various purposes, aesthetic in the first place. (A poem might also have a moral or political purpose, which is less true of a symphony.) In some sense a poem might also constitute a reason for action, when it gives the reader a reason to act in a way that is different from how they would act had they not read the poem. But a poem is not normative in the (strong) sense in which law is normative. Law is made of norms, rules, and principles. Law is made of standards of conduct, obligations, prohibitions, rights, immunities, permissions, etc. Nothing of this sort characterizes poems and symphonies, let alone tables and chairs.

Note I'm not discussing the issue of law's normativity in the justification perspective. I'm not asking whether and under what circumstances the law gives true reasons for action that provide a justification for one's conduct, in some strong sense of "justification." I'm not arguing about the binding value of law either. I'm just remarking that what we call "law" is made of such normative standards of conduct: obligations, prohibitions, rights, etc. established in legal rules and principles by legal authorities, according to legal procedures, etc.

I think that nothing of this sort is true of other kinds of artifacts. You might raise children educating them to admire poems and symphonies, but you don't teach them how to act using poems and symphonies. You teach them moral and social norms in the first place, then legal ones when they are able to grasp the subtleties of legal issues and the possible divergences of law and morality. Such teaching might go along with significant examples, provided by yourself or by others. Examples have a persuasive force that abstract rules lack. But this doesn't change the point I'm making here: the rules

[25] Consider this point on norms as reconstructed out of signs: "norms never leave our mind: we cannot exchange them directly; we merely exchange signals from which we reconstruct in our mind the norm present in someone else's mind" (Amselek, "Law in the Mind" (n. 16) 20–1).

that are taught, via examples or not, have a normative dimension by definition. So, if law is a kind of artifact, it is a peculiar one also in this respect.

3.3 A Social Artifact

Third, law is different from an individual creation because it's social: it exists only in, and for, a society. Things like collective intentionality and shared cooperative activity are necessary for the constitution of legal entities and these serve social purposes or functions. This might appear as a move from product-ontology to process-ontology, or an implicit avowal that this distinction is not tenable, for the focus here is on the social conditions of the existence of law. Now it is true that focusing on the relevant intentionality and activity shifts the attention to the process of law-making, but the point on the relevant product is this: law serves social purposes, or social functions. So it has a social origin and a social point. Le me expand on these various features.

In writing a poem or a symphony authors can use and almost always use some material artifacts: pencils, pens, paper, etc. At least they need one artifact that traces the relevant signs and a support for the signs. In some categorization of objects these are the real artifacts, whereas the poem and the symphony are not, having no material consitution.[26] (However, intellectual creations have their own structure or "logic": poetry lines, symphony movements, code articles, etc.) This process usually involves a society, for one has to learn some language and some mastery of signs in the first place. Then, in the second place, if composers use pencils and paper, they need someone else who produces these things and someone who sells them, unless poets and music composers produce their own writing instruments (which is unlikely, to say the least). But poems and symphonies are not necessarily social objects. Composers could keep them for themselves and destroy their works before others come to know about them. One can compose a poem in his or her mind only, without paper and pen. If the author does not disclose it to anyone, poetry inevitably disappears with the death of its author, or when his or her memory is unable to recall it. (Poets know well what it means to be with a line in mind but unable to trace it and later unable to remember it exactly, which is why they tend to carry notebooks with them—but today some of them write directly on electronic devices.)

Law is different, because it only exists in a society and for social purposes. Legal norms regulate social interactions, economic transactions, political

[26] See again Marconi, "Artefatti e oggetti sociali" (n. 23).

issues. They do not have a point apart from the coordination and ordering of social action. A Robinson on a lone island would not need legal norms. He would need some kind of economic rule and rationality for the use of his scarce resources.[27] But no law.

Of course, an individual can imagine a piece of law to regulate some form of social behavior. An individual can even articulate a whole legal code (as Bentham did with his codification projects). But that would only be imaginary law. Actual law requires a society.

Law involves law-making authorities, law addressees, officials for law application, and various social arrangements. All of this would be unnecessary were law just an individual and mental creation. If it is a kind of artifact, it is a social kind.

We might also put it this way: ask yourself why there are no patents and copyrights on law. Part of the answer lies on the social dimension of law. It's not an individual's creation. The question may appear misdirected because patents and copyrights are legal measures themselves. But try to make abstraction from this and ask why the law, though being an artifact, does not raise any intellectual property right (or at least a moral right to this). Because it is a social artifact is part of the answer.

3.4 An Interpretive Artifact

Fourth, and last, as a social artifact law cannot be reduced to some authors' intentions, nor to some users': in fact, it is the interplay of different social actors (such as legislators, scholars, judges, etc.) that makes up the law. In particular, as I will claim below, law is an interpretive artifact.

It is reported that French composer Erik Satie used to collect umbrellas but cared so much about them that he kept them closed in a room where no one else could enter. Obviously he didn't use them as umbrellas, perhaps out of fear of damaging them or having them stolen. This is a bizarre example, but notice that many artifacts undergo a similar process: some wheelbarrows become flowerpots, some medicines become popular soft drinks, some cars are used as refuges, some photographs taken for fun become evidence in a trial, and so forth.

This is a phenomenon that some scholars call the "recycling" of artifacts.[28] It goes along with a discussion on what counts more in the characterization

[27] See Lionel Robbins, *An Essay on the Nature and Significance of Economic Science* (3rd edn., Macmillan 1984) 10–12, 35.

[28] Ehrenberg, *The Functions of Law* (n. 12) 124–5.

of an artifact: whether it is the author's intention or rather the user's.[29] Contemporary philosophy of technology has a much more sophisticated (and controversial) account of artifacts than the received one of something intentionally designed for a specific purpose.

Law is no exception in this respect. It happens that a legal rule or institution is created for a certain purpose and later is used for a different one. But law is "a strange kind of artifact" insofar as it is created by different persons, in different places, at different times, and with different purposes. Some artifacts can change and do actually change their function along with their history, but for law that is more than a possibility. In our contemporary legal systems, legislative bodies are made of many individuals with different opinions and interests. These bodies often deal with materials that the government gives them, asking for their approval; so they vote on legal provisions that before were set by the government or by a parliamentary commission and that later, if approved, are sometimes enacted by a different authority (for instance, the President of the Republic in Italy). Then such provisions are interpreted by legal scholars discussing their merits and demerits. Finally the enacted provisions are interpreted and applied by legal officials, judges in particular, dealing with concrete cases and disputes, arguing with the parties about the best reading of the relevant texts in the case at hand.[30]

One can focus on some element of this complex picture, for instance, on the intention of the government when it submits a certain proposal to the parliament in order to fix a given social problem. But that would only be a part of the complex process. Once approved and enacted, legal measures usually undergo some process of interpretation, which is crucial for what we call "law in action" as opposed to "law in books."

Legal theory captures this difference, distinguishing a legal *provision* from a legal *norm*: the former is the text, the latter is the content or meaning of the

[29] On function ascription to technical artifacts, see Pieter E. Vermaas and Wybo Houkes, "Ascribing Functions to Technical Artefacts" (2003) 54 *British Journal for the Philosophy of Science* 261 (favoring designer function) and Beth Preston, "Of Marigold Beer: A Reply to Vermaas and Houkes" (2003) 54 *British Journal for the Philosophy of Science* 601 (favoring user function). Cf. Beth Preston, "Why Is a Wing Like a Spoon? A Pluralist Theory of Function" (1998) 95 *The Journal of Philosophy* 215; Ruth Millikan, "Wings, Spoons, Pills, and Quills: A Pluralist Theory of Function" (1999) 96 *The Journal of Philosophy* 192; Eric Margolis and Stephen Laurence (eds.), *Creations of the Mind: Theories of Artifacts and Their Representation* (Oxford University Press 2007).

[30] See among others Karl Olivecrona, *Law as Fact* (2nd edn., Steven & Sons 1971) 86ff on the formation of legal rules and the legislative process in particular.

text.[31] Interpretation is the process of determining the content or meaning of authoritative legal texts and documents.

To be sure, the property of being subject to interpretive processes is structural to law (as a linguistic artifact) whereas it's merely contingent to other kinds of artifacts. Also poems are structurally subject to interpretation. But remember they are neither normative nor social artifacts. Hence law and poetry are analogous in some respect but quite different in others.

Some scholars underscore the institutional, or "institutionalized," dimension of law.[32] Indeed my previous point on the social nature of law and the present point on its interpretive dimension qualify as ways to point out that institutional dimension. Various bodies, arrangements, and institutions contribute to what we call "law." Some individuals or bodies write legal texts, some vote on them, others enact them, and still others interpret and apply them.

It's a complex social process and the picture of it must be complex as well to be an accurate one. As John L. Austin once said, "It's not things, it's philosophers that are simple."[33] Philosophy often tries to provide clear-cut, simplified pictures of reality, which is good for the sake of clarity and understanding; but we need a trade-off between simplicity and accuracy.

All this being said, let me add some reflections on the importance of functions to the identification of artifacts in general and of law in particular—assuming it is a kind of artifact, though "strange."

4. Nature and Function of Law: Two Kindred Questions

The boundary between natural entities and artifacts is not as definite as we might think at first glance. Is a nest an artifact? Well, yes and no. It is built by birds following their instinct, which suggests that we should qualify it as a natural thing. But it's built with such amazing craft that one might be inclined to think of it as an artifact, an animal artifact. And what about pizza and spaghetti? Is food a natural kind?

[31] See among others Riccardo Guastini, "Rule-Scepticism Restated" in Leslie Green and Brian Leiter (eds.), *Oxford Studies in Philosophy of Law, vol. 1* (Oxford University Press 2011); Riccardo Guastini, *Interpretare e argomentare* (Giuffrè 2011) 63.

[32] Ehrenberg, *Functions of Law* (n. 12) 106: law's "institutional nature is captured by Searle's theory; its abstract nature is captured by Shapiro's claim that law is a plan and hence an abstract entity; and seeing it as an artifact is meant to call up more clearly the notion that the law is a tool created by human beings to address specific tasks so it is to be understood and identified in terms of its functions"; "institutionality gives more endurance to the plans than its makers and subjects psychologically need to accept." Ibid. 111.

[33] John L. Austin, *Philosophical Papers* (3rd edn., Oxford University Press 1979) 252.

In this world belonging to the geological epoch that some call "Anthropocene," with genetic engineering, biotechnologies, anthropogenic hybrids, GMOs, and various interactions and combinations of nature and technology, the line between nature and artifacts becomes more puzzling indeed. But, of course, the ocean and the stars are still there, the earth is populated by a huge number of ants, and in no way can I conceive of my laptop as a natural thing. We can maintain some conceptual distinction between natural and artifactual kinds, even if the dividing line is increasingly blurred. We have things like water at one extreme and cellphones at the other, with a variety of stuff in the middle. (If you like analogy, consider the distinction between mountain and flatland: to apply the relevant concepts you don't need to know where the former ends and the latter starts, exactly.)

One of the troubling philosophical issues about natural kinds is whether they have any function.[34] It's easy to claim they have the functions we ascribe them; for instance, in this sense, one might claim that apple trees have the function of providing us with food. The interesting question is whether they have their own functions, that is, any function independent from what we think about them and do with them. Some think this is the case with respect to the blood-pumping function of the heart and other biological traits.

Fortunately, that question is not a pressing one when we deal with artifacts. For artifacts are created precisely with the intent of making them serve a function we are interested in. Forks are made to spear food, cellphones to communicate at distance, laws to guide and coordinate social behavior, etc. So they definitely have the functions we ascribe them. Or, if you think that in some cases an intentional ascription is not necessary, they have the functions they are used for. They would not exist otherwise, because they are created and used for those functions. (As the reader can see, I'm using "function" in a broad sense, encompassing both intentional and unintentional use, or manifest and latent functions; if you prefer you may distinguish purposes, as being intentional, from functions, understood as unintentional.)

So, is law analogue to an artifact having a function imposed by a designer or a user, or analogue to a biological trait having a function independent of any intentional state? Perhaps this is too categorical a question, but a standard supporter of positivism does not hesitate in joining the intentionalist party. However, I think it utterly plausible to claim that some positive laws have unintentional effects and functions. The point I'm going to make is not

[34] Cf. Larry Wright, "Functions" (1973) 82 *The Philosophical Review* 139; Robert Cummins, "Functional Analysis" (1975) 72 *The Journal of Philosophy* 741; Ruth Millikan, "In Defense of Proper Functions" (1989) 56 *Philosophy of Science* 288.

dependent on that, though. I leave to others the determination of the part of law which is characterized by intentional functions and the part which is instead characterized by unintentional ones.

The theoretical point I would like to make in this last section of the present work concerns the relationship between the nature and function of artifacts, including law if we take it as an artifact. (Of course I'm using "nature" in a loose ontological sense and "function" in the broad sense indicated above.)

Questions about function are typically "why-questions," namely questions about the reasons for producing or using a given kind of artifact, or about the causes that determine its use or production.[35] Questions about nature are typically "what-questions."[36] Now, the theoretical point about artifacts is this: why- and what-questions are intimately connected. It's hard to understand what a given artifact is if you don't grasp its function. Archeologists dealing with relics of a long lost civilization know the problem quite well. But it's also true that it is hard to determine the function of something you cannot individuate apart from function. It would be the function of what? With artifacts, nature and function are intimately connected: it's hard to determine the one if you don't determine the other. Our concepts of them integrate both aspects. As Jules Coleman put it, the hammer's function is likely integral to our concept of it, notwithstanding the fact that it might have other uses.[37]

Therefore the questions on nature and function of artifacts are kindred. They are interdependent. But this is puzzling as soon as you realize that the argument seems to run into a vicious circle: in order to know about the nature of an artifact you must know about its function and vice versa. Let me

[35] "Despite the differences in the form of the questions asked by scientists from the form of the questions asked by inventors, there is no reason to believe that the cognitive processes underlying questioning in the two contexts are fundamentally different. Scientists encounter a puzzling X and try to explain it: inventors identify a desirable X and try to produce it.... Both kinds of question are produced in response to surprise, curiosity, need, and other questions, and both kinds involve emotions such as puzzlement and excitement" (Paul Thagard and David Croft, "Scientific Discovery and Technological Innovation: Ulcers, Dinosaur Extinction, and the Programming Language Java" in Lorenzo Magnani, Nancy J. Nersessian, and Paul Thagard (eds.), *Model-Based Reasoning in Scientific Discovery* (Kluwer 1999) 134).

[36] I leave aside the status of how-questions, but I guess that some of them can be reduced to what-questions while others (e.g., those dealing with knowledge-how) cannot. On the idea that law is "modal," in that it is a *way* of performing some functions, see Leslie Green, "The Functions of Law" (1998) 12 *Cogito* 117.

[37] Jules Coleman, *The Practice of Principle: In Defence of a Pragmatist Approach to Legal Theory* (Oxford University Press 2001) 194. Note that functionalism as conceptual analysis is different from functionalism as an empirical theory (providing functional explanations and functional predictions). Cf. Kenneth M. Ehrenberg, "Defending the Possibility of a Neutral Functional Theory of Law" (2009) 29 *Oxford Journal of Legal Studies* 91, 94–5.

illustrate this point with respect to law before suggesting a possible way-out of the trouble.

What-questions are posed to grasp the nature of what is concerned and why-questions to grasp its functions. The problem is that what-questions about law are intertwined with why-questions, so that we cannot answer the one without answering the other. For if we want to respond to the second we must answer the first, as to identify the functions of law we have to know what it is. But to answer the first we have to answer the second, because it does not seem possible to know what law is without identifying its functions. So the difficulty is this: *to say what law is we need to know what it is for; but to say what it is for we need to know what it is.*

It is true that in general we know, at least pretheoretically, what law is and what it is for. It is also true that, for many positivists, a purposive or functional account of law is not needed to answer the what-question about it; or at least it is true that, for some positivists, to answer that ontological question one would just need an unspecific functional account such as the idea that law serves to guide human behavior.[38] So far so good. But explicit answers to one type of question usually come with implicit answers to the other, or with explicit but very unspecific answers to the other. So I think that theoretically we cannot be satisfied with this.

Much contemporary analytical theory of law neglects indeed why-questions and the topic of the functions of law, which is addressed instead by legal sociology; however legal sociology is often deaf to what-questions and does not engage in a thorough theoretical reflection about the nature of law. If this is correct, these disciplines should be more integrated than they currently are.[39]

What-questions require ontological answers, or at least an analysis of the relevant concepts. What is law? In the literature there is a number of answers to this simple question. You know many of them. Let me mention a few: a product of the human spirit; the set of commands of the sovereign; a set of judicial decisions; a system of rules sanctioned and institutionalized; a social practice; a kind of artifact. If we say it is an artifact, we must specify the features which make it different from other artifacts such as chairs and symphonies. If what we said above is correct, law is an intellectual, normative, social and interpretive artifact, for the reasons we have discussed. That

[38] See H.L.A. Hart, *The Concept of Law* (2nd edn., Oxford University Press 1994) 248–9. I must add that Hart's apparatus of primary and secondary rules is presented as a functional account, for different types of rule perform different social functions. Ibid. 27ff.

[39] See Kenneth E. Himma, "Do Philosophy and Sociology Mix? A Non-Essentialist Socio-Legal Positivist Analysis of the Concept of Law" (2004) 24 *Oxford Journal of Legal Studies* 717; Ehrenberg, *Functions of Law* (n. 12) 144–6.

this will be enough to distinguish it from other normative kinds, such as morality, is not what I intend to discuss. I would rather stress the assumption we already pointed out: to the extent that law is a kind of artifact, it is a man-made kind of entity. So if this is the point and it's true that generally human activities and creations are designed to some purpose, it is reasonable to assume that law is made for some purpose. With this we see how a what-question is quickly transformed into a why-question, to the extent that it is important to understand for what purposes or functions law is produced in its various branches (civil, criminal, administrative, constitutional, etc.) which can be explained in terms of different functions. To say that law is an artifact without saying what it is for is not a satisfying account of it.

I believe that such considerations can be applied, *mutatis mutandis*, to other ways to answer the what-question about law, but I cannot show it here. The point is particularly obvious if we assume that law is a kind of artifact, meaning no adequate account of law can be given if we limit ourselves to the what-question about it. Without having identified its particular functions, it is hard to understand what law is.

Why-questions require teleological or functional answers, or at least an explanation of the causes or reasons why a certain entity exists. Legal sociology often deals with this. One of the most common responses in sociology to the why-question about law is the functionalist one that tries to distinguish the functions of the legal system from other social systems, and the functions of certain types of law from other types of law (civil, criminal, etc.).[40] It is true that the term "function" is ambiguous and must be carefully specified; but once this is done (for example, distinguishing the intentional aspects of the creation of artifacts from the unintentional aspects of their actual operation) it does not seem impossible to conduct an investigation into the functions of law.

Law is a human artifact endowed with some properties that are peculiar to it (it is a "strange kind of artifact") and a definite structure designed or developed to perform certain social functions.

So, what are the functions of law? In the sociological literature there are many answers, including the following: the function of social control; the function of social orientation; the legitimation of power; the promotion of social change; the resolution of social conflicts; the allocation of resources. It is plausible to think that these functions are not incompatible with each other, and that on the contrary law satisfies more than one.

[40] See among others Talcott Parsons, *The Structure of Social Action* (McGraw-Hill 1937), and T. Parsons, *The Social System* (The Free Press 1951); Lawrence M. Friedman, *The Legal System: A Social Science Perspective* (Russell Sage 1975).

I do not wish to take a position on the merits and say what the (main) functions of law are. The thing that I find interesting is that the focus on one or the other of such functions is closely related to the type of legal theory that one wants to defend. Our ideas on the functions of law are largely implicit in our ideas on law.[41] A theory of the spontaneous formation of law (legal evolutionism) argues that the function of law is to stabilize social expectations (rather than to guide behavior), while an imperativist theory states that its main function is to direct the behavior of its addressees, yet some realist theory highlights the function of promoting social change, and the economic analysis of law focuses on resource allocation. Then the point seems to be this: if we take functional explanations seriously we cannot really say what law is if we do not understand what it is for; but we soon realize that it is not easy to say what it is for if we have no idea of what it is. Then the why-question and the what-question seem interdependent.[42]

These difficulties are well known to those who deal with functionalism in philosophy of mind. Take the standard sense of "function" used in that context: the functions of a mental state are its typical causes and effects.[43] In a standard functionalist account a mental state is identified by its typical causes and effects, not by any intrinsic feature of it. Similarly, a functional explanation of law looks for its typical causes and effects. It works on the assumption that law is an artifact that is typically produced in certain ways and typically produces certain consequences.[44] The functional method makes them explicit.[45] And yet—this is one of the objections—to identify such causes and effects you must already have identified the state or thing in question!

[41] See Roscoe Pound, *An Introduction to the Philosophy of Law* (first published 1954, Yale University Press 1982) 25ff.

[42] One reviewer has stressed that such an intertwining is related to the intertwining of process- and product-ontology, since one cannot provide an answer to the why-question about a legal institution without going deep into the process that generates it. I take this to be true, but I am unclear about the connection between the two issues and I suspect that both ontologies can pose both questions (respectively, on the nature and function of law and of law-making processes).

[43] See among others Hilary Putnam, *Mind, Language and Reality* (Cambridge University Press 1975) ch. 14 and Jerry Fodor, "Fodor's Guide to Mental Representation" (1985) 94 *Mind* 76, 81ff. But see also Hilary Putnam, *The Threefold Cord: Mind, Body, and the World* (Columbia University Press 1999) 118 for a critique of his previous functionalism.

[44] See Felix S. Cohen, "The Problems of a Functional Jurisprudence" (1937) 1 *Modern Law Review* 5, 15–23.

[45] Felix S. Cohen, "Transcendental Nonsense and the Functional Approach" (1935) 35 *Columbia Law Review* 809, 834: "The significance of the functional method in the field of law is clarified if we consider the bearings of this method upon four traditional legal problems: (1) The definition of law; (2) The nature of legal rules and concepts; (3) The theory of legal decisions; and (4) The role of legal criticism." See also Cohen, "The Problems of a Functional Jurisprudence" (n. 44) 8: "Functionalism as a method may be summed up in the directive: If you want to understand something, observe it in action."

The functionalist can reply that whatever it takes to achieve a certain function is identifiable as the kind of thing you need to satisfy that function. Let me present an everyday example: according to some functionalist orthodoxy, everything that can be used to spear food and bring it to the mouth is a fork, regardless of whether it has a certain structure. This argument is somewhat puzzling: in front of a subject who spears food with a screwdriver or with a long nail we would not say that they are using a fork; we would say instead that they are using a screwdriver or a long nail *as* a fork. This reaction implies two things: (i) the behavior of our imaginary subject satisfies the fork function, but does not do it with a fork; (ii) that function is not sufficient to define what a fork is, because to this end we can not neglect some structural properties of the artifact. Note that functions depend somehow on the structure of an artifact: a wheelbarrow can be used as a flowerpot in virtue of its form and structure; it may be made of the same metal of a fork but only the second can be used to spear food; and among the things that can be used to spear food a definite structure identifies a fork. So it is a combination of structure and function that usually defines an artifact.[46]

I think this also applies to law. Suppose the (main) function of law is to resolve conflicts (or more cautiously, to deal with them). Could we say that anything capable of solving conflicts is law? I'm afraid not. Flipping a coin would be a way to resolve a conflict, but I do not think that most of us would be willing to consider it a way of proceeding according to the law. Not to mention the extreme solution, which would be to eliminate one of the parties or even both. What an extraordinary effect this method would have! It would be functionally perfect, since every conflict would be resolved, with the elimination of the conflicting parties. Yet, we may plausibly react, this way of resolving conflicts would not be according to the law. This reaction would imply two things, again: (i) the elimination of the parties would achieve the function at stake (to resolve conflicts), but it would not do it according to the law; and (ii) that function is not sufficient to define what law is, since for definitional purposes we cannot neglect some structural properties of this kind of artifact, such as being a system of abstract and general rules to be applied to specific and concrete cases, through officials and definite authorities, following certain procedures, etc.[47]

[46] In addition you may stress the *point* for which one uses one artifact instead of another performing the same function; see Diego Marconi, "Pencils Have a Point: Against General Externalism about Artifactual Words" (2013) 4 *Review of Philosophy and Psychology* 497.

[47] Green, "The Functions of Law" (n. 36) 120–1 would probably say this is the "modal" aspect of law: He thinks that law is less a functional kind than it is a modal kind, because it is distinguished less by what it does than by how it does it.

I believe that similar considerations can be made assuming that the (main) function of law is not the resolution of conflicts, but another of the functions mentioned and mentionable. Suppose it is that of social control: Could we achieve this function by influencing the behavior of citizens through the systematic distribution of conditioning drugs (as in *Brave New World* with "soma"), or by programming their minds from birth? Yes, but we feel it would not be a way to operate through law. Examples can easily be made for each function of law to support the argument that to say what law is for is not enough to say what it is.

What we have been saying can be rephrased with respect to specific legal institutions and measures. Consider for instance forfeiture, which is the deprivation of money or property without compensation by the State or some legal authority. This is the main structural trait of the measure. And this answers a what-question. But why is forfeiture used? It is used as a consequence of a breach or nonperformance of some legal obligation, or the commission of a crime. The measure has in fact different functions:[48] from a precautionary one in favor of the promisee in a contract, to a compensatory one in case of an offense, and a punitive one both in administrative and criminal law. So to rephrase the point on what- and why-questions, structure and function are connected insofar as structure serves function and function depends on structure. With old and long-standing institutions and measures, carrying historical stratification with them, it's hard to say what came first. The "recycling" phenomenon we saw above (some artifacts are created for some use and later are put to different uses) makes things quite complex. Repurposing processes, modifications of existing structures, filling in of incomplete plans and so on make it difficult to say what comes first. But an artifact is always created for some purpose or function. So functions have some primacy in the explanation of artifacts. However, we must individuate the artifact at stake, independently from any function ascription, as a preliminary step of function ascription. And again we seem to be running in circles.

The theoretical solution I would like to suggest as a way-out is a difference in methodology. We must treat questions and answers differently. I praise *atomism concerning questions*. Questions must point at specific features; to be fruitful they must address specific issues of the topic one is about. Hence we must distinguish why-questions from what-questions. If we don't, only conceptual confusion will ensue. On the contrary answers must be integrated. To have a full understanding of a given phenomenon, we must put together

[48] See, e.g., in Italian law, *Cass Sez Un Penali* no. 26654/2008.

the answers to the different questions about it. So I praise *holism concerning answers.*

For the purpose of conceptual clarity our questions should be as distinct as possible; but for the purpose of understanding, the answers should be as integrated as possible.

Take the examples I used above, fork and forfeiture. A why-question about the fork artifact receives an answer in terms of function: it is made to spear food. But we saw that this is insufficient to distinguish it from other things that can be used to spear food. So a what-question is needed to specify some structural properties of the artifact. And a combination of the answers gives a full understanding of it. Similarly for the legal institution of forfeiture: if we ask a what-question about it, the simple answer is that it is the authoritative deprivation of money or property without compensation; but this answer tells you nothing about the function the measure has, which in fact can be diverse. So a why-question about this legal institution is needed if you wish to have a full understanding of it, while the relevant what-question is necessary to distinguish it from other (legal) measures that perform the same functions.

Question-atomism and answer-holism are methodological recipes for our understanding of the world and of artifacts in particular. The answer to a why-question and the answer to a what-question illuminate each other and the phenomenon at stake. We must try to do this with law as well, in order to integrate and harmonize our understanding of what it is and of the causes or reasons why it is created, used, interpreted, and applied.

12

Not All Law Is an Artifact

Jurisprudence Meets the Common Law

*Dan Priel**

1. Introduction

Brian Leiter has recently suggested that anyone who denied law's artifactuality, "the extravagance of their metaphysical commitments would . . . be a subject for psychological, not philosophical investigation."[1] There is a sense in which he is unquestionably right. If by artifact we mean the product of human effort, the claim is obviously true, indeed so obviously true that I do not know anyone who denies it. After some light interrogation it turns out that even some of the usual suspects have to be released without charges. It is accepted by John Finnis, who described law as "a cultural object, constructed, or . . . posited by creative human choices, [which] is an instrument, a technique adopted for a moral purpose, and adopted because there is no other available way of agreeing over significant spans of time about precisely how to pursue the moral project well."[2] Lon Fuller is not guilty either: he spoke of the lawyer as an "architect of social structures" and gave a central role in his writings, far more than his critics have, to the importance of institutional

* I thank Luka Burazin and two anonymous referees for their detailed comments on earlier drafts. Space limitations have forced me to cut more than a third of the original manuscript. The excised part provided a far more detailed demonstration of the way attempts to explain the common law within the law-as-artifact ideological framework lead to artificial and unconvincing accounts of the common law. The longer version is available upon request.

[1] Brian Leiter, "The Demarcation Problem in Jurisprudence: A New Case for Skepticism" in Jordi Ferrer Beltrán et al. (eds.), *Neutrality and Theory of Law* (Springer 2013) 161, 164.

[2] John Finnis, "Natural Law and Legal Reasoning" in Robert P. George (ed.), *Natural Law Theory: Contemporary Essays* (Oxford University Press 1992) 134, 141.

design to the traditional questions of jurisprudence.[3] Even everyone's favorite punching bag, Ronald Dworkin, can plead innocence.[4] Unless one is willing to argue that Finnis, Fuller, and Dworkin were all deeply confused about their own views, their examples show that the artifactuality of law, if understood as the claim that law is the product of human efforts, is an uncontentious claim.

I think there is a different way of understanding law's artifactuality. It is (roughly) that law is the product of purposive action, that it is the product of design. Understood in this way, the claim that law (in general) is an artifact is, I think, by no means trivial. In fact, I will argue that with respect to one familiar form of law it is false. Before proceeding to defend my claim, let me assure the tough-minded reader that my claim that not all law is an artifact in no way depends on any commitment to the idea that some law exists as a brooding omnipresence in the sky waiting patiently through the eons for humans to first evolve and then, several millennia later, to discover it. I can be spared psychological examination because the view I present is meant to convince even the most hardened of jurisprudential naturalists. I consider the uber-naturalist Jeremy Bentham an ally in the argument I present below.

To say that not all law is an artifact may be controversial enough; to make things worse I will further argue that the claim that all law is an artifact is not a neutral, hard-headed description of what law really is, arrived at after we rid ourselves of metaphysical excesses, aspirations, idealizations, and confusions. Rather, the claim that law is an artifact is an ideological claim. It is an ideology that many contemporary legal theorists, of very different stripes, consider so obvious that they elevate it to the level of a conceptual truth about what they call "the nature of law." I will not challenge this ideology for no other reason that I am sympathetic to it. Nevertheless, I recognize it for what it is: not a universal truth about law wherever and whenever we find it, but a normative stance.

As should be obvious from this chapter's title, my example of non-artifactual law is the common law. To demonstrate this conclusion I begin by explaining what I mean by artifact. I argue that artifacts are functional

[3] See Lon L. Fuller, "The Lawyer as an Architect of Social Structures" in *The Principles of Social Order* (rev. edn., Hart Publishing 2001) 285; Lon L. Fuller, *The Morality of Law* (rev. edn., Yale University Press 1969) 178 (talking about the "architectural design of legal institutions").

[4] Dworkin's analogy between law and the chain novel, where each participant has a creative role, is one indication. Contrary to popular belief, Dworkin did not think that law pre-exists humans who discover it. He ridiculed the idea in no uncertain terms. See Ronald Dworkin, *Taking Rights Seriously* (rev. edn., Harvard University Press 1978) 216, 337. As he also said, the sense of interpretation central to his conception of law is "creative." See Ronald Dworkin, *Law's Empire* (Harvard University Press 1986) 50.

designed objects. On the basis of this definition I argue in Section 3 that the common law, or at least some of its central manifestations, is not an artifact. In Section 4 I turn to explaining the broader jurisprudential significance of this point. I argue that the dominant view today that all law is an artifact is not a conceptual truth, but an ideological claim. It reflects a particular view of law as a tool for improving society. This view ignores a competing ideology (on which much common law thinking is based) which rejects this conception of law. I briefly conclude by suggesting that recognizing the ideological nature of this view, together with the particular view of law as a tool should help reorient jurisprudence in a new direction—away from description and understanding, and toward construction and engineering.

2. Design, Function, and Artifactuality

In this section I present the analytical framework that will serve me for the jurisprudential argument that follows. This is not an exercise in conceptual analysis in the sense of trying to capture what artifactuality really is. It is meant to help clarify and define the terms I will use in the remainder of the chapter. Though I cannot prove it, I think it reflects prevailing linguistic usage, but as I explain below, my argument is not affected in a significant way even if it does not.

2.1 Physical Artifacts

Artifacts, as I understand them, are *functional* objects, which are *purposely designed*. This definition has three elements. *Designed* objects are non-randomly organized. Part of the explanation of a designed object calls for identifying a *design mechanism* that explains how the object's design came about. The most obvious design mechanism is a conscious, intentional being—a designer—that is responsible for the non-random organization. For a long time it was thought that a designer is the only design mechanism (hence, for example, the argument from design to the existence of God), but we now know of design mechanisms that dispense with a designer: Adam Smith's invisible hand and natural selection are probably the best-known ones, but there are others as well. To use a well-known example, a path can come into existence without any purposeful design.[5] In this example, a non-randomly organized object

[5] T.E. Holland, *The Elements of Jurisprudence* (12th edn., Oxford University Press 1917) 57, which also draws the analogy between the formation of a path and the emergence of custom.

(path) can emerge without a designer because of the advantage, however slight, conferred on any individual in following on the footsteps of others. Notice that in this case even though the design depends on the intentional actions of individuals, none of them may have any intention to create a path. Other design mechanisms (for example, natural selection) are less intuitive, because they show how order can emerge in the absence of any intentional action.

Within the domain of designed objects, then, we can distinguish between those that are purposely and those that are non-purposely designed. Within the category of purposely designed objects we can further distinguish between functional and non-functional objects. On my definition, works of art are artifacts only if they are functional. That may be controversial, but it seems to me a plausible distinction, allowing us to distinguish between so-called "decorative arts" and crafts, which are artifacts, and other artistic creations (for instance, symphonies) which are not. However, this distinction ultimately depends on a question I will not address, whether some or even all art has a function (improving morals, increasing happiness, or whatever). Depending on one's answer to this question, some (or even all) works of art may count as artifacts.

Function is normative in the sense that it is (or provides) an evaluable standard of success. Given a function, some artifacts will perform it better than others. In some cases, an object will be so poor at performing the function it was intended to perform, that we will not consider it a specimen of an artifact type. One may genuinely intend to build an airplane, but the object he produces is so spectacularly incapable of flying that it will not be an airplane. This standard of success may seem straightforward, but there is a twist. In my classification crafts and other decorative objects are artifacts, but they are a special kind of artifact, because their function is aesthetic, and as such it is determined by contingent cultural standards. The success of a decorative item is assessed against certain aesthetic standards of a particular community, or of objects of that type. To be sure, even in the case of other artifacts, there is a particular cultural context in which the function of the artifact makes sense (a screwdriver can perform its function only in an environment where screws exist), but one can give a description of the way the design serves the function without invoking the cultural context. By contrast, with cultural artifacts their description of the way they perform their function must include this context. Neckties, for example, perform a decorative function but also signal seriousness or respectability on the part of their wearer. That they perform this function is a purely conventional signal understood within a particular culture. The very idea that wearing a necktie has this meaning, as well as the particular designs that convey that meaning, cannot be understood without invoking neckties' cultural context. When this is the case, we can call the function in question "cultural function" to distinguish such a function from the function performed by other artifacts, which I will call "teleological function."

Obviously, there are many artifacts with both cultural and teleological functions, and the balancing of the two elements is a familiar design problem (think of watches), one that may be exacerbated by the fact that there may be disagreement over whether a given function is teleological or cultural. The important point for the discussion that follows is that the two kinds of function are normatively different. They employ different notions of success and employ different methods for achieving their respective modes of success.

Table 12.1 gives a rough guide of what I take to be the scope of artifactuality.

In my definition artifacts are objects that are functional and purposely designed. I don't treat this definition as an attempt to capture "the" concept of an artifact, because I do not think such a thing exists. The definition aims to capture a useful category. I do not consider debates over the scope of artifactuality—whether it includes all works of art, whether it includes humans (or "designer dogs," humans who underwent plastic surgery, genetically modified foods, reproductions of original paintings, or rocks that are being used as door stops)—to be particularly important, for there is no nature of artifactuality to identify and demarcate. Some may think that some of these objects are artifacts and others will not. There is no way of showing one person is correct on such matters while someone else is wrong (unless by "correct" we mean more prevalent among people). What exists is human language, used to communicate thought and guide action. Humans apparently succeed in doing that with imperfectly regimented, and somewhat differently regimented concepts. The view that behind this linguistic diversity there is a single category is not warranted; and even if such categories exist, it is not explained how the methods of philosophers (wholly conducted within the language they are supposed to transcend) are useful, or even relevant, to discover such categories.

Table 12.1 Identifying artifacts

	Design	Conscious design	Function	Artifact
Rock	No	No	No	No
Tiger	Yes	No	No	No
Heart	Yes	No	Teleological	No
Kandinsky's *Composition VII*	Yes	Yes	Controversial	Depends on functionality
Necktie	Yes	Yes	Cultural	Yes
Tea kettle	Yes	Yes	Teleological	Yes

Reflection or debate on category-boundaries may lead some people to change their mind, but this is not because one categorization is correct while others are not; it is because one becomes convinced that a particular categorization is more useful.[6] *The study of categories and classifications should not be understood as an attempt to find "real" categories; it is valuable for what it reveals about those who categorize the world in this way.* This is the central assumption that underlies the argument in the remainder of this chapter.

With all this in mind, I can state that I believe my definition roughly corresponds to prevailing usage, but it is unlikely that there will be perfect agreement on such matters. I already mentioned that on my definition not all art is necessarily an artifact, a claim that others are likely to contest. For another example of possible disagreement, consider Daniel Dennett's provocative suggestion that organisms and organs are artifacts.[7] He did this in order to emphasize the fact that the *mechanism* of design does not matter for the end-product being designed. Dennett did not commit a "conceptual" or "category" error when he said that humans are artifacts. Nevertheless, Dennett's usage is probably unusual, as the typical contrast is between artifacts and natural objects, and in this contrast humans (together with the rest of the biological world) belong firmly in the "natural." Nevertheless, it is perfectly legitimate for him to define artifactuality the way he did to stress the sense in which humans are designed objects, even if they had no designer.

2.2 Intellectual Artifacts

It is not obvious that in everyday usage "artifact" includes purely intellectual objects, but we can extend the scope of the term to such objects if we understand intellectual artifacts as the creation or organization of objects with meaningful semantic content. Intellectual artifacts can thus refer to the creation or organization of propositions (information) or of prescriptions (algorithms). The value of limiting artifactuality to products of conscious design is even more evident in the domain of intellectual objects than in the domain of physical objects. If we use the word "artifact" to refer to all human creations, then every thought, every idea, every sentence, perhaps even grunts and hums,

[6] All this is, of course, controversial, and within legal philosophy, a minority view. For a defense of these views see Dan Priel, "The Misguided Search for the Nature of Law," available at <https://papers.ssrn.com/sol3/papers.cfm?abstract_id=2642461> accessed June 15, 2017.

[7] See Daniel C. Dennett, "The Interpretation of Texts, People, and Other Artifacts" (1990) 50 *Philosophy and Phenomenological Research* (Supplement) 177, 187. Contrast this with Risto Hilpinen, "Authors and Artifacts" (1993) 93 *Proceedings of the Aristotelian Society* 155, 156–7, adopting the opposite view.

would count as artifacts. More significantly for the argument below, such a definition of artifactuality will also include many social norms. Even if they are not the product of any conscious design, they are still human creations.

Limiting artifactuality to functional *conscious* design helps identify a narrower and more useful category of intellectual artifactuality, one according to which thoughts and spoken sentences are not artifacts, but academic papers and legislation are.[8] Legislation is the product of conscious design and it is typically functional in the same way that physical artifacts are, to achieve a particular goal: "Why do we allow people to deduct their charitable donations?" "Because we want to encourage such donations." Unlike legislation, social norms (customs) are also a kind of order (design), but it is not typically conscious. Such norms typically emerge without any conscious decision by any single person to adopt them. The norm that putting one's belongings on a table in a cafeteria designates that table as "taken" even before one sits down need not be pronounced by anyone, indeed need not even be consciously noticed by those who adhere to it. For all we know there was never a moment in which such a norm was "authored."

As mentioned, the element of function in artifactuality is normative: it both explains actions and can be used to justify or criticize them. "Why does the airplane's wing look the way it does?" "Because this shape reduces drag." "But if that is the aim, a somewhat different design would have served that goal better." The same is true of intellectual artifacts: "Why was the advertisement written in this way?" "Because our studies have shown that it is an effective way of getting people to buy the new product." "It would have been even more effective if it had been written differently."

The distinction between teleological and cultural function encountered in the discussion of physical artifacts is significant in relation to intellectual objects as well. Teleological justification is a familiar form of explaining legislation: "Why does the Affordable Care Act contain an individual mandate?" "Because without one healthy people will not sign up in sufficient numbers and that would lead to adverse selection." "In that case, the law should have included a public option, as that would have pushed down premiums even

[8] In the text I treat academic papers and legislation as purely intellectual artifacts. In reality, they have physical existence in addition to their meaningful content. This may seem a contingent fact, for their content could be memorized. While strictly speaking this is true, given the limitations of human cognition, I believe the physical instantiation of intellectual artifacts is important for understanding their "nature." Some of what I say below about the difference between common law and legislation relates to this issue, but it deserves a much more focused discussion than is possible here. If I am right, then attempts to provide a timeless account of the nature of law are flawed to the extent that they ignore the extent to which technological change has changed the physical boundaries of law.

further." Customary norms, however, are often justified differently. As many have noted, when talking about custom, we do not just talk about a convergence of behavior; we talk about a *justified* convergence of behavior, with the justification primarily being that others behave in the same way. More people go to the beach on warm, sunny days than on cold, rainy ones. That convergence, however, does not in itself establish a custom. Each person may individually think it more enjoyable to be out on a warm day, regardless of others' behavior. By contrast, what counts as appropriate attire on the beach is (partly) determined by the changing of customs known as "fashion." Here, the justification for the design of items to make them fashionable, as well as acting according to the prevailing custom, are explicable from within a particular culture and not for the sake of promoting a goal.

Obviously, here too there are often cases of mixed functions. There are often good teleological reasons for the existence of a custom over no custom; and there are many illuminating studies dedicated to showing how a seemingly pointless custom in fact does promote a goal. For example, there may be good reasons for preferring the norm according to which the order of boarding a bus will be based on the order of arrival at the bus station (rather than, say, on the basis of passenger height, age, or by drawing lots). What is interesting about such explanations is that they are often made with scant reference to the attitudes of those who engage in the custom. They assume a non-conscious design mechanism that has led people to adopt a certain norm with little awareness of whatever goal the norm serves. This is an important facet of such norms. It is the existence, and strength, of cultural function that explains why customs may persist even when they cannot be shown to serve a teleological function (anymore), or even in the face of evidently bad consequences. Indeed, in some cases, the lack of a point becomes one of a custom's defining characteristics. Defenders of a custom will then criticize those who argue for abandoning it for lack of a point, for missing the custom's (lack of) point.

Gathering these points, Table 12.2 provides a rough summary of the way my definition of artifactuality relates to two types of intellectual objects:

Table 12.2 Identifying intellectual artifacts

	Design	Conscious design	Functional	Artifact
Legislation	Yes	Yes	Teleological	Yes
Social norms	Yes	No	Cultural	No

This is the basic analytic framework for my argument below regarding the common law. Before proceeding, three important clarifications are due. First, I presented paradigmatic cases of legislation and customary norms in order to draw a sharp contrast between intellectual artifacts with non-artifacts. Reality is often more complex. Dress norms are often customary, but some people ("fashion gurus") may acquire a quasi-authoritative role that may shape norms in a conscious way. Similarly, rules of etiquette may emerge as purely customary, non-consciously designed norms, but at some point certain individuals may attain such authoritative status on etiquette that their say-so may be able to change behavior. Therefore, it is fair to say that the status of a norm as customary is not binary, but a matter of degree. Second, my argument below will be that the common law is custom, but it is worth stressing in advance that it is a special kind of custom. This will require some further refinement of some of the points made so far. Third, the jurisprudential argument that follows does not depend on linguistic (or "conceptual") niceties. As mentioned, I think the definition I adopted corresponds to prevailing linguistic usage, but nothing changes from the argument below if it turns out my usage is unusual, or even deemed wrong. Instead of an argument about whether the common law is an artifact, my argument can be recast in terms of two different kinds of artifact. The rest of the argument can then proceed in roughly the same way. Instead of my critique of legal theorists who all think of law as an artifact when some of it is not, the argument can be restated as a critique of the view that law is made up of one kind of artifact when in fact it consists of (at least) two. What matters is that these two categories, however labeled, correspond to two different (political) ideologies.[9]

3. The Common Law Is Not an Artifact

On the basis of the definition of artifactuality in the previous section, in this section I consider whether the common law is an artifact. My argument will be that on a prominent understanding of the common law it is not. I will argue that the common law's design level is low, whatever design it has is not conscious, and a teleological function does not often play a

[9] Jonathan Crowe, "Law as an Artifact Kind" (2015) 40 *Monash University Law Review* 737 recognizes that customary law poses a difficulty to most accounts of the artifactuality of law. He addresses it by offering a disjunctive definition of artifact (ibid. 747), in which artifacts are either the products of human design or natural objects "adopted" by humans. Customary law for him belongs to the latter category, and so by his definition it is an artifact roughly as a rock "becomes" an artifact when someone decides to use it as a door stop. With respect to the common law, all Crowe says is that it is an artifact, because "judicial decisions have authors" (ibid. 739). Even if accepting Crowe's classification of artifacts, my argument seeks to show that (a) the common law is closer to customary law, and (b) that the distinction between his two kinds of artifact is normatively significant.

significant role in its design and development. All these points call for a detailed explanation.

3.1 The Common Law Is Custom

To begin the discussion, consider the following argument outline:

(1) The common law is law.
(2) The common law is custom.
(3) Custom is not an artifact.
Hence, (4) Not all law is an artifact.

I will take (1) for granted,[10] and in the previous section I argued for (3). Custom is undoubtedly the product of human intentional actions (even if some of them may have their origins in innate psychological traits), even though it is not an artifact in the narrower sense I specified above. That leaves defending (2) to complete the argument. It is tempting to add that the truth of (2) is similarly uncontroversial for there is a long history of analyzing the common law as custom.[11] This seems to lead straightforwardly to the conclusion that not all law is an artifact.

An argument along these lines should be appealing to anyone who accepts that the path formed by the unplanned, uncoordinated actions of many individuals is not an artifact, even though it is unquestionably human made. While something like this is the conclusion I ultimately reach, I think the argument outlined above requires further defense, for what is meant by saying that the common law is custom is unclear. In particular, the argument will have to address the following objections: First, one might argue that despite the long provenance of claims about the customary nature of the common law, it is not in fact a custom. It is far too elaborate, or far too organized, to be similar in any important sense to customary norms like table etiquette. Second, even if the common law is in some sense customary, it might be argued that the word "custom" in (2) and (3) has a different meaning. If this is the case, the argument outlined above is invalid, for it rests on the fallacy of equivocation.

Discussions on the common law as custom often confuse two related but distinct issues: the adoption of customs into the common law, and common-law practice *itself* as custom. The two issues are not always easy to disentangle, but they must be kept apart for I am interested here in the second. The first

[10] Bentham on occasion denied (1). He was not wrong to do so, because he was not making a conceptual claim, or was not trying to capture prevailing attitudes. See the discussion in the concluding paragraphs of Section 4.3.

[11] See Gerald J. Postema, *Bentham and the Common Law Tradition* (Clarendon Press 1986) 3–14, 63–80; C.K. Allen, *Law in the Making* (7th edn., Clarendon Press 1964) chs. 1–2, especially at 71–9.

question is of particular interest to legal historians writing on medieval and early modern English common law and debating the extent to which it relied on local custom. My argument focuses on the different question of the way common law norms are designed and justified. It takes as its object common-law practice itself, as it exists up to this day, even when the adoption of customary norms by common-law judges has become a relatively rare occurrence.

With respect to the latter question, to say that the common law is not an artifact is to say that it fails to exhibit at least one of the three features of artifactuality. The common law satisfies, to a limited degree, the requirement of design. The common law is a non-random organization of intellectual content, but because of its relative complexity compared with social norms, its design level is quite low. There are several mechanisms that help make it more organized, but even with those in place, there are countless examples, familiar to anyone who studied any common law area, of obscurity, confusion, and contradiction within the common law.[12] The more significant sense in which common-law practice is customary, and as such non-artifactual, relates to the two other elements of artifactuality, *conscious* design and *functionality*, as the common law is lacking in both. This statement may seem odd: the common law may not be an example of great design, but whatever design we find in it looks like it is arrived at through the conscious decisions of judges. Isn't reasoned justification a staple of common-law adjudication? These days it is (although this is, significantly, much less true of its past), but what matters is the *kind* of explanation we find of common law decisions.

To understand this point we must have a clearer sense of what we mean by the common law. At the most basic level when we talk about the common law, we talk about law constructed in some way from judicial pronouncements made in the context of the resolution of disputes. That requires having a *theory of authority* explaining in virtue of what these pronouncements are in some way binding, and a *theory of content* explaining how these discrete pronouncements are taken together to generate legal norms. To say that the common law is custom implies certain answers to both questions that can be derived from its practice. Now, it is important to stress that it is wrong to expect "the common law" to speak with a unitary voice on these issues. For the same reasons the common law is often messy at the level of particular legal doctrines, it is messy also at the level of its own working theory. The product of a multitude of largely uncoordinated individuals working at different

[12] See, e.g., the critical comments (made by both commentators and judges) on the English law of defamation collected in Simon Deakin et al., *Markesinis and Deakin's Tort Law* (7th edn., Oxford University Press 2013) 696. Likewise, the state of the economic torts in twentieth-century English law has been described as a "mess and [a] muddle" in Hazel Carty, "The Economic Torts in the 21st Century" (2008) 124 *Law Quarterly Review* 641, 644.

periods and in different places is unlikely to produce a perfectly coherent legal doctrine; similarly, such product is unlikely to be grounded in identical views on authority and content. What I say below is therefore not the whole truth in the sense that not all common-law practice fits it, but it reflects a prominent theory underlying much of that practice.[13] If the rest of my argument is successful, that is enough to show that not all law is an artifact.

Perhaps the most notable aspect of the common law is that in constructing an answer to novel questions the common lawyer is primarily looking to existing practice: "this case should be resolved in such-and-such a way, *because* this is how we decided similar cases in the past." Typically these past cases are relatively recent, but even when the cases cited and discussed are old, it is their present understanding (often quite different from the original one) that matters. It is this understanding that is "the law." More significantly, judges follow precedents not just in "settled" cases, but also in "novel" ones where there is (supposedly) no law governing them. Even in these cases, judges do not search for some metaphysically right answer, one that is true before or outside of the law. There are, in fact, often more citations to past cases in appellate cases (which presumably deal with matters on which there is no settled law) than in trial cases. The reason is that even in such cases, judges seek an answer constructed from an understanding of an existing practice. On many occasions there is some attempt to justify the decision in terms of certain goals the law seeks to promote: "Policy" arguments, as such arguments are typically called, have a long history in the common law, but they remain controversial and are typically conducted without much information or expert knowledge on the issues. Moreover, such arguments are rarely the only kind of argument used. In short, there is rarely an attempt to construct answers to outstanding questions by examining directly some goal to be achieved; the typical mode of justification in the common law is "we decide this case in this manner, because this answer fits the way we do things around here."

Other familiar features of common-law practice reinforce this point. One well-known aspect of the common law is that it develops incrementally. It is not incrementalism per se that undermines its artifactuality; historians of technology have demonstrated (and as anyone who has gone through several mobile phones in the last decade will attest), that technological advance is also incremental.[14] The evolution of physical artifacts is typically the result of an

[13] Elsewhere I identify four different conceptions of common law authority. See Dan Priel, "Conceptions of Authority and the Anglo-American Common Law Divide" (2017) 65 *American Journal of Comparative Law* 609.

[14] See George Basalla, *The Evolution of Technology* (Cambridge University Press 1988); Henry Petroski, *The Evolution of Useful Things* (Knopf 1992).

attempt to improve an existing artifact by measuring it against its purported teleological function. By contrast, because common-law justification is often "internal"—cultural rather than teleological—the kind of incrementalism we find in the common law is different. It develops by way of fitting a current answer within a pattern created by an existing practice. The difference between the two may be put this way: artifact design is often based on attempts to identify problems with past design and solve them; common-law justification typically involves the opposite approach of acting in a particular way because of past practice. In the former, past design is relevant in that it may limit one's design space, it is an unfortunate constraint. In the latter, on the other hand, the past may be a reason in itself to do certain things in a particular way. The difference is that only in the latter the fact that things have been done in a certain way confers normative value on them.

This point can be further explicated in relation to the adage that the common law "works itself pure." This phrase can be (and has been) rendered more modern as the idea that common-law practice aims at internal coherence. Coherence is, at best, a puzzling moral ideal for the law when one thinks that law exists to help maintain and promote some external goal and is to be evaluated by its success in doing so.[15] But the common law's coherentism makes more sense against an internal mode of justification in which particular instantiations of the practice are measured against some evaluation of the practice as a whole. This involves a constant movement between particular instantiations (called "cases" in the common law) to a broader picture of the whole practice (called "principles"), which are then used to re-evaluate cases. Thus, cases are not evaluated for their success in promoting some goal, but for their fit into an existing pattern of past cases or some aims extracted from them. Within this conception of law, the correctness of a decision, no matter how novel, cannot be determined independently of an existing practice.

The fact that the common law is culturally rather than teleologically functional is still consistent with it being an artifact. (The significance of the distinction will become clearer later.) But the common law is particularly lacking with respect to the element of conscious design. There are numerous statements from commentators (and often judges as well) who complain about the messiness, confusion, contradictoriness, and obscurity of many of their constituent parts.[16] This is true not just of the common law

[15] For a clear example of this puzzlement see Joseph Raz, *Ethics in the Public Domain: Essays in the Morality of Law and Politics* (rev. edn., Clarendon Press 1994) ch. 13, especially at 299–301.

[16] Here are two examples: Peter H. Schuck, *Suing Government: Citizen Remedies for Official Wrongs* (Yale University Press 1983) 51 ("The historical legacy of public tort remedies is a jerry-built structure, a patchwork, a doctrinal stew. It is a pastiche of policies, precedents, and perspectives

today: commentators fail to identify a clear plan in the common law even in the days when it was the product of a tiny bench and bar all concentrated in London.[17] Given the craft that goes into the writing of judicial opinions, such statements may seem too strong, but as I have argued above, intentional individual actions can co-exist with no overall conscious design. That the common law is not the result of a plan should be no more difficult to accept than the fact that a path can be created without conscious design, even though individual actions leading to its creation are intentional.

3.2 Two Objections Answered

We can now return to the idea that the common law is a kind of custom and, in turn, that it is not an artifact. When I argue that common-law practice is best understood as a kind of custom, what I meant, and arguably what can be gleaned from the writings of the classical exponents of the common law, is that its mode of development and especially its mode of justification is customary. A central feature of custom is that its primary mode of justification is cultural rather than teleological. We see the same distinction in common-law thinking, except that instead of the contrast between "cultural" and "teleological" functions, we find a distinction between "internal" and "external" justification.

If true, the argument outlined in the beginning of this section appears sound. To substantiate this conclusion let me respond here to the two objections mentioned above. The first was that the well-known claims by classical exponents of the common law to its customary nature were mistaken. To further explain, it might be argued that though the likes of Matthew Hale or William Blackstone were involved in the development of the common law, they do not enjoy any privileged understanding on what they were doing.

drawn primarily from three distinctive legal realms and overlaid with features of its own."). Anon. [Nicholas St. John Green], "Slander and Libel" (1871) 6 *American Law Review* 593, 597 ("As the English law upon any subject was never constructed upon a plan, it cannot be resolved into one. It is a mass which has grown by aggregation, and special and peculiar circumstances have, from time to time, shaped its varying surfaces and angles.").

[17] S.F.C. Milsom, "Reason in the Development of the Common Law" (1965) 81 *Law Quarterly Review* 496, 497–8 ("There has been no plan in the development of the common law, even less . . . than legal historians have sometimes thought"); Roscoe Pound, "The Development of American Law and Its Deviation from English Law" (1951) 67 *Law Quarterly Review* 49, 50 ("the common law is little systematized . . . . The law books of Anglo-American common law are typically alphabetical abridgements, digests, and cyclopedias."). More generally see Michael Lobban, "Mapping the Common Law: Some Lessons from History" [2011] *New Zealand Law Review* 21; Geoffrey Samuel, "Can the Common Law Be Mapped?" (2005) 55 *University of Toronto Law Journal* 271.

On this question (so the argument goes), it is legal theorists with their greater analytical skills, who can provide a better understanding of the practice.

The problem with this argument is that it treats all claims by common-law practitioners as external observations on the practice, made in a purely theoretical mood. In fact, however, these views should be understood as an attitude that these practitioners brought to the practice, and hence helped define it. As Joseph Raz put it, "the way a culture understands its own practices and institutions is not separate from what they are ... [T]hey ... are in part shaped by the way they are understood by the people whose practices and institutions they are."[18]

Raz's claim needs to be carefully parsed. A judge may genuinely think that he is being impartial, treating all defendants in the same way regardless of their ethnic backgrounds or gender, but research can reveal him to be unconsciously biased. The belief that one is unbiased is not itself part of the practice of adjudication; it is an evaluation of one's actions, and such evaluations are many times incorrect.[19] The belief that common-law justification is customary in nature is different to the extent that it shapes the practice itself. As the illustrations above show, to conceive of the common law as custom affects how it is actually practiced, the kind of arguments deemed acceptable within it, and the way it develops. To argue that despite all this common-law practice is not custom requires showing that there exists a certain mythology that is entirely divorced from the practice. This is possible, but for such an argument to be convincing, it has to be the case, first, that the practice is completely different from the way its practitioners understand it. In the case of unconscious bias, such a claim will not be convincing without empirical evidence; in the case of the common law, it will require providing an alternative explanation for the customary features of common-law practice. The discussion above was meant to show that familiar features of the practice fit its theoretical understanding. Second, to the extent that such explanations differ from the way practitioners understand the practice, it calls for an explanation of the difference, one that is likely to involve either global delusion or massive fraud.

A further problem with this challenge in this context is that it is self-defeating. The question under consideration is the possibility of countering

[18] Joseph Raz, *Between Authority and Interpretation: On the Theory of Law and Practical Reason* (Oxford University Press 2009) 96–7.

[19] See generally Timothy D. Wilson, *Strangers to Ourselves* (Harvard University Press 2002). The full implications of this view have not been adequately acknowledged in much contemporary legal philosophy. See further Dan Priel, "Action, Politics, and the Normativity of Law" (2017) 8 *Jurisprudence* 118.

my view that the common law is not an artifact. Its ultimate goal is therefore to show that the common law is an artifact in the sense that it is a *conscious* attempt at law-making. But it is inconsistent to argue for this conclusion with the arguments that those who think of law as custom are actually mistaken about what they are doing. *Even if they are mistaken*, the element of conscious, purposive, creation remains lacking.

The second objection was that the common law may be a kind of custom, but it is an unusual kind of custom. If so, it is wrong to draw from the fact that the common law is custom and that custom is not an artifact the conclusion that the common law is not an artifact. I think this objection is correct in that the common law does indeed have some features that set it apart from most customs. It is more complex than other customs; and it is a custom backed by the power of the state, something that is not true of most customs. Most notably, the common law today is written and analyzed ("theorized") in a way that other customs are not, and it is often analyzed in terms of its ability to protect certain "external" goals. All this may imply that the common law is such an unusual custom that the argument presented above is invalid.

Though there are real differences between the common law and other customs, they do not set the common law apart from other customs in any sense relevant for the argument made above. As mentioned earlier, other customs sometimes have quasi-authoritative guides; and though not typically enforced by the state, other customs often have very powerful enforcement mechanisms behind them. A powerful social taboo can be far more effective than a weakly enforced legal norm. It must also be remembered that those who seek to provide a general theory of law must account not just for contemporary common law, one that has been much affected and to some extent shaped by the dominance of legislative design (more on this below). They must also be able to account for the common law as it existed for much of its history, including in those times when it was, as common-law historians insist, almost entirely lacking in theoretical literature and its most common organizing principle was the alphabetical ordering of cases.

4. Law-as-Artifact as Ideology

The reader may wonder why the conclusion of the last section is significant. Indeed, she may even consider it rather obvious. After some toing and froing its conclusion was that the common law is custom; and that is not exactly news. The purpose of this section is to explain the broader jurisprudential significance of this conclusion. I contend that the view that law is an artifact is not a conceptual truth about law (in general), but an ideological one. And though common-law practice is not ideologically uniform,[20] a very central strand in it rejects the ideology to which the law-as-artifact view belongs. The result is unconvincing accounts that attempt to explain the common law as something it is not.

To suggest jurisprudence is "ideological" may seem not just obviously false but inflammatory. To call a view "ideological" is sometimes a form of criticism: "His opposition to the new plan had nothing to do with its merits, it was purely ideological." Used in this way, ideology is seen as an irrelevant consideration, a prejudice. This is not the way I use the term. As I use it, it is a set of organizing ideas that individuals use to make sense of the world, a way of organizing brute facts, of giving particular events meaning within a larger conceptual scheme. Ideology, to use Clifford Geertz's term, is a "cultural system."[21] My claim is that the law-as-artifact is part of a broader, evaluative, worldview. Still, even in this sense my claim will likely be resisted. General jurisprudence is said by many of its champions to be "conceptual," "descriptive," "universal," "morally neutral"—all designations suggesting it is non-ideological even in the non-pejorative sense. It is an attempt to provide a description of the nature or essence of law wherever and whenever it is found. In the prevailing view the claim that law is an artifact may be true or false, but it is not right or wrong.

I have no doubt that those who make these claims believe that they are a morally neutral description of law as it is. What I attempt to explain is why such views are mistaken and why such views make more sense when their hidden ideological assumptions are made explicit. Does this show that there is no conceptual part to jurisprudence? It does not, though the argument still casts doubt on this project.[22] What it purports to show is that even if there are some purely conceptual truths about law, there is value in showing that their scope is narrow and that certain features of law currently accepted as conceptually true, are not.

4.1 The Dominant Ideology in Contemporary Jurisprudence

What I take to be a dominant ideology in contemporary jurisprudence consists of two components, both of which are often taken for granted as

[20] See Priel, "Conceptions of Authority and the Anglo-American Common Law Divide" (n. 13).

[21] See Clifford Geertz, "Ideology as a Cultural System" in *The Interpretation of Cultures* (Basic Books 1973) ch. 8.

[22] Elsewhere I do argue that there is no conceptual part to jurisprudence. See Dan Priel, "The Scientific Model of Jurisprudence" in Beltrán et al. (eds.), *Neutrality and Theory of Law* (n. 1) 239; Priel, "The Misguided Search for the Nature of Law" (n. 6).

conceptual truths about law. The first, one which by now should be familiar, is the thought that law is an instrument consciously designed to solve problems. It treats law having a teleological function as a conceptual truth about it, and that an important measure of law's success is the extent to which it fulfills that function. The second component is a more concrete view about the *kind* of problems that law is designed to solve, and correspondingly the primary aim of law. On the view in question the primary aim of the law is to solve *moral* problems, when morality is understood as a kind of fixed set of norms for lawyers to match. It follows from putting these two views together that law has to match this pre-existing, eternally unchanging set of norms, and that law fulfills its (teleological) function when it matches these moral norms, thereby serving as an instrument for the better enforcement of morality. Notice that this instrumental view of law is consistent with thinking that the morality law exists to promote is non-consequentialist.

To illustrate this point consider the views of three contemporary legal theorists. Their views differ in fundamental respects, and yet all three endorse both points. John Gardner says that "[n]atural law is the same thing as morality. It is the higher thing to which human law answers."[23] This view depends on the claim, that "[b]eing subject to morality is an inescapable part of being rational .... And being rational ... is part of being human."[24] The link between law and morality is thus established in this way: "[morality] binds us by our nature as human beings, while law binds us, to the extent that it does, only by the grace of morality,"[25] and in that "[l]aw answers to all moral norms in proportion to their ordinary moral importance."[26]

Morality is the fixed star, something that any human being, in virtue of being a rational animal, can discover; it is something that in virtue of the normative demands of rationality all humans ought to follow; and it is the standard against which we measure law. In Gardner's view laws are artifacts[27] one of whose measures of success is their ability to guide people: "Whatever other purposes law may have, it clearly has the purpose of providing

[23] John Gardner, *Law as a Leap of Faith: Essays on Law in General* (Oxford University Press 2012) 175. Strictly, these words are attributed to natural lawyers, but as far as I can tell, Gardner accepts it, as long as the term "natural law" is replaced with "morality." Gardner's problem with the natural law view seems to be that they mistakenly think of morality as a kind of law, not with other aspects of this view. See ibid.

[24] Ibid. 150. [25] Ibid. 175. [26] Ibid. 192.

[27] Ibid. 193. Gardner does not define artifact, but it seems he takes artifacts to include all products of human action. He explicitly includes in the definition works of art (ibid. 182). Since he considers all law an artifact, and considers some laws to be the product of accidents (ibid. 70–1), it follows that he thinks artifacts include also the accidental products of intentional action. That suggests he considers the wood shavings created in the process of creating a wood carving an artifact. (This example is taken from Hilpinen, "Authors and Artifacts" (n. 7) 159–60.)

law-subjects, including the government, with normative guidance; that is to say, of subjecting their conduct to the governance of norms."[28] But, crucially, law is not about any kind of guidance: the "morally successful law" is one that helps us resolve "moral problems."[29]

Scott Shapiro's central idea of law as a plan is, of course, a straightforward endorsement of the first aspect of the ideology in question: law, just like all planning, "seeks to accomplish the same basic goals that ordinary, garden-variety planning does, namely, to guide, organize, and monitor the behavior of individuals and groups."[30] But law for Shapiro is not just any kind of plan. It is, he says, a conceptual truth that law is a plan with the aim "to remedy the moral deficiencies of the circumstances of legality."[31] Although "the sheer diversity of political objectives that actual legal systems have attempted to secure throughout human history suggests that the law often fails in its primary mission,"[32] Shapiro still maintains that "it is part of the identity of law to have a moral mission."[33] Shapiro is less direct on the second component of the ideology I consider, but it is quite clear he accepts it as well. When he talks about morality, Shapiro reflects the view of morality as an unchanging pre-existing entity when he states that "it makes no sense to talk about incrementally developing ... morality."[34] In a similar vein Shapiro writes that "moral norms are not able to solve coordination problems because morality concerns itself with principled action and coordination problems arise because of their arbitrary nature."[35]

These claims are unconvincing as conceptual claims supposedly true of all law whenever and wherever we find it. There are many things unquestionably considered as laws that are difficult to reconcile with the idea that they are there to address the kind of situations Shapiro talks about. One need not be committed to everything said by public choice theorists to acknowledge that many laws are enacted with different aims. Such cases are not instances of an unfortunate failure (due to a miscalculation, lack of foresight, etc.) to fulfill law's purported conceptual aim, but cases in which the

[28] Gardner, *Law as a Leap of Faith* (n. 23) 209.

[29] Ibid. 163. If being moral is akin to being rational, what counts as a "moral problem" is not entirely clear.

[30] Scott J. Shapiro, *Legality* (Harvard University Press 2011) 200.

[31] Ibid. 213.

[32] Ibid. 213–14.

[33] Ibid. 215.

[34] Ibid. 128.

[35] Ibid. 201. These claims are by no means obvious. See, e.g., Philip Kitcher, *The Ethical Project* (Harvard University Press 2011) 2, *passim* ("Ethics emerges as a human phenomenon, permanently unfinished. We, collectively, made it up, and have developed, refined, and distorted it, generation by generation."). The view that at least parts of morality have emerged as responses to coordination problems is also familiar. See, e.g., Robert Sugden, *The Economics of Rights, Co-Operation and Welfare* (2nd edn., Palgrave Macmillan 2004).

conscious aim motivating the legislation is not moral. The puzzle is not just empirical: surprisingly for a project intended to defend a version of legal positivism, Shapiro seems committed to the view that a duly enacted statute that was adopted with an immoral aim is *thereby* not law. This sounds like an affirmation of a variant of natural law theory rather than a challenge to it: it is the view that while a putative law that is in fact unjust remains valid law, a law designed to be unjust (thereby lacking in moral aim) is not law, perhaps even if it is in fact just.

At the other end of the positivist/natural law divide, Allan Beever is similarly committed to the two ideas that dominate contemporary jurisprudence. In an attempt to explain the declaratory theory of the common law, he distinguishes between positive law and some kind of higher, "enduring," law. The latter for him is simply a different name for interpersonal morality. It is not a human creation, it is unchanging, and it can be discovered by reason. Beever also states that it is the aim of human law to match the natural law and help enforce it. The two elements of the prevailing ideology are captured by his claim that "the law that remains unaltered is not positive law but something more abstract and enduring. Fulfilling the law is a matter of making the positive law more accurately reflect this abstract and enduring law."[36] It follows, as Beever also says, that the common law is merely the public record of successive human efforts to discover this unchanging law.[37] Reflecting on this higher law aims to "provide principles capable of guiding (not determining) deliberations" on novel cases.[38] Once we separate a functional conception of law from consequentialist morality, it is easy to see that Beever too is committed to the idea that law should match, and is ultimately necessary in order to maintain, this unchanging law.

4.2 The Ideological Space

Perhaps the single most important aspect of this dominant contemporary ideology is that law is about guidance. The view of law as an artifact fits

[36] Allan Beever, "The Declaratory Theory of Law" (2013) 33 *Oxford Journal of Legal Studies* 421, 428–9.

[37] See Allan Beever, "How to Have a Common Private Law: The Presuppositions of Legal Conversation" in Andrew Robertson and Michael Tilbury (eds.), *The Common Law of Obligations: Divergence and Unity* (Hart Publishing 2016) 215, 227; but see Dan Priel, "The Philosophies of the Common Law and their Implications: Common Law Divergences, Public Authority Liability, and the Future of a Common Law World" in ibid. 233, for casting doubt on this view.

[38] Beever, "The Declaratory Theory of Law" (n. 36) 442.

right into this view, as it presents law as a kind of signpost for confused humans to follow. It is a view of law as a tool designed by humans to ultimately attain a better life. In legal philosophers' discourse (and this may reflect the influence of natural-law thinking) as far as the law is concerned, a "better life" means a more moral life. This is why law's success is measured by its correspondence to, and ability to maintain and promote, morality. Of course, different scholars may have different views about morality and what it requires, but in the way the boundaries between legal and moral philosophy are drawn, this debate is not part of jurisprudence. Disagreement on this latter question (a question of political philosophy) is consistent with agreement that law is (primarily, essentially) a tool for maintaining and promoting morality. Against this agreement, the remaining jurisprudential disputes between legal positivism and natural law theory are concerned with fairly marginal points. The questions whether morally faulty specimens of putative law are not law or merely are a "perversion of law," or the question whether the unchanging norms that law should match are to be considered a kind of law ("natural law") or something else ("morality"), are fairly insignificant against a backdrop of vast agreement.[39] What matters for the present discussion is that because so much is shared across the supposedly wide chasm that separates legal positivism and natural law theory, it is natural to think of it as "conceptual" truths.

I identified two components that make up the dominant law-as-artifact, on the basis of which we can identify four theoretical possibilities (only three of them are realized).

Table 12.3 The ideological space around law-as-artifact

	Law as non-artifact	*Law as artifact*
The ideal for law is the imitation of morality	N/A	Contemporary legal positivism, contemporary natural law theory
Constructivism	Common law theory, Ronald Dworkin	Classical legal positivism: Thomas Hobbes, Jeremy Bentham

[39] Gardner is thus correct to call his position "nearly natural law" in Gardner, *Law as a Leap of Faith* (n. 23) ch. 6.

Table 12.3 identifies two alternatives to the law-as-artifact view. As this chapter is concerned with the common law, I will say little about one of them, the one I call "classical legal positivism," except to note that unlike contemporary legal positivism, this view is a real alternative to natural law theory.[40] There are many important differences between classical and contemporary legal positivism, but they share the Enlightenment idea of the possibility of progress through human endeavor. Law fits into this picture as a tool ("artifact"), perhaps the primary tool by which such progress is to be attained.[41]

Once identified, this idea can also be seen in Hart's account of the change from the prelegal to the legal society, explained in terms of the gains in efficiency it provides. Hart insists that for law to exist, there has to be a legal *system*, which comes into being when some institutional mechanisms are introduced, almost inevitably by design, to improve the pre-legal norms' efficiency at providing guidance. The same commitment is even more evident in the Razian "service conception" of authority. On the basis of this view Raz presented law's authority as grounded in its "superior knowledge" and likened the law to a "knowledgeable friend."[42] At other times, the law co-ordinates the actions of different individuals. Either way, this is an instrumental conception of law in which the law's raison d'être is its ability to direct people's action in a way that will help people comply with reasons that exist regardless of the law. It is for this reason that the ability to guide conduct is so central to his view of law and has also been central to his well-known argument in support of exclusive legal positivism.

Raz made the link between this view and the ideology of improvement clear when he said: "We take legislation as the base [of an account of law] because of its centrality to the understanding of law and of the governance of human affairs by deliberate decisions of human institutions appointed to control and give direction to human conduct and to social change."[43] This view, which sees conscious acts of legislation as the paradigmatic case for law *because* they are human devices to "control and give direction to human conduct" inevitably treats customary law and the common law as less central cases of law.

Not only does this view make legislation a more central case of law, it is quite difficult to account for the common law within it, because the

[40] See Dan Priel, "Toward Classical Legal Positivism" (2015) 101 *Virginia Law Review* 987. See also the remark on Bentham in the concluding paragraph of this section.

[41] Recent years have seen the proliferation of so many "Enlightenments" that the term almost lost all meaning. Even thinkers like Edmund Burke and Adam Ferguson, which I posit in opposition to the Enlightenment idea I discuss in the text, have been described by some as adherents to a more "moderate" or "pragmatic" Enlightenment, in contrast to a more "radical" or "rigid" Enlightenment. The labels matter less than the difference in ideas.

[42] Raz, *Ethics in the Public Domain* (n. 15) 348.

[43] Ibid. 301; cf. Raz, *Between Authority and Interpretation* (n. 18) 320.

suggestion that judges are some kind of moral experts, or experts in solving co-ordination problems, is implausible. It is hard to think of any judge, including the acknowledged "great judges" of the common law (Mansfield, Holmes, Cardozo, Atkin) as a moral expert, and it is hard to think of any of their decisions as great essays in moral philosophy. The suggestion that they possessed any special knowledge or insight on coordination problems is, if anything, even less plausible. Now, it is true that Raz's view is consistent with the possibility that the common law claims such authority but is uniformly failing at actually having it. While theoretically possible, I think such a conclusion suggests an alternative, one in which the authority of the common law is best explained as a rejection of this ideology of improvement, rather than a failed embrace of it.

4.3 The Common Law as Tradition

One prominent strand in common-law thought is best understood as reflecting an ideology that fundamentally rejects the idea of rational design as a guiding principle for the improvement of civil society. Correspondingly, it is also based on a competing theory of authority. Hayek challenged the Enlightenment idea of the organization of society, which he associated with Hobbes and Bentham; he contrasted it with a view he found reflected, among other places, in "a tradition rooted in the jurisprudence of the common law," and he quoted Scottish philosopher Adam Ferguson for the idea that human institutions are "the result of human action but not the execution of human design."[44] This remark parallels the distinction between the broad (and trivial) sense of law's artifactuality (law is the product of human action) and the non-trivial sense of its artifactuality (law is the product of conscious design). Hayek thus contrasted legal design with "rules [that] have never been deliberately invented but have grown through a gradual process of trial and error .... In most instances ... [of such law-making] nobody knows or has ever known all the reasons and considerations that have led to a rule being given a particular form."[45]

According to another statement of this view, coming from Michael Oakeshott,

> [t]he laws of civil association ... are not imposed upon an already shaped and articulated engagement, they relate to the miscellaneous, unforeseeable choices and transactions of agents each concerned to live the life of a 'man like me', who are

[44] F.A. Hayek, *The Constitution of Liberty* (Routlege & Kegan Paul 1960) 56, 57, quoting Adam Ferguson, *An Essay on the History of Civil Society* (A. Kincaid and J. Bell 1767) 187. Ferguson also wrote: "No constitution is formed by concert, no government copied from a plan." Ibid. 188.

[45] Hayek, *The Constitution of Liberty* (n. 44) 157.

joined in no common purpose or engagement, who may be strangers to one another .... Nor do they [i.e., these laws] impose any such common purpose upon those who fall within their jurisdiction: they are not devices for engineering the promotion of a common interest.[46]

How do we explain the contrast between this view and the law-as-artifact view? One possibility is to say that this is a competing conceptual claim about law, but one that happens to be false. If that was indeed Oakeshott and Hayek's aim, then they are equally guilty of confusing the ideological with the conceptual. But I think this is an implausible reading of these thinkers. Oakeshott presented his view of law as part of a broader avowedly "conservative" political theory. In his writings Oakeshott repeatedly chastised what he called—always in scare quotes—"rationalism," the view that perceives of politics as a science in which external goals are defined and then uses various means (including, prominently, laws) to pursue them.[47] The idea of law as an artifact designed to match pre-existing morality or natural law is the jurisprudential manifestation of the rationalistic worldview that he rejected.

Common-law practice fits this view. To put this bluntly, most common-law practice does not look like lawyers and judges care much whether universal moral truths exist; and even if they exist, there is rarely a suggestion that to find them is relevant, let alone decisive, to solving "novel" cases. Lord Justice Scrutton emphasized this point almost a century ago when he said that, "justice is not what we strive after in the Courts, paradoxical as it may seem .... We are not trying to do justice, if you mean by justice some moral standard which is not the law of England."[48] Of course, the statement of a single judge, influential though he may have been, is not proof of my argument, but I contend that what Scrutton said is a fair representation of common law practice, definitely in England at the time he was writing.

Beyond such exegetical matters, to dismiss this view as a misunderstanding of the authority of the common law is theoretically problematic. It is true that one may consistently hold that some people believe that tradition is a source of legitimate authority and that such beliefs are mistaken. But if people hold such a view they are likely to shape their practices accordingly. Thus,

[46] Michael Oakeshott, *On Human Conduct* (Clarendon Press 1975) 129. See also Michael Oakeshott, "The Rule of Law" in *On History and Other Essays* (Blackwell 1983) 119, 136: "The expression, 'the rule of law', taken precisely, stands for a mode of moral association exclusively in terms of the recognition of the authority of known, non-instrumental rules (that is, laws) which impose obligations to subscribe to adverbial conditions in the performance of self-chosen actions of all who fall within their jurisdiction."

[47] This is a recurring theme in Michael Oakeshott, *Rationalism in Politics and Other Essays* (expanded edn., Liberty Fund 1991).

[48] T.E. Scrutton, "The Work of the Commercial Courts" (1921) 1 *Cambridge Law Journal* 6, 8.

even if one believes that a traditionary view of authority can *never* provide a successful basis for legitimate authority, the fact that people believe that it is, is important for understanding a practice that involves people who do. This point was implicitly accepted by Raz when he said that,

> since our own concept is liable to be forever in flux, since legal theory is itself part of the culture to which 'our' concept of law belongs, it is inevitable that legal theory is no mere passive mirror of the concepts of that culture. To the extent that legal theorists acquire influence their views tend to be self-verifying. This led some post-modernists to identify theory with advocacy. This is a misleading view. Theory aims at understanding. By and large, only bad theory can lead to change. *If its wrong conclusions are accepted their acceptance may lead to a change in the self-understanding of the culture which will make the bad theory true.* But such bad theories succeed only by not trying, i.e. by claiming—however erroneously—that they state how things are, and not that they advocate change. Once they avow that they advocate change they lose the claim they have on our attention, they join reformers in an activity to be judged by different standards altogether.[49]

Raz is almost correct here. He is right that when people offer certain understandings of the practice they can alter the practice and with it its underlying philosophy. But he is wrong to say that this is true only in the case of "bad theory," one that is mistaken. All accounts of the practice have potential to influence it, even when they do so by affirming a prevailing understanding of it. This is particularly clear when we remember that there is never a single account of a practice. What always exists are competing views presented more-or-less simultaneously. "Correct" and "incorrect" accounts thus compete in the marketplace of ideas; and since these competing views are held by practitioners, they constantly push the practice in different directions. In any case, even if one accepts Raz's view that only "bad theory" can change the practice, it follows from what he says that if a bad theory becomes sufficiently influential, it can change the practice to such a degree that it eventually will become the "good theory" of the practice. This means that the prevalence of traditionary ideas about the common law can influence (and as a historical matter, has influenced) the practice of law. If it is shown that much common-law practice has in fact been based on this traditionary ideology, to maintain the view that all law is an artifact implies that much of the common law is not law. While possible, that would be a radically revisionist view of law, not one that supposedly captures (roughly) all phenomena humans have identified as law throughout history.

[49] Raz, *Between Authority and Interpretation* (n. 18) 98–9 (emphasis added).

So this way of responding to this view fails. A second response might be that the traditionary view is based on a particular political ideology, and as such it comes into play only after the non-ideological, conceptual analysis of law has been completed.[50] This response will thus argue that this clearly ideological view of the common law rests on a universal conceptual basis. But this second response is also implausible. One way of demonstrating this is by pointing out that Raz's words quoted earlier about legislation as central to understanding law are correct when read against the background of the Enlightenment ideology of improvement through law. But this view is not a neutral basis on which conservative political thinkers then added a second, political layer. For some, legislation is not the paradigm of law, but a degenerate, perverse, example of it.[51]

Similarly, Hayek and Oakeshott did not think that their favored conception of law (in which it is not an object designed for guidance) is a politically motivated layer added onto a conceptual, morally neutral truth that law is about guidance. They rejected the idea of law-as-artifact designed to guide altogether. On the traditionary view, law is not a solution to a problem that can be identified in advance and then acted upon when the right time comes. Rather, it is a standard that reflects, as Oakeshott put it, "current moral activity" within a particular community. To use his example, what counts as "reasonable care" is "not something that can be known in advance" (thus ruling out the idea of guidance); instead it reflects "knowledge of how to behave well which belongs to our way of living."[52] This view is not political disagreement added to a layer of conceptual agreement; it is a challenge to the "conceptual" foundation. Law on this view is not put in place where custom fails; it is a continuation of, a manifestation of, custom. It is thus not a way of guiding people for the sake of attaining some teleological ("external") function, but a cultural ("internal") one.

I think the most plausible way of understanding this disagreement is also the most straightforward one, namely as reflecting two conflicting views about law, both of which are derived from conflicting ideologies. This claim, if accepted, raises another set of questions. When Oakeshott made these claims, they were by no means novel. The association of the common law with the

[50] Cf. Julie Dickson, "Ours Is a Broad Church: Indirectly Evaluative Legal Philosophy as a Facet of Jurisprudential Inquiry" (2015) 6 *Jurisprudence* 207, 215, 229.

[51] See, e.g., James C. Carter, *The Proposed Codification of our Common Law* (Evening Post Job Printing Office 1884) 51 ("The decadence [of Rome] was marked by a corresponding decline in jurisprudence, and the extension of the province of legislation over the proper domain of the unwritten law.").

[52] Oakeshott, *Rationalism in Politics and Other Essays* (n. 47) 130, also 117. Oakeshott explicitly rejects the idea that law should match natural law. Ibid. 51, 67, 423.

political theory of tradition is at least as old as Edmund Burke, if not older.[53] Given this long historical provenance, it is a good question why it has been largely ignored by legal philosophers. To the little extent that they even paid attention to proponents of this view, they apparently did not see them as having any bearing on their own work. I think there are three main reasons that together go a long way toward an explanation. The first is the prevailing (albeit mistaken) view that jurisprudence is a value-neutral search for the nature of law. This attitude has blinded many contemporary writers to the ideological basis of contemporary jurisprudence. As a result, writings that were perceived as clearly ideological could be ignored as irrelevant to the enterprise of general jurisprudence. The second is the relative lack of interest among contemporary legal philosophers in legal practice (and the occasional denigration of legal theorists who took an interest in it as not really legal philosophers), as well as their lack of interest in the history of law and jurisprudence. This allowed jurisprudential debates to be conducted at a level of abstraction at which realities about the practice did not adequately inform the theories that were supposed to describe it. Insufficient attention to legal history has led to the elevation of familiar features of contemporary western law to the level of conceptual truths about all law. Even the most fervent admirer of the common law will admit that it is far less significant today than it once was,[54] and the dominance of statutes has influenced thinking on the common law as well. But these are contingent facts about the present-day regulatory state, not timeless verities.

The third reason has more to do with the fact that the traditionary ideology is relatively unpopular among legal academics. For all their differences (jurisprudential as well as, I suspect, political), Gardner, Shapiro, and Beever, whose work I briefly discussed earlier, share the view that morality is an unchanging set of norms, which law should match. They may disagree on what this independent unchanging morality requires, but not on its "nature." A view that depended on a fundamentally different understanding of morality could thus be ignored, or when not ignored, misunderstood.

This is enough to show that even if contemporary legal philosophy is ethically neutral, it is not metaethically neutral. For the sake of my argument,

[53] For various formulations of the idea see J.G.A. Pocock, "Burke and the Ancient Constitution: A Problem in the History of Ideas" (1960) 3 *Historical Journal* 125; Anthony T. Kronman, "Precedent and Tradition" (1990) 99 *Yale Law Journal* 1029; Gerald J. Postema, "Philosophy of the Common Law" in Jules L. Coleman and Scott J. Shapiro (eds.), *The Oxford Handbook of Jurisprudence and the Philosophy of Law* (Oxford University Press 2002) 588; David Strauss, *The Living Constitution* (Oxford University Press 2010); cf. Martin Krygier, "Law as Tradition" (1986) 5 *Law and Philosophy* 237.

[54] Cf. Dan Priel, "The Political Origins of English Private Law" (2015) 40 *Journal of Law and Society* 481, 501–2.

it does not matter whether this metaethical view is correct; it matters, however, whether it was accepted by important practitioners of the common law. I have attempted to demonstrate that it was; my subsequent discussion was meant to show that this approach goes beyond mere difference in law-making technique (some laws happen to be made by legislatures, others by courts). It reflects a different view about the nature of political authority, and arguably also the nature of morality.

These last remarks put Bentham's views on the common law in clearer light. Bentham had many bad things to say about Blackstone, and he characteristically spelled those out in exhaustive detail over hundreds of pages. But he did not think that Blackstone's definition of law was conceptually wrong. Blackstone, he said, "has a right to put into his idea of [municipal Law] what he pleases."[55] This explains why Bentham did not contradict himself when he said that the common law is not real law.[56] When he said this, he was not making a conceptual claim, but a normative one. Bentham was openly dismissive of the authority of tradition, calling it the "wisdom of the cradle,"[57] and based his entire corpus on an overriding commitment to the Enlightenment ideal of social improvement through the rational application of the scientific method to human affairs. Not being able to fit the common law within this, patently normative view, he rejected it. But it is not that his dislike for the common law was political, while his dismissal of it as non-law was conceptual. Both were part of the same ideological view.

5. The Implications of Thinking about Law as an Artifact

I began this chapter by drawing a distinction between two possible definitions of artifactuality. On the broader definition, something is an artifact if it is the product of human efforts. I said that this view is trivial and not contested by any present-day legal theorist. But it does have an interesting implication: if law is an artifact even in this broad sense, it makes as much sense to think that there is a philosophical task of discovering its nature as there is a philosophical task of discovering the nature of cars. It is not (just) that such a task seems utterly pointless, it is that the answer to it is one to which philosophers

[55] Jeremy Bentham, *A Comment on the Commentaries and a Fragment on Government* (Clarendon Press 1977) 38.

[56] See, e.g., Jeremy Bentham, *"Legislator of the World": Writings on Codification, Law, and Education* (Oxford University Press 1998) 193, where he talks about the "unreal, not really-existing, imaginary, fictitious, spurious judge-made law ... [known by the] unexpressive, uncharacteristic and unappropriate names of common law and unwritten law."

[57] Jeremy Bentham, *The Book of Fallacies* (Oxford University Press 2015) 173.

have little to contribute. Cars, and humans' attitudes about them, have a history, a sociology, a technology, not self-evident "truisms" to be discovered by philosophical reflection. If law is an artifact, it is hard to see why it should be any different.

This chapter has attempted to show one way in which thinking about law as an artifact changes the way we should analyze it. More generally, I think openness to law's artifactuality should lead legal philosophers to realize that science, essential nature, and discovery are not the right models for jurisprudence. As with other artifacts, it is engineering, development, and construction.

Index

The manufacturer's authorised representative in the EU for product safety is Oxford University Press España S.A. of el Parque Empresarial San Fernando de Henares, Avenida de Castilla, 2 – 28830 Madrid (www.oup.es/en or product.safety@oup.com). OUP España S.A. also acts as importer into Spain of products made by the manufacturer.

www.ingramcontent.com/pod-product-compliance
Lightning Source LLC
LaVergne TN
LVHW011748200926
848484LV00003B/648

* 9 7 8 0 1 9 8 8 2 1 9 7 7 *